THE CAREER
FITNESS PROGRAM

EXERCISING YOUR OPTIONS

TENTH EDITION

Diane Sukiennik

Lisa Raufman

William Bendat

PEARSON

Boston   Columbus   Indianapolis   New York   San Francisco   Upper Saddle River
Amsterdam   Cape Town   Dubai   London   Madrid   Milan   Munich   Paris   Montreal   Toronto
Delhi   Mexico City   Sao Paulo   Sydney   Hong Kong   Seoul   Singapore   Taipei   Tokyo

VP/Editor in Chief Student Success & Career Development: Jodi McPherson
Acquisitions Editor: Katie Mahan
Editorial Assistant: Clara Ciminelli
Executive Marketing Manager: Amy Judd
Development Editor: Jenny Gessner
Production Editor: Karen Mason
Production Coordination and Electronic Composition: Cenveo Publisher Services/
Nesbitt Graphics, Inc.
Text Design and Illustrations: Cenveo Publisher Services/Nesbitt Graphics, Inc.
Cover Coordinator: Diane Lorenzo
Cover Photo: Jupiter Images
Interior Photos: Author photos: Michael Reiss, Van Nguyen, and Ken Bendat; interior photos
from: Shutterstock.com

Library of Congress Cataloging-in-Publication Data

Sukiennik, Diane.
   The career fitness program : exercising your options / Diane Sukiennik, Lisa Raufman,
   William Bendat. – 10th ed.
      p.   cm.
   Includes bibliographical references and index.
   ISBN 0-13-276233-1
1.   Vocational guidance.   2.   Job hunting.   3.   Personality assessment. I. Raufman, Lisa.
      II. Bendat, William. III. Title.
   HF5381.S914 2013
   650.14--dc23

2011046819

10 9 8 7 6 5 4 3 2

ISBN-13: 978-0-13-276233-5

ISBN-10: 0-13-276233-1

About the Authors

Dr. Diane Sukiennik is a career counselor, a licensed marriage and family therapist, and an internationally recognized lecturer and workshop facilitator. She holds advanced degrees from Columbia University and Nova Southeastern University and has extensive postgraduate training in industrial psychology, management, and organizational development. Dr. Sukiennik was on the faculty of Moorpark College in California for 37 years. Her areas of expertise are career development, personal and professional presentation skills, and managerial effectiveness. She is a consultant, has a private practice, has contributed to the development of a nationally distributed telecourse on career and life development called "Career Advantage" distributed by PBS, and is an executive career coach. Dr. Sukiennik walks her talk by turning a lifelong passion into a popular website, **www.foodandwineaccess.com**.

Dr. Lisa Raufman has been Dean of Counseling and Career Center Coordinator at El Camino College in Torrance, California. She is a career counselor and consultant, as well as a licensed marriage and family therapist. Her master's degree is in counseling with a specialization in the community college and vocational rehabilitation. Her doctoral degree from the University of California at Los Angeles focused on higher education, work, and adult development. Previously, Dr. Raufman coordinated the Career Transfer Center at Moorpark College. She is past president of the Los Padres chapter of the American Society for Training and Development (ASTD) and the California Community College Counselors Association. Over the past decade, Dr. Raufman has been a member of the California Community College Chancellors Office State Advisory on Career Development. She is a lifelong member of state and national counseling associations such as ACA, NCDA, ACCA, CCDA, CCCCA, and CAC and she blogs regularly on **www.careerthoughtleaders.com website**.

Dr. William Bendat was a recognized leader and innovator in career development theory. While serving as Dean of Student Services at Moorpark College, he managed the award-winning counseling and career programs that gained recognition in both California and nationally. The counseling and career program at Moorpark College was awarded the Stanford University H.B McDaniel Award for comprehensive career services. Dr. Bendat used his advanced degrees in counseling psychology, with emphasis in decision making and self-concept, to greatly enrich *The Career Fitness Program*. He was the director of Careerscope, offering specialized career workshops to public and private agencies. He was also a licensed therapist, past president of the California Managers of Counseling, and a contributor to numerous workshops and professional journals.

Brief Contents

Contents

3   Confirming Core Values: Strengthen Your Balance   41

4   Assessing Your Personality and Interests: Express Your Real Self   57

7 Exploring Career Information: Expand Your Horizons   135

8 Developing Your Decision Making: Strategize Your Game Plan   157

PART 3

Execute Your Game Plan: Job Search Strategy and Team Huddle   181

9 Targeting Your Job Search: Mobilize Your Network   183

10 Crafting a Winning Resume and Portfolio: Market Your Unique Brand

11 Interviewing Strategically: Become Your Own Coach   249

12 Focusing on the Future: Keep the Momentum Going   267

Career Fitness Portfolio · 275

Preface

Welcome to the tenth edition of *The Career Fitness Program: Exercising Your Options.* We are immensely gratified by the positive feedback from the field, which tells us that we are contributing to the quality of life for the thousands of students who use our book. We say *use our book* rather than *read our book* because the process of career planning is action oriented. We have balanced the text with a variety of exercises incorporated into each chapter to encourage you to "get into the process" and allow it to unfold in the many unexpected ways that careers take shape. We are committed to the process of career planning, which is part science and part art, part logic and part intuition, part inspiration and part perspiration. We recognize the critical role of the teacher/counselor/coach in this process as the voice of experience, reassurance, validation, and wisdom. Just as a personal trainer keeps a well-intentioned exerciser on track, the instructor keeps students moving forward in a process that tends to be circuitous rather than linear and straightforward.

Our book is a comprehensive and current compendium of the best art and science in the field of career planning. This tenth edition incorporates the use of the electronic medium into every aspect of the planning process without implying that the Internet is the only tool in the process. In fact, the book's emphasis on the importance of human relations skills sets it apart. This combination of high tech and high touch will help you integrate the best of both worlds to maximize the impact of your career-planning efforts.

New to This Edition

The tenth edition introduces a new four-color layout and graphic format, new titles, topics, discussions, exercises, and features. The new layout and design will capture the attention of visually perceptive students; the new titles more clearly reflect the content and outcomes for each chapter.

- **Process, challenge and commitment to career planning have been added.** Chapter 1 emphasizing what is necessary from the reader to fully engage in the process.
- *Student Learning Outcomes.* The opening chapter objectives have been renamed to more directly emphasize the intent of having students experience a shift in understanding, practice and focus.
- New *Tips From the Pros* feature. Anchors concepts and discussion with real world street smarts.

TIPS FROM THE PROS

SKILLS SETS FOR THE HEALTHCARE INDUSTRY

Although each career in the field of health care has its own unique requirements, you can be sure that there are common health-care career skills required of everyone in this rapidly expanding field. Most positions require excellent interpersonal and communication skills, some level of technical or quantitative thinking capacity, and a strong work ethic. Additionally, most positions entail a great deal of responsibility and maturity. Health-care workers must be willing to learn and to continue to learn, because constant updating and recertification are the norm in this constantly changing field with the development of new technology, advanced procedures, experimental treatments, and even new diseases.

WHAT DO *YOU* THINK?

1. From this description, what skills mentioned do you already possess?
2. What can you do now to develop any of the skills mentioned?

- **New Decision-making questions.** In each chapter, these questions have been added to strengthen decision-making skills for every "Fact and Figures", "Success Strategies" and "Real Stories" feature.
- **New *Exercising Your Options* end-of-chapter feature.** Elicits application specific action steps from the reader.

EXERCISE your options

If someone offered you a valuable prize for stating your mission right now, what would you say it is? Take a stab at stating it now, knowing full well that it and you are a work in progress, subject to revision as you move through the process. We all have a purpose that we can pursue that will allow us to actualize our values.

MY MISSION STATEMENT: _____

_____

Congratulations, the prize is self-knowledge and you are on your way!

- **New *Reinforcing Your Learning Outcomes.*** Each chapter ends with this new exercise, where students evaluate their own progress.
- **New *Career Fitness Portfolio.*** Students write their answers at the end to reflect on what they are learning.

Career Fitness Portfolio

Putting it all together to create a Career Fitness Portfolio and reach a tentative career goal.

A career portfolio is an essential tool in your career fitness program. It will help you track your thinking, collect your work products and prepare you to present your most professional self to the work world. It will be useful to you as you begin your career planning and search. Create a file on your computer and/ or a hard copy in a binder in which you can collect information about yourself—your skills, interests, and abilities. Get into the practice of collecting and documenting information about yourself. Include any reports, projects, job appraisals, notes or awards of recognition or other information that will support your self-assessment.

You will note that many of the following exercises are excerpted from their respective chapters in the text. This is done deliberately. This is your opportunity to review your responses and reflect on how true they are for you today. If your responses today are different from those you recorded when you initially completed these exercises, note your current responses below. These summaries will help you integrate the information from each chapter and put together your unique Career Fitness Portfolio. ***Note:*** Use extra paper as necessary to complete exercises.

CHAPTER 1 Testing Your Career Savvy

Refer back to original Chapter 1 answers.

1. I am _____

2. I need _____

3. I want _____

4. My generational preferences that may influence the career I select can be summarized as _____

5. The Holland Type most like me is:
   ___ Realistic   ___ Investigative
   ___ Artistic   ___ Social
   ___ Enterprising   ___ Conventional

6. Five adjectives that best describe me are _____

7. My favorite school subjects include _____

- **The year 2012 and beyond.** Explored in discussions, charts, graphs, and projections. Helps students prepare for how they fit into the world of the future.
- **Incorporates the latest practice, terminology, and content designed to address current economic realities.** Teachers, counselors, and students need to be aware of and engaged by questions now embedded throughout the text to stimulate interest and add relevancy.
- **Reorganized and streamlined content to increase usability of the material.** Streamlined chapters and exercises in the chapters; formatted all the exercises so they can be done individually or in collaboration with others; each chapter can stand alone but also builds on each other.
- **The Career Fitness Program** addresses specific National Occupational Information Coordinating Committee (NOICC) competencies necessary for the transition from school to career.

New material shows students how to optimize their career fitness program in light of current realities and global opportunities:

- Generational differences
- Branding
- Competitive advantage
- Understanding the value of a personal mission statement
- Trends related to STEM (Science Technology, Engineering and Mathematics) careers
- Freelance/temp/contingent workforce
- Expanding role of social media on every aspect of job search strategy, portfolio and digital resume alternatives
- Emerging resume, portfolio and interview formats
- Importance of persistence and resiliency (ie. mental fitness) to sustain a prolonged job search
- Strategic positioning in a global economy

The learning objectives that open each chapter are now called "Student Learning Outcomes" to more directly emphasize the intent of having students experience a shift in understanding, practice, and focus. With that goal in mind, each chapter ends with a new exercise called "Reinforcing Your Learning Outcomes." In this exercise, students evaluate their own progress.

- In an effort to strengthen decision-making skills in each chapter, we have added decision-making questions to "Fact and Figures," "Success Strategies," and the "Real Stories" features.
- We are further engaging readers by embedding questions in the text to keep their interest and add relevancy to the content.
- To keep current, we relate the content to the current economic realities with an eye toward the indication of positive change that is being reported.

Acknowledgments

We would like to thank the following people who reviewed this project in various stages of completion and offered suggestions on how it might be improved. The book is better as a result of their efforts.

For the 10th edition: Ailene Crakes, San Diego Mesa College; Jonathan Brent Ellis, Hillsborough Community College—Dale Mabry, Florida; Cheryll LeMay, Diablo Valley College, California; Rechelle Mojica, Miramar College (part of San Diego CC district); Robert Morris, University of Illiniois; Dr. Katie Scott-Garcia, Santa Fe College, Florida; Belen Torres-Gil, Rio Hondo College, California; Martha Vargas, Santa Ana College, California; and Wendy Walker, Dutchess Community College.

For previous editions: Barbara Allen-Burke, Clackamas Community College; Howard J. Bachman, Creighton University; Phyllis Bickers, Auburn University; Bruce Bloom, DeVry Institute of Technology, Chicago; Michael Brooks, Texas Christian University; Beverly Brown, Southern Illinois University; Dora Clarke, Whittier College; Pam Conyngham, Kent State University; Mariah Daniel-Platt, Rancho Santiago College; David Davis, Delta College; Rita Delude, New Hampshire Community Technical College; Ricardo Diaz, Chaffey Community College; Angela Dillavou, Westwood College of Technology; Sally Dingee, Monroe Community College; Sue Eckberg, Career Focus; Robert Ehrmann, Santa Barbara City College; Susan Ekberg, Webster University; Nancy Elk, Anoka Ramsey Community College; Theresa Green Ervin, The University of Mississippi; John Evans, Hillsboro Community College; Christina Friedman, Triton College; Sue Gannon, Vista Community College; Sheila Goethe, Hillsborough Community College; Laura Goppold, Central Piedmont Community College; Kathy Hanahan, Harper College; Tim Haney; Karen Hardin, Mesa Community College; Mary Harreld, McHenry County College; Kenneth Harris, College of DuPage; Jacqueline Hing, Rice University; Marilyn Joseph, Florida Metropolitan University; Sandi Krantz, Moorhead State University; Patsy Krech, University of Memphis; Gina Larson, Doane College; Christine Laursen, Westwood College of Technology; Robert D. Lewallen, Iowa Western Community College; Jackie Lewis, Minnesota State University–Mankato; Lea Beth Lewis, California State University at Fullerton; Carole Mackewich, Clark College; Cheryl Matherly, Rice University; Ruth McCormick, Edmonds Community College; Kathleen McGough, Broward Community College; Carmen McNeil, Solano College; Cynthia, Moore The University of Alabama; Carla Mortensen, Simmons Graduate School of Management; Paul Neal, Sierra College; C. Michael Nina, William Patterson University; Judy Patrick, Community College of Aurora; Sonjia Peacock, Lewis and Clark Community College; Bob Peters, College of DuPage; Hue Pham, Orange Coast College; Jenny Beasley Preffer, Flagler College; Susan Rhee, College of DuPage; Joe Ritchie, Indiana University of Pennsylvania; Dennis, Sadler, Rancho Santiago College; Judith Fine, Sarchielli, for editorial assistance in the ninth edition; Patrick Schutz, Mesa State College; Geri Shapiro, Los Angeles Mission College; Victoria Sitter, Milligan College; Joseph Spadafino, Arizona Department of Transportation; Bob Stanelle, Tulane University; Peggy Sullivan, Purdue University; Belen Torres-Gil, Rio Hondo College; Tanya Wahl, Inver Hills Community College; David White, College of San Mateo; Laurie Williamson, Appalachian State University; and David Young, Cerritos College.

We thank Janis Pizer of Cerritos College for her help in developing case stories and other content. We also appreciate the input of many other professional contacts and colleagues throughout the country and are grateful for the stimulating opportunities to share ideas. In particular, we want to mention our colleagues at Moorpark College, Cheryl Matherly of Rice University and the entire academic team who steered the development of the "Career Advantage" telecourse available through PBS. These contacts have served to influence and enhance our book. Additionally, we extend our sincere thanks to all those instructors who have used the book throughout the past nine editions. We hope you find this tenth edition even more comprehensive and helpful to your students in their career search. As always, we are interested in hearing your feedback.

Finally, we are indebted to our friend and previous publisher, John Gorsuch, for his encouragement throughout our many years of association. Special acknowledgment is given to our past executive editor Sande Johnson; our new executive editor, Jodi McPherson; our development editor Jenny Gessner; Jodi's editorial assistant, Clara Ciminelli; our production editor, Karen Mason; and our publisher, Jeffery Johnston, for their enthusiasm, support, and dedication to making this edition of *The Career Fitness Program* the best ever!

Last but not least, on a personal note, we dedicate this tenth edition to the memory of our dearly missed coauthor, Dr. Bill Bendat, who died recently doing what he loved, cruising! We are deeply indebted and enriched by his spirit, leadership, and contributions. We extend special thanks and heartfelt appreciation to each of our significant supporters and partners: Masha Fleissig, Dr. Bernard Natelson, and Dr. Michael Reiss.

Introduction

On Your Mark... Get Set...

The world of work is spinning at a dizzying pace. The job market is more unpredictable than ever. Companies are downsizing, rightsizing, restructuring, outsourcing, and undergoing radical technological change. Bigger mega-mergers are occurring and more small businesses are being created. The globalization and outsourcing of industries and organizations present us with competitive challenges and unprecedented opportunities. You can benefit from becoming aware of the changing job market by keeping up with trends, and by identifying how they fit your personal preferences. The following major trends are shaping the workplace:

1. The majority of jobs are created by small businesses employing fewer than 50 employees.
2. The traditional hierarchical organization is changing into a variety of forms, with a flat (reduced middle management) organizational chart becoming more common. Flexible networking of specialists who come together for a short-term project and then form again into a new group for the next project will be commonplace.
3. Smaller companies are able to expand and contract with the changing economy by employing temporary and contract employees.
4. Just as manufacturing used to be our mainstay, the United States is now considered a service economy that depends on knowledge workers. (See the section in Chapter 6 titled "The Need for Knowledge Workers.")
5. Lifelong learning is the rule; getting a degree to get a job may allow you entry into a company, but if you don't continually upgrade your knowledge, you will lose your competitive edge. Those who stay employed are rethinking, reinventing, and reengineering products, ideas, and services to meet continually changing needs.
6. Global competition and multinational corporations will influence more and more companies. The most valuable employee will be the one most familiar with several languages and cultural customs. The number of women and immigrants will continue to increase in the workforce.
7. Web 2.0 will continue to influence the way we think, act, learn, do business, and manage our careers. Social media will expand into all areas of work.
8. Those entering the workforce should expect to change their career path more than five times in their lifetime. Many will have 9 to 13 jobs by the time they reach age 35.
9. Workers are increasingly looking for meaning and purpose in their jobs. Seeking a new career is now about finding balance and meaning in one's life. This becomes a spiritual (not necessarily religious) component of job satisfaction.
10. Long-term unemployment is influencing many to take any job for immediate income. This book will help you to vision and plan beyond any current economic constraints to a time when career choice will be a viable option.

When you finish this Career Fitness Program, you will be able to see the long-term possibilities that will offer you a variety of career options.

A broad sweep of change and upheaval makes this a challenging time in history. Many of us are overwhelmed by lack of knowledge about our choices and our place and purpose in the world. One thing that is certain is change. It is essential to prepare now to expect change, accept it, and plan for it. You can best prepare for it by learning "who you are" in terms of lifetime goals and by taking responsibility for shaping your life. As you gain information about yourself and begin to make your own decisions, you develop self-confidence. In a deep, personal way, you begin to realize that no matter how drastically the world changes, you can deal with it.

The expectations and demands of today's job market require you to be physically agile, mentally alert, and psychologically able. *The Career Fitness Program* will prepare you to exercise your options whether you are planning for your first job, reentering the workforce, or rethinking your career. This program will help you build the mental stamina and psychological strength you need to be successful and satisfied today. You will also develop the mind-set and develop the tools for continuing success despite the inevitable surprises and challenges you will face. *The Career Fitness Program* is designed to assist you in the process of self-discovery and realization. The main goal of this book is to lead you through the process of career planning, which includes self-assessment, decision making, and job-search strategy. This process will help you make satisfying and fulfilling career choices throughout your life. By following the chapter-by-chapter program, you will learn more about yourself and how self-knowledge relates to your emerging career plan.

Let's preview the content of this book to see how it will help you achieve your career goals. The career-planning process is divided into three main parts: personal assessment (Chapters 1 to 5), the world of work (Chapters 6 to 8), and job search strategy (Chapters 9 to 12).

- In Chapter 1, you will come to understand how the process of self-assessment begins the process of career planning. You will explore the reality of many generations working together and examine how that affects you. Chapter 1 also discusses the difference between a job and a career. Most importantly, Chapter 1 compares the challenge of building a career to building your body.

- In Chapter 2, you will learn how building self-esteem impacts your actions. This chapter helps you develop confidence and maintain a positive approach to life and career planning, and it introduces you to the powerful concepts of branding and competitive edge.

- In Chapter 3, you will identify your needs, wants, and values and explore how these motivators influence your career choice. You will also explore value differences across generations.

- In Chapter 4, you will develop an understanding of and appreciation for your own unique personality and interests—factors that will influence your career choice.

- In Chapter 5, you will learn to recognize different types of skills and you will learn to identify and describe your own skills and their transferability in the workplace.

- In Chapter 6, you will explore societal and cultural norms and biases that may affect your career choices. You will also read about workplace trends, promising occupations, and salary predictions, and you will be given some excellent websites for career information.

- In Chapter 7, you will investigate websites and published sources of information about careers and specific jobs, including government publications and Internet resources.

- In Chapter 8, you will identify how people make decisions and learn how to improve your own decision-making skills. This process includes learning to set and pursue short- and long-term goals, establish and maintain financial fitness, and choose a major.

- In Chapter 9, you will learn about job-search strategies to find the hidden job market, including using college career centers, networking, informational interviewing, social media, and online job search techniques.

- In Chapter 10, you will learn how to craft winning resumes, portfolios, and cover letters.

- In Chapter 11, you will prepare for job interviews. This chapter discusses all aspects of the interview process, includes sample questions that you may encounter, and advises you about handling an employer's illegal questions.

- In Chapter 12, you will address the transition from college to career and learn what it takes to manage your career and embrace the philosophy of career fitness as a way of life.

Even if you are not yet in the full-time job market, the job-search strategy chapters (9–12) are a valuable resource. If you are in school, planning to work part-time, already employed, seeking an internship, or preparing for graduate school, you can begin to build your resume and portfolio and practice interviewing skills.

You will find your Career Fitness Portfolio at the end of the book. After completing each chapter, go to the portfolio section of the chapter to summarize your learnings and develop an ongoing journal. You will reflect back on your learnings, add to and change some of your responses as you go through the process of discovering your career fitness profile. This will help you exercise your options and strengthen your career fitness.

Supplemental Resources

INSTRUCTOR SUPPORT – Resources to simplify your life and support your students.

Book Specific

Online Instructor's Manual – This manual is intended to give professors a framework or blueprint of ideas and suggestions that may assist them in providing their students with activities, journal writing, thought-provoking situations, and group activities. The test bank, organized by chapter includes: multiple choice, true/false and short-answer questions that support the key features in the book. This supplement is available for download from the Instructor's Resource Center at www.pearsonhighered.com/irc

Online PowerPoint Presentation – A comprehensive set of PowerPoint slides that can be used by instructors for class presentations or by students for lecture preview or review. The PowerPoint Presentation includes bullet point slides for each chapter, as well as all of the graphs and tables found in the textbook. These slides highlight the important points of each chapter to help students understand the concepts within each chapter. Instructors may download these PowerPoint presentations from the Instructor's Resource Center at www.pearsonhighered.com/irc

MyTest Test Bank – Pearson MyTest offers instructors a secure online environment and quality assessments to easily create print exams, study guide questions, and quizzes from any computer with an Internet connection.
Premium Assessment Content
  • Draw from a rich library of question testbanks that complement the textbook and course learning objectives.
  • Edit questions or tests to fit specific teaching needs.
Instructor Friendly Features
  • Easily create and store questions, including images, diagrams, and charts using simple drag-and-drop and Word-like controls.
  • Use additional information provided by Pearson, such as the question's difficulty level or learning objective, to help quickly build a test.
Time-Saving Enhancements
  • Add headers or footers and easily scramble questions and answer choices all from one simple toolbar.
  • Quickly create multiple versions of a test or answer key, and when ready, simply save to Word or PDF format and print!
  • Export exams for import to Blackboard 6.0, CE (WebCT), or Vista (WebCT)!
    Additional information available at www.pearsonmytest.com

MyStudentSuccessLab – Are you teaching online, in a hybrid setting, or looking to infuse technology into your classroom for the first time? It is an online solution designed to help students build the skills they need to succeed for ongoing personal and professional development at www.mystudentsuccesslab.com

Other Resources

"Easy access to online, book-specific teaching support is now just a click away!"
Instructor Resource Center – Register. Redeem. Login. Three easy steps that open the door to a variety of print and media resources in downloadable, digital format, available to instructors exclusively through the Pearson 'IRC'. www.pearsonhighered.com/irc

"Provide information highlights on the most critical topics for student success!"
Success Tips is a 6-panel laminate with topics that include MyStudentSuccessLab, Time Management, Resources All Around You, Now You're Thinking, Maintaining Your Financial Sanity, and Building Your Professional Image. Other choices are available upon request. This essential supplement can be packaged with any student success text to add value with 'just in time' information for students.

ALWAYS LEARNING

Supplemental Resources

Other Resources

"Infuse student success into any program with our "IDentity" Series booklets!" - Written by national subject matter experts, the material contains strategies and activities for immediate application. Choices include:

- Financial Literacy (Farnoosh Torabi)
- Financial Responsibility (Clearpoint Financial)
- Now You're Thinking about Student Success (Judy Chartrand et.al.)
- Now You're Thinking about Career Success (Judy Chartrand et.al.)
- Ownership (Megan Stone)
- Critical Thinking: A Career Choice (Paul Schuler)
- Identity (Stedman Graham).

"Through partnership opportunities, we offer a variety of assessment options!"
LASSI – The LASSI is a 10-scale, 80-item assessment of students' awareness about and use of learning and study strategies. Addressing skill, will and self-regulation, the focus is on both covert and overt thoughts, behaviors, attitudes and beliefs that relate to successful learning and that can be altered through educational interventions. Available in two formats: Paper ISBN: 0131723154 or Online ISBN: 0131723162 (access card).

Noel Levitz/RMS – This retention tool measures Academic Motivation, General Coping Ability, Receptivity to Support Services, PLUS Social Motivation. It helps identify at-risk students, the areas with which they struggle, and their receptiveness to support. Available in paper or online formats, as well as short and long versions. Paper Long Form A: ISBN: 0135120667; Paper Short Form B: ISBN: 0135120659; Online Forms A, B & C: ISBN: 0130981583.

Robbins Self Assessment Library – This compilation teaches students to create a portfolio of skills. S.A.L. is a self-contained, interactive, library of 49 behavioral questionnaires that help students discover new ideas about themselves, their attitudes, and their personal strengths and weaknesses. Available in Paper, CD-Rom, and Online (Access Card) formats.

SmarterMeasure Learning readiness indicator (formerly Readiness for Education at a Distance Indicator or READI) – is a web-based tool that assesses the overall likelihood for online learning success. It generates an immediate score and a diagnostic interpretation of results, including recommendations for successful participation in online courses and potential remediation sources. Please visit www.readi.info for additional information. ISBN: 0131889672.

Pathway to Student Success CD-ROM – The CD is divided into several categories, each of which focuses on a specific topic that relates to students and provides them with the context, tools and strategies to enhance their educational experience. ISBN: 013239314X.

"For a truly tailored solution that fosters campus connections and increases retention, talk with us about custom publishing."
Pearson Custom Publishing – We are the largest custom provider for print and media shaped to your course's needs. Please visit us at www.pearsoncustom.com to learn more.

STUDENT SUPPORT – Tools to help make the grade now, and excel in school later.

"Now there's a Smart way for svtudents to save money."
CourseSmart is an exciting new choice for students looking to save money. As an alternative to purchasing the printed textbook, students can purchase an electronic version of the same content. With a CourseSmart eTextbook, students can search the text, make notes online, print out reading assignments that incorporate lecture notes, and bookmark important passages for later review. For more information, or to purchase access to the CourseSmart eTextbook, visit www.coursesmart.com

"Today's students are more inclined than ever to use technology to enhance their learning."
MyStudentSuccessLab will engage students through relevant YouTube videos with 'how to' videos selected 'by students, for students' and help build the skills they need to succeed for ongoing personal and professional development. www.mystudentsuccesslab.com

"Time management is the #1 challenge students face."
Premier Annual Planner - This specially designed, annual 4-color collegiate planner includes an academic planning/resources section, monthly planning section (2 pages/month), weekly planning section (48 weeks; July start date), which facilitate short-term as well as long term planning. Spiral bound, 6x9.

"Journaling activities promote self-discovery and self-awareness."
Student Reflection Journal - Through this vehicle, students are encouraged to track their progress and share their insights, thoughts, and concerns. 8 1/2 x 11. 90 pages.

MyStudentSuccessLab

Start Strong. Finish Stronger.

www.MyStudentSuccessLab.com

MyStudentSuccessLab is an online solution designed to help students acquire the skills they need to succeed for ongoing personal and professional development. They will have access to peer-led video interviews and develop core skills through interactive practice exercises and activities that provide academic, life, and professionalism skills that will transfer to ANY course.

It can accompany any Student Success text or used as a stand-alone course offering.

How will MyStudentSuccessLab make a difference?

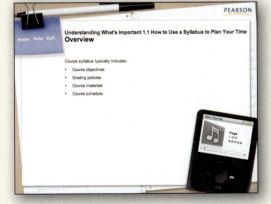

Is motivation a challenge, and if so, how do you deal with it?

Video Interviews – Experience peer led video 'by students, for students' of all ages and stages.

How would better class preparation improve the learning experience?

Practice Exercises – Practice skills for each topic - leveled by Bloom's taxonomy.

What could you gain by building critical thinking and problem-solving skills?

Activities – Apply what is being learned to create 'personally relevant' resources through enhanced communication and self-reflection.

MyStudentSuccessLab
Start Strong. Finish Stronger.
www.MyStudentSuccessLab.com

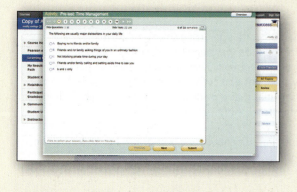

As an instructor, how much easier would it be to assign and assess on MyStudentSuccessLab if you had a Learning Path Diagnostic that reported to the grade book?

Learning Path Diagnostic

- For the **course**, 65 Pre-Course questions (Levels I & II Bloom's) and 65 Post-Course questions (Levels III & IV Bloom's) that link to key learning objectives in each topic.

- For each **topic**, 20 Pre-Test questions (Levels I & II Bloom's) and 20 Post-Test questions (Levels III & IV Bloom's) that link to all learning objectives in the topic.

As a student, how much more engaged would you be if you had access to relevant YouTube videos within MyStudentSuccessLab?

Student Resources

A wealth of resources like our FinishStrong247 YouTube channel with 'just in time' videos selected 'by students, for students'.

MyStudentSuccessLab Topic List -

1. A First Step: Goal Setting
2. Communication
3. Critical Thinking
4. Financial Literacy
5. Information Literacy
6. Learning Preferences
7. Listening and Taking Notes in Class
8. Majors and Careers
9. Memory and Studying
10. Problem Solving
11. Professionalism
12. Reading and Annotating
13. Stress Management
14. Test Taking Skills
15. Time Management

MyStudentSuccessLab Feature set:

Learning Path Diagnostic: 65 Pre-Course (Levels I & II Bloom's) and 65 Post-Course (Levels III & IV Bloom's) / Pre-Test (Levels I & II Bloom's) and Post-Test (Levels III & IV Bloom's).

Topic Overview: Module objectives.

Video Interviews: Real video interviews 'by students, for students' on key issues.

Practice Exercises: Skill-building exercises per topic provide interactive experience and practice.

Activities: Apply what is being learned to create 'personally relevant' resources through enhanced communication and self-reflection.

Student Resources: Pearson Students Facebook page, FinishStrong247 YouTube channel, MySearchLab, Online Dictionary, Plagiarism Guide, Student Planner, and Student Reflection Journal.

Implementation Guide: Grading rubric to support instruction with Overview, Time on Task, Suggested grading, etc.

PEARSON

Pearson Success Tips, 1/e

ISBN-10: 0132788071 • ISBN-13: 9780132788076

Success Tips is a 6-panel laminate that provides students with information highlights on the most critical topics for student success. These topics include MyStudentSuccessLab, Time Management, Resources All Around You, Now You're Thinking, Maintaining Your Financial Sanity, and Building Your Professional Image. Other choices are available upon request via our www.pearsoncustomlibrary.com program, as well as traditional custom publishing. This essential supplement can be packaged with any student success text to add value with 'just in time' information for students.

Features

- **MyStudentSuccessLab** — Helps students 'Start strong, Finish stronger' by getting the most out of this technology with their book.
- **Time Management** — Everyone begins with the same 24 hours in the day, but how well students use their time varies.
- **Resources All Around You** — Builds awareness for the types of resources available on campus for students to take advantage of.
- **Now You're Thinking** — Learning to think critically is imperative to student success.
- **Maintaining Your Financial Sanity** — Paying attention to savings, spending, and borrowing choices is more important than ever.
- **Building Your Professional Image** — Students are motivated by preparing for their future careers through online and in person professionalism tips, self-branding, and image tips.
- **Additional Topics** — Topics above are 'default.' These topics include MyStudentSuccessLab, Time Management, Resources All Around You, Now You're Thinking, Maintaining Your Financial Sanity, and Building Your Professional Image. Other choices are available upon request via our www.pearsoncustomlibrary.com program, as well as traditional custom publishing. This essential supplement can be packaged with any student success text to add value with 'just in time' information for students.

Topic List

- MyStudentSuccessLab*
- Time Management*
- Resources All Around You*
- Now You're Thinking*
- Maintaining Your Financial Sanity*
- Building Your Professional Image*
- Get Ready for Workplace Success
- Civility Paves the Way Toward Success

- Succeeding in Your Diverse World
- Information Literacy is Essential to Success
- Protect Your Personal Data
- Create Your Personal Brand
- Service Learning
- Stay Well and Manage Stress
- Get Things Done with Virtual Teams

- Welcome to Blackboard!
- Welcome to Moodle!
- Welcome to eCollege!
- Set and Achieve Your Goals
- Prepare for Test Success
- Good Notes Are Your Best Study Tool
- Veterans/Military Returning Students

NOTE: those with asterisks are 'default' options; topic selection can be made through Pearson Custom Library at www.pearsoncustomlibrary.com, as well as traditional custom publishing.

PEARSON

PERSONALIZE THE EXPERIENCE WITH

PEARSON LEARNING SOLUTIONS

FOR STUDENT SUCCESS AND CAREER DEVELOPMENT

The Pearson Custom Library Catalog

With Pearson Custom Library, you can create a custom book by selecting content from our course-specific collections. The collections consist of chapters from Pearson titles like this one, and carefully selected, copyright cleared, third-party content, and pedagogy. The finished product is a print-on-demand custom book that students can purchase in the same way they purchase other course materials.

Custom Media

Pearson Learning Solutions works with you to create a customized technology solution specific to your course requirements and needs. We specialize in a number of best practices including custom websites and portals, animation and simulations, and content conversions and customizations.

Custom Publications

We can develop your original material and create a textbook that meets your course goals. Pearson Learning Solutions works with you on your original manuscript to help refine and strengthen it, ensuring that it meets and exceeds market standards. Pearson Learning Solutions will work with you to select already published content and sequence it to follow your course goals.

Online Education

Pearson Learning Solutions offers customizable online course content for your distance learning classes, hybrid courses, or to enhance the learning experience of your traditional in-classroom students. Courses include a fully developed syllabus, media-rich lecture presentations, audio lectures, a wide variety of assessments, discussion board questions, and a strong instructor resource package.

In the end, the finished product reflects your insight into what your students need to succeed, and puts it into practice. Visit us on the web to learn more at www.pearsoncustom.com/studentsuccess or call 800-777-6872

Introducing CourseSmart, The world's largest online marketplace for digital texts and course materials.

A Smarter Way for Instructors

▶ **CourseSmart saves time.** Instructors can review and compare textbooks and course materials from multiple publishers at one easy-to-navigate, secure website.

▶ **CourseSmart is environmentally sound.** When instructors use CourseSmart, they help reduce the time, cost, and environmental impact of mailing print exam copies.

▶ **CourseSmart reduces student costs.** Instructors can offer students a lower-cost alternative to traditional print textbooks.

▶ **"Add this overview to your syllabus today!"** REQUIRED COURSE MATERIALS - ALTERNATE VERSION AVAILABLE:

CourseSmart is an exciting new choice for students looking to save money. As an alternative to purchasing the printed textbook, students can purchase an electronic version of the same content. With a CourseSmart eTextbook, students can search the text, make notes online, print out reading assignments that incorporate lecture notes, and bookmark important passages for later review.

A Smarter Way for Students

▶ **CourseSmart is convenient.** Students have instant access to exactly the materials their instructor assigns.

▶ **CourseSmart offers choice.** With CourseSmart, students have a high-quality alternative to the print textbook.

▶ **CourseSmart saves money.** CourseSmart digital solutions can be purchased for up to 50% less than traditional print textbooks.

▶ **CourseSmart offers education value.** Students receive the same content offered in the print textbook enhanced by the search, note-taking, and printing tools of a web application.

CourseSmart is the Smarter Way
To learn for yourself, visit www.coursesmart.com

This is an access-protected site and you will need a password provided to you by a representative from a publishing partner.

PART

1

Your Career Fitness Profile

Survey Your Strengths

Testing Your Career Savvy

Get Into Shape

Do you want to have a career that meets your needs, complements your personality, inspires you to develop your potential, and supports your vision and purpose? Are you someone who deliberately chooses the type of life you live rather than settling for what's convenient and available? If so, you need to set goals that will lead you from where you are now to where you want to be. However, to be achieved, goals must reflect your experiences, desires, attitudes, needs, interests, values, mission, and vision of the future. Collectively, these comprise your unique personal profile, which acts as a GPS, helping you navigate your way to your destination through uncharted paths, detours, and the uncertainties of the job market. Your personal assets also tap into your deepest, most authentic self, sparking the fire of motivation that you need to move you along your path with courage and conviction.

> Yesterday is the past, tomorrow is the future, but today is a gift. That's why they call it the present.
>
> —Bil Keane

Personal Assessment

As the first step in self-assessment, this chapter helps you examine your personal experiences, who you are right now, your current stage of career and life development, and your ability to deal with new information. As you begin to identify who you are and what energizes you about life, you will begin to incorporate those insights into a career. Self-awareness is the first stage of both the career choice and the career change process. As you look for insights that will help you chart your career, it is helpful to consider career development theories. Renowned psychologist Donald Super is credited with developing the theory that a career makes it possible for you to actualize or express your self-concept throughout your life span and life space. Your **self-concept** is essentially *how you see yourself*. Review the following principles of Super's theory on career development; and as you read, determine how they relate to you at this point in your career journey.

> Self-awareness = first step

▲ Personal assessment leads to job satisfaction.

Super's Self-Concept Theory

1. We differ in abilities, interests, and personalities.
2. Every occupation requires a characteristic pattern of abilities, interests, and personality traits. Within each occupation are workers with varying degrees of these characteristics.
3. Each of us is qualified for a number of occupations.
4. Vocational preferences and skills, the situations in which we live and work, and our self-concepts change with time and experience. These factors make choice and adjustment a continual process based on our maturity and lifestyle.
5. Selecting a career involves the following stages. As we discuss later in this chapter, many people experience these stages more than once in life. Thus, although Super discusses the stages in a more traditional sense, remember that you may return to the stages discussed here at various times in your life.
   a. Growth. This includes both physical and emotional growth as you form attitudes and behaviors that relate to your self-concept. What did you learn about yourself from childhood games or family roles? For example,

"I am a team player," "I am an individualist," "I am a mediator," or "I would rather read than play games." A child begins having fantasies during this period (e.g., a dream of becoming a doctor).
   b. Exploration. This is divided into *fantasy* (e.g., a child's dream of becoming a doctor), *tentative* (e.g., high school and post–high school periods of exploration in which ideas are narrowed down), and *reality testing* (e.g., in high school or early college, working part time or volunteering in a hospital, taking math and science classes, or raising a family). You start learning about the kind of work you enjoy and the kind of worker you are. For example, "I am good with detail," "I enjoy working with people," "I enjoy working alone," "I take criticism well."
   c. Establishment. This includes initial work experience that may have started only as a job to earn a living but that offers experiences for growth so it becomes part of the self-concept. For example, "I am an assistant manager, I am responsible for the bookkeeping, and I look forward to becoming the manager," rather than, "This is just a job, and I will be doing

bookkeeping until I can finish my bachelor's degree and get into law school." Very often several changes in jobs will occur over a few years.

d. Maintenance. This is a time when we maintain or improve in our career area. Advancement can be to higher levels or laterally across fields. For example, you may start thinking, "I am extremely competent," "I can compete with others," "I can cooperate and share my knowledge," or "I can train others."

e. Disengagement. Super defines disengagement as the stage just before retirement or one when we see no new challenges or chances for mobility. Traditionally, it is a period during which there is a shift in the amount of emphasis you place on your career; you may even seek a reduction of the hours you work. Disengagement may also occur some time before retirement. You may think, "I have many things other than this job I want to do," "I want to spend more time at home," "I want to work on my hobbies," "I want to travel more," or "I want to make a living from my leisure pursuits." Job or career changes are a form of disengagement,

whether prompted by personal choice or circumstances beyond your control (a layoff, for instance).

6. The nature of any career pattern is influenced by parental socioeconomic level, mental ability, personality characteristics, and opportunities to which the individual is exposed. Both limitations and opportunities may be apparent as a result of these factors. People are affected by the realities of everyday life. A teenager living in an affluent suburb may have unlimited opportunity to focus on schoolwork because of ample financial support. A teenager living in the inner city with several siblings, in contrast, may work 20 hours or more each week to help out with the family finances and thus have limited time and energy for schoolwork.

7. The process of career development is essentially that of self-concept development and implementation. All of us try to maintain a favorable picture of ourselves.

8. Work satisfaction and life satisfaction depend on the extent to which our work and our life provide adequate outlets for our abilities, interests, personality traits, and values.

SUCCESS strategies — Relevance of Super's Theory of Career Development

Theories are helpful in understanding and putting into perspective what we are experiencing in our own lives. In terms of career choice, you might feel confused, lost, alone, different, and concerned about your current status; however, after you have become familiar with Super's theory, you understand that it's normal to feel this way. Whether you are in a particular stage of career development or you are in a transition and between stages, knowing about Super's theory helps you deal with the anxiety that accompanies any stage of development.

What has influenced your self-concept? Have you assessed your likes and dislikes, desires, attributes, limitations, needs, wants, and values? An accurate and current self-assessment will enable you to make better career decisions by increasing your personal awareness and understanding. Self-awareness improves your ability to seek and select jobs that fit your unique self-concept or to shape whatever job you have, given your own unique assets. Super's theory applies each time you make a career change: You will reexperience the stages of growth, exploration, establishment, maintenance, and disengagement.

Our discussion of Super's theory briefly mentioned the general career stages that many people have experienced: growth, exploration, establishment, maintenance, and disengagement. Because you are probably somewhere between the stages of exploration and maintenance right now, it is useful to understand that you are also experiencing the transitional stages that relate to your age and affect your career planning. To start the critical step of personal assessment, complete Exercise 1.1.

1.1   First Impressions

Here is your first chance to think about yourself and record your responses. Fill in each blank carefully and honestly. Be true to yourself; don't try to please anyone else with your answers. Try to be spontaneous; the longer you think before answering, the more likely you are to censor your answers.

1. I am _____

2. I need _____

3. I want _____

4. I would like to change _____

5. If all goes well in the next five years, I will be doing the following things:

   _____

   _____

6. If things go poorly in the next five years, I will be doing

   _____

   _____

7. Reviewing past jobs or volunteer experiences I have had, what did I like best/least about each one? Is there a pattern?

   _____

   _____

UNDERSTANDING LIFE STAGES

Many authors, including Gail Sheehy, have explored how people change as they age, and they have found that as longevity has increased, so have concepts and definitions of career and retirement. There is no longer a clear-cut point when we end our training or move into retirement. Finding challenging or rewarding employment may mean retraining and moving from a stale or boring job in order to find your passion and pursue it. The idea is to think long range and anticipate an active lifestyle into later years—perhaps into one's 80s or 90s. Being personally productive may now mean anticipating retiring in stages. This might indicate going to an alternate plan should a current career end by choice or economic chance.

Because we are living longer, we have longer to grow up and grow old. We need to constantly review and renew the meaning of our existence and be to new experiences. These can include hobbies, learning, nonprofit ventures, volunteering, hobbies turned into businesses, or part-time work to help others and increase earnings. Taking risks to supplement and expand our personal horizons can help us at any age to avoid becoming vulnerable, feeling stuck, or being directed by unforeseen events. In essence, our later adulthood will be a time of renewal, discovery, leisure, service to society, adventure, and productivity.

Remember that life stages are based on social norms that are in constant flux. People are changing careers and employment frequently, and the world is changing at such a pace that social norms will surely continue to adjust. For example, two-career families, single-parent households, later marriages and/or alternative lifestyles, longer life spans, and in addition, fewer good entry-level jobs and the need for lifelong learning, will all influence the direction of people's lives and will lead to more fluidity and ambiguity between life stages. Decisions will vary greatly, with some people still choosing early marriages or delaying career and professional plans or decisions regarding childbearing for more education or training. A future scenario may incorporate more fully a flexible and adaptive work schedule both permitting and addressing leisure, longevity, and family.

APPRECIATING GENERATIONAL DIFFERENCES

Never before in the workplace have so many different generations worked side by side. Each generation is defined by a time frame in which they were born. As a group, each of these populations live through specific periods in time that affect the way they see life and develop their value systems. Their values, perceptions, attitudes, and expectations have been formed as a result of historic events, wars, politics, and economic and cultural influences. By looking at each of the four generations currently in the labor pool, we can better understand ourselves and our fellow employees and thus be more effective and productive. The birthdates and population of each group varies slightly depending on the research.

As you look at each group, remember that not every descriptor applies to every individual in the group. We are not trying to label or pigeonhole people but to provide some generalizations that may be useful in understanding yourself and those with whom you work.

MILLENNIALS: GEN Y (BORN 1982–2000)

This generation is composed of the newest members of the workforce. They are called *millennials, gen y, gen next, the google generation, the echo boom,* and *the tech generation.* Because their numbers are similar to those of the baby boomers, their impact will be significant. They have been raised with three other generations and they feel comfortable with all age levels, often texting parents and grandparents regularly to keep in touch. They are the digital natives who have grown up with technology and the Web. Gen Y is a generation of multitaskers who value flexibility and freedom as much as money. They want a job on their own terms with the opportunity to make a difference, learn, grow, and have fun. They will often choose meaningful work over high-paying work if pushed to make a decision based on those factors. These young people are well educated, globally aware, civic minded, polite, and tolerant of authority. They are natural team players who are eager and confident about making a contribution despite being the youngest on the team. They value and learn from their peers and are more inclusive and group oriented than any other generation.

GEN X (BORN 1961–1981)

The Gen X generation represents almost a third of the workforce, and they will take over as the baby boomers retire. Because they are smaller in numbers than are the boomers, they will have multiple options, as evidenced by their comfort in job hopping. They bring a breadth of experience with a strong independent spirit; they are unimpressed with authority and titles and might come across as cynical. These employees are loyal only as long as they get what they want from the job or company. If not, they are comfortable moving on. Unlike their parents, the motto of Gen X is "Work to live." They insist on a life and work balance and are willing to leave a job to get it.

(BABY) BOOMERS (BORN 1943–1960)

According to *FutureWork Institute/Society for Human Resource Management,* boomers are 46 percent of the current workforce and as such they make up the largest population within the workforce. Because of the current economic situation and the satisfaction they derive from working, this group intends to stay in the workforce in significant numbers. Boomers' focus has been on personal goals and achievement. They have been willing to sacrifice for success and worthwhile causes and are often labeled workaholics whose motto is "Live to work." They have been called the *me generation,* and they sometimes view the two younger generations as unwilling to "pay their dues" to succeed. They excel in teams and make decisions by consensus. These employees are currently beginning to retire from one career; but a recent AARP survey reports that 70 percent will keep working, and they will most often be reporting to the two younger generations.

SILENT: MATURES/TRADITIONALS (BORN 1925–1942)

There are 34 million people in this generation, often called *traditionalists* or *matures*. This group values history, work experience, the company legacy, and a strong tradition based on loyalty, hard work, and conformity. Matures/traditionalists are civic minded and help oriented. They are sometimes perceived as authoritarian and unwilling to accept new ideas or change. They are also valuable mentors to the younger generations and will continue to fill in the gaps in the labor pool. This generation wants respect and the opportunity to continue to make a contribution.

 **FACTS & FIGURES** **Generations in the Workplace**

According to generational historians Neil Howe and William Strauss, the following defines the generations:

Silent (Traditional /Mature)	born 1925–1942	34 million
(Baby) Boomers	born 1943–1960	76 million
Generation X	born 1961–1981	41 million
Millennials (Gen Y)	born 1982–2000	75 million

WHAT DO *YOU* THINK?

1. As you consider some of the defining differences in each of these generational groups, think of yourself. What is your generation called?
2. How closely do you resemble some of the descriptors?
3. If you are currently working, think about your boss and supervisors as well as your fellow employees. How closely do they fit the descriptions? Does this help you understand and work better alongside each other?
4. You will undoubtedly have to work on a team or perhaps you will hold a leadership position at some point in your future career. Why do you think it would be beneficial for you to understand the generational makeup of your colleagues, subordinates, or managers?
5. How might this help you become a more effective supervisor or boss?
6. How might this information affect your choice of employers?

 **SUCCESS strategies** Identifying Generations by Their Behaviors

For each workplace scenario, identify which generation might be represented and why. Then think about how an employer from each generation might be likely to respond to the scenario. Finally, how would you personally react to each scenario if the person was a colleague? How about if you were managing this person? Would you have any advice to share if this person asked, "How can I get ahead in this organization?"

1. In an interview, when a candidate was asked what questions she had, her first question was, "How much vacation do I have and when can I start taking it?"
2. An employee refuses the opportunity to work from home, stating that he's always put in his time at the office and he isn't about to change his routine at this point in his career.
3. A professor on a college campus started bringing her dog to her office and to class without asking for permission. She was the only one on campus to do so.
4. An employee regularly leaves work to attend his son's soccer games.
5. A salesperson offers to brief a colleague about a meeting with a prospective new client. The colleague declines, certain that all will go well.
6. After working for a year, an employee asks for a two-month leave to take advantage of a unique travel opportunity.
7. Someone who has been at the company for a while offers to show a new employee around and fill her in on the office politics.
8. Although not part of the company culture, an employee requests working from home three days a week.
9. An employee volunteers to stay late and close up for the night when the rest of the group is attending a training session.

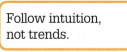

Differentiating between a Job and a Career

We will be using the words *job* and *career* throughout this book, so let's define them. There is an important difference between them. Basically, *a job is a series of tasks or activities that are performed within the scope of what we call work.* These tasks relate to a career in that a career is a series of jobs. But more than jobs, a career is a sequence of attitudes and behaviors that are associated with work and relate to our total life experience. *A career is the integration of our personality with our job activities.* Therefore, our career becomes a primary part of our identity or our self-concept.

> A career is the integration of personality with work activities.

In the past, people chose their careers early in life, and they stayed in those careers most of their lives. Farmers worked on their farms, bookkeepers stayed in the office, and teachers taught until retirement. Today, the trend in the United States has shifted toward multiple careers. We can now expect to have four or more careers in our lifetimes. Furthermore, with the rapid changes in society as well as in economic conditions, jobs, and technologies, many traditional jobs are becoming obsolete. In fact, William Bridges in his book *Managing Transitions: Making the Most of Change* suggests that jobs as we know them will evolve to meet the current needs. He means that a person hired to take a particular job can be certain the job tasks will change rapidly. Even if the job title remains the same, new and different skill sets will continually be required. The original position may become dramatically different or even disappear altogether.

> Follow intuition, not trends.

TIPS FROM THE PROS

Today, a phrase like "that's not my job" will never be uttered by anyone who wants to keep their job! The most valued employees are those who are flexible and do what is required regardless of job title or job description.

This is markedly different from the world in which the Silents and Baby Boomers worked. Thus, the expectation that once you find a job, you are home free, secure, or set for life is no longer realistic. The traditional employee contract, although unwritten, implied an honest day's work for an honest day's wage, employee loyalty in exchange for job security, and raises and promotions in return for seniority. Today's new employee contract simply implies continued employment for individuals who possess skills that continue to meet a business need.

More than ever it is important to give considerable thought to what you want to do and to structure your training and education to be relevant both to your interests and to trends in the job market. Knowing yourself and developing a plan of action based on your needs

> Be prepared to manage your career.

as well as the needs of the job market will help you embark on the career most satisfying for you rather than just following the latest trends in one field or another.

Demands in the job market rapidly shift. Some time ago, teachers were in great demand. Then, for about a decade, a glut of teachers was on the market. Now, although there is a need for teachers, they are being furloughed because of economic issues, and this is happening in many other fields today. If you base your career decision primarily on current trends, by the time you obtain the training necessary to get into the hot field, it may well have cooled down. This strategy leaves you with slim prospects for a job that can lead to a career, and quite possibly with skills and training in a field that you weren't terribly excited about in the first place (except as a quick opportunity).

Each of us has the potential to be satisfied in any number of occupations. Getting to know yourself better through personal

▲ Teamwork across generations makes for success.

assessment will help you identify careers that are best suited to your personality. People who are not prepared for change allow that change to influence their decisions. They are often frustrated and unhappy because they are forced to work at jobs they don't enjoy. They may never have realized they have choices, or perhaps they never took the time or energy to become aware of their preferences. They settle for less than what might be best for them. Dad says "get a job in business," even though his child has a special talent in art. The high school adviser recommends engineering because scholarships are available. The employment department directs an unemployed applicant into a computer training program because there's an opening. Granted, in tough economic times, you might be forced to take a job for pure survival on a temporary basis until more possibilities open up. But, by knowing your own preferences, you will be ready to manage your career and get back on your path instead of merely following others' suggestions. Complete the following exercises to jump-start your personal assessment by thinking about your current preferences in Exercise 1.2 and by describing yourself in Exercise 1.3.

EXERCISE
1.2 Identify Your Interests

1. What subjects in school do I like most / least?
   _____
   _____

2. What books or magazines do I read? What kinds of music, art, theater, and cinema do I like? What are my favorite websites?
   _____
   _____
   _____

3. What do I like to do for fun? How do I spend my spare time?
   _____
   _____
   _____

4. What jobs have I had (including volunteer work), and what did I like most and least about them? _____
   _____

5. What interests do I have that reflect my generation? _____
   _____

EXERCISE
1.3 Describe Yourself

Circle those adjectives that best describe you. Place an "X" in front of those adjectives that are least like you.

REALISTIC (R)		INVESTIGATIVE (I)		ARTISTIC (A)	
____ practical	____ persistent	____ careful	____ introverted	____ emotional	____ impulsive
____ athletic	____ conforming	____ achieving	____ confident	____ expressive	____ flexible
____ rugged	____ down to earth	____ curious	____ analytical	____ imaginative	____ idealistic
____ stable	____ self-reliant	____ precise	____ intellectual	____ unordered	____ original
____ frank		____ independent		____ creative	

SOCIAL (S)

____ helpful	____ understanding
____ insightful	____ popular
____ kind	____ cooperative
____ friendly	____ responsible
____ tactful	____ flirtatious

ENTERPRISING (E)

____ energetic	____ adventurous
____ driving	____ powerful
____ ambitious	____ persuasive
____ assertive	____ competitive
____ enthusiastic	

CONVENTIONAL (C)

____ conscientious	____ moderate
____ persistent	____ orderly
____ organized	____ efficient
____ obedient	____ detailed
____ dependable	____ thorough

Next, review the adjectives you circled. Note the list is divided into six clusters: Realistic, Investigative, Artistic, Social, Enterprising, and Conventional (RIASEC). This is called the Holland Code. Which groups of adjectives best describe you? Also note that most of the words are positive personality traits. This exercise gives you a chance to acknowledge your positive attributes.

From which three of the six groups do most of your adjectives come? Rank the groups from which most of them come as 1, second most as 2, and third most as 3.

1 _____   2 _____   3 _____

This three-letter code is your preliminary Holland Code. It helps you organize information about yourself so you will be in a position to make informed career decisions. Each group of adjectives describes a certain kind of person. What kinds of people do you like to be around? Rank the top three types here using the three-letter code.

1 _____   2 _____   3 _____

How similar are the letters you selected for people you like to be around to those you selected to describe yourself? Dick Bolles, author of *What Color Is Your Parachute?*, suggests the code you selected for people you like to spend time with is a good indicator of the code that relates to occupations you would also enjoy the most. You will have the opportunity to further analyze and use this code in your career fitness program as we go through the process.

STRIVING FOR CAREER SATISFACTION

Survey after survey on job satisfaction among American workers indicates that well over 50 percent are dissatisfied with their jobs. In a study for *U.S. News & World Report*, people were asked to name the three things that contribute most to their quality of life. The top categories for men and women were "job/career satisfaction," "relationship with family," and "money." Because you will likely be changing jobs and careers several times in your life, it is more important than ever before to have accurate knowledge about yourself and the world of work.

The Gallup Poll organization analyzed its massive database and determined that 55 percent of employees have no enthusiasm for their work! In another Gallup survey, two-thirds of a group of adults said if they were starting all over, they would try to get more information about their career options. In Gallup's annual worker satisfaction survey, job stress has consistently ranked near the bottom along with other factors, including job security, and health and retirement benefits. The largest decline in overall satisfaction was from 35- to 44-year-olds. Interestingly, people in this age group were once among the happiest group in the American workforce.

You will face the need to continually evaluate yourself and your career path. It is useful to know about the changing world of work and which occupations in which industries allow you to best express yourself and best use your strengths and talents. When analyzing your personal assets, it is to your advantage to think ultimately about the total job market. Search for jobs that will lead you into a career. You will benefit greatly from identifying a variety of alternatives that allow you to express your personality. Once you have looked within yourself and identified what you want and need in a job, changes will be easier to make because you'll know when you have outgrown one job and need a new one. You will develop the personal insights to help you make decisions about career changes and transitions with greater ease and confidence. For most of us, career planning is not a simple, straightforward, linear process in

> Be prepared to revise your career plan continually.

> There is no single "right" career.

which we follow certain prescribed steps, end up at a specific destination, and live happily ever after. It is instead a feedback loop that continues to self-correct as you add information about your changing self and the world around you. We are constantly revising our career plan as we grow and change. This means there isn't any one "right" career. Instead, there are many careers in which we could be equally happy, equally successful, equally satisfied.

We are looking, then, not for the *one* right career but for the series of alternatives and career options that seem to make sense for each of us given our background, our personality, our career and life stages, and the changing world.

REAL stories   Meet Sandra

After graduating from high school, Sandra didn't know what she wanted to do. Many of her friends were enrolling in college, but Sandra wasn't interested in continuing with her education; she was tired of going to school and wanted to experience the "real world." Because she did well in her high school business classes, she thought that administrative assistant work might be interesting. With the help of a friend, Sandra put together a resume and went on the Internet to search for jobs. There were many administrative assistant positions, but Sandra didn't know the type of business she might find interesting, so she decided to go back to her high school counselor for some help. The counselor said that to make a career or job decision, it was important for Sandra to determine her interests, values, and goals. Once she had an idea of "who" she was, she could then investigate the kind of business that would be right for her. The counselor suggested that she make an appointment with the career counselor at the local community college.

The counselor at the community college gave Sandra several assessments, and they revealed an interest in the legal field. Sandra went back to the Internet, but she soon discovered that the jobs that interested her required special skills. Sandra had a decision to make: return to school or look for work in a different field. Because Sandra thought she would really like the legal field, she decided to do both. She began looking for general office positions and enrolled in a community college to begin a legal secretary certificate program. Sandra found a job as a receptionist with Transamerica Corporation. She learned the work quickly and found the hours allowed her to attend school and study. Although the pay did not allow her to live

on her own, she took advantage of the opportunity to live at home and save money for her own apartment. After two years, Sandra was close to receiving her certificate.

One day at work she was reading her legal terminology text when one of the executives walked by. Sandra liked Mr. Owens; he was always interested in her opinions and she enjoyed talking to him about her studies. When she told him her career plans, he indicated that he knew several attorneys and perhaps he could be of help when she was ready. Over the next few months, Sandra worked hard, and in early April she felt ready to make a move. She called Mr. Owens and said, "I wanted you to know that I will be completing my legal secretary certificate in May, and I remember you mentioned to me that if I needed any assistance in finding employment you might be able to help. I was wondering if I could meet with you to discuss my qualifications." Mr. Owens told Sandra how proud he was of her and that he would be happy to meet with her.

WHAT DO *YOU* THINK?

1. Do you think Sandra made a wise choice by not attending a four-year college? List the pros and cons of her decision.
2. If Mr. Owens had not offered to help Sandra, what other resources could she have investigated?
3. While Sandra was attending college, what organizations could she have joined that would have given her networking connections?
4. What other types of jobs or careers could Sandra have selected based on her high school diploma?

Choosing and Changing Careers

> Preparation = short-term and long-term goals

Each one of us, regardless of our stage in life, is in some phase of career development. You may be starting your first job or looking for a job. You may be planning for your first career, reentering the job market after some time at home, considering your next career, planning for part-time employment, or looking for meaningful volunteer experience.

Because there is no crystal ball that will predict the one right career for you, you will want to consider several options as you explore career development. The examples in the

"Real Stories" box describe people who reassessed their needs and made satisfying changes. It is also possible to survey your needs, values, interests, skills, aptitudes, and sources of information about the world of work to create a broader career *objective*. Some careers do have established or common career paths. In teaching, one often starts out as a tutor, works up to student teacher, and then becomes an assistant teacher before becoming a full-time teacher. In the marketing profession, people often start in sales. Therefore, we need to think about career goals in the sense of their being both short term and long term. A short-term career goal is one that can be rather quickly attained. For instance, in the process of career planning, you may discover you want to be a lawyer. We would normally consider law a long-term career option because it generally takes many years of study and preparation. However, a short-term career goal related to law might be obtaining a job as a legal secretary or a paralegal. Either of these would give you the opportunity to work in an environment that excites and energizes you long before you actually achieve your final and ultimate career goal. In addition, relevant experience enhances your appeal to future employers.

REAL stories — Career Changers Across Generations

Here are some examples of the kinds of career decisions we've been discussing:

PROFESSOR NGUYEN had reached his life goal, or so he thought. He was one of the few professors of religion at a small college in the San Francisco area. One day he woke up with stomach pains and body aches and had little energy. He dragged himself out of bed. When the pains lasted longer than three days, he visited his family physician only to find there was no medical reason for his discomfort. He then began some soul searching. His pains and nightmares continued over a period of months and seemed to occur only during the workweek. On weekends, when he was with his family or volunteering at a hospital, he felt energetic and healthy. Soon he took a leave of absence from his job and devoted more time to his hospital avocation. The physical ailments mysteriously disappeared. He spent a year examining his needs, consulting with a career counselor, and talking things over with friends. He found that his real satisfaction came from helping people in the hospital rather than from teaching religion.

Shortly thereafter, a friend told him about a job opening as an ombudsman in a hospital. He was selected for the job and now lectures to local classes in career development on the hazards of keeping a job that is making you ill! Professor Nguyen needed to reexamine his original goals to discover why his career as a professor wasn't meeting his needs.

DAVID CHAN spent two years at a state college with a major in prelaw but a love for art. He wished to choose a career with strong financial potential that would be acceptable to his parents. During his junior year David realized he constantly daydreamed about a career in art. So he enrolled in an evening community college class and then transferred full time to a technical art school where he specialized in drawing and sketching. David completed his degree, sought career counseling, and decided to try for his dream job. Within two years, he had a part-time job with an animation studio. He is now a full-time animator, creating characters for feature films. David was able to find a career that used his artistic talents and surpassed his financial goals.

If you examine enough options during the career-planning process, you may be able to use career experiences such as job shadowing, part-time jobs, and internships to move into related areas.

There is a final, very important reason that this effort at personal assessment is crucial as the first step in your career-planning process. Once you know who you are and what your preferences and talents are, you can better make sense of the information that continually bombards you regarding the world of work. It's almost impossible to read a headline, listen to a news broadcast, visit a website, or watch a television show that does not have some implication for you and your career. In fact, you may feel you suffer from information overload. Surfing the Web, looking at the classified ads, and reading about employment projections and trends can cause confusion, frustration, and often discouragement about what place you might have in this elusive job market.

One of the best ways to achieve a sense of control of and perspective on this constant stream of information is knowing precisely who you are. Then, when you are surfing, listening,

REAL stories — More Career Changers Across Generations

TAYLOR JORDAN is a sophomore at a community college. For the past two years, largely on the advice of her parents, she has been preparing to transfer to the local university to complete a degree in business. Taylor now realizes she wants to follow her true talents and interests, and pursue a career in interior design. Although she has spent much time and effort accumulating credits toward a bachelor's degree in business, she knows that many of her core courses will apply toward her associate's degree in interior design. She is determined to do what is necessary to achieve her new goal. To prepare for her discussion with her parents, Taylor has researched local job opportunities with furniture and home improvement stores, home builders, and interior design firms. She has talked to a college adviser about possible internships and volunteer work. Most important, she believes her decision is the right one and is determined to follow through with it.

JOSE MARCADO emigrated to the United States in the 1990s. In 2000, after improving his language skills by attending adult school, he enrolled in a restaurant and hotel management program at a community college and began working as a parking attendant. Jose was very sociable and positive, often making friendly conversation with his customers. By the time he finished his schooling, he was the supervisor of parking facilities. One of his customers told him about a job possibility with a large hotel chain and recommended he apply. Jose not only got the job, but within three years was managing the hotel's restaurant. His ability to network, be friendly, learn on the job, and combine studies and work experience led him to a great job.

RHONDA SPEER spent five years in college completing a bachelor's degree program in teaching with an emphasis in special education. After two and a half years working in the field, she decided she needed a change. Working with children all day was making it difficult for Rhonda to concentrate at the end of the day on her own young daughter. She found a job as a stockbroker trainee. Within six months she was a full-fledged stockbroker. Now she's a corporate financial adviser.

reading, watching, and experiencing, you will have a means of processing information through your consciousness, through your personality and preferences, and through your values and skills. Eventually, you will be able to recognize and reject information that does not apply to you, and to internalize and add to your career plan information that does. If a group setting such as a career class is available to you, all the better! The opportunity to discover yourself and expand your horizons is multiplied by the added benefit of group interaction. Exercise 1.4 is best done in a group setting because it gives you the opportunity to compare your ideas on occupational status with others. There are no correct or right answers to these questions, but doing this exercise helps you clarify what societal bias may be influencing your career preferences. Bringing this information to light and discussing it may free you up to consider a wider range of options.

EXERCISE

1.4 Consider Occupational Status

Rank the following occupations in numerical order according to the *status* you attribute to them. Number 1 should be the occupation that in your mind is most significant. How you define *significant,* of course, is up to you. For example, a police officer could appear as number 1 on your list if you place most value on societal order and safety. Number 20 should reflect the occupation you regard as least significant.

_____ administrative assistant	_____ engineer	_____ plumber
_____ auto technician	_____ farmer	_____ police officer
_____ barista	_____ hairdresser	_____ psychiatric nurse
_____ computer operator	_____ lawyer	_____ public school teacher
_____ construction worker	_____ landscape designer	_____ restaurant manager
_____ dental hygienist	_____ movie director	_____ robotics technician
_____ doctor	_____ musician	

Think about the aspects of these positions that impress you or seem of value to you. Next, think about how you define *status*. Is it based on probable income, amount of education required, societal standards? How individualistic do you think your rankings are? For example, was *musician* ranked in your top five because you appreciate music? There are no correct or incorrect answers in this exercise. However, your rankings may reflect some of your basic preferences. If most of your top-ranked occupations were higher-salaried or if your rankings were based on potential for high pay, you may be motivated by a need for security; if your highest rankings were for service-related occupations (e.g., doctor, public school teacher), your motivation might be different.

THE PROCESS

In many ways, the process of preparing to meet job and career challenges is much like the process athletes use to prepare to compete in their particular sport. It involves establishing a fitness program in which the competitor sharpens existing skills, adds needed skills, and, most importantly, develops a mental attitude of success.

Any good fitness program is a combination of theory and exercise, and our career fitness program maintains this balance. For each step of the planning process, we explain the theory behind that step, how it relates to the previous and next steps, and how it moves you closer to your final goal of identifying career options. We provide you with **Learning Outcomes, Facts and Figures, Success Strategies, Real Stories,** and **Tips from the Pros** to reinforce the relevancy of the material to your life.

The chapters include a series of exercises designed to bring each step of the process to life. These exercises will make you more aware of your strengths, weaknesses, and attitudes, and they will also help you summarize what you think is important to remember after each chapter. Each chapter ends with an activity called **Exercising Your Options**. This feature synthesizes the key points of the chapter and emphasizes the fact that no matter what the circumstances, we all have choices.

Note that the end of each chapter also contains a section called **WWWebwise**. These web links will build your skills in using the Internet to broaden your exposure to the information presented. Remember that reading a chapter or a book or viewing a website is a passive activity. However, responding to questions makes you an active participant in the career exploration process. We urge you to spend the time to think through and respond to the questions in the book. At the end of each chapter, we refer you to the Career Fitness Portfolio. This exercise asks you to review and record many of the most critical personal responses that you reported as you read through each chapter. You may find that some of your initial reactions have changed because of the new information in the text or other related activities. This summary section will afford you the opportunity to revisit your initial responses and pull together current and accurate information about yourself. We recommend that you catalog this information (either online or in a binder) and begin to collect supporting documents you may use to create a career portfolio. You can use this portfolio to assist you in your career planning process, as well as in your job search. As you go along in the process and begin to reflect on the content and exercises, you will find that it helps to share your answers with at least one other person; a classroom setting in which group discussion is encouraged is ideal because other perspectives expand your own awareness.

It is easy to sit back and read about career planning and simply agree with the text, theories, and exercises. *But until you make the commitment to actually get involved in the process, to actively participate, and to experience both progress and occasional discomfort along the way, you will not be able to reap the benefits of the process. No one ever "got fit" by sitting on the sidelines!*

THE CHALLENGE

Yes, we did mention the word *discomfort* just now. What do we mean by that? Anytime you begin a new exercise program, even if you start cautiously and sensibly in relation to your current level of activity, new muscles are stretched, and they let you know it. They feel awkward.

They ache. You become aware of parts of your body that you may never have noticed before. You can also expect this to happen in the process of career planning. Along the way, confusion and some discomfort may occur. We will ask questions to help you dig deep into yourself for answers. In this process of enhancing self-awareness, you will discover much about yourself that you like, as well as some characteristics you would like to change.

Because of this self-discovery process, at certain points along the way in our fitness plan you may feel a bit confused, a bit anxious, a bit impatient. All of these feelings are a normal part of the process. When you start out on a physical fitness program, you idealistically hope that in a week or two you will have the body that you visualize in your mind, even though you know realistically that developing a good physique is going to take a lot longer. Similarly, with your career plan you may begin to feel impatient and want things to move along more quickly or more clearly. Remember that any change or growth typically includes some discomfort, uneasiness, or anxiety. Frankly, if you begin to experience some of those feelings, it is a good sign! It indicates you are stretching, you are growing, and you are moving toward a newly developed awareness of who you are and how you relate to the world of work.

COMMITTING TO THE PROCESS

Whether you are taking the time at the beginning of your adult career to examine your options carefully and thoroughly or are finding at midlife that it is time to explore new directions, you will reap tremendous benefits in the future. The satisfaction you experience at "the finish line" will be directly proportional to your willingness and ability to deal with the anxiety and uncertainty you will experience at some points in the career-planning process. In essence, the more you put into any activity, the more you are likely to get out of it. Except for the short-lived fame of reality TV "stars," stories we have heard and read about our cultural heroes and heroines, whether athletes, performers, scientists, or political figures, tell us that the results they achieve are not easily accomplished. Their triumphs, which look so easy and so glamorous, are always the consequence of tremendous sustained effort, commitment, and perseverance. A statement attributed to famed artist Michelangelo seems to say it all: "If people knew how hard I had to work to gain my mastery, it wouldn't seem so wonderful after all."

Your career search requires a similar commitment. It requires your willingness to go with the process, to seek out specialized assistance, and to move through points of frustration, uncertainty, and confusion in the belief that you will come out with more awareness and a good sense of the next steps to take along your career path. We invite you to participate in an adventure and endeavor that we believe is every bit as exciting and rewarding as preparing for the Olympics. You are identifying your own mountain peaks and are setting out to climb them. Among your resources is this career-planning textbook, which incorporates the insights and experience of successful career planners. Most of all, the important attributes of your own spirit, vitality, and intuition, together with the desire to improve yourself, will serve you well throughout your search. This career fitness program will help you master the inevitable changes that occur within yourself and are associated with your evolving career choices and the work world around you. It will help you identify options that are consistent with who you are. It will enable you to be the champion of your own career.

EXERCISE your options

Are you prepared to engage in the enterprise of your life, YOUR CAREER? What is one thing you can do today to commit to your career? _____

Summary

The best approach to the process of career planning is first to examine who you are, what you know about yourself, and what you need and want, and next to mesh that information with the world of work. You then have the distinct advantage of being able to choose training for a career about which you are truly excited and enthusiastic. These two qualities are among the most important to potential employers. Even if the job market for the field you have chosen is extremely competitive, you will have an edge because of your sense of commitment, your passion, and your enthusiasm for what you are doing.

PURPOSE OF EXERCISES

The exercises from this chapter helped you explore your current feelings and attitudes and thus better understand yourself. Exercise 1.1, "First Impressions," assisted you in taking stock of where you are and what you are feeling. Exercise 1.2 asked you to begin thinking about your interests, and Exercise 1.3 asked you to identify your personal strengths. Exercise 1.4 encouraged you to identify job preferences by ranking occupations according to how you perceive their status. Next, you will find **WWWebwise**, a web-based research activity that will enhance your understanding. **Reinforcing Your Learning Outcomes** will reinforce what you learned in this chapter.

EXERCISE 1.5 WWWebwise

Go to **www.careerjournal.com/**. Choose one article that interests you to read and report on in class. Include in your report why you selected the article, information that was new and surprising or that confirmed something for you, and how you can apply that information to your own career fitness program.

(Note: Please be aware that websites can change without notice. If a link does not work, find a similar site to complete the activity.)

REINFORCING YOUR LEARNING OUTCOMES

Review and Rate Your Chapter Outcomes. Indicate in the right-hand column how well you do the following items (1 = very well, to 5 = not at all). If you rated yourself 4 or 5, review the material on the pages in parentheses to ensure your career success.

How Well Can You Do the Following?

- Differentiate between a job and a career. (pp. 9–10) 1 2 3 4 5
- Identify and apply Super's theory to your career development. (pp. 4–5) 1 2 3 4 5
- Determine how generational differences affect the workplace. (pp. 7–8) 1 2 3 4 5
- Discuss why personal assessment is the key factor leading to career satisfaction. (pp. 11–15) 1 2 3 4 5
- Understand the process, challenge, and commitment necessary to exercise your career options. (pp. 15–17) 1 2 3 4 5

Go to the Career Fitness Portfolio at the end of the book and complete this chapter summary to build and record your personal Career Fitness Portfolio.

Additional Opportunity: Your instructor may choose to assign the Career Fitness Portfolio for in class or online completion. If so, they will provide the handout or link for you to access.

Building Your Career Success Profile

Discover Your Personal Power

STUDENT LEARNING OUTCOMES

At the end of the chapter you will be able to . . .

- Understand that **positive** self-esteem is essential to a successful career plan.
- Identify specific assets that comprise the career success profile.
- Practice the approaches and techniques necessary to develop a career success profile.

Through the process of career planning, you discover how to use what you've learned about yourself (values, skills, interests, aptitudes, qualities, talents, and limitations), and apply it to the world of work (workplace savvy) and do what it takes (job search strategy) to reach your career goal. This is the formula for career success. We begin the process of career development with an assessment of your self-esteem and your attitudes because your mental outlook is the crucial variable that will move you toward (or keep you from) identifying and achieving your career goals.

No book, set of exercises, system, counselor, teacher, coach, or mentor will affect your future as much as your own belief system and your own commitment to achieving success. Your beliefs are reflected by your actions.

How many times have you told yourself, "I'm going to start on a new exercise program today" and then found a "legitimate" excuse to postpone your efforts? Are you really ready to work on your career fitness? If so, let's examine some of the beliefs and attitudes that can assist you with your plan.

Because we believe in positive attitude and imagery, we have used positive statements to begin each section in this chapter. This is done to provide you with models of statements that reflect and reinforce attitudes that lead to successful behavior and outcomes. This chapter describes each component of the success profile, stated as an affirmation. Read about each one and complete the exercises to determine your strengths and areas for development.

> Act as if it were impossible to fail.
>
> —*Dorothea Brande*

I Am Building Positive Self-Esteem

I maintain a positive outlook.

- I am assertive.
- I have a sense of humor.
- I am self-confident.
- I am enthusiastic.
- I use positive self-talk (affirmations).
- I visualize success.
- I have multiple intelligences.
- I learn from role models.
- I initiate action.
- I am persistent.
- I am disciplined.
- I demonstrate emotional intelligence.
- I set goals.
- I am self-reliant and career resilient.
- I am flexible.
- I have passion.
- I am responsible.
- I have vision.
- I am an innovator.

The ultimate goal is to know yourself and feel comfortable in your skin, to like yourself. The more you appreciate yourself, the more likely you will be to achieve your personal and career goals. Our sources of self-esteem are deeply rooted; at a very young age, we begin to formulate a concept of ourselves based on our upbringing, our schooling, our culture, and our life experiences. This book contains resources that will help you develop positive self-esteem and project it into your personal and career development and in essence create your unique brand. The concept of personal and career branding was originally introduced a decade ago by Tom Peters, a well-respected author of successful business books. His idea is that branding yourself as unique will contribute to your success. He called it "Me, Inc." It's essentially the same process that large companies use to develop a brand like Nike, Starbuck's, or Apple. The goal and outcome of developing your career fitness profile will be to identify "You, Inc." You will clarify what makes you stand out so that your uniqueness becomes part of what others think of you and why others seek you out. Your brand, or reputation, reflects your philosophy, your values, and your consistent demonstration of who you are, so that people in your personal and professional life know they can count on you for consistent performance. This reliability of character and action makes you a valuable and desirable asset both personally and professionally.

Dan Schwabel, an expert personal branding blogger, says that before establishing your brand and taking it online via a blog, website, or participation in social networks, you must go through the process of self-discovery so that you know your worth and your competitive advantage in the work world. Your competitive advantage is your unique self, distinct from anyone else in the job market. As you begin to understand and hone your personal assets, you become more able to set yourself apart from the pack and differentiate your brand so that you stand out from the crowd and you become the obvious choice for the job.

▲ Positive self-esteem is critical as you move forward with your career.

TIPS FROM THE PROS

Employers have an idea of who they want to hire. It is always someone with a combination of the personal assets that you will explore in this chapter. Cultivate these assets to gain your unique competitive edge.

This chapter, as well as every other chapter in the book, helps you in this self-discovery and branding process. Your career success will be accelerated and enhanced to the degree that you know yourself and are able to communicate your uniqueness and brand in the marketplace. The building blocks of positive self-esteem are listed in the sidebar and discussed next.

As you read each section, make a quick assessment. How would you rate yourself on each of these essential assets? Which of these assets have you already developed? Which do you need to work on? As you identify the areas in your life that need work, pay attention to the suggestions for improvement. The exercises in the chapter will help you build positive self-esteem and a success profile. These are both essential components of your ultimate goal in reading this book, which is to identify, develop, and enjoy a successful, satisfying career. Although the word success means many things to many people, success in general usually means the progressive external demonstration of internalized life goals. In other words, success refers to the step-by-step movement toward the attainment of an object, quality, or state of mind that we value and wish to possess.

Establish small goals that you can meet along the way, and give yourself credit for small successes. For example, although at this point, you may not know what you want to do careerwise, you are reading this book, one chapter at a time, you are thoughtfully completing the exercises, and you are taking a course in career development to further your chances of identifying a satisfying career that fits you.

TIPS FROM THE PROS

Even when you're not sure of your goal or the final destination, the process of moving forward, doing something that you sense might help, will serve to ultimately clarify your path. You are, in fact, leaning into your goal.

Congratulate yourself for taking this first step toward reaching your goal. Now complete Exercise 2.1, which will help you take the pulse of your self-esteem.

EXERCISE
2.1 Past Actions and Influences

This review will help you apply the building blocks of self-esteem to your life and future career. Fill in each blank carefully and honestly. Be true to yourself; don't try to please anyone else with your answers.

1. I am proud that _____.

_____

_____

2. One thing I can do now that I couldn't do a few years ago is _____.

_____

_____

3. Name the person you most admire. This person can be living, historical, or fictional. Write down the specific characteristics that you admire in this person.

_____

_____

EXERCISE 2.1   Past Actions and Influences   *CONTINUED*

4. Name a person who is like you, and describe this person in your own words.

_____

_____

5. In the last two weeks, which activities gave you

the greatest feeling of being energized?_____

the greatest feeling of importance? _____

the greatest feeling of self-worth?_____

6. What have you always wanted to do in your life? What's keeping you from doing it? What action could you take in the next year to get closer to this goal?

_____

_____

I Use Positive Self-Talk (Affirmations)

Positive self-talk improves self-image.

One of the most effective ways to improve your self-image is the deliberate use of positive self-talk. You already talk to yourself; we all do, and probably more often than we'd like to admit! But we usually are not consciously aware of our internal dialogue. Sometimes we are prone to self-defeating, negative messages that promote a poor self-image. Raising this internal dialogue to a conscious level can enable you to take charge of your self-talk. By repeating positive messages, you will be more apt to reinforce a positive self-image. These messages are commonly called **affirmations**.

An affirmation is a statement or assertion that something is already so (Gawain, 2000). It is an existing seed or thought in the present that reinforces your desires and aspirations. It is not intended to change what already exists but to create new possibilities. Remember, all events begin with a thought. If you think you can, and you apply yourself as if you can, you can! Anything a person can conceive can be achieved. Top performers build not only their bodies but also their minds. The thoughts you are thinking motivate your actions. Negative thoughts adversely affect your ability and strength. You have the power to influence your career path. Therefore, a career in which you can imagine yourself being happy and successful is a realistic and achievable goal.

However, while you develop your affirmations, remember you are planting a seed that must carry information about the exact thing you want to grow into, or produce—the result you desire. When you become specific about what you want, you are focusing the power of your mind's energy (your thoughts) on your desires. The more specific you are about your goals, the more focused you become about what must be done to reach them. You know you are being specific enough when you can visualize details about what you want. For example, if you want to become a college professor, you must be able to visualize yourself on a college campus in a specific classroom, working with students, interacting with other professors, and doing all the preparation work before class, including correcting papers!

Let's put this technique into action. Think of a quality you want to develop in yourself; we'll use enthusiasm as an example. Your first instinct might be to say or think, "I'm not very enthusiastic." As soon as this thought comes to mind, replace it with the opposite thought: "I am enthusiastic." Repeat the phrase over and over, day and night, until you feel you own it; soon it will feel comfortable. At the same time, picture yourself doing something with enthusiasm. Imagine that you are explaining to your boss why you deserve a day off, starting a conversation with a stranger, or confidently disagreeing with an instructor during class. Picture yourself as you make your statement and are positively reinforced: Your boss says, "Yes, you deserve it"; the stranger becomes a friend; the instructor praises you for your insight.

Now, take this opportunity in Exercise 2.2 to create and incorporate affirmations into your success profile.

EXERCISE

2.2 Positive Self-Talk Affirmations

1. Write six affirmations related to being successful in your career and life planning. Put them on 3 × 5 cards (one per card), create electronic reminders as your screen saver, put them on your mirror or wall. You can use the affirmations that are part of this chapter (see the examples here) and add some of your own. Apply the same technique that was outlined in the text in the example of enthusiasm. Then review suggestions 2 and 3 here to further cement your new affirmations.

   SOME SAMPLE AFFIRMATIONS
   I am a confident and competent person.
   I have many transferable skills.
   I am a valuable employee.
   I am a risk taker.
   I am skilled at networking.
   I enjoy talking to people about their careers.

   Now add your own affirmations here and write each one on 3 × 5 cards:

   a. _____

   b. _____

   c. _____

   d. _____

   e. _____

   f. _____

2. Read your affirmations to yourself several times during the day, in the morning as you awake and just before you go to sleep. Share your affirmations with a close friend or a classmate to verbalize your commitment. Consider posting them on your favorite social networking site, tweet about how you are demonstrating them.

3. To accelerate their effectiveness, try the following suggestions:

   a. Write your affirmations in longhand while speaking them aloud to yourself 10, 20, or more times. Wallpaper your computer screen with your affirmations.

   b. When writing, use different persons, such as "I, Marilyn, am highly employable"; "You, Marilyn, are highly employable"; "She, Marilyn, is highly employable."

   c. Record your affirmations and listen to them as you drive or while you do chores around the house.

   d. Before going to sleep at night or on arising in the morning, visualize yourself as the person you are becoming. For example, see yourself as more assertive, organized, social, enthusiastic.

   e. Chant or sing your affirmations aloud while driving or during any appropriate activity.

   f. Meditate on your affirmations.

   g. Tape them up around the house, on the telephone, on mirrors, on the refrigerator, on the ceiling above your bed, on the dashboard of your car, in your dresser drawers.

   h. Use affirmations as bookmarks.

4. Finally, ask yourself, "Is it what I really want?" George Bernard Shaw once commented, "The only thing worse than not getting what you want is getting what you want!"

I Visualize Success

Use mental rehearsal for success.

Visualization, much like affirmation, is mental practice. It is the conscious implanting of specific images in your mind. Through repetition, these images will become part of your unconscious and then conscious mind, evoking and enhancing abilities, habits, and attitudes. Visualization differs slightly from affirmations because it involves specific mental imagery as opposed to *verbal expression* of positive thoughts. Indeed, visualization is referred to as *mental imagery* or mental rehearsal.

When we marvel at the mastery of an expert, we often assume the person was born with extraordinary talents or skills. We forget that every champion athlete, every great performer, every skilled surgeon, and every professional developed expertise through endless hours of physical and mental practice. They visualize their performance, engage in positive self-talk ("I can," "I'll do better each time"), and, through repetition, they become closer to the example of what they desire to be.

Until you begin to understand yourself, it is difficult to contemplate success fully, in both personal and professional matters. Choose your own vision in which specific results, qualities, and abilities are evident and consistent with your definition of success.

Visualization is one of the most powerful tools that promote personal change. It is the process of maintaining a thought long enough for the mental picture we create to evoke an emotional response. This emotion causes conviction, and conviction influences reality. Thus, change in reality begins with visualization, which generates emotion, sparks conviction, and results in action.

SUCCESS strategies   Creating Effective Affirmations

Here are some hints to follow when stating or writing down your own affirmations:

1. Always phrase the affirmation in the *present*, never in the future; otherwise it may remain in the future. For example, if your goal is to be less tense or nervous in challenging and stressful situations, use an affirmation such as "I am calm; I am in control of my feelings in this situation," rather than "I *will* be calm."

2. Phrase your affirmation in the positive rather than the negative. In other words, don't affirm what you don't want. Instead of writing, "My present job doesn't bother me anymore," it would be more effective to write, "My work is wonderful" or "I enjoy my job."

3. Maintain the attitude that you are creating something new and fresh. You are not trying to manipulate, redo, or change an existing condition.

Thus, even before you implement your affirmation by enthusiastically taking some action, you have prepared yourself mentally for a positive outcome of your action. Your chances of experiencing the positive outcome improve because you are projecting a positive self-image. Try it!

Visualization can have a profound impact on your mind. Your subconscious does not distinguish between *imagining* something and actually *experiencing* it. (Try imagining you are biting into a lemon; can you taste it?) You can change your opinions, beliefs, aspirations, and levels of expectation by vividly imagining the circumstances and experiences you select. Of all the species on earth, only human beings can visualize the future and believe it can happen (Dyer, 1992).

A pessimist says, "I will believe it when I see it," whereas an optimist says, "I always see it when I believe it." What you see is what you get. The critical first step is a mental one. You must believe in and be able to see the possibilities and outcomes in your mind before you can hope to realize them in your life.

A high jumper visualizes a successful route to clear the bar; a golfer sees the putt dropping into the cup and follows that vision. Strong visual messages are reinforced with appropriate positive affirmations. This process will assist you in achieving what you want to accomplish. Conscious visualization of yourself as a success is a key step toward a positive self-fulfilling prophecy.

Those who use visualization successfully do so regularly over a period of time. This is the key to the success of mental rehearsal. Research indicates that a goal must be visualized a minimum of 30 minutes a day for at least a month to obtain results. This discipline distinguishes visualization from random daydreaming, an effortless activity in which we all engage from time to time! It is no secret and no surprise to learn that Michael Phelps, who won eight gold medals in the 2008 Summer Olympics, used both affirmations and visualization to reach his goal.

I Maintain a Positive Outlook

Do you have your own personal definition of success? Regardless of the particular goals you have in mind, you need to think positively to attain them. Have you ever heard the saying, "It's all in your head"? The people who say this believe our mental attitudes have control over our body and our life and can, therefore, program our success or failure. Although many of our attitudes and beliefs come from early messages we received from our parents and teachers, as adults we can choose to keep or change these messages, depending on how helpful they are to us in achieving success and satisfaction in life. Examine your philosophy of life. How you see life in general is how you lead your life. A quick way to identify your philosophy is to examine how you visualize the future. Read the following scenarios and select the one that best relates to your point of view.

The future is a great roller coaster on a moonless night. It exists, twisting ahead of us in the dark, although we can see each part only as we approach it. We can make estimates about where we are headed, and sometimes see around a bend to another section of track, but it's pointless because the future is fixed and determined. We are locked in our seats, and nothing we may know or do will change the course that is laid out for us.

The future is a mighty river. The great force of history flows inexorably along, carrying us with it. Most of our attempts to change its course are mere pebbles thrown into the river: They cause a momentary splash and a few ripples, but they make no *true* difference. The river's course can be changed, but only by natural disasters like earthquakes and landslides, or by massive, concerted human efforts on a similar scale. But we are free as individuals to adapt to the course of history either well or poorly. By looking ahead, we can avoid sandbars and whirlpools, and pick the best path through any rapids.

Remember the times you've thought the following:

- "That's just the way I am."
- "I can't control what I do."
- "I just can't seem to finish anything I start."
- "I would like to do that differently, but it's just too hard to change."
- "Yes, it happened again."
- "I've never been good at that."

The future is a great ocean. There are many possible destinations, and many different paths to each destination. A good navigator takes advantage of the main currents of change, adapts the course to the capricious winds of chance, keeps a sharp lookout posted, and moves carefully in fog or uncharted waters. Doing these things will get the navigator safely to a destination (barring a typhoon or other disaster that one can neither predict nor avoid).

The future is entirely random, a colossal dice game. Every second, millions of things happen that could have happened another way and produced a different future. A bullet is deflected by a twig and kills one person instead of another. A scientist checks a spoiled culture and throws it away or looks more closely at it and discovers penicillin. A newly renovated home is destroyed by an earthquake. Because everything is chance, all we can do is play the game, pray to the gods of fortune, and enjoy what good luck comes our way.

One of these scenarios may reflect your own perception of life. Is your life a roller coaster, beyond your control; a mighty river to which you must adapt; a great ocean with many directions and options; or just a game of chance? Are you a positive thinker or a negative thinker? The second and third scenarios represent more positive reflections. Your belief system will affect how you see your life. If one of the first two scenarios is more representative of your philosophy, you may find it more difficult to create the results you want. Your mind tends to believe what you tell it. And, yes, you can if you think you can. Cultivating a positive, assertive outlook on life is the most crucial factor in the difference between those people who have successful, satisfying careers and lives and those who don't. In other words, your most dominant attitudes and thoughts influence what happens to you. In a sense, you create your reality by how you choose to think about what happens to you. This phenomenon is called the **self-fulfilling prophecy.**

Let's examine some of the aspects of a positive philosophy and outlook so you can build a mind-set for career success. Employers often say they can teach anyone the skills of a job; but if applicants do not have the mind-set for success, they cannot teach this and therefore these applicants are not hired or promoted. To ensure you are a competitive candidate, you must assess your success quotient, identify and develop any aspects of your success profile that need attention, and demonstrate this positive attitude in your interviews and on the job.

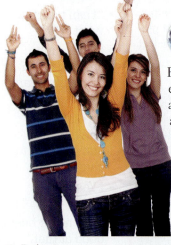

▲ Enthusiasm is contagious.

Employers rate enthusiasm highly.

🌐 I Am Enthusiastic

Building on the example of enthusiasm that you completed in Exercise 2.2, when employers are asked what traits they look for in prospective employees, enthusiasm is always among those at the top of the list. What kind of people do you want as friends, associates, and colleagues? Chances are you want people who are optimistic and have a zest for life. They are people who support each other through praise, encouragement, and networking. When asked about their career goals, instead of saying, "I don't know," they say, "I'm in the process of discovering my career goals," or they list specific goals knowing that they may change given new information and life experiences.

You can become more enthusiastic about life by getting involved in something that has meaning for you. A hobby, volunteer work, mastery of a skill, or a new relationship all provide opportunities to generate and express enthusiasm. On the job, displaying a professional attitude includes acting as if things are fine even when you feel upset or depressed. Although it may seem phony, you will find that acting positively pays off. Not only do you come across as mature and professional, but as you begin to act with enthusiasm, you receive positive feedback from others. The smiles, nods, and positive words of others begin to make you feel enthusiastic, and you soon discover you are no longer acting: You genuinely feel better! This is another example of the self-fulfilling prophecy at work.

What Makes Workers Succeed?

In a study by Judge and Hurst done in conjunction with the data compiled by the Bureau of Labor Statistics, approximately 12,000 people were studied between 1979 and 2004. The results indicated that those who rated themselves most highly on traits related to positive self esteem experienced more success and quicker career advancement both early on and throughout their careers (a span of 25 years) than those whose self evaluations were lower. Positive self esteem does pay off!

WHAT DO *YOU* THINK?

1. Review the 19 strategies to develop positive self-esteem that are explained in this chapter. Review your answers to Exercise 2.6, which help you analyze your current success profile and strategize a plan to increase your success.

2. As you look at your areas to develop and identify the action steps you need to take, what one step can you commit to taking today to jumpstart your effort?

3. Who can you look to as a mentor and coach in developing your success profile?

4. Looking at your top six success factors, who might benefit from your expertise in these areas? Who can you mentor?

Source: From a study by Timothy A. Judge and Charlice Hurst, "How the Rich (and Happy) Get Richer (and Happier): Relationship of Core Self-Evaluations to Trajectories in Attaining Work," *Journal of Applied Psychology*, 93 (4): 2008. Information accessed 8/18/11 from Strategy+Business, **http://www .strategy-business.com/article/re00046?gko=ed2a4**.

I Have Passion

People who are passionate about life express an enthusiasm and zest for living that is noticeable and enviable. They are focused and committed to their purpose. Passion comes from loving what you are doing and wanting to do it whether or not you are paid. As Confucius said, "Find something you love doing, and you will never work a day in your life." Ideally, you will find this kind of work through the purposeful career planning in which you are currently engaged. Outside of work, passionate people are doing what makes their heart and soul sing. They are in tune with their inner needs and find ways to express them. Oprah Winfrey is a prime example of an individual who has used her passion to reach her goals. There are people in all walks of life who exude a passion for their work and play. Can you think of three others you know?

Passionate people understand their purpose, the "why" underneath whatever it is they are doing at the moment. They realize some activities that might otherwise be viewed as "have to's" are simply steps along the way to their chosen passion. They view these tasks as choices, and their attitude about completing them is positive and purposeful. They have adjusted their attitudes to maximize their enjoyment and enthusiasm. Passionate people attract others who want to work with them and support their goals. Would Bill Gates have been able to accomplish what he has without passion? How did he attract others who supported his goals? Think about the difference between a passionate teacher and a teacher who is not passionate about teaching. What a difference in impact!

I Am Flexible

The world of work has never offered a greater array of choices and possibilities. A common response to this seemingly endless horn of plenty is to look desperately for the one right choice that will offer certainty and stability. Although it is an understandable response to want to relieve the anxiety of uncertainty, it is unrealistic in today's turbulent, fast-paced, global economy. Instead, we must cultivate a sense of acceptance regarding the ambiguity, uncertainty, and change that challenge our every plan. We must learn to recognize and accept the fact that life happens as we're making plans and that everything that happens influences our decisions.

The ability to appreciate and incorporate the unexpected twists and turns along the path is the secret to success in today's economy. Rather than resisting change and the unexpected, learn to adapt to the unpredictable. Cultivate the ability to incorporate new information quickly and with ease into your current or emerging career plan. Challenge yourself, not only to experience the unsettled feeling that comes with surprise, but to think positively about the unanticipated possibilities that present themselves.

I Have a Sense of Humor

Learn to laugh at yourself.

According to journalist Norman Cousins, laughing is "internal jogging," and when you laugh, you are exercising all your internal organs. Not only does laughter feel good, it is essential to good health and a sense of well-being. Cousins had good reason to believe this. Some years ago he was diagnosed with a terminal illness and given just two months to live. Instead of spending his precious time remaining in the hospital, he checked into a hotel and watched, read, or listened to every humorous movie, book, CD, and DVD he could get his hands on. He virtually laughed himself well. Many years later, still in excellent health, Cousins was convinced, as were his doctors, that laughter accounted for his recovery! In fact, even though he wasn't a doctor, the medical school at UCLA invited him to join its faculty to teach interns how to lighten up.

Cousins's amazing story holds a lesson for all of us. We would all benefit from lightening up a little—to find the genuine humor in an embarrassing moment, in a mistake, in a situation that is so serious we need to laugh to keep from crying. Humor at its best means being able to laugh at yourself and your situation. Look for opportunities to see the lighter side of life and to share the experience of being human with others who can laugh with you, not at you. Cultivate the habit of walking on the light side of life. Not only will this improve your outlook on life, but it will help you choose a career that fits your personality. Humor also helps get you through those days when work seems especially frustrating or difficult, or when your job hunting seems fruitless. You also need humor to help you lighten up as you go through the career fitness program and encounter the inevitable rough spots along the path.

I Am Assertive

Positive, assertive behavior shows self-confidence.

One of the basic choices we make moment to moment is whether to be assertive, aggressive, or passive in response to life situations. Being assertive means being the ultimate judge of our own behavior, feelings, and actions and being responsible for the initiation and consequence of those actions. In essence, assertive people choose for themselves and build themselves up without putting others down. Aggressive people choose for themselves *and* others; they build themselves up by putting others down. Passive people allow others to choose for them; they put themselves down or allow others to do so.

An assertive attitude will help you maintain your self-esteem in today's competitive job market. An assertive outlook enables you to be persistent, seek more information when you run out of leads, weigh all alternatives evenly (incorporating both your logic and your intuition), revise your goals when necessary, and pursue your goals with commitment and purpose. Assertiveness specifically enables you to say what you feel, think, and want. It allows you to be expressive, be open, and be a clear communicator. You are able to say no under pressure, recognize and deal with manipulation, and stand up for your rights in negative, confrontational situations. You gain the ability to be a better listener. Others appreciate your directness and ability to hear them. You enjoy more positive interactions with people and feel more positive about being able to handle life situations.

Assertive personal traits include body language as well as words. It is believed that 93 percent of the meaning of any message is communicated nonverbally. Look at your appearance, facial expressions, and typical physical movements and posture when you are feeling assertive compared with when you are feeling passive. What does your style of dress say about you? Can changing the color or style of your outfit change the mood you project to others? Have you ever noticed your gestures? Assertiveness is often associated with confident gestures rather than timid ones. For example, begin to notice how people shake hands. A strong, firm hand shake conveys a confident, assertive stance, whereas a soft, limp handshake conveys a sense of timidity and uncertainty. Check out your own handshake by asking friends or classmates to give you feedback on your handshake. If it lacks strength and confidence, practice until it communicates what you want it to.

Positive, assertive behavior suggests that you have confidence in yourself. This behavior conveys verbally and nonverbally that you believe in your own abilities and worth. That positive, confident, and enthusiastic self will set you apart, give you a competitive advantage, make people take notice of you, and ultimately enable you to exercise control over your career and your life.

I Am Persistent

Persistent people refuse to give up. Particularly in the face of difficulty, they maintain their resolve and push on. They realize that accomplishing any goal takes time and tenacity. They know setbacks occur and that blaming genes for an out-of-shape body or calling it fate when they don't get a job is simply copping out. They recognize that perseverance pays off. What appears to be luck is usually opportunity met by preparation. Persistence is stick-to-itiveness, not just initiating and taking action, but following through because of commitment, conviction, and pure drive.

> Luck = opportunity + preparation + persistence.

Perhaps nowhere is this more evident than in the Olympics. Only the most persistent and committed athletes are chosen to participate, and all know full well the slim chance of coming home with a medal. Nevertheless, many return time after time, and some eventually triumph. Those who compete gain public acclaim, knowing their participation places them in elite company. Successful people keep trying after not reaching a goal or after experiencing rejection, they push on until their dream is attained. While being persistent and experiencing the unexpected events that occur, they also take advantage of unexpected opportunities and new possibilities. "Unsuccessful" Olympians may get to endorse a product they believe in, scout and coach other hopefuls, broadcast and report on sports events, support causes they believe in, and touch the world in many unimagined ways while pursuing a goal.

In today's unpredictable economy, many of us feel as if we, too, are preparing for the Olympics; this especially holds true for students and job seekers who must face such hurdles as degree and training decisions, financial hardships, interviews, and rejections along the way. Talent and education are not automatic keys to success. Tenacity, determination, and consistent effort are keys to success.

I Identify My Goals

People who succeed have clearly defined plans and objectives that they refer to regularly to keep in mind their lifetime goals, as well as to order their daily priorities. Clearly defined, written goals help move us to goal completion. The reason most people don't reach their goals is that they don't identify them. They don't know what they want. If you don't know where you are going, you probably won't get there. Even though you're just embarking on your career fitness plan and you may not have a specific career in mind as yet, you can still begin the process by leaning into your goals. Your first goal might be to read this entire book (one chapter a week), and complete all the exercises with the intent to learn more about yourself, so you can move in the direction of making appropriate career choices. Another goal that you can work on immediately is to build your network. The majority of jobs are found through networking, which means contacting people you know and asking them to put you in touch with people they know who might be able to assist you with whatever you need. Although there are many ways to network, the Web provides limitless access through social networking sites that are specifically set up for this purpose. Which are your favorite sites? Have you used them for job/career networking? Try facebook.com and linkedin.com to begin this process. Although you may be texting, tweeting, and socially networking for fun, set aside a specific amount of time each week, so you will get into the habit of working on your career fitness plan goals in the same way you would work on a physical fitness plan—with focus, consistency, and commitment.

I Initiate Action

Successful people realize that goals *activate* people and fears *stop* people. If you dwell on your fears, whether real or imagined, you will be slowed down in the pursuit of your goals. If you concentrate on your goals, you will move toward them. People who are afraid to tell the world what they want, don't get what they want. In what direction are you going—away from or toward your goals? Goals enable you to frame your process in a positive light, whereas fears tend to foster a negative outlook on the possibilities before you. Imagine yourself in your dream job, your fantasy career, the kind of job you would pay to do. Take the job of cruise ship director, for example. Now identify someone who has that occupation. If you don't know of anyone, use your social network and ask your friends, relatives, neighbors, and classmates, all of whom are part of your extended network. Ask if they know someone who actually has your dream job. Next, contact that individual in person, if possible, and arrange a brief informational interview to determine if your dream job really is a good fit.

TIPS FROM THE PROS

Build your network by asking every contact if he or she can refer you to anyone else in the field. If so, ask the same questions until you have a clear idea of what the job or profession entails. Remember to send thank you notes to anyone who has given you their time.

After you have gathered the facts about your fantasy career, ask yourself if it still holds its appeal for you. If so, you've got a career goal! If not, choose another fantasy career to investigate. Complete Exercise 2.3 now to determine what fantasy careers may relate to your success profile.

EXERCISE 2.3 Your Fantasy Careers

"Wouldn't It Be Great to Be a . . . What? "

CURRENT FANTASY CAREERS

List your current fantasy careers below. Then think back chronologically to earlier age levels and try to recall some of your past fantasy careers; list them as well. We develop fantasy careers at a very young age. Most children see cartoons, television dramas, and movies about doctors, lawyers, police officers, firefighters, astronauts, teachers, and scientists, to name a few popular careers. Books about solving mysteries create an image of excitement about being a detective. Current movies influence many to dream of being a jet pilot or a gifted performer. What have you read about, seen in the movies, or dreamed about doing as a career?

1. For each career on your list, ask yourself this question: "What about this career appeals to me?" Many of us might have the same fantasy career but for different reasons.

Current Fantasy Career: What About This Career Appeals to Me?

a. _____

b. _____

c. _____

d. _____

PAST FANTASY CAREERS

Take time to think back to any fantasy careers you had in earlier years.

Past Fantasy Careers: What Appealed Most to Me about This Fantasy Career?

Ages 1–10 _____

_____

_____

Ages 11–15 _____

_____

_____

Ages 16–20 _____

_____

_____

Ages 21–30 _____

_____

_____

Ages 31–40 _____

_____

_____

Ages 41–50 _____

_____

_____

Ages 51 plus _____

_____

_____

2. Now choose the one fantasy career that is most appealing. Use your social networking sites. Try to locate someone who earns a living in this career. If you are part of a class, ask your instructor and classmates if they can refer you to someone. Otherwise, try to make a connection by asking people you know at school, work, and social gatherings. Do your investigative work to determine how well this job fits you.

_____

MAKING A FANTASY REAL

1. Find a newspaper or magazine article that describes a job that seems like a fantasy job to you. Or find a story about a person you consider to be truly successful. (Remember: Go beyond the societal stereotypes of success. Develop your own definition of success.)

2. Summarize the features that make the job or the successful person appealing to you. What are the personality traits of the person holding the job? What adjectives best describe this person?

_____

_____

🌐 I Have Vision

Just as Martin Luther King Jr. said "I have a dream," so, too, do those who have a vision. This vision is a mental model of the truth of the current moment and what you want that moment to be. It is a detailed description of where you want to arrive. For a balanced, successful life, your vision needs to address as many aspects of your life as possible. These include education, leisure, career, finances, health, relationships, personal and spiritual goals, and contributions to your community.

When you identify, describe, and stay focused on your vision, you will begin to encounter the people, resources, and circumstances that will bring you closer to your dream. This is called *synchronicity*. It's important to think big, even if you are not at all certain how you will get there. Bill Gates dreams of a world where every home has a computer connected to the Internet. Lance Armstrong dreamed of *repeated* Tour de France victories. The world is filled with ordinary people who dream and live out extraordinary visions. Expect naysayers who will try to talk you out of your dreams. Recognize that they are coming from their own sense of limitations and move on.

▲ Share your vision with people you trust.

Share your vision with people you trust. Even if your vision seems outrageous, you will encounter people who will offer to help make it a reality. They will make suggestions and introduce you to others who can support and nurture your vision. Most important, when you share your vision, you reinforce as well as clarify it, and you strengthen your belief that it can be achieved. At the start of his career, Jim Carey, then a struggling actor, wrote himself a check for $10 million and promised himself that in 10 years he would be able to cash it. He framed it and looked at it daily, and sure enough, in 10 years he had sufficient funds to cash his "vision check." Exercise 2.4 will give you the opportunity to clarify your ideal success profile so that you can work toward making it a reality.

EXERCISE

2.4 Two Perfect Days: Your Future Vision

1. **Written description.** To be clear about what you want in life, write a one-page description of two ideal days in your future. One day should be related to leisure, and one day should be related to work. Think about where you would be; what you'd be doing; who, if anyone, would be with you; and so on. Try to be as detailed as possible.

Use this space for notes:

_____

_____

_____

_____

_____

_____

2. **Summary.** Write down three or more words or phrases that capture the essence and quality of each of these two days (e.g., peaceful, challenging, fun, harmonious, exciting, restful, productive).

Leisure day . . .

_____

_____

Workday . . .

_____

_____

I Am an Innovator

Stephen M. Shapiro, author of *24/7 Innovation: A Blueprint for Striving and Thriving in an Age of Change*, states that if you want to separate yourself from the pack and become a valued player in our fiercely competitive marketplace, work to develop your innovative ability. He distinguishes *invention*, which is discovering something totally new, from *innovation*, which is discovering a new way to add value. Not everyone is an inventor, but we all have the innate ability to innovate. Think about the many times when you have said to yourself, "I could do this better." That's the seed of innovation, and you must not only think about how to improve it but actually step up and do it. Can you think of a time when you have, in fact, suggested a better way to do something instead of just thinking to yourself about how you could do it better?

TIPS FROM THE PROS

Innovators act on their thoughts and ideas.

Shapiro suggests that you can foster your innovative capacity by focusing on results and how your job contributes to reach those goals, so you begin to take responsibility not only for your job but also for the larger outcomes and the best ways to achieve them. In essence, this requires you to adopt an entrepreneurial mind-set—the ability to act, think, and feel like an owner so you constantly think about adding value, serving customers, improving operations, and exploiting new opportunities.

I Am Responsible

Responsible people assume personal accountability for their lives. You realize you are in control of your thoughts, decisions, behaviors, and outcomes. After every important event, you analyze what went well and what could be done better next time, rather than shift the blame to someone or something for the past or current situation. You are self-reliant and action oriented. You realize that time is your most precious resource, and you avoid procrastination, recognizing that a prompt response is the most efficient way to handle most situations. Responsible individuals always ask themselves, "What's the best use of my time right now?" and use their purpose, passion, and goals to determine their priorities.

Responsible people know that life is a self-fulfilling prophecy. You expect the best from every situation. You choose to respond to circumstances with a glass-half-full attitude rather than a negative, blameful, or victimlike mentality of the glass half-empty. As former U.S. president Harry S. Truman said, "I studied the lives of great men and famous women, and I found that the men and women who got to the top were those who did the jobs they had in hand, with everything they had of energy and enthusiasm and hard work."

I Have Multiple Intelligences

Scientists used to believe there were only two ways to demonstrate intelligence, either verbally or mathematically. The research of Dr. Howard Gardner (1999) indicates that there are at least eight distinct areas of intelligence. Gardner proposes that each person possesses all eight intelligences to a greater or lesser degree, and that everyone can more fully develop each of the eight. As you read about each intelligence, ask yourself which you have already well developed and which you would like to develop further:

 **VERBAL/LINGUISTIC INTELLIGENCE** focuses on the use of language and words. Individuals with this type of intelligence tend to enjoy school subjects such as English, foreign languages, history, and social sciences. They participate in debate, drama, TV and radio work, newspaper and yearbook editing, writing blogs, newsletters, and magazine articles. Common career choices include attorney, teacher, salesperson, writer, and religious leader.

 **MUSICAL/RHYTHMIC INTELLIGENCE** focuses on the ability to be aware of patterns in pitch, sound, rhythm, and timbre. These individuals enjoy such school subjects as music and dance. They are involved in band, orchestra, choir, and dance productions. Some common career choices include singer, composer, dancer, conductor, disc jockey, and sound engineer.

 **LOGICAL/MATHEMATICAL INTELLIGENCE** includes the ability to think abstractly, to problem-solve, and to think critically. Favorite school subjects for these individuals include math, science, economics, and computer programming. They tend to be involved in science projects and enjoy reading maps, spreadsheets, budgets, and blueprints. Common career choices include engineer, scientist, mathematician, banker, economist, accountant, and computer programmer.

 **VISUAL/SPATIAL INTELLIGENCE** includes the ability to create mental images and transform them into an art form. Individuals with this intelligence enjoy art, shop, drafting, and photography. They enjoy projects such as designing brochures, ceramics, costumes, structures, and websites. Common careers include visual artist, designer, architect, and webmaster.

 **BODILY/KINESTHETIC INTELLIGENCE** involves the ability to connect mind and body, and often relates to excelling at sports. Popular subjects include dance, drama, sports, and culinary arts. Common career choices include athlete, coach, personal trainer, dancer, and chef.

 **INTRAPERSONAL INTELLIGENCE** involves the ability to comprehend one's feelings. Popular school subjects related to this intelligence include psychology and creative writing. These individuals enjoy reading and journal writing. Common careers include psychologist, detective, coach, author, lawyer, and religious leader.

INTERPERSONAL INTELLIGENCE involves the ability to comprehend others' feelings. Individuals who possess this intelligence enjoy such school subjects as literature, psychology, and sociology. Typical career choices include counselor, life coach, psychologist, nurse, social worker, teacher, manager, salesperson, and politician.

NATURALISTIC INTELLIGENCE involves the ability to understand and work effectively in the natural world of plants and animals. This is exemplified by careers such as landscape architect, botanist, zoologist, and animal trainer.

Because each person possesses some of all eight intelligences, it's useful to recognize which are most highly developed, which come naturally, and which you should consciously target for improvement. Most research on career satisfaction suggests that to be satisfied with your career, you need to identify and capitalize on areas that seem to come naturally and take advantage of your multiple intelligence preferences. If you had to make a career choice right now, just considering this information on multiple intelligences and the various careers listed under each, which of the eight areas would be in your top three? Which careers might fit you best? How you respond to these questions will indicate how these various intelligences might impact your future career. You are likely to be more satisfied and less stressed in a career that uses your natural preferences.

 ## I Demonstrate Emotional Intelligence

Our competitive and achievement-oriented society places great value on intellectual ability. Early in your life your parents and teachers may have tried to determine your IQ (intelligence quotient). The results of such tests are sometimes highly regarded in academic circles, even though these tests are often judged to be inaccurate and incomplete. The results are often unreliable predictors of future success in life because they don't take the whole

▲ If your primary intelligence is bodily/kinesthetic, consider careers that involve *movement*.

person's unique set of abilities, interests, talents, skills, and motivators into account. In addition, being labeled often sets limits on performance and potential or sets up unrealistic expectations. Were you labeled an overachiever or underachiever? Average or below average? Were you inspired by these labels—or did they cause you to lose motivation? We have all heard stories of high-IQ individuals who were not successful at chosen paths or who were unhappy in life. In contrast, people with low to average "intelligence" have defied all predictions and become successful by any definition of the term. In fact, research on college grade-point average as a predictor of success indicates that the B to C student often enjoys more success, financially and in terms of lifestyle and relationships in later life than the solid A performer! What explains this apparent paradox? At times, the A student is so intent on getting good grades that other critical aspects of life such as the development of friendships and hobbies, and attention to physical, emotional, and spiritual development are overlooked. Of course, we are not advocating that you should not strive for A's, but we are suggesting that other parts of life that lead to emotional intelligence are critical and can be cultivated as well.

TIPS FROM THE PROS

It is most often the individual who demonstrates emotional maturity, EQ—the ability to control your emotions—to tune into others' feelings and the ability to get along with others who is promoted or retained in a tight job market instead of the person who may demonstrate A-level performance on the job but does not demonstrate the qualities of emotional intelligence.

Research by Daniel Goleman, discussed in his books on emotional intelligence, offers insight into the dimensions of and ways to cultivate emotional intelligence. The common sense, wisdom, maturity, humor, and street smarts that distinguish successful individuals are the manifestation of emotional intelligence (EQ). The awareness of and ability to monitor and control our emotions, thoughts, and feelings and the ability to be sensitive to others define emotional intelligence.

Complete Exercise 2.5 to test your own EQ. The better developed your EQ, the more successful you are likely to be. Although you are born with IQ, you can learn and cultivate EQ. Check out the websites for EQ listed in the WWWebwise exercise for more information on how to develop EQ. It may be IQ that gets you the job, but it's EQ that *keeps* you employed and gets you promoted!

EXERCISE

2.5   Emotional Intelligence Checklist

Answer the following questions from A to Z, for a better idea of how your attitude is reflected in your actions. Ask several important people in your life to respond to these questions about you as well. Compare their answers with yours. The more areas you are satisfied with, the greater your EQ. Choose two or three areas that you think are important to work on to improve your emotional intelligence.

a. Do I always do my best?

b. Do I tend to look on the bright side of things?

c. Am I friendly and cooperative?

d. Am I prompt and dependable?

e. Do I do my share (or more than my share)?

f. Do I appear confident, poised?

g. Am I believable?

h. Do people ask my opinions?

i. Am I trustworthy?

j. Am I well mannered, tactful, and considerate of others?

k. Do I dress appropriately?

l. Am I a good team player?

m. Do I listen more than I speak?

n. Do I incorporate others' suggestions and feeling in my decision?

o. Do I consider the long term consequences rather than the immediate benefit to my actions?

p. Do I put others before myself? To what extent?

q. Can I accept compliments?

r. Do I give compliments?

s. Do I make suggestions?

t. Can I say no?

u. Do I wait for others to decide for me?

v. Do I try to understand how others feel?

w. Do I control my negative emotions?

x. Am I able to laugh at myself?

y. Do I take responsibility for my actions?

z. Do I consider other's feelings before taking action?

 I Am Disciplined

Self-discipline can also be called self-control. It is the ability to control or manage some aspect of your life, to have power over it. A simple example is that most of us have the self-discipline to get out of bed every morning at a particular time even though we'd probably prefer to sleep later.

> Discipline yourself for success.

Self-discipline is a vital component of success. If you lack the discipline to complete a task or spend the hours needed to accomplish your immediate goal (e.g., to contact four potential employers, study for an important test, complete the exercises in this book, etc.), your long-term goals are less likely to be accomplished. Each time we allow a task to go undone or a goal to go unaccomplished, we train ourselves to believe it is okay, that there's always tomorrow. In the meantime, someone else is out there doing it. Self-discipline is part of the foundation for success.

I Am Self-Reliant and Career Resilient

In the face of events such as layoffs and downsizing, outsourcing and global competition for jobs that can now be done electronically from anywhere in any country, successful employees need to demonstrate self-reliance and resilience. These involve the ability to continually learn and develop new skills, initiate activities, demonstrate flexibility, and continuously align work with the business need. It is essential to ask constantly—and be able to answer—this question: "How does my work add value to the organization?" The question conveys a sense of commitment and a sense of purpose to your current project. As the job tasks and business needs change, those who want to remain employed must be in a continuous learning mode. Simply doing a good job is no longer enough!

I Learn from Role Models

So far, we have explored the components necessary to develop a positive self-image—that is, personal behaviors and attitudes that help us identify and best use our values, skills, and interests. Now it's time to look outside ourselves at people who display the qualities of success we want to cultivate. This is an important part of our development because as human beings, we are socially minded. We learn from and emulate others. If we consciously think about whom we admire and want to be like, we are more likely to begin thinking and acting in similar ways. We can choose our coaches and role models rather than simply be affected by the people who happen to be part of our current lives for better or worse. Think about the people you admire and begin to make a list. First, think globally about prominent individuals on the national and international scene. Then, think locally about people with whom you work; individuals who are part of your community, your neighborhood, or your religious affiliation; those who attend your school; or those who share your hobbies. Finally, think of the people who are closest to you—your family and friends. Which of their qualities do you admire? In what ways do you want to be more like them?

Spend time observing these people in action. Consider telling them what you admire about them, and asking them to tell you how they developed those qualities. Ask them for insights and suggestions that you might use to develop your own success profile. Make these people part of your network of contacts. You will probably find that even the most successful people have struggled with moments of self-doubt or crises of self-confidence. Ask them what they do when the going gets rough.

Choose your friends and associates deliberately and carefully, knowing that you are influenced by the attitudes of the company you keep. Similarly, when you seek out individuals and acknowledge the qualities you admire in them, you are giving them the gift of recognition and appreciation, a valuable commodity in today's fast-paced, often all-too-impersonal world. Also, when you speak with your role models, you are practicing informational interviewing and thus developing your networking skills.

In fact, this is a good time to do some volunteer work, explore internships, and get involved in the community. This will be beneficial to you because you will meet and observe potential role models who are outside of your daily life. This will help you expand your horizons so you will have more types of people to relate to, to admire, and to emulate. You may continue to interact with some of these people for years to come, and they may become part of your network of friends and supporters who can help you when it comes time to job-hunt. You may be wondering how to meet these people. Always start with your own interests or think about a talent or an area you would like to know more about. Then use campus resources, the Internet, the newspaper, or local magazines to find leads and meet people who are involved in these interests. Look for articles that describe successful people and interesting jobs. Then call these people and interview them about how they chose and trained for their careers. Their strategies may also work for you. Now that you have reviewed all of the qualities that make up a success profile, Exercise 2.6 will help you identify those that you already exhibit and those that you want to develop.

EXERCISE 2.6   Building Your Success Profile

1. Review all of the affirmations (topics) in this chapter. Together, they comprise the formula for your success profile. Identify the six affirmations that are *most true* of you today (e.g., I have a sense of humor, I am persistent). Write them on the lines provided. They are already part of your success profile.

MY TOP SIX SUCCESS FACTORS

(1)_____   (4)_____

(2)_____   (5)_____

(3)_____   (6)_____

2. Now, identify the three affirmations that need further development. List them here. These are the three that are most likely to keep you from experiencing optimal success. Think about one action step you could take this week to develop each of these three areas

THREE AREAS TO DEVELOP   **THREE ACTION STEPS TO TAKE**

(1)_____   (1)_____

(2)_____   (2)_____

(3)_____   (3)_____

REAL stories   Meet Alan

Alan began working for Sony's Music Division in Hollywood, California, after he received his associate degree. He started out as an assistant to the sound cutter and then was promoted to lead sound cutter. After 12 years, his division was reorganized and Alan was laid off. Not knowing exactly what he wanted to do, Alan went to see a career counselor offered to him through Sony. The counselor used a variety of career resources to uncover Alan's interests, skills, and values.

After several meetings and some serious soul searching, Alan realized that surfing the Web and spending time in the library were two of his strongest interests. The counselor suggested that he check out his local library for volunteer opportunities while he was trying to decide what career direction he would take. With his current skills, Alan was less than confident about his ability to volunteer in the library, and he was sure he didn't want to return to school to become a librarian. Alan secured unemployment benefits and got a temporary job as a clerical assistant while he pursued his career search.

Alan worked on his self-esteem and got up the courage to talk to the volunteer coordinator at the library about his interests. The coordinator was happy to have Alan volunteer; however, the work he was initially assigned was not very challenging or interesting. He was stocking shelves and erasing pencil marks from the children's books. He expressed his frustration to one of the other volunteers, who asked him what he really wanted to do in the library. Alan thought that working with the library's media collection would be interesting. Alan's volunteer friend suggested that he call the media specialist and meet with him.

After thinking about it, Alan decided he had nothing to lose so he made an appointment. The two men established an instant rapport. After checking with the volunteer coordinator,

the specialist decided that Alan could work in the media department. After several months, Alan was making a significant contribution to the department. One day the media specialist and Alan started to brainstorm ideas to create a permanent job for Alan. They decided to explore writing a grant. They spoke with the grant writer associated with the library and discovered several grants they could apply for. After six months, the grant was submitted and the library received $250,000 to update the media center. The library management was so impressed with Alan's initiative and abilities that they offered him a position.

WHAT DO *YOU* THINK?

1. What positive success attitudes found in this chapter did Alan use to get to his eventual new job?
2. How did networking help Alan pursue his goal?
3. What affirmations might Alan have used while he was going through his career search?
4. How did visualization help Alan when he started working with the media specialist?

EXERCISE your options

You now know what the attributes of the success profile are. You have assessed which ones you possess and which you need to develop. You know that your success depends on your demonstrating these qualities. Are you motivated enough by your desire to succeed to practice these behaviors even when the going gets tough? What might stop you? If you can anticipate and plan for your weaknesses before they occur, you will be better able to recognize them and overcome them. What will get in the way of your success? Is it procrastination, fear of success or failure, lack of discipline, nonsupport of key people? These are just a few of the most common barriers to success. Identify your own right now and make a plan to address them before they overcome all your best intentions. The first crucial step is awareness, then you must resolve and plan to counteract your weaknesses. The best defense is a good offense. Can you remember when you were able to rise above your weakness and exhibit one of these attributes of success? What did you do? How did it feel? These are your personal Olympic trials, just do it!

Summary

Career success is based on a knowledge of self. The more you understand and accept your uniqueness, your brand, the better able you will be to make appropriate life and career choices.

Branding yourself for success is the first step of your personal assessment program. As you cultivate and engage in each of the practices addressed in this chapter, you will raise and reinforce your self-awareness and self esteem. Your opinion of yourself will grow in proportion to the time and energy you give to develop your most valuable asset—yourself—and you will develop a competitive edge that will give you an advantage in today's job market.

PURPOSE OF EXERCISES

Exercise 2.1 enabled you to take the pulse of your self-image before reading the chapter. Exercise 2.2 asked you to create and incorporate affirmations into your success profile. Exercise 2.3 helped you determine what fantasy careers may relate to your success profile. Exercise 2.4 gave you the opportunity to clarify your ideal success profile so that you can work toward making it a reality. Exercise 2.5 asked you to test your own EQ. Exercise 2.6 enabled you to identify those affirmations that you already exhibit and those that you want to develop. We close the chapter with Exercise, 2.7, **WWWebwise**, a web-based research activity that will enhance your understanding. The last exercise, **Reinforcing Your Learning Outcomes**, will reinforce what you learned in this chapter.

EXERCISE
2.7   WWWebwise

Go to **http://www.cybernation.com/victory/quotations/**. Click on "View Quotes by Subject". Choose a subject and read some of the quotes. Find one that really speaks to you. Write a brief summary explaining what it means to you. Consider signing up for the quote of the day to keep the inspiration coming. (*Note:* Please be aware that websites can change without notice. If a link does not work, find a similar site to complete the activity.)

REINFORCING YOUR LEARNING OUTCOMES

Review and Rate Your Chapter Outcomes. Indicate in the right-hand column how well you do the following items (from 1 = very well, to 5 = not at all). If you rated yourself 4 or 5, review the material on the pages in parentheses to ensure your career success.

How Well Can You Do the Following?

- Understand that **positive** self-esteem is a critical component of a successful career plan. (pp. 19–22)   1   2   3   4   5

- Identify specific components of the career success profile. (pp. 22–38)   1   2   3   4   5

- Practice through exercises the approaches and techniques necessary to develop a career success profile. (pp. 22–40)   1   2   3   4   5

Go to the Career Fitness Portfolio at the end of the book and complete this chapter summary to build and record your personal Career Fitness Portfolio.

Additional Opportunity: Your instructor may choose to assign the Career Fitness Portfolio for in class or online completion. If so, they will provide the handout or link for you to access.

Confirming Core Values

Strengthen Your Balance

STUDENT LEARNING OUTCOMES

At the end of the chapter you will be able to . . .

- Define and clarify your values.
- Discuss how your values motivate you.
- Describe how your values affect your career decisions.
- Understand the value of a mission statement.

What is it that causes someone to study for years to enter a career such as medicine or law while others are looking for the quickest, easiest way to make money? What causes someone to switch careers midstream after spending years developing mastery and a reputation in a field? The answer to these questions is most often **values.** Your values are the intangible forces that guide and influence your decisions throughout your life. Values are *the deeply held convictions that influence your thinking when you are faced with choices*. They provide you with a frame of reference for evaluating information and options. If you value fitness and good health, you make time for daily exercise, positive self-talk, and proper nutrition. If you value career satisfaction, you take time to examine your values and make choices consistent with them.

> Destiny is not a matter of chance. It is a matter of choice.
>
> —*William Jennings Bryan*

Defining Values

Values are the self-motivators that indicate what you consider most important in your life. Values are reflected in what you actually do with your time and your life. This chapter will help you identify what is needed in your work environment to make you feel satisfied with your job. Individuals often discover that the reason they are dissatisfied with their current job is that it incorporates few of their values and interests.

At times it may be necessary to settle for a job just to pay the bills; in such circumstances you may feel empty, frustrated, and unfulfilled by the job. Once you learn how to identify your values, it will be natural for you to take them into account and make meaningful and satisfying decisions about jobs. It will also be possible to improve a less than ideal situation by recognizing what values are missing and incorporating them into your work or into some other part of your life. In other words, your decisions can be based on what's really important to you. If you are determined to follow your chosen career path and stay committed to your values, you will find that even when times are tough, you will make every effort to stick to your long-range goal.

▲ Your values reflect your daily choices as well as your long-term goals and actions.

Clarifying Your Values

As you begin to take charge of your career success profile, identifying your values is a critical step in your personal assessment program. By the age of 10, most preadolescents have unconsciously adopted the values of their parents, teachers, and friends. By their teens, adolescents have begun to sort out which of these adopted values they want to choose freely as their own. This process of rejecting some family values and developing their own is often called "teenage rebellion." Parents, in particular, often take offense when their children question or reject a value they believe is important. In fact, however, this process of values clarification is an essential part of growing up. Mature, independent, successful individuals act on their own values rather than those of others. This frees them from unnecessary guilt ("What would my mother say if . . . ?") and indecision ("What would my boss do in this situation?"). It fosters satisfaction, self-esteem, and self-confidence ("Regardless of the outcome, I'm in control of my life").

Adults often fail to reassess their values as life goes on when, in fact, adults can and do make dramatic changes in their personal and career lives based on changes in circumstances and changes in values. This process of change can be less traumatic for everyone involved if, as adults, we periodically review and reassess what is important to us.

How can you identify your values? The more intense your positive feelings are about some activity or social condition, the more you value it. Is there an issue currently in the news that excites you or makes you angry? Are there certain activities that energize you? Are there circumstances in your life that lead you to certain activities? All of these are indicators of your values.

More specifically, the following criteria will help you determine your values. Values that are alive and an active part of you have the following qualities:

Prized and Cherished. When you cherish something, you exude enthusiasm and enjoyment about it. You are proud to display it and use it. Mark Zuckerberg, Facebook founder and CEO, is just one example of successful people who prize and cherish their values of discipline, tenacity, and focus.

Publicly Affirmed. You are willing and perhaps even eager to state your values in public. Mother Teresa took every opportunity to refer to her faith as a cherished and publicly affirmed value.

Chosen Freely. No one else is pressuring you to act in a certain way. You own these values. They feel like a part of you. Some examples include people who choose a vegetarian diet and individuals who decide to follow a religion or spiritual path that was not a part of their backgrounds, but they chose it freely and deliberately.

Chosen from Alternatives. If given a choice to play a leading role in a Hollywood film or be provided with a full scholarship to study at Harvard Business School, which would you choose? Choosing to act in Hollywood highlights such values as creativity, prestige, glamour, monetary returns, and risk taking, whereas choosing to earn a Harvard MBA suggests prestige, monetary returns, education, intellectual stimulation, and security.

Chosen after Consideration of Consequences. We usually consider the consequences before we make an important decision. What impressions come to mind when you consider the following scenarios?

- You have been offered a job at a firm across the country far from the place you've lived all your life.
- You are offered a well-paying job at a defense contractor in your town.
- You are presented with a dinner check that doesn't charge you for all the food ordered.

What values come into play as you think about the decisions involved and their possible consequences?

Acted On. Again, values are reflected in what you do with your time and your life; they are more than wishful thinking or romantic ideals about how you *should* lead your life.

Acted On Repeatedly and Consistently, Forming a Definite Pattern. The premise here is that you repeatedly engage in activities that relate to your highest values. To identify specific examples for yourself, complete the Values Grid in Exercise 3.1. List five aspirations or goals you have achieved in your lifetime (e.g., high school diploma, a volunteer project, active member of a team or club or civic or church group, an internship, a trip, planned a successful activity, found a job) and then check the values that were involved in each goal. When you're done, the values with the most checks are those most important to you.

EXERCISE

3.1   Values Grid

1. Fill out the following Values Grid

   Above the numbers 1 through 5, list five accomplishments you have achieved anytime throughout your life. Use only a key word or two to represent the accomplishment. If you wish, use the space below to describe your accomplishments in more detail. Check the values that were involved in each accomplishment. Then add up the number of checks for each value and write this number in the last column.

   _____

   If you wish, describe your accomplishments 1 through 5 in more detail here:

   (1) _____

   (2) _____

   (3) _____

   (4) _____

   (5) _____

2. List your top five values. (1 is the value that received the greatest number of checks.)

   (1) _____   (4) _____

   (2) _____   (5) _____

   (3) _____

ACCOMPLISHMENTS

Value	Definition	1	2	3	4	5	Total checks
accomplishment	knowing you've done well						
advancement	moving up						
aesthetics	caring about beauty and harmony						
cooperation	living in harmony with others						
creativity	developing new ideas or things						
economic return	working at a job that pays well						
education	appreciating learning						
family	caring about parents, children, and relatives						
freedom	having free choice of thoughts and actions						
health	feeling emotional/physical/spiritual well-being						
helping others	being of service to people						
independence	planning your own schedule						
integrity	displaying behavior consistent with beliefs						
loyalty	showing devotion to someone or something						
management	planning and supervising work						
pleasure	seeking enjoyment or gratification						
power	having influence and the ability to act on it						
prestige	becoming well known and respected						
recognition	gaining respect and admiration						
security	being certain of something						
teamwork	working together productively						

REAL stories Meet Maria

Maria was the oldest of four siblings. Her parents owned a small mortgage brokerage company. Maria was an excellent student in high school, but her parents never encouraged her or discouraged her from attending college. They felt that Maria would always be able to make a living no matter the circumstance. Before Maria graduated from high school, her counselor told her she had a very good chance of getting a scholarship to attend college, but Maria never took advantage of the opportunity.

After graduation, she went to work in her parents' business and her life changed very little. Being a shy, quiet young woman, Maria usually let decisions happen to her, or she let others make them for her. One morning Maria awoke and she couldn't get out of bed. She felt very tired and had a bad headache. Her mother told her to see the doctor, who told her she was probably starting to get the flu, but weeks went by and she was still feeling poorly.

One night Maria was having dinner with a friend and she started to cry. With some encouragement, Maria started to talk about how unhappy she was with her work and her life in general. Her friend suggested that she talk with a career counselor who might be able to help her look at career options. Not knowing how to find a career counselor, Maria decided to call her local community college. She discovered that she could meet with the counselor in the career center.

The counselor spent some time talking with Maria and together they felt it would be beneficial for Maria to take some assessments to examine her interests, personality preferences, values, and skills. The assessments revealed a pattern of interests that were very different from the type of work Maria was doing and a value system that supported a strong moral code,

creativity, and self-expression. After several appointments with the counselor, Maria began to understand why she was so unhappy.

The counselor suggested that Maria develop some goals and objectives to help her move from her current situation. She also suggested that Maria speak with her parents to help them understand her feelings. A year later, Maria had made some specific changes in her life. She enrolled in college and discovered she was really interested in psychology. Because she was still very close to her parents, she kept her job, but with school and more social activities, she felt she had some balance in her life.

WHAT DO *YOU* THINK?

1. Do you think Maria was unhappy with her job because it didn't satisfy her values, her interests, or both? Why?

2. Do you think values or interests are more important when it comes to making career decisions? Explain your answer.

3. Why do you think Maria had problems with decision making?

4. How do you know when you have made a poor decision?

5. What values are most critical to your career satisfaction right now?

6. To what extent does your current job or lifestyle support your most critical values?

7. Can you recall a recent decision that you've made that supported these values?

8. How easy was it to make that decision? Were you aware of the role that your values played?

As you begin to think about it, you will come to realize how much you rely on your values to make decisions. People facing career planning often wonder how they will ever choose a career when they have so many possibilities in mind or when they haven't got a clue about what to do. This is precisely the time when knowing your values is most useful. Let's say you've discovered that economic return, helping others, and security are your top three values. You are thinking about becoming an artist, an actor, or a speech teacher. You might well be able to do all three, even simultaneously!

TIPS FROM THE PROS

Eliminate either/or thinking. It's always wise to ask yourself how you can combine rather than limit your options. However, to choose one direction, try deciding which career would best satisfy your top three values. You are likely to experience the most success and happiness from this kind of choice.

In this case, speech teacher most closely incorporates the values mentioned. Now complete Exercise 3.2, which will help clarify what is important to you in all aspects of your life, from hobbies to work environments. The job descriptions are actually general descriptions of both jobs and values. Try to figure out the name of the value and job described. The answers can be found at the end of the chapter. This exercise will give you some additional ways to discover your values besides the accomplishments you identified in Exercise 3.1.

EXERCISE

3.2   Explore Your Values

1. List five things you love to do. What values are reflected in these activities? (See Exercise 3.1, Values Grid, for ideas.)

   _____

   _____

   _____

   _____

   _____

2. What is one thing you would change in the world? _____

   _____

   In your town? _____

   _____

   About yourself? _____

   _____

3. What is something you really want to learn during your lifetime?

   _____

4. List several values that will be most important to you in your career (e.g., independence, creativity, working outdoors).

   _____

   _____

5. Work environments are people environments. Some people add to your energy, productivity, and self-esteem; others drain you. Think of three influential people in your life (family members, friends, peers, teachers) and describe their impact on you,

   _____

   _____

   _____

6. If you had unlimited funds so that you would not have to work:

   a. How would you spend your time? (Think beyond a summer vacation; envision a daily lifestyle.)

   _____

   _____

   b. To what charities or causes would you contribute?

   _____

   _____

JOB DESCRIPTIONS

From the following list of 15 job descriptions that you might find in the classified section of the newspaper or a website, choose the 3 that you find most interesting as career possibilities. Then list what appeals to you most about each one.

1. Here's an opportunity to help people in a personal way. Meet and deal with the public in a meaningful relationship. Help make the world a better place to live. Pay and benefits in accordance with experience.

2. Do your own thing! Work with abstract ideas. Develop new ideas and things. Nonroutine. A chance to work on your own or as a member of a creative team. Flexible working conditions.

3. Looking for a position of responsibility? Administrative assistant provided. Pay dependent on experience and initiative. Position requires a high level of education and training. Job benefits include high pay and public recognition.

4. Here's a job with a guaranteed annual salary with a secure, stable company. Minimum educational requirement is high school. Slightly better pay with one or two years of college or vocational training. Position guarantees cost-of-living pay increases annually. Good retirement benefits.

5. Looking for an intellectually stimulating job? One that requires research, thinking, and problem solving? Do you like to deal with theoretical concepts? This job demands constant updating of information and ability to deal with new ideas. An opportunity to work with creative, bright people.

6. We're looking for an extraordinary person! The job demands risk and daring. Ability to deal with exciting tasks. Excellent physical health a necessity. You must be willing to travel.

7. Looking for an ideal place to work? An opportunity to work with people you really like and—just as important—who really like you. A friendly, congenial atmosphere? Get to know your coworkers as friends. Pay and benefits dependent on training and experience.

8. Work in a young, fast-growing company. Great opportunities for advancement. Starting pay is low, but rapid promotion to mid-management is possible for the right candidate. From this position, there are many opportunities and directions for further advancement. Your only limitations are your own energy and initiative. Pay and benefits related to level of responsibility.

9. Set your own pace! Set your own working conditions. Flexible hours. Choose your own team or work alone. Salary based on your own initiative and time on the job.

10. Start at the bottom and work your way up. You can become president of the firm. You should have the ability to learn while you work. Quality and productivity will be rewarded by rapid advancement and recognition for a job well done. Salary contingent on rate of advancement.

11. Do you like telling others what to do? This job requires leadership in managing a workforce and maintaining production schedules, coordinating a team, instructing a workforce and evaluating work completed. Hiring and firing responsibilities included in the job.

12. Great opportunity for high income! Salary, expense account, stock options, extra pay for extra work. End-of-year bonus. All fringe benefits paid by company. High pay for the work you do.

13. Are you tired of a dull, routine job? Try your hand at many tasks, meet new people, work in different situations and settings. Be a jack-of-all-trades.

14. Does the thought of a desk job turn you off? This job requires brisk and lively movement and is for the active person who enjoys using energy and physical abilities.

15. Here's an opportunity to express your personal convictions in all phases of your job. Devote your lifestyle to your work.

List your top three choices by number and identify what appeals to you most about each one. Then look at what the jobs represent on page 55 at the end of the chapter.

1. _____

_____

2. _____

_____

3. _____

_____

EXERCISE 3.2   **Explore Your Values** *CONTINUED*

Using the Values Grid (Exercise 3.1) for a list of values, identify 5 jobs from the list of 15 on page 55 that best express your values, then five that least express your values.

BEST EXPRESS MY VALUES

(1)_____

(2)_____

(3)_____

(4)_____

(5)_____

LEAST EXPRESS MY VALUES

(1)_____

(2)_____

(3)_____

(4)_____

(5)_____

SUCCESS *strategies*   True Values

To help you identify your true values:

1. Think about 10 decisions you've made this week. Consider how you spent your money and your time, what you watched on TV, what you surfed on the Web, what you read, and with whom you spent time.

2. As you review your choices, observe the patterns that emerge.

3. Compare what you say your values are with what you actually choose.

4. Reflect on any differences that may surface as you do your comparison.

5. Consider adjusting your decisions to reflect your values more closely, or reevaluate what you thought were your values and identify those that do reflect your decisions.

6. This process of values clarification will help you identify your true values so you can make wise career choices that are consistent with those values. This will confirm who you are and give you a deeper sense of satisfaction when you act on your true values.

🌐 Needs and Motivators

So far we have discussed motivation based on personal attitudes and values. In addition, inner drives or needs also influence how you choose a career. People experience psychological discomfort when their needs are unmet. We best satisfy our needs by identifying them and then engaging in behaviors that meet them. Once our needs are met, tension and discomfort are reduced. In Exhibit 3.1 (see p. 49), you will read about five primary types of needs as identified by Abraham Maslow (1987), a famous psychologist.

These needs progress from the most basic and biologically oriented (survival needs) to more complex and socially oriented levels of needs. When people are preoccupied with finding ways to put food on the table and a roof over their head (physiological needs), they have little time or desire to work on developing relationships or to search for a job that can use their talents. Rather, they tend to work at any job that will immediately bring in money. A person becomes aware of a higher-order need only when a lower-order need has been met. These basic needs are primary and intense self-motivators that often eclipse our core values when we are struggling to meet primary needs.

One example of changing needs often occurs among divorcing couples with children. Most newly single parents have to readjust from the shared responsibilities of a two-parent family and the greater financial security of a two-person income. For some, the reduction in

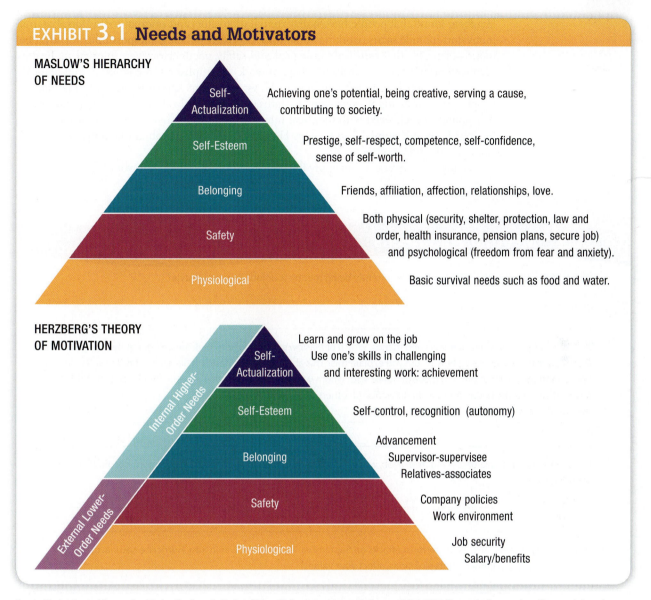

EXHIBIT 3.1 Needs and Motivators

MASLOW'S HIERARCHY OF NEEDS

- Self-Actualization — Achieving one's potential, being creative, serving a cause, contributing to society.
- Self-Esteem — Prestige, self-respect, competence, self-confidence, sense of self-worth.
- Belonging — Friends, affiliation, affection, relationships, love.
- Safety — Both physical (security, shelter, protection, law and order, health insurance, pension plans, secure job) and psychological (freedom from fear and anxiety).
- Physiological — Basic survival needs such as food and water.

HERZBERG'S THEORY OF MOTIVATION

Internal Higher-Order Needs
- Self-Actualization — Learn and grow on the job. Use one's skills in challenging and interesting work: achievement
- Self-Esteem — Self-control, recognition (autonomy)

External Lower-Order Needs
- Belonging — Advancement / Supervisor-supervisee / Relatives-associates
- Safety — Company policies / Work environment
- Physiological — Job security / Salary/benefits

Source: Motivation and Personality, 3/e, by Abraham H. Maslow (Robert D. Frager and James Fadiman, eds.), © 1997. Electronically reproduced by permission of Pearson Education, Inc., Upper Saddle River, NJ.

income and addition of responsibilities may be so great that the individual can focus only on meeting survival needs such as securing food and shelter. If parents in this situation are out of work and job hunting, they will likely be far less concerned about meeting all their values than with simply finding a job to bring in enough money to survive.

It is also important to assess needs from a cultural perspective and to realize that people may function and see things differently, depending on their cultural context. For example, recent immigrants need time to adapt or adjust to a new environment. Even if their survival needs for food, clothing, and shelter are met in the new culture, their lack of familiarity with local customs and their homesickness for familiar people and surroundings may diminish their sense of security, psychological well-being, and competence, as outlined by Maslow.

When your ability to meet your physiological and safety needs is stable, you may find that you demand more feedback (satisfaction of social needs) in your work environment. Industrial psychologist Frederick Herzberg examined the factors that produce or contribute to job satisfaction for most workers. His research is still used to explain job satisfaction. We have already discussed how a job that reflects your top values contributes to job satisfaction.

Herzberg found that people have both external motivators and internal motivators. External motivators include salary, working conditions, company policies, and possibility for advancement—elements that fulfill physiological and safety needs. However, internal motivators involving amount of responsibility, type of work accomplished, recognition, and achievement—also contribute to job satisfaction. These motivators appear to be most important for people with values and needs related to status and self-actualization. People do not necessarily respond to each need with identical intensity or desire. What brings *you* satisfaction on the job? Look at Exhibit 3.1 to see how Herzberg's research on job satisfaction overlaps with Maslow's identification of needs.

Complete Exercise 3.3 to apply the concepts from Exhibit 3.1 to your life.

EXERCISE

3.3 Meeting Your Needs

1. Which of the needs outlined by Maslow are currently being met by your job? By your lifestyle?

   _____

   _____

2. Now think of several family members and friends. Which of Maslow's needs do you think are being met by their jobs? If they are different from your needs, how would you explain this? This ability to apply Maslow's hierarchy of needs will help you understand your motivations and those of others with whom you work. The more you are able to understand and empathize with others, the better able you are to work with others and eventually lead others.

   _____

   _____

3. If you were suddenly laid off or fired from a job, what would likely happen to your needs? What might become foremost in your mind?

   _____

   _____

4. How do world events, such as the terrorist attacks on September 11, 2001, the war in Iraq, Hurricane Katrina, or the numerous reports of global human rights violations, affect your values?

   _____

   _____

Work–Life Balance

VALUES ACROSS GENERATIONS

Each generation brings with it a set of values that tend to characterize the group. **Generation Y, the Millenials,** born from 1982 to 2000, are optimistic and tolerant; they value diversity, challenge, and creativity. They are self-confident, technological wizards and multitaskers who value a fun, team-oriented work environment. **Gen Xers,** born from 1961 to 1981, want to know "What's in it for me?" They are independent, self-reliant, flexible, technologically confident, informal, quick paced, and often irreverent. Although they have high performance expectations and want to be rewarded for merit alone, they are unwilling to sacrifice life balance for work. **Baby Boomers,** born from 1943 to 1960, value achievement, accomplishment, hard work, the traditional work ethic, and a democratic work environment

FACTS & FIGURES   Life Balance

In a survey conducted by PricewaterhouseCoopers of graduating business students from 11 countries, 57 percent said that balancing work and personal life is their top career goal.

Companies are starting to meet the needs of those people who say they intend to put family ahead of work. The most progressive corporations are striving to let men and women work flexible schedules, take time off after the birth of a child, and go home at a normal hour, without fear of job loss.

WHAT DO *YOU* THINK?

If you were continually asked to sacrifice your leisure time to ensure job promotion in the future, would you find this an acceptable arrangement? Why or why not?

where anything is possible given enough effort expended. **The Matures,** born from 1925 to 1942, are disciplined, responsible, conservative and loyal, and willing to sacrifice. They value security, history, tradition, and a clearly defined set of rules and hierarchy. Of course, there is more that each generation has in common than what differentiates them. They all want to be respected for their contributions despite their age. They all want challenging work; the opportunity to learn, grow, and try new ways of doing things; and to be recognized and appreciated for a job well done. They all want to work in an environment that honors their personal and family values and one in which integrity and economic rewards are offered.

FINDING BALANCE

Balance is the ability to include all your top priorities and values in your career and life plan. Some people who live to work (*workaholics*) and claim to be happy may not experience balance.

In today's challenging economic environment, it may seem more difficult than ever to consider your values, interests, and overall happiness when making career decisions. Nevertheless, as you learn more about what makes you happy and successful, you are indeed more likely to take all factors into account when choosing schooling or training and when making job and career decisions, even in tough economic times.

▲ Finding balance is a constant juggling act.

ROLE OF LEISURE

At one time, an employee who diligently honored family obligations and pursued leisure and other nonwork activities may have been considered uncommitted. The workplace now, however, acknowledges and often encourages these pursuits, sometimes providing fitness, recreational, meditation, and child-care facilities. A satisfied, balanced individual is likely in the long run to be a more productive employee, as mentioned in the next "Facts and Figures" box. Leisure activities allow individuals to let go, be spontaneous, and nurture their creativity, self-expression, and personal growth. All these qualities enhance performance on the job and counteract the negative effects of stress in many work situations. (In addition, many people have turned leisure pursuits into careers. Consider Michael Phelps and his swimming, Serena Williams and her tennis, Ashley Qualls and her Whateverlife.com.) The more an individual can balance the demands of family, work, and personal leisure, the better he or she can embrace the inevitable changes that challenge us daily.

FACTS & FIGURES

Work–Life Balance Leads to Greater Productivity

In the current economic environment, work–life balance now ranks as one of the most important workplace attributes—second only to compensation, according to research conducted by the Corporate Executive Board (2009) among more than 50,000 global workers. Employees who feel they have a better balance between life and work tend to work 21 percent harder than those who do not.

WHAT DO *YOU* THINK?

Can you think of an example of when you worked harder in a situation where you had more control of your work life?

Source: Bloomberg-Business Week, March 2009 "Work-Life Balance"
http://www.businessweek.com/managing/content/mar2009/ca20090327_734197.htm?chan=careers_special+report+--+work-life+balance_special+report+--+work-life+balance

Creating Your Mission Statement

Now that you have clarified your top values and you understand how critical they are to your optimal career fitness, it's time to translate this understanding into your mission statement. Although it may sound like a lofty challenge, your mission statement is simply an expression of your most important values put into action to achieve a goal.

Our mission statement as authors of this book is *to engage, inspire, enlighten, and empower our readers to execute their goals toward choosing, changing, or confirming their career.* This statement adds clarity, meaning, and purpose to our writing. It helps us keep on track, keep our focus, and eliminate anything that does not directly address our mission. It enables us to be efficient and effective in accomplishing our goal. What do you think Bill Gates's mission was when he started Microsoft in his garage? What is it now? What do you think Mark Zuckerberg's mission was in starting Facebook while he was in Harvard? What is it now?

As you consider your top five values, think about how you want to use them. In the service of what need, will you put your values to work? It takes conscious thought over time to discover and hone your mission statement. Your continued engagement in the career fitness program through your reading, exercise completion, and actions will help you clarify and create your own unique mission. You will be discovering and developing your mission as you continue to exercise your options.

EXERCISE your options

If someone offered you a valuable prize for stating your mission right now, what would you say it is? Take a stab at stating it now, knowing full well that it and you are a work in progress, subject to revision as you move through the process. We all have a purpose that we can pursue that will allow us to actualize our values.

MY MISSION STATEMENT: _____

_____

Congratulations, the prize is self-knowledge and you are on your way!

Summary

Your values act as your internal compass. They help you navigate the turbulence and complexity of challenging times and they keep you stable during uncertainty and transition. Keep tuned in to your core, internal selves and remain true to the values that will ensure you a satisfying work and personal life despite any external factors that you might encounter.

PURPOSE OF EXERCISES

This chapter's exercises are designed to help you identify your own values. As you complete the exercises, look for the values that occur repeatedly in your answers. By the end of the exercises you will have identified the five values that come up most often. These are your primary work values. You will note them in Exercise 3.5.

Exercise 3.1, the Values Grid, demonstrated how activities that you consider accomplishments reflect your values. It also showed you how your highest values recur and are implemented repeatedly in a variety of activities. Exercise 3.2 helped you clarify what is important to you in all aspects of your life, from hobbies to work environments. Exercise 3.3 asked you to reflect on your needs and values. Exercise 3.4

asks you to rank your values in the order of importance. Often, in our careers and in life, we must give up something desirable to get something *more* desirable. Exercise 3.5 asks you to examine what you say you want to do in your life. If you haven't taken any action to get what you want, your goals need to be reevaluated. The premise is that what is really valued serves as a driving force that motivates you to take action. Exercise 3.6 explores the relationship between values and ethics. At the end of the chapter's exercises, you will find Exercise 3.7, **WWWebwise**, a web-based research activity that will enhance your understanding, as well as **Reinforcing Your Learning Outcomes** that will reinforce what you learned in this chapter.

3.4   Your Values: Some Hard Choices

In this exercise you are asked to choose the best and worst among sets of options, all of which are more or less undesirable. Rank the situation and individual, however unpleasant, that you could best and most easily accept as number 1, and the worst case, the situation you would find hardest to accept, as number 5, with the intervening cases ranked accordingly.

JOB SITUATIONS

_____ To work for a boss who knows less than you do about your work and over whom you have no influence.

_____ To be the key person in a job while someone else gets better pay and all the credit for what you do.

_____ To work with a group in which trust is very low.

_____ To work in an organization whose job is to serve the poor but that wastes huge amounts of its resources on red tape.

_____ To work day to day with someone who is always doing second-rate work.

ENVIRONMENT

_____ The desert (120° F) with a well-paying job.

_____ A small subsistence-level farm in Appalachia.

_____ An efficiency apartment in New York on a tight budget.

_____ A congested, smoggy urban area that is a short walk to work from your comfortable low-rent apartment.

_____ A middle-income suburban housing development, with an hour commute (one way) that depends totally on a freeway route.

RISKS

_____ Bet $10,000 on a gambling wager.

_____ Put $10,000 into a new and uncertain business venture.

_____ Go into business for yourself, with minimum resources.

_____ Without an assured job, move to a place where you always wanted to live.

_____ Risk arrest in a public demonstration for something you feel strongly about.

EXERCISE

3.5 Top Five

List five things you want in life. Examine each of these to see what is most important to you. What have you done to support or express these values? What actions have you taken or do you need to take to move toward what you most want in life? The difference between what you say is important and what you are actually willing to do deserves close examination.

1. _____

2. _____

3. _____

4. _____

5. _____

EXERCISE

3.6 Values Related to Ethics

1. In a class or group setting, discuss how values affect ethical behavior. Consider current events and prominent figures in these worlds:

athletics	entertainment	military
business	government	science
education	law enforcement	

2. Choose one example from a newspaper or magazine article, and explain how you would act if you were in the same situation. For example, consider an athlete who suffers a physical disability but continues to push on and excel at her sport, or a model who starves herself to meet an image of success. What values are reflected in your actions?

   _____

   _____

   _____

   _____

   _____

   _____

   _____

3.7 WWWebwise

Go to **http://careerservices.rutgers.edu/OCAvaluesassessment.html/**. Complete the values assessment to further identify what is important to you in your career fitness program. Briefly describe what you learned. (*Note:* Please be aware that websites can change without notice. If a link does not work, find a similar site to complete the activity.)

REINFORCING YOUR LEARNING OUTCOMES

Review and Rate Your Chapter Outcomes. Indicate in the right-hand column how well you do the following items (from 1 = very well, to 5 = not at all). If you rated yourself 4 or 5, review the material on the pages in parentheses to ensure your career success.

How Well Can You Do the Following?

- Define and clarify your values. (pp. 37–44)   1 2 3 4 5
- Discuss how your values motivate you. (pp. 44–46)   1 2 3 4 5
- Describe how your values affect your career decisions. (pp. 47–52)   1 2 3 4 5
- Understand the value of a mission statement. (p. 52)   1 2 3 4 5

Go to the Career Fitness Portfolio at the end of the book and complete this chapter summary to build and record your personal Career Fitness Portfolio.

Additional Opportunity: Your instructor may choose to assign the Career Fitness Portfolio for in class or online completion. If so, they will provide the handout or link for you to access.

ANSWERS TO JOB DESCRIPTIONS IN EXERCISE 3.3

Job Number	Value	Job Title (Examples)
1	Helping others	Social worker, teacher, counselor, coach
2	Creativity	Writer, artist, graphic designer, animator, designer
3	Prestige	Executive, politician, doctor, police officer, lawyer
4	Security	Educator, government employee, administrative assistant
5	Intellect	Researcher, mathematician, scientist,
6	Adventure	Archaeologist, CIA investigator, firefighter
7	Association	Educator, tour guide, public relations
8	Advancement	Manager, engineer
9	Independence	Landscape artist, contract worker, consultant, entrepreneur
10	Productivity	Sales representative, clerk, bookkeeper, author, pilot
11	Power	Manager, team leader, company president, coach
12	Money	Stockbroker, accountant, real estate developer
13	Variety	Electrician, plumber, lawyer, freelance editor
14	Physical activity	Game warden, physical trainer, physical education teacher, parks and recreation worker, construction worker
15	Lifestyle	Minister, guidance counselor, consultant

Assessing Your Personality and Interests

Express Your Real Self

4

STUDENT LEARNING OUTCOMES

At the end of the chapter you will be able to . . .

- List differences in personality types.
- Explain your own personality type.
- Recognize how personality type relates to career planning.

- Identify college majors that interest you.
- Match your interests to occupations and potential majors.

The more you know about your natural tendencies and preferences, the easier it will be for you to identify a career path that enables you to maximize what comes naturally. If you take your personality and interests into account when starting down your career path, you are much more likely to enjoy your work and find it fulfilling.

Many of us dismiss the notion that we can have careers based on who we are and what we like to do. Somewhere along the way, we lose track of early dreams inspired by our true selves and begin focusing on more practical matters: What degrees are offered and what classes are needed? What occupation offers security and good pay? In many cases, we might have been able to explore careers much more closely aligned with our interests than we thought possible. For example, a young man who loves baseball might not enjoy the many hours of practice needed to become a professional ballplayer and might abandon the field altogether. Yet he might be able to pursue a career related to his interests, perhaps as an athletic trainer for a team, a facility manager at a ballpark, or a park recreation leader. These careers might be more congruous with his personality and interests than that of ballplayer or a completely unrelated position.

This chapter will help you explore some aspects of your own personality and interests. You will learn how to interpret this knowledge and apply it to your career decisions. Perhaps you will identify a career path you hadn't considered before, based on who you are and what you really like to do. Or perhaps you'll confirm what you already knew about yourself and this confirmation will further your resolve to follow your unique path. This chapter will provide tools to help you look at yourself and answer the questions: "Who am I?" and "What types of careers are compatible with my personality?"

> I am a great believer in luck, and I find the harder I work the more I have of it.
>
> —*Thomas Jefferson*

Exploring Personality

Have you ever said to a friend, "That's not like you"? Has anyone ever said to you, "You're not acting like yourself today"? These are common ways for us to talk about the complex set of tendencies, behaviors, attitudes, and characteristics that make each of us unique. The sum total of these qualities is called your *personality*.

The more you know about yourself and your personal preferences, the better able you will be to identify work and outside activities that complement your personality type. Several different assessment instruments are available to help you learn about yourself. Like the upcoming activity, some of these instruments are based on the work of noted Swiss psychologist Carl Jung (1923), who developed a way to help us understand and categorize our inborn tendencies. Katherine Briggs and Isabel Briggs Myers (Myers, 1962) later expanded on Jung's theory to develop an assessment tool that helps identify personality preferences. This widely used survey is called the Myers-Briggs Type Indicator instrument (MBTI).[1] It might be possible for you to arrange through your instructor or career center to take this or some other survey to learn more about your personality type. You may also try out similar surveys such as "Typefocus" or "Humanmetrics" that are available online.

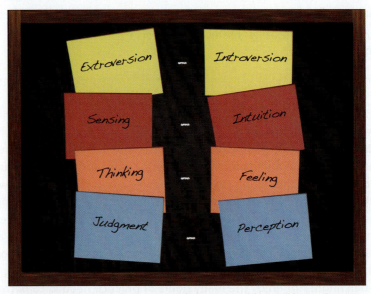

▲ The more you learn about yourself, the better able you'll be to choose work that you enjoy and that complements your personality type.

The following activity is not intended to give you an exact description of your personality or to indicate that a certain personality fits exactly within a certain career. In fact, there is debate about the extent to which personality relates to career choice or satisfaction. Instead, this discussion and the accompanying exercise are intended to make you aware of some characteristics of your personality and give you some insight into what types of interactions and activities might be more comfortable and satisfying for you than others.

The information you gain about your personality can help you make practical decisions about the types of classes to take and the career you pursue. Career success is based on a knowledge of self. The more you know, understand, and accept your unique self, the better able you will be to make appropriate life and career choices. Learning about personality will also make you better able to understand and accept differences in others.

Identify your personal preferences from the four parts in the following activity.

---

[1]MBTI, Myers-Briggs, and Myers-Briggs Type Indicator are trademarks or registered trademarks of the MBTI Trust Inc. in the United States and other countries.

The work of Jung, Myers, and Briggs provides us with a four-part framework in which to examine our inborn tendencies; thus, this exercise consists of four parts. In each part, you will determine which of two characteristics or preferences better describes you. Briefly, in Parts 1 through 4 you will select items that indicate personality tendencies toward (1) extraversion or introversion, (2) sensing or intuition, (3) thinking or feeling, and (4) judging or perceiving. All of these characteristics are explained below.

INSTRUCTIONS: Read the following pairs of descriptions and check the item in each pair that is like you *most of the time.* (All of us have aspects of all of these qualities to some degree.)[2] To help you decide, think of your most natural self, your behavior if no one were looking.

PART 1. In describing your *flow of energy*, review the descriptions and circle the pattern that resembles you more closely, **E** or **I**.

E Extraversion, which means outward turning	**I** Introversion, which means inward turning
_____ Likes action and variety	_____ Likes quiet and time to consider things
_____ Likes to do mental work by talking to people	_____ Likes to do mental work privately before talking
_____ Acts quickly, sometimes without much reflection	_____ May be slow to try something without understanding it first
_____ Likes to see how other people do a job, and to see results	_____ Likes to understand the idea of a job and to work alone or with just a few people
_____ Wants to know what other people expect of him or her	_____ Wants to set his or her own standards

E's interest turns mostly outward to the world of action, people, and things. **I**'s interest turns more often to the inner world of ideas and personal concerns. Of course, everyone turns outward to act and inward to reflect. You too must do both, but you are more comfortable doing one or the other and rely on one more often than the other, just as right-handers are more comfortable using their right hands.

SAMPLE EXTRAVERSION TYPE

Jesse is a computer consultant. He thrives on attending meetings at which several people at a company explain their computer needs, and he loves providing training for clients on their upgraded systems. His hobbies include attending conferences and serving as a Boy Scout leader for his son's troop, which he has also taken on weekend outings. Jesse gets energy from being around groups of people.

SAMPLE INTROVERSION TYPE

Jennifer is a computer consultant. She works in computer systems design. She meets individually with a company's computer networking specialist, who provides her with a list of company needs; then she manipulates the company's system until it is operating as requested. She lets others train the staff. Jennifer gets her energy from working intensively with a technical system. She also gets recharged by spending time alone. Her hobbies include reading and exploring new ways of learning through the Internet and other distance-learning programs.

PART 2. In describing the ways in which you take in information, review the descriptions and circle the pattern that resembles you more closely, **S** or **N**.

---

[2]The checklists in this exercise are adapted from *People Types and Tiger Stripes: A Practical Guide to Learning Styles*, 4th edition, 2009, by Dr. Gordon Lawrence, Center for Applications of Psychological Type, Gainesville, FL. This exercise is not a type indicator, nor does it replicate the Myers-Briggs Type Indicator® instrument, which is a validated instrument. MBTI, Myers-Briggs, and Myers-Briggs Type Indicator are trademarks or registered trademarks of the MBTI Trust, Inc. in the United States and other countries. Parts of this exercise are also based on an exercise in *Building Self-Esteem: Strategies for Success in School and Beyond,* 3rd edition, 2001, by Bonnie Golden and Kay Lesh (Upper Saddle River, NJ: Prentice Hall).

S Sensing	**N** iNtuition
_____ Pays most attention to experience as it is	_____ Pays most attention to the meanings of facts and how they fit together
_____ Likes to use eyes, ears, and other senses to find out things	_____ Likes to use imagination to come up with new ways to do things, new possibilities
_____ Dislikes new problems unless there are standard ways to solve them	_____ Likes solving new problems, and dislikes doing the same thing over and over
_____ Enjoys using skills already learned more than learning new ones	_____ Likes using new skills more than practicing old ones
_____ Is patient with details but impatient when the situation gets complicated	_____ Is impatient with details but doesn't mind complicated situations

     S and **N** represent two kinds of perception—that is, two ways of finding out or giving attention to experiences. Everyone uses both sensing and intuition, but we are likely to use one more than the other. **S** pays most attention to the facts that come from personal experience. **S** can more easily see the details, whereas **N** can more easily see the big picture. **N** pays most attention to meanings behind the facts.

SAMPLE SENSING TYPE

Georgette has a good memory for numbers and has been a book-keeper at a car dealership for several years. One day, she commented to her boss that spoilers and dash covers were selling well. Upon reviewing the sales figures, the boss confirmed Georgette's observations and promoted her to work with inventory management. The boss found it helpful that Georgette enjoyed keeping track of materials.

SAMPLE INTUITIVE TYPE

Santos is a freelance writer and teaches scriptwriting at a community college. He uses his creative and real-life experiences to assist others in creating scripts for independent producers. He often gets ideas while daydreaming or exercising at the gym. Santos keeps a journal on his iPad and in his car to capture his thoughts, and he teaches others how to keep track of their ideas for writing assignments.

PART 3.   In describing your ways of *making decisions,* review the descriptions and circle the pattern that resembles you more closely, **T** or **F**.

T Thinking judgment	**F** Feeling judgment
_____ Likes to decide things logically	_____ Likes to decide things with personal feelings and human values, even if they aren't logical
_____ Wants to be treated with justice and fair play	_____ Likes praise, and likes to please people, even in unimportant things
_____ May neglect and hurt other people's feelings without knowing it	_____ Is aware of other people's feelings
_____ Gives more attention to ideas or things than to human relationships	_____ Can predict how others will feel
_____ Doesn't need harmony	_____ Gets upset by arguments and conflicts; values harmony

     T makes decisions by examining data, staying less personally involved with the decision. **F** makes decisions by paying attention to personal values and feelings. Each of us uses both **T** and **F** judgments every day, but we tend to use one kind of judgment more than the other.

SAMPLE THINKING TYPE

Malcolm is a student trying to decide if he wants to major in business. He is basing his decision on the facts that he has collected: He has talked to a college counselor, researched his interests in the career center, taken classes related to business, and visited work-places that hire people with such majors. He has even investigated graduate degrees related to the types of business specialties that employers have suggested they need.

SAMPLE FEELING TYPE

Shareen has always wanted to be a model but was influenced by her husband and adult children to get a college degree. She stays in shape and is taking modeling classes in the community while also attending college full time. After meeting with a college counselor, she's decided that majoring in fashion merchandising will allow her to study something related to her ideal job as well as please her family.

PART 4. In describing your day-to-day lifestyle, review the descriptions and circle the pattern that resembles you more closely, **J** or **P**.

J Judgment	**P** Perception
_____ Likes to have a plan, to have things settled and decided in advance	_____ Likes to stay flexible and avoid fixed plans
_____ Tries to make things come out the way they "ought to be"	_____ Deals easily with unplanned and unexpected happenings
_____ Likes to finish one project before starting another	_____ Likes to start many projects but may have trouble finishing them
_____ Usually has mind made up about situations, people	_____ Usually looks for additional information about situations, people
_____ May decide things too quickly	_____ May decide things too slowly
_____ Wants to be right in forming opinions, making decisions	_____ Wants to miss nothing before forming opinions, making decisions
_____ Lives by standards and schedules that are not easily changed	_____ Lives by making changes to deal with problems as they come along

J people show to others their thinking or feeling judgment more easily than they show their sensing and intuitive perception. The opposite is true of **P** people; they show their sensing or intuition rather than judgment in dealing with the world outside themselves. People who tend to prefer "judgment" usually like deadlines and to get closure, whereas people who prefer "perception" usually like flexibility with deadlines.

SAMPLE JUDGING TYPE

Chan is a film editor. His appointment calendar is programmed with alarm beeps to remind him about important dates. All of his clients know that when he makes a deadline to finish a project, the project will be delivered on time. He lets nothing interrupt his plans. Rush jobs, given to his department by higher-level management, drive him crazy; he doesn't want to start a new project before he finishes his current obligations.

SAMPLE PERCEIVING TYPE

Sarla is also a film editor. Some colleagues think that Sarla is scattered. She works on several projects at the same time. Even though her office is a mess, she seems to be able to find the DVDs, telephone numbers, and accessories she needs. She often takes on new assignments before she is finished with old ones because she doesn't want to miss out. She gets irritated when her supervisor reminds her that a project should have been completed yesterday and tends to get projects done just in time.

EXERCISE

4.1   Your Personality Type

Reviewing each of the four areas, which do you resemble most closely in each pair? (Choose one from each pair and write it in the boxes below.)

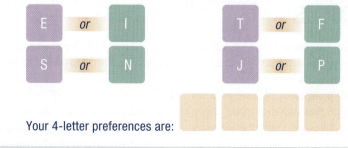

Your 4-letter preferences are:

You now have a four-letter personality preference based primarily on the work of Jung and of Myers and Briggs. This preliminary self-assessment offers one way to appreciate and value your natural individuality. Although we all represent combinations of each characteristic described, we have natural preferences, revealed in our type, that have implications for our career choices. To understand your preferences further, arrange to take the Myers-Briggs Type Indicator instrument (MBTI) at your college counseling or career center.

Now that you have selected the four letters representing your first impressions of your personality preference, review the characteristics related to your four letters in Exhibit 4.1, answer the questions in the "Facts and Figures" module and confirm if the general descriptions in the Success Strategies relate to your personality preferences. Determine if these descriptions of your four letters fit how you see yourself. *Be sure to answer the questions at the end of the "Facts and Figures."*

EXHIBIT 4.1 Personality Typology

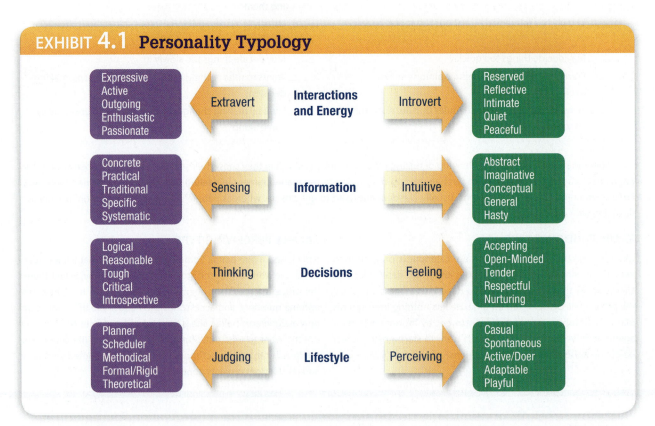

Source: Sherfield, Robert M.; Moody, Patricia G., *Cornerstone: Creating success through Positive Change,* 6th Edition, © 2011, p. 176. Reprinted by permission of Pearson Education, Inc., Upper Saddle River, NJ.

FACTS & FIGURES   Decisive Types

The first and last letters of your personality type often indicate your preferred style of exploring majors. A study of college students (Hammer, 1996) has shown that developing a sense of purpose is associated with **EJ** preferences. Also, when career counselors ranked students on how well they made appropriate educational plans, the following order of preferences emerged: **EJ, EP, IJ,** and **IP.**

Hammer's study showed that **EJ** types are the most decisive about their majors and careers, whereas **IPs** are the least decisive. In two other studies, the **ISTPs** were the most likely types to have undecided majors, and the **IPs** were the most likely to be attracted to special advising programs.

WHAT DO *YOU* THINK?

1. Which type best describes you? (If not listed under "Decisive Types," see types under the upcoming "Success Strategies" and choose from that list.)
2. In what ways does your type fit your personality?
3. If you could change your type, which of the types listed would you choose and why?

Your career choices may be based in part on your temperament or personality preferences. If you enjoy detail and structure, fields such as accounting, engineering, math, sciences, law, and health sciences might interest you. If you prefer unstructured, global thinking, then majors and fields such as the creative arts and social sciences may better suit your temperament. It is essential to note, however, that all types are found in all fields. To truly do well, you must stretch yourself in areas that do not come as naturally for you. This stretching takes extra effort above and beyond the demands of the occupation. Keep this in mind as you experience yourself responding to various work settings and demands.

Be aware that choosing a major or making a career choice that does not mesh with your personality preferences typically takes more energy and concentration than one that more closely matches your preferences. The purpose of understanding personality type in relation to your classes and major is not to discourage you from pursuing a specific career, but to help you become more aware of why you might master certain subjects more easily than others, be attracted to certain careers over others, and use your strengths in any work or life situation.

SUCCESS strategies | Exploring Majors

The descriptions here may help you become more aware of your preferred style or suggest alternative strategies. Remember that the first and last letters of your personality type often indicate your preferred style of exploring majors.

EJ Types (ESTJ, ESFJ, ENFJ, ENTJ)

"I want to decide and get on with my life."

EJ students often put choosing a major on their to-do list soon after reaching college. It is not uncommon for them to seek career counseling early, hoping to declare a major before the first semester ends. Early decision making can have its drawbacks, however. For example, an EJ student may decide at an early age to be a doctor, lawyer, or engineer but then discover he or she lacks the necessary ability or the continuing interest. The student may then become disappointed and want to hurry up and choose another major because "I don't want to waste any more time." Ironically, what such students often need to do is slow down and collect more information. Managers, school administrators, and organizers are found in this category.

EP Types (ESTP, ESFP, ENFP, ENTP)

"I want to experience it before deciding."

For **EP** types, deciding tends to be an ongoing process. They often decide by trial and error. They typically want, and try, to do it all—every course, major, or extracurricular activity that appeals to them. Changing their mind helps to reassure them they still have options open, but they often don't know how to choose among the options. Their style, however, can be very difficult for their parents to understand, especially parents who have a Judging style. EP types can become better decision makers by accepting that the decision is part of a journey, not the final destination. Psychologists, counselors, authors, and helping types are often found in this category.

IJ Types (ISTJ, INFJ, ISFJ, INTJ)

"I want to be sure about my selection."

The **IJ** types probably spend a lot of time researching and reflecting before reaching a final decision. They often consult books and other resources on majors and careers. Because they tend to stick with a decision once it's made, the information they collect must be carefully considered. Because their thinking is done alone, however, they may surprise people when they announce their plans. Accountants, computer programmers, and engineers are often found in this category.

IP Types (ISTP, ISFP, INFP, INTP)

"I wonder what I'll be when I grow up."

IP students often want to delay a decision about a major until they can consider all options, which they do at their own pace. Although they may resist deadlines imposed by others, they sometimes need the outside influences to help them make a decision. When they can tell themselves that no decision is ever final, they can move ahead. Even in midlife, they often say they don't know for sure what they want to be when they grow up. Their style of decision making often reflects a struggle between the vast amount of information they are exploring from the outer world (which can be overwhelming) and their need to be true to their inner world. The world's artists and creative types are often found in this category. A career path for them is a never-ending quest for more knowledge, facts, or inspiration.

REAL stories Meet Holly

"I've taken several inventories now and have gotten the results! My results for the Myers-Briggs were ENFP, which means that I am extraverted, intuitive, feeling, and perceptive. On the Interest Inventory, my results were mainly high in Social and Enterprising areas, with a medium interest in Investigative and Conventional-type activities.

The MBTI results suggest that I like to use my creativity to help others reach goals and realize their dreams. I like to solve problems using a person-oriented approach, and I make decisions by relying on my values and the values of others. I prefer to solve problems as part of a team rather than deciding alone. Because I am social, I will benefit from working with people, especially people who are friendly and who like to socialize outside of work too. Because I am intuitive and perceptive, I like to be able to connect my daily routine to a bigger picture. I need to know why I am doing my work, and I am able to help others see the bigger picture too. Because I am social, enterprising, and global, I enjoy leading others while helping them see the bigger picture.

The inventories indicate that I would enjoy teaching, counseling, social work, managing community organizations, and human resource management. I also was reminded that dietitian and athletic trainer fit my personality. It is important to me that my career will allow me to work with a cooperative, supportive group of people who are committed to helping, nurturing, and caring for others.

The results of these inventories really fit me because I have always been a helper-type person and an organizer. In high school, I was the junior class secretary and the senior class vice president in charge of special events. I was a tutor, and I helped organize the tutorial program. I also planned recognition activities for clubs at my high school. The reminder about dietitian and athletic trainer relates to my early life as a gymnast, which I gave up when I sprained my back at age 12. I have read about and used almost every diet there is! But I also know that I do not want to take the science and math classes necessary to be a nutritionist or athletic trainer major. At this point, with the help of these assessments, I am leaning toward being a teacher or a counselor."

WHAT DO *YOU* THINK?

1. What are your Myers-Briggs and Interest Inventory results? Are your results as true about you as Holly's were for her?
2. Which descriptors from these results, as well as those listed in the "Success Strategies" box, are true for you?
3. Which descriptors are not true for you?
4. Which of the occupations suggested by your results might you consider?
5. What other information do you need to consider before making an informed decision about your career?

Identifying Fields of Interest

The rest of this chapter explores the ways that interests can be grouped into job categories or clusters so you can begin to select specific fields of interest to investigate.

We highlight two different approaches to identify interests. The first is the *Holland Interest Environments* (or categories) (Holland, 1985), which are Realistic, Investigative, Artistic, Social, Enterprising, and Conventional. The second system, *career clusters*, is provided by the American College Testing (ACT) Program. The ACT clusters, as well as the tech-prep and school-to-career clusters listed later in this chapter, are used in secondary-school career centers.

Although you may have access to career inventories, remember that the information gathered by printed or online assessments is not magic. Assessments simply provide a quick, efficient way of gathering and organizing the information that you know about yourself—the answers come from you. In the absence of an inventory, you are still able to collect the same information by completing the exercises, activities, and links to available inventories online provided throughout this book.

Holland Interest Environments

Interest clusters, known as *personality types* or *environments*, are based on the following assumptions:

- People express their personalities through their vocational choices.
- People are attracted to occupations that they feel will provide experiences suitable to their personalities.

- People who choose the same vocation have similar personalities and react to many situations in similar ways.

We have listed the categories in the next section for your review and for you to use to assess yourself informally. Each of the six Holland categories (Realistic, Investigative, Artistic, Social, Enterprising, and Conventional) is described by the following characteristics:

1. Adjectives
2. Hobbies
3. Abilities and interests
4. Sample careers
5. Sample majors

Most interest inventories relate your interests to the six Holland categories and provide a list of jobs connected to these interests. If you are in a class that uses the Self-Directed Search or the Strong Interest Inventory, your instructor will explain which jobs are related to these six environments. If you don't have access to separate inventories, several online assessments can be found at **www.cacareerzone.com** (go to Assess Yourself, then go to Quick Assessments). These inventories should give you a general idea of how your interests and values relate to potential jobs. *Be sure to summarize the results of your inventories in Exercise 4.2 and to share your results with several of your classmates.*

▲ Lifelong interests can become future careers.

TIPS **FROM THE PROS**

Once you have identified your interests, you will notice how much more enthusiastic and alive you feel when you are involved in activities involving your interests. Ideally, your work will relate to your interests. If that is not currently the case, get involved in something that interests you for at least 4 hours per week—for example, if you love helping kids, tutor a child or volunteer at a childcare center.

INSTRUCTIONS Using the descriptions in each section, select the category that best describes you.

DOERS

(Realistic—R) Doers like jobs such as automobile mechanic, air traffic controller, surveyor, farmer, and electrician. They like to work outdoors and to work with tools. They prefer to deal with things rather than with people. They are described as:

conforming	humble	natural	shy
frank	materialistic	persistent	stable
honest	modest	practical	thrifty

Hobbies	Building things	Growing	Repairing	Using hands
Abilities/Interests	Operating tools	Planting	Playing sports	Repairing
Sample Careers	Air conditioning mechanic (RIE)	Automotive mechanic (RIE)	Electrical engineer (RIE)	Police officer (SER)
	Anthropologist (IRE)	Baker/chef (RSE)	Fiber-optics technician (RSE)	Radio/TV repair (REI)
	Archaeologist (IRE)	Biochemist (IRS)	Floral designer (RAE)	Software technician (RCI)
	Architectural drafter (RCI)	Carpenter (RCI)	Forester (RIS)	Truck driver (RSE)
	Athletic trainer (SRE)	Commercial airline pilot (RIE)	Industrial arts teacher (IER)	Ultrasound technologist (RSI)
	Automotive engineer (RIE)	Construction worker (REC)	Optician (REI)	Veterinarian (IRS)
		Dental assistant (RES)	Petroleum engineer (RIE)	

THINKERS

(Investigative—I) These types like jobs such as biologist, chemist, physicist, anthropologist, geologist, and medical technologist. They are task oriented and prefer to work alone. They enjoy solving abstract problems and understanding the physical world. They are described as:

analytical	curious	introverted	precise
cautious	independent	methodical	rational
critical	intellectual	modest	reserved

Hobbies	Collecting rocks Collecting stamps	Doing puzzles	Participating in book clubs	Visiting museums
Abilities/Interests	Doing complex calculations	Interpreting formulas	Solving math problems	Using a microscope or scientific instrument
Sample Careers	Actuary (ISE)	Chemical technician (IRE)	Hazardous waste technician	Petroleum engineer (RIE)
	Anesthesiologist (IRS)	Commercial airline pilot (RIE)	Industrial arts teacher (IER)	Physician (ISE)
	Anthropologist (IRE)	Computer analyst (IER)	Landscape architect (AIR)	Psychologist (IES)
	Archaeologist (IRE)	Dentist (ISR)	Librarian (SAI)	Statistician (IRE)
	Automotive engineer (RIE)	Ecologist (IRE)	Medical technologist (ISA)	Technical writer (IRS)
	Baker/chef (RSE)	Electrical engineer (RIE)	Nurse practitioner (ISA)	Ultrasound technologist (RSI)
	Biochemist (IRS)	Geologist (IRE)		Veterinarian (IRS)
	Biologist (ISR)			Writer (ASI)
	Chemical engineer (IRE)			

---

[3] To explore Holland's ideas more fully, ask your instructor or counselor for the Self-Directed Search, available from Psychological Assessment Resources, Inc., P.O. Box 990, Odessa, FL 33556.

CREATORS

(Artistic—A) These types like jobs such as composer, musician, stage director, writer, interior designer, and actor/actress. They like to work in artistic settings that offer opportunities for self-expression. They are described as:

complicated	idealistic	impulsive	nonconforming
emotional	imaginative	independent	original
expressive	impractical	intuitive	unordered

Hobbies	Drawing/photography Performing	Playing music Sewing/designing	Visiting museums	Writing stories, poems
Abilities/Interests	Designing fashions or interiors	Playing a musical instrument	Singing, dancing, acting	Writing stories, poems, music; being creative, unique
Sample Careers	Actor (AES) Advertising (AES) Artist (AES) Broadcasting executive (EAS) Clothing designer (ASR) Copywriter (ASI)	Dancer (AES) Drama/music/art teacher (ASE) Economist (IAS) English teacher (ASE) Fashion designer (ASR) Fashion illustrator (ASR)	Floral designer (RAE) Furniture designer (AES) Graphic designer (AES) Interior designer (AES) Journalist (ASE) Landscape architect (AIR)	Librarian (SAI) Medical illustrator (AIE) Museum curator (AES) Nurse practitioner (ISA) Writer (ASI)

HELPERS

(Social—S) These types like jobs such as teacher, clergy, counselor, nurse, personnel director, and speech therapist. They are sociable, responsible, and concerned with the welfare of others. They have little interest in machinery or physical skills. They are described as:

convincing	generous	insightful	sociable
cooperative	helpful	kind	tactful
friendly	idealistic	responsible	understanding

Hobbies	Caring for children	Participating in religious activities	Playing team sports	Volunteering
Abilities/Interests	Expressing oneself	Leading a group discussion	Mediating disputes	Teaching/training others
Sample Careers	Air traffic controller (SER) Athletic coach (SRE) Chaplain (SAI) College faculty (SEI) Consumer affairs director (SER) Cosmetologist (SAE) Counselor (SAE)	Dental hygienist (SAI) Historian (SEI) Homemaker (S) Hospital administrator (SER) Mail carrier (SRC) Medical records administrator (SIE)	Nurse (SIR) Occupational therapist (SRE) Paralegal (SCE) Police officer (SER) Radiological technologist (SRI)	Real estate appraiser (SCE) Schoolteacher (SEC) Social worker (SEA) Speech pathologist (SAI) Youth services worker (SEC)

PERSUADERS

(Enterprising—E) These types like jobs such as salesperson, manager, business executive, television producer, sports promoter, and buyer. They enjoy leading, speaking, and selling. They are impatient with precise work. They are described as:

adventurous	domineering	optimistic	risk-taking
ambitious	energetic	pleasure-seeking	self-confident
attention-getting	impulsive	popular	sociable

PERSUADERS   *(continued)*

Hobbies	Campaigning	Leading organizations	Promoting ideas	Starting own service or business
Abilities/Interests	Initiating projects Leading a group	Organizing activities	Persuading people	Selling things or promoting ideas

Sample Careers	Advertising
	   executive (ESA)
	Automobile sales
	   worker (ESR)
	Banker/financial
	   planner (ESR)
	Buyer (ESA)
		Claims adjuster (ESR)
		Credit manager (ERS)
		Financial planner (ESR)
		Flight attendant (ESA)
		Food service
		   manager (ESI)
		Funeral director (ESR)
			Hotel manager (ESR)
			Industrial engineer (EIR)
			Insurance agent (ECS)
			Journalist (EAS)
			Lawyer (ESA)
			Office manager (ESR)
				Politician (ESA)
				Public relations
				   representative (EAS)
				Real estate agent (ESR)
				Stockbroker (ESI)
				Urban planner (ESI)

ORGANIZERS

(Conventional—C) These types like jobs such as bookkeeper, computer technician, banker, cost estimator, and tax expert. They prefer highly ordered activities, both verbal and numerical, that characterize office work. They have little interest in artistic or physical skills. They are described as:

careful	conservative	orderly	reserved
conforming	efficient	persistent	self-controlled
conscientious	obedient	practical	structured

Hobbies	Arranging and organizing household	Collecting memorabilia	Playing computer or card games	Studying tax laws Writing family history
Abilities/Interests	Keeping accurate records	Organizing	Using a computer	Working within a system Writing

Sample Careers	Accountant (CSE)
	Administrative
	   assistant (ESC)
	Bank teller (CSE)
	Budget analyst (CER)
	Building inspector (CSE)
	Business teacher (CSE)
		Claims adjuster (SEC)
		Clerk (CSE)
		Computer operator (CSR)
		Congressional-
		   district aide (CES)
		Court reporter (CSE)
		Customer inspector (CEI)
			Elementary
			   school teacher (SEC)
			Financial analyst (CSI)
			Insurance
			   underwriter (CSE)
			Internal auditor (ICR)
			Legal secretary (CSA)
				Librarian (CSE)
				Medical records
				   technician (CSE)
				Paralegal (SCE)
				Tax consultant (CSE)
				Travel agent (ECS)

Sample Majors Related to Holland Types

Now that you are familiar with Holland Interest Environments, this chart will help you review some sample majors that may be of interest to you. **INSTRUCTIONS: Underline or circle those areas that seem to fit you.** Note that this is just a sample list of available majors.

REALISTIC

Air conditioning and heating	Construction technology	Engineering technology	Industrial engineering
Architectural/mechanical	Criminal justice	Fire technology	Mechanical engineering
Auto technology	Dietitian	Forestry	Medical technology
Civil engineering	Drafting technology		

INVESTIGATIVE

Biological science	Economics	Earth sciences	Mathematics
Biology	Electrical engineering	Environmental sciences	Materials science
Chemical engineering	Electrical engineering	Geography	Paralegal
Chemistry	technology	Geology	Physics
Computer sciences	Electronics	Law	Psychology
Dental hygiene			

ARTISTIC

Advertising art	Computer animation	English	Music
Art	Computer graphics	Graphic technology	Studio art
Art history	Design drafting	Instructional media	Theater
Commercial art	Design technology	Multimedia technology	

SOCIAL

American studies	Elementary and secondary	Home economics	Pre-law
Anthropology	education	Medical assistant	Religious studies
Child care	English	Nursing	Sociology
Classical studies	Foreign languages	Nutrition	Special education
Communications	Health	Physical education	Speech
Dental hygiene	History	Political science	

ENTERPRISING

Advertising technology	Finance	Industrial management and	Marketing technology
Business administration	Industrial and transportation	retail marketing	Public administration
Business education	management	Law enforcement administration	Real estate
Business management		Management engineering	

CONVENTIONAL

Accounting	Computer technology	Legal/medical office	Transportation management
Administrative assistant	Court reporting	management	technology
Computer information	Executive technology	Library science	Office administration
systems			

EXERCISE

4.2 Your Holland Interest Environment

Share your results with two or three classmates; explain how your first impressions are similar or different from results from inventories you have taken:

1. Check your top three Holland Environments (pp. 66–68):
   - ❏ Realistic
   - ❏ Artistic
   - ❏ Enterprising
   - ❏ Investigative
   - ❏ Social
   - ❏ Conventional

2. What adjectives from these environments best describe you (pp. 66–68)?

   _____

   _____

   _____

   _____

   _____

3. List three interesting jobs or careers from your top categories (pp. 66–68):

   _____

   _____

   _____

   _____

   _____

4. List three interesting majors from your top three categories (pp. 68–69):

   _____

   _____

   _____

   _____

   _____

Career Clusters

Career centers often organize their materials by the following career clusters (U.S. Office of Career Education "Career Pathways" used in tech-prep or school to career programs):

Agriculture and Natural Resources
Architecture and Construction
Arts and Communication
Business and Administration
Education and Training
Finance and Insurance
Government and Public Administration
Health Science
Hospitality and Tourism
Human Service
Information Technology
Law and Public Safety
Manufacturing
Marketing, Sales, and Service
Science, Engineering, and Math
Transportation, Distribution, and Logistics

The American College Testing Program (ACT) has also devised a useful system of organizing jobs into career clusters (see Exhibit 4.2). If you are attending school and trying to choose a major or have chosen a major, you might research the cluster in which your major falls or your interests are located. Otherwise, explore the area that seems to relate to your interests, values, and skills. The definitions of each cluster found in Exhibit 4.2 and also at the ACT website (**http://www.act.org/wwm/overview.html**) will help you answer the questions found in Exercise 4.3 related to identifying career interest areas.

Understanding your interests will be a great aid to you in making satisfying educational and career choices. Exhibit 4.3 arranges career clusters into 12 "regions" based on primary work tasks that are found in jobs: dealing with data, people, ideas, and things. Please note that this figure also uses the letters RIASEC (Realistic, Investigative, Artistic, Social, Enterprising, and Conventional) to show the relationship of each region to Holland's Interest Environments, discussed earlier in this chapter.

▲ Once you assess yourself, you need to explore which careers are the best fit or create a career to fit all the pieces together.

The more you are able to incorporate your interests into your work, the more you will enjoy your work. Once you have completed an interest inventory, plan to explore those occupations associated with your interests. Find out what people actually do, and compare these jobs to your interests.

EXHIBIT 4.2 ACT Career Clusters and Career Areas (A–Z), Illustrating How Jobs Can Be Clustered into Related Categories

ADMINISTRATION AND SALES CAREER CLUSTER

A. **Employment-Related Services** Managers (human resources, training/education, employee benefits, etc.); recruiter; interviewer; job analyst.

B. **Marketing & Sales** Agents (insurance, real estate, travel, etc.); buyer; sales/manufacturers' representatives; retail salesworker; telemarketer.

C. **Management** Executive; executive secretary; purchaser; general managers (financial, office, property, etc.); specialty managers (retail store, hotel/motel, food service, etc.). For other managers, see specialty—e.g., Social service (Career Area Y).

D. **Regulation & Protection** Inspectors (customs, food/drug, etc.); police officer; detective; park ranger; security manager; guard.

BUSINESS OPERATIONS CAREER CLUSTER

E. **Communications & Records** Receptionist; secretary (including legal and medical); court reporter; clerks (order, billing, hotel, etc.).

F. **Financial Transactions** Accountant/auditor; cashier; bank teller; budget/credit analyst; tax preparer; ticket agent.

G. **Distribution & Dispatching** Shipping/receiving clerk; warehouse supervisor; mail carrier; dispatchers (flight, cab, etc.); air traffic controller.

TECHNICAL CAREER CLUSTER

H. **Transport Operation & Related** Truck/bus/cab drivers; locomotive engineer; ship captain; aircraft pilot; sailor; chauffeur.

I. **Agriculture, Forestry, & Related** Farmer; nursery manager; pest controller; forester; logger; groundskeeper; animal caretaker.

J. **Computer & Information Specialties** Programmer; systems analyst; information systems manager; computer repairer; desktop publisher; actuary.

K. **Construction & Maintenance** Carpenter; electrician; brick-layer; tile setter; painter; plumber; roofer; firefighter; custodian.

L. **Crafts & Related** Cabinetmaker; tailor; chef/cook; baker; butcher; jeweler; silversmith; hand crafter.

M. **Manufacturing & Processing** Tool & die maker; machinist; welder; bookbinder; photo process worker; dry cleaner.

N. **Mechanical & Electrical Specialties** Mechanics/technicians (auto, aircraft, heating & air conditioning, electronics, dental lab, etc.); repairers (office machine, appliance, electronics).

SCIENCE AND TECHNOLOGY CAREER CLUSTER

O. **Engineering & Technologies** Engineers (aerospace, agriculture, nuclear, civil, computer, etc.); technicians (electronics, mechanical, laser, etc.); surveyor; drafter; architect; technical; illustrator.

P. **Natural Science & Technologies** Physicist; astronomer; biologist; statistician; soil conservationist; food technologist; crime lab analyst.

Q. **Medical Technologies** Pharmacist; optician; prosthetist; technologists (surgical, medical lab, EEG, etc.); dietitian.

R. **Medical Diagnosis & Treatment** Physician; psychiatrist; pathologist; dentist; optometrist; veterinarian; physical therapist; audiologist; physician's assistant.

S. **Social Science** Sociologist; experimental psychologist; political scientist; economist; criminologist; urban planner.

ARTS CAREER CLUSTER

T. **Applied Arts (Visual)** Artist; graphic artist; photographer; illustrator; floral/fashion/interior designers; merchandise displayer.

U. **Creative & Performing Arts** Writer/author; musician; singer; dancer; music composer; movie/TV director; fashion model.

V. **Applied Arts (Written & Spoken)** Reporter; columnist; editor; ad copywriter; P. R. specialist; TV announcer; librarian; interpreter.

SOCIAL SERVICE CAREER CLUSTER

W. **Health Care** Administrator; nurse; occupational therapist; psychiatric technician; dental hygienist/assistant; geriatric aide.

X. **Education** Administrator; teachers & aides (preschool, elementary, & secondary, special education, PE, etc.). For others, see specialty—e.g., Physics teacher (Career Area P).

Y. **Community Services** Social service director; social worker; lawyer; paralegal; home economist; career counselor; clergy.

Z. **Personal Services** Waiter/waitress; barber; cosmetologist; flight attendant; household worker; home health aide; travel guide.

EXHIBIT 4.3   The World-of-Work Map

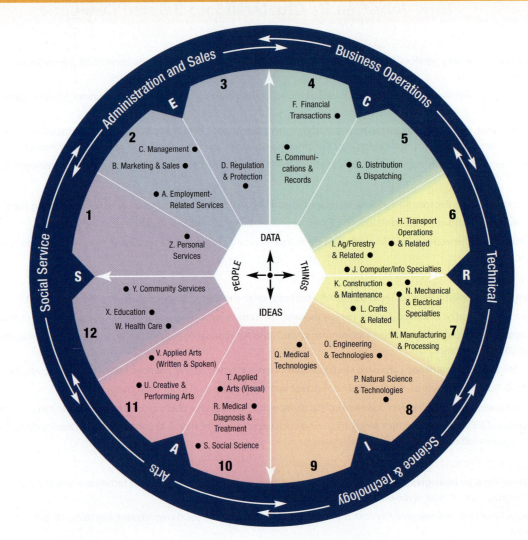

ABOUT THE MAP

- The World-of-Work Map arranges 26 career areas (groups of similar jobs) into 12 regions. Together, the career areas cover all U.S. jobs. Most jobs in a career area are located near the point shown. However, some may be in adjacent map regions.
- A career area's location is based on its primary work tasks. The four primary work tasks are working with

  Data: Facts, numbers, files, accounts, business procedures.

  Ideas: Insights, theories, new ways of saying or doing something, for example, with words, equations, or music.

  People: People you help, serve, inform, care for, or sell things to.

  Things: Machines, tools, living things, and materials such as food, wood, or metal.

- Six general types of work (Holland Interest Environments) are shown around the edge of the map. The overlapping career cluster arrows indicate overlap in the occupational content of adjacent career clusters.
- Because of their People rather than Things orientation, the following two career areas in the Science & Technology cluster are located toward the left side of the map (Region 10): Medical Diagnosis & Treatment and Social Science.

Website: http://www.act.org/wwm

Source: Copyright © 2011 by ACT, Inc. All rights reserved. Reproduced with permission. No further use of these materials is authorized without specific permission from ACT, Inc.

EXERCISE

4.3 Identifying Career Interest Areas

Check off the three areas listed in 1, 2, and 3 below that you find most interesting.
List the interest areas you have checked off, as well as the subjects you find most interesting in the space provided.
If you had two hours to research careers, what would you select?

_____

_____

_____

1. What Fields Interest You?

- **Mechanical**   Do you like to fix things? Do you use and repair

  (R) _____   machines, appliances, equipment? Do you like to make or build things?

- **Scientific**   Are you curious about ideas and abstract processes?

  (I) _____   Do you like to experiment, research data, and solve problems?

- **Artistic**   Do you like music, dance, art, literature, photography, decorating?

  (A) _____   Do you like to express yourself creatively?

- **Social**   Do you like to work with people? Do you help others?

  (S) _____   Are you active in social events?

- **Sales–Verbal**   Do you like to sell, convince, persuade, influence, lead?

  (E) _____   Do you like to talk, write, read?

- **Computational–Clerical** Do you like to keep things organized? Do you like to keep records, use a computer,

  (C) _____   know software? Are you a detail person?

The letters next to the field refer to the six Holland Types.

2. Categories According to the Six Holland Types

- **Realistic**   Careers include jobs in industrial trades, repair, and

  (R) _____   outdoors (e.g., firefighter and police officer).

- **Investigative**   Careers include jobs in the fields of science, health

  (I) _____   science, law, and technology.

- **Artistic**   Careers include jobs in the fields of art, music,

  (A) _____   and literature and related fields.

- **Social**   Careers include jobs in the fields of education,

  (S) _____   human resources, and social welfare.

- **Enterprising**   Careers include jobs in sales, entrepreneurship, law, and

  (E) _____   management.

- **Conventional**   Careers include accounting, banking, office, organizing,

  (C) _____   and clerical jobs.

3. A.C.T. Career Clusters related to Holland Types

Technical	Administration and Sales	Artistic
Science and Technology	Business Operations	Social
Arts	Realistic	Enterprising
Social Service	Investigative	Conventional

EXERCISE your options

Successful students have personality traits and interests that are related to a variety of possible majors in college.

- What have you learned about your personality type and your interests that will help you select a major?

Summary

Now that you have completed this chapter, you are aware that your satisfaction in a career is related to how much you can incorporate your unique personality and interests into your work. With this information, you are now closer to identifying your career fitness profile!

PURPOSE OF EXERCISES

The following exercises will help you summarize information you have learned about interests. You have already learned about your Holland Code and how it relates to careers and majors. In Exercise 4.3 you identified career interest areas; this focus will continue in Exercises 4.4 and 4.5 (from Exhibit 4.3). Exercise 4.6 will ask you to record the results of any additional assessments you have taken. In Exercise 4.7 you will be asked to list interesting jobs found in the classified ads; Exercise 4.8 will ask you to make a list of interesting courses taken from a college catalog. In Exercise 4.9, you will put your information together and describe a dream/ideal job or set of activities that best reflects who you are. Exercise 4.10, **WWWebwise**, is an online exercise that assists you in finding careers and majors related to your interests. **Reinforcing Your Learning Outcomes** will reinforce what you learned in this chapter.

EXERCISE
4.4   Your Career Interest Areas

List the interest areas you have checked off in Exercise 4.3.

_____

_____

_____

_____

EXERCISE
4.5   ACT Career Clusters

List any additional ACT jobs from the World of Work in Exhibits 4.2 and 4.3 that are most interesting to you.

1. _____

2. _____

3. _____

EXERCISE

4.6   Interest Inventories

Record here the results of any other interest or personality inventories you have taken (e.g., top three career choices):

_____

_____

_____

EXERCISE

4.7   Classified Careers

Locate the Sunday classifieds section from two or three weeks of newspapers in hard copy or on the Internet. These do not need to be recent or local papers. Scan the entire section of the Sunday job classifieds and identify those jobs that look interesting, *regardless of whether you consider yourself qualified.* Review the jobs you identified and look for patterns in the announcements that caught your eye. Write the job titles and industries that interested you in the space provided. This prepares you to connect your interests with real jobs.

_____

_____

_____

_____

_____

EXERCISE

4.8   College Catalogs

Locate the general catalog for the college or university you are currently attending or for a local college. The general catalog is the publication that contains the entire listings and descriptions of courses offered at that college. Read the catalog and course descriptions, marking those classes on topics about which you would like to learn more. *Review the classes you have marked and notice which subjects seemed most interesting.* Write the subject areas here:

_____

_____

_____

EXERCISE

4.9   Dream/Ideal Job

What kinds of activities or job descriptions would your ideal job reflect, based on what you have learned about your personality and interests? (Maybe you found an almost ideal job in the want ads.)

_____

_____

_____

EXERCISE

4.10   WWWebwise

Go to http://www.cacareerzone.org (West Coast) or http://www.nycareerzone.org (East Coast).

When you get to the site, "Quick Assessments" are divided into Holland's six broad interest areas. Knowing your combination of interests can help you determine which jobs will suit you. Click on the graphics version and then go to "Assess Yourself." Select "Quick Assessments" and read the instructions. Choose three of the six RIASEC environments and find three careers that interest you. After reading about those three careers, write down the one that best fits you now. Briefly discuss what makes you interested in this career.

_____

_____

_____

_____

(Note: Please be aware that websites can change without notice. If a link does not work, find a similar site to complete the activity.)

REINFORCING YOUR LEARNING OUTCOMES

Review and Rate Your Chapter Outcomes. Indicate in the right-hand column how well you do the following items (from 1 = very well, to 5 = not at all). If you rated yourself 4 or 5, review the material on the pages in parentheses to ensure your career success.

How Well Can You Do the Following?

- List differences in personality types. (pp. 58–63)   1 2 3 4 5
- Explain your own personality type. (pp. 58–63)   1 2 3 4 5
- Recognize how personality type relates to career planning. (p. 63)   1 2 3 4 5
- Identify college majors that interest you. (pp. 63, 68–69)   1 2 3 4 5
- Match your interests to occupations and potential majors. (pp. 66–74)   1 2 3 4 5

Go to the Career Fitness Portfolio at the end of the book and complete this chapter summary to build and record your personal Career Fitness Portfolio.

Additional Opportunity: Your instructor may choose to assign the Career Fitness Portfolio for in class or online completion. If so, they will provide the handout or link for you to access.

Evaluating Your Skills

Accentuate Your Assets

STUDENT LEARNING OUTCOMES

At the end of the chapter you will be able to . . .

- Discuss the importance of skills in your career search.
- Define and identify your skills.
- Recognize the power of the transferability of your skills.
- Use the language of skills in writing your resume and preparing for an interview.

The next step in the career-planning process is to identify your skills. Skills are the building blocks of your future career, just as muscles are the building blocks of your future body shape. A career fitness program helps you identify your current skills and those you want to develop. A thorough skills analysis is a critical component of the career-planning process.

Skills are the currency used by job seekers. In the job market you receive pay in exchange for skills. Individuals who can describe themselves to a potential employer in terms of their skills are the people most likely to enjoy their careers because they are the most likely to obtain jobs that use their particular talents. People who enjoy their work tend to be more productive and healthy. After completing this chapter, you will be able to analyze a potential job on the basis of how the skills required by the job compare with both the abilities you possess and enjoy using and the skills you want to develop. Furthermore, you will have a broader vocabulary to use in describing your strengths when you prepare your resume and when you are interviewed for jobs.

> Skills are the currency of the job market.

> Ability is what you are capable of doing. Motivation determines what you do. Attitude determines how well you do it.
>
> —Lou Holtz

Defining Skills

Skills include the specific attributes, talents, and personal qualities that we bring to a job as well as the tasks we learn on the job. We also develop our talents simply through the process of living, by interacting with others and going through our daily routines. Our personal preferences often affect our skills and abilities. We tend to be motivated to use skills repeatedly that are part of enjoyable activities. Our recurring use of and success with certain preferred skills identifies them as our *self-motivators*. Self-motivators are skills we enjoy and do well.

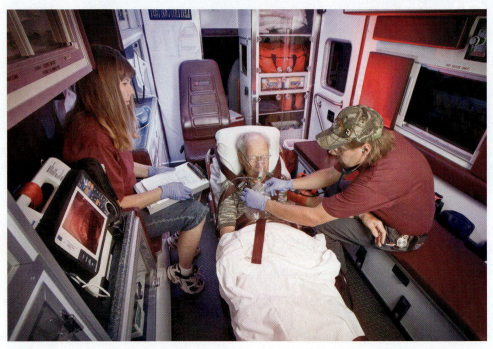

▲ Most jobs call for both functional and work-specific skills, and self-management skills are a crucial part of any job.

By learning the vocabulary of skills, you can recognize the hundreds of skills that may be within your grasp. Skills are generally divided into three types: functional, work content, and adaptive. All of these can be considered transferable.

- *Functional skills* are those that may or may not be associated with a specific job, such as maintaining schedules, collecting data, and diagnosing and responding to problems. They are called functional skills because they are used to accomplish general tasks or functions of a job.

- *Work-content skills* are specific and specialized to one job (e.g., bookkeeping is done by bookkeepers, assigning grades is done by teachers, interpreting an electrocardiogram is done by specific medical practitioners).

- *Adaptive or self-management skills* are personal attributes; they might also be described as personality traits or soft skills. The ability to learn quickly, to pay close attention to detail, and to be task oriented, self-directed, congenial, and cooperative are some examples of adaptive skills.

Identifying Your Skills

If you were asked right now to list your skills, what would your list look like? It might be a short list, not because you do not have skills but simply because you have never been asked to identify them and are not accustomed to thinking and talking about them. Reflecting on your skills may also be difficult because most of us have been taught to be modest and not to brag. We often feel that something we do well doesn't take any special skills; that is, we discount our own special talents. We may also feel that if we are not currently using a skill, we can no longer claim it—that somehow it has escaped us. Or, if we haven't been paid to use the skill, we may not recognize its value.

All of these false assumptions make it difficult to list our skills honestly and accurately. Your goal now will be to recognize the many skills you possess that make you valuable in the job market. You have acquired hundreds of skills just by virtue of your life experiences, and, paid or not, they are part of your portfolio!

Once you begin to recognize your skills, you will become more aware of your identity as extending beyond the narrow limits you tend to apply to yourself. We all unconsciously tend to categorize ourselves too narrowly. For instance, you might typically answer the question "Who are you?" with statements such as "I am a student," "I am a history major," "I am a graphic artist," "I am a conservative," or "I am a homemaker." The problem with these labels is that they tend to stereotype you. This is especially true when you are interviewing for a job. If you say you are a student, the interviewer might stereotype you as not having enough experience. If you say you are a secretary, the interviewer may consider you only for a secretarial job or may insist that you start as a secretary. But suppose you say your experience has involved public speaking, doing organizational work, coordinating schedules, managing budgets, researching needs, problem solving, following through with details, motivating others, resolving problems caused by low morale and lack of cooperation, and establishing priorities for allocation of available time, resources, and funds. Not only does this sound impressive, but you appear eligible for many positions that require these skills.

Homemakers and the long-term unemployed face a particular challenge because they have been out of the job market and often believe they have no transferable or marketable skills. To the contrary, homemaking and working out of your home (while looking for full time employment) is a full-time job requiring a wide range of skills that can translate into paid employment. In fact, "stay at home" parents develop skills in the areas of management, leadership, coaching, personnel, finances, logistics, event planning, asset allocation, negotiations, mediation, and purchasing (just to name a few). Can you think of other skills to add to this list? Scan the list in the following activity for suggestions. All of these skills can be included in a list of transferable skills that relate to paid employment.

Complete the Activity "Assessing Your Skills" checklist. This list includes more than 200 skills in 13 different categories. These categories are useful because they're familiar to employers and often show up in job announcements as keywords. As you complete the checklist, carefully consider how each skill applies specifically to you.

If you are currently working, think of ways to use those skills you identify in the activity checklist as your self-motivated skills as often as possible to give you job satisfaction. Talk to your supervisor and identify additional ways to use these skills now or in the future. For example, if you were hired because of your computer or technical skills, you might suggest that you become the company expert on formatting documents and reports to give them a consistent look. If your people skills are one of your strengths, make sure your boss keeps you in mind for office supervisor, or as a member of a committee, or as the company liaison with an important client. Don't take your skills for granted and don't let others do so!

Employers look for employees who are task oriented and who think and talk in terms of what they as employees can do to make the employer's operation easier, better,

▲ Transferable skills: You can develop new skills and improve on current identified skills throughout your life.

ACTIVITY Assessing Your Skills

For each item in this table, mark a plus (+) next to each skill you enjoy using (even if you aren't expert at it!). Then go back over the list and place a check (✓) next to each skill that you perform particularly well. Place an O next to any skills that you have never used. Finally, place an X next to any skills that you would like to develop or acquire. Under personal qualities, check all that apply to you.

Once you have completed these steps, review those skills that are marked with both an X and a check-mark. These are your *self-motivated* or preferred skills. These skills represent your areas of mastery and probably your areas of greatest interest as well. If you use these skills on the job whenever possible, and look for additional ways to use them, you will increase the enjoyment and satisfaction you derive from your job.

+ = skills you enjoy using	**X** = skills you would like to develop or acquire
✓ = skills you perform especially well	**O** = skills you have never used

CLERICAL SKILLS

____ Examining
____ Evaluating
____ Filing
____ Developing
____ Improving
____ Recording
____ Collating
____ Computing
____ Recommending
____ Following
____ Bookkeeping
____ Keyboarding
____ Transcribing
____ Indexing
____ Arranging
____ Systematizing
____ Tabulating
____ Photocopying
____ Collaborating
____ Sorting
____ Retrieving
____ Organizing
____ Purchasing
____ Handling people
____ Problem solving

TECHNICAL SKILLS

____ Financing
____ Evaluating
____ Calculating
____ Adjusting
____ Aligning
____ Observing
____ Verifying
____ Drafting

____ Designing
____ Cataloging
____ Examining
____ Adjusting
____ Problem solving
____ Creating
____ Detailing
____ Restructuring
____ Reviewing
____ Revising
____ Synthesizing
____ Structuring
____ Solving
____ Refining
____ Reviewing
____ Following specifications

PUBLIC RELATIONS SKILLS

____ Planning
____ Conducting
____ Informing
____ Consulting
____ Writing
____ Researching
____ Representing
____ Negotiating
____ Collaborating
____ Communicating
____ Promoting
____ Convincing
____ Hosting
____ Entertaining
____ Mediating
____ Performing
____ Endorsing

____ Recruiting
____ Demonstrating
____ Creating
____ Problem solving

AGRICULTURAL SKILLS

____ Inspecting
____ Costing
____ Lifting
____ Cultivating
____ Assembling
____ Problem solving
____ Devising
____ Scheduling
____ Demonstrating
____ Inspecting
____ Evaluating
____ Estimating
____ Diagnosing
____ Repairing
____ Maintaining
____ Replacing
____ Constructing
____ Operating

SELLING SKILLS

____ Contacting
____ Persuading
____ Reviewing
____ Inspecting
____ Informing
____ Promoting
____ Positioning
____ Influencing
____ Convincing
____ Comparing

____ Differentiating
____ Representing
____ Asking
____ Closing
____ Costing
____ Negotiating
____ Communicating
____ Calculating
____ Advising
____ Contracting
____ Recommending
____ Problem solving

MAINTENANCE SKILLS

____ Operating
____ Repairing
____ Maintaining
____ Dismantling
____ Adjusting
____ Cleaning
____ Purchasing
____ Climbing
____ Lifting
____ Assembling
____ Problem solving
____ Devising
____ Scheduling
____ Demonstrating
____ Inspecting
____ Evaluating
____ Estimating

MANAGEMENT SKILLS

____ Planning
____ Organizing
____ Scheduling

_____ Assigning
_____ Delegating
_____ Directing
_____ Hiring
_____ Measuring
_____ Administering
_____ Conducting
_____ Controlling
_____ Coordinating
_____ Enabling
_____ Empowering
_____ Initiating
_____ Formulating
_____ Supervising
_____ Sponsoring
_____ Modeling
_____ Supporting
_____ Negotiating
_____ Decision making
_____ Team building
_____ Conceptualizing
_____ Problem solving

COMMUNICATION SKILLS

_____ Reasoning
_____ Organizing
_____ Defining
_____ Writing
_____ Listening
_____ Explaining
_____ Interpreting
_____ Reading
_____ Speaking
_____ Editing
_____ Instructing
_____ Interviewing
_____ Collaborating
_____ Presenting
_____ Formulating
_____ Proposing
_____ Synthesizing
_____ Integrating
_____ Connecting
_____ Summarizing
_____ Articulating
_____ Interpreting

_____ Translating
_____ Problem solving

RESEARCH SKILLS

_____ Recognizing
_____ Interviewing
_____ Questioning
_____ Synthesizing
_____ Writing
_____ Diagnosing
_____ Compiling
_____ Reviewing
_____ Designing
_____ Theorizing
_____ Testing
_____ Equating
_____ Evaluating
_____ Investigating
_____ Summarizing
_____ Communicating
_____ Collaborating
_____ Demonstrating
_____ Analyzing
_____ Refining
_____ Problem solving

FINANCIAL SKILLS

_____ Calculating
_____ Projecting
_____ Budgeting
_____ Recognizing
_____ Accounting
_____ Processing
_____ Computing
_____ Correlating
_____ Costing
_____ Forecasting
_____ Comparing
_____ Compiling
_____ Examining
_____ Leveraging
_____ Verifying
_____ Problem solving

MANUAL SKILLS

_____ Operating
_____ Monitoring

_____ Controlling
_____ Setting up
_____ Driving
_____ Cutting
_____ Assembling
_____ Drafting
_____ Drawing
_____ Inspecting
_____ Programming
_____ Tabulating
_____ Constructing
_____ Creating
_____ Repairing
_____ Problem solving

SERVICE SKILLS

_____ Counseling
_____ Guiding
_____ Leading
_____ Listening
_____ Coordinating
_____ Teaching
_____ Responding
_____ Collaborating
_____ Facilitating
_____ Monitoring
_____ Integrating
_____ Motivating
_____ Persuading
_____ Evaluating
_____ Summarizing
_____ Planning
_____ Correcting
_____ Mediating
_____ Encouraging
_____ Contracting
_____ Demonstrating
_____ Problem solving

PERSONAL QUALITIES

_____ Adaptable
_____ Adventuresome
_____ Aggressive
_____ Alert
_____ Ambitious
_____ Assertive
_____ Calm

_____ Capable
_____ Confident
_____ Conscientious
_____ Creative
_____ Cooperative
_____ Candid
_____ Dependable
_____ Determined
_____ Diplomatic
_____ Discreet
_____ Dominant
_____ Efficient
_____ Energetic
_____ Enterprising
_____ Enthusiastic
_____ Flexible
_____ Forceful
_____ Frank
_____ Idealistic
_____ Initiating
_____ Innovative
_____ Logical
_____ Loyal
_____ Methodical
_____ Objective
_____ Optimistic
_____ Organized
_____ Patient
_____ Persistent
_____ Practical
_____ Precise
_____ Quiet
_____ Realistic
_____ Reliable
_____ Resourceful
_____ Risk taking
_____ Self-starting
_____ Sensitive
_____ Serious
_____ Sincere
_____ Tactful
_____ Tenacious
_____ Versatile

Can you talk about your skills?

more profitable, and more efficient. The best way to describe what you can do for an employer is to talk about your skills and how they apply to the job. People tend to discount their accomplishments and their related skill development. Here's your opportunity to become more aware of the skills you already have that are part of your success profile. They will give you a competitive edge in the job market. Although climbing a mountain and running a four-minute mile are noteworthy accomplishments, so are the following:

Sample accomplishments. Use past accomplishments to reveal skills.

raising a child	raising funds for a cause
getting into college	giving a speech
delivering papers on a route	writing a term paper
using a software program	getting a job
repairing a car	consoling a child
playing sports	graduating from high school
designing a costume	planning a trip and traveling
developing a blog	working as a food server
completing a computer course	mastering a sport
planning a surprise party	overcoming a bad habit
creating a webpage	designing a website
completing a degree	

In reviewing this list, you may be thinking that some of these activities are simple, no big deal. Some are activities you can do without much thought or preparation. However, just because they don't take much preparation does not mean they aren't accomplishments that are filled with skills. Start thinking of goals that you have set and then later met as accomplishments!

ANALYZE YOUR ACCOMPLISHMENTS

You can begin to recognize your skills by identifying and examining your most satisfying accomplishments; indeed, it is your skills that led you to those accomplishments. By analyzing these accomplishments, you are likely to discover a pattern of skills (your self-motivators) that you repeatedly use and enjoy using. Again, accomplishments are simply completed activities, goals, projects, or jobs held.

There are several ways to analyze accomplishments. One way is to describe something that you are proud of having completed, and then list the skills that were required to complete it. Exercises 5.2 and 5.3 ask you to list 10 accomplishments and then to describe a few of them in detail. Exercise 5.4 allows you to identify the skills used in the accomplishments described in those two previous exercises.

Before thinking about accomplishments, however, let's begin by thinking about your life. Exercise 5.1 asks you to write about several major experiences in your life with enough detail so that you will be able to analyze each experience for the particular skills used.

EXERCISE

5.1   Experiography

To explore your past experiences and relate them to your career plan, write an account of the significant experiences in your life—an *experiography*. Think of this as describing your own life story. The best way to go about this task is to think of three or four major experiences in your life from any three of the following categories and then describe each of them, in writing, in as much detail as you can. Describe not only what happened but also your feelings (good or bad) about the experience or person and what you learned from the experience:

1. Work experience
2. Activity experience—school, clubs, etc.
3. Life events
4. Leisure time or hobbies

5. People in your life
6. Life's frustrations
7. Life's rewards

Remember, neither the chronology nor the order of significance is important. What is critical is to describe people or events that have had an impact on who you are right now and how you have had an impact on others. Keep the writing specific enough so you can analyze these experiences for particular skills you have demonstrated.

EXERCISE 5.2 Accomplishments

Make a list of up to 10 of your accomplishments. Exercise 5.1 may have reminded you of several other important activities in which you identified accomplishments you can use here.

1. _____   6. _____
2. _____   7. _____
3. _____   8. _____
4. _____   9. _____
5. _____   10. _____

EXERCISE 5.3 Description of Accomplishments

Select one or two of the accomplishments you listed in Exercise 5.2 and describe each of them in detail. Use one sheet of paper for each accomplishment. To be as detailed as possible in your description of the event, try to elaborate on *who* influenced you, *what* you did, *where* it happened, *when* it occurred, *why* you did it, and *how* you did it. Your detailed description will now be comparable to the "Real Stories" feature you are about to read. After reading about John in "Real Stories," you will be able to identify skills in your own descriptions.

EXERCISE 5.4 Your "Self-Motivated" Skills

Using the Skills Checklist (see pp. 80-81), list the skills you used in the Accomplishments in Exercise 5.3.

_____
_____
_____
_____
_____

EXERCISE 5.4   Your "Self-Motivated" Skills   CONTINUED

Review your list from your checklist and accomplishments, and identify five skills that interest you and you would like to develop.

1. _____
2. _____
3. _____
4. _____
5. _____

Think of ways you can develop these skills, such as taking a course or class, getting on-the-job training, joining a club, volunteering, or asking a friend, associate, colleague, or mentor for help. To further clarify your responses, complete Exercise 5.7 at the end of the chapter

Let's now look at John, whose life story includes a detailed description of several events, people, life rewards, and accomplishments. After you have read about John, reread the list of skills that John identified in the third paragraph. See if you can think of any that he missed. We all have many more skills than we credit ourselves with having!

REAL stories   Meet John

In high school, John was always someone friends went to when they needed a plan. When he was younger, John was known as a schemer, and most of the time he was in trouble for his schemes, but as he got older he learned to turn his schemes into plans. Well liked, John never thought of himself as anything special, but his friends thought he had a real talent for making things happen.

John's girlfriend, Alicia, was turning 18 and he wanted to throw a really great surprise party for her. He called all their friends told them his ideas. He divided everyone into groups to cover the food, entertainment, transportation, and decorations. The party was a huge success (even though Alicia says she knew about it all along).

The following week when John had to write a paper for his career class describing an accomplishment, he used the party. He described his initial plan and how he organized and divided the work, made a checklist, and communicated with everyone. From a list of skills given to each student by the teacher, John identified *leadership, creativity, communication, determination, organization, dependability,* and *attention to detail* as the skills in putting together the party.

In his senior year, a friend told John of an internship opportunity with a congressional representative in his district. The friend felt that John's organizational skills would make him a perfect candidate. Because John did not have any real work experience, he used the party-planning activity on his resume to demonstrate his skills. His resume got him an interview, and his outgoing personality and strong organizational skills got him the internship.

One of John's assignments was to organize meetings and special events. He loved the work, and he was able to use the full resources of the congressional office to put together impressive events.

After graduation, John felt more confident than he ever felt before. With an excellent reference letter from the legislator, John decided to enroll in community college. He took some marketing classes and looked for another internship. He was lucky to land a position with an ad agency that promoted Miley Cyrus. He learned a great deal working with the ad agency and the people associated with Ms. Cyrus.

When the internship ended, John began researching careers to see what education and training he needed to continue with this type of work. He discovered that event planning fit with his interests and his skills; however, the salary was not as much as he had expected. John met with a counselor and they agreed that to do the type of work he loved and make a decent salary, he would need a four-year degree. The counselor helped John create an educational plan to prepare him to transfer to the university.

WHAT DO *YOU* THINK?

1. Other than event planning, what other types of jobs require the skills that John possesses?
2. Are some people born with organizational skills? If not, how can people develop these skills?
3. What gave John the confidence to attend college?
4. List an activity or project you have accomplished and indicate the skills you used to complete it. Discuss your accomplishment and skills with a friend.
5. Write yourself a letter of reference.

Another shorter method to identify skills is to simply write a story about one task completed and then list the skills used. Dick Bolles popularized this approach in his *Quick Job Hunting Map* (2006), a booklet that lists hundreds of skills. Following is an example of one student's project and the skills involved. The student's classmates listened to her story and helped her identify 21 skills.

Completing a Team Research Report

It was necessary for me to learn new software and Web-based tools to communicate to my team and to format my findings on a spreadsheet. As the team leader, I had to find a time when all members could meet in person to share findings and formulate the final report before the due date. The skills used in this team research project include the following:

1. Learn quickly
2. Display flexibility
3. Meet challenges
4. Direct self and others
5. Follow through
6. Face new situations
7. Proof and edit
8. Translate concepts
9. Use technology
10. Organize
11. Get the job done
12. Display patience
13. Attend to detail
14. Overcome obstacles
15. Communicate clearly
16. Work under stress
17. Display persistence
18. Ask questions
19. Use new software and web-based technology
20. Exercise leadership skill
21. Manage time effectively

Identifying Transferable Skills

Transferable skills are those you carry from one job to another and can use in many occupations. Perhaps you are concerned about a lack of paid job experience, or you may have chosen a liberal arts major (such as English or History) and are concerned you will not be trained for a job when you graduate. This section discusses three ways to identify your transferable skills:

1. Reviewing a traditional national report on skills considered necessary by employers (SCANS skills)
2. Reviewing skills one develops while being a secondary school student as well as a college student
3. Reviewing a national Bureau of Labor Statistics website (O*NET) that connects skills to occupations

SCANS is the acronym for Secretary's Commission on Achieving Necessary Skills. The U.S. Department of Labor issued the report back in the 1990s, and this list has stood the test of time. Many colleges require that curricula for new classes include a list of the skills and competencies listed in the report that can be learned while a student is taking the class.

The Conference Board, along with The Partnership for 21st Century Skills, Corporate Voices for Working Families, and the Society for Human Resource Management, conducted a survey in 2007 of more than 400 employers across the United States to identify skill sets that will be needed by new workplace entrants to succeed. A key finding of the survey reinforces the SCANS Report, indicating that the "three R's" alone are not sufficient to succeed on the job, and that applied or soft skills are essential for success. Among the most important soft skills needed by entrants into today's workforce are the following:

- Professionalism/Work ethic
- Communications (written and oral)
- Teamwork/Collaboration
- Critical thinking
- Creative problem solving

The Conference Board, The Society of Human Resource Management, The President's Council on Competitiveness, The National Center on Employment and the Economy, and The American Management Association all confirm a widening global skills gap related to the core skills mentioned above. Studies conducted regularly by these professional organizations indicate that the United States will have a shortage of 14 million skilled workers by 2018!

▲ Whether you work as an engineer, an interior designer, or a school teacher, you will employ such transferable skills as computer technology, communication, teamwork, and problem solving.

By reading the list of SCANS skills on the following pages, note how many SCANS skills you use in daily life and in school. Read Exhibit 5.1 and the "Success Strategies" feature both of which show that by completing exercises in this book related to resume writing, career information searching, information interviewing, and making a budget, you will be using many skills that employers have identified are important for success in the workplace (see "Using SCANS Skills," p. 90).

EXHIBIT 5.1	Tasks from Diverse Occupations Representative of Level of Performance in SCANS Know-How Skills Required for Entry into Jobs with a Career Ladder

Position and Tasks

Resources	*Travel Agent:* Sets priorities for work tasks on a daily basis so that travel arrangements are completed in a timely manner.	*Restaurant Manager:* Prepares weekly sales projections; conducts inventories of food supplies; calculates the costs of purchased and on-hand food; determines sales.	*Medical Assistant:* Acquires, maintains, and tracks supplies on hand—inventories supplies and equipment, fills out reorder forms, and obtains extra supplies when merchandise is on sale.	*Quality Control Inspector:* Establishes a system for inspecting items within a given area and time frame while allowing for contingencies.	*Chef:* Performs a cost analysis on menu items in order to turn a profit.
Interpersonal Skills	*Childcare Aide:* Works as a member of a team in the classroom.	*Outside Equipment Technician:* Coordinates with a peer technician to install a point-to-point data circuit in two different cities.	*Carpenter:* Shares experiences and knowledge with other workers, and cooperates with others on a variety of tasks to accomplish project goals.	*Accounting/ Financial Analyst:* Teaches a coworker the procedure for sending bimonthly statements.	*Customer Service Representative:* Assists customers in selecting merchandise or resolving complaints.
Information	*Travel Agent:* Uses online software to retrieve information relating to customer requests, plans itineraries, and books airline tickets.	*Office Supervisor:* Records and maintains purchase requests, purchase invoices, and cost information on raw material.	*Childcare Aide:* Compiles accurate written records including all facets of the child's play for the office and the parents.	*Order Filler:* Communicates a downtime situation to coworkers and explains the situation so that everyone can visualize and understand it.	*Cosmetologist:* Keeps abreast of new and emerging styles and techniques through magazines and attendance at fashion shows.
Systems	*Medical Assistant:* Understands the systems of the organization and the organization's ultimate goal (i.e., excellent patient care).	*Accounting/ Financial Analyst:* Performs analyses comparing current expenditures with projected needs and revenues.	*Shipping and Receiving Clerk:* Unloads and directs material throughout the plant to storage and the assembly line in accordance with company policy.	*Food Service Worker:* Evaluates the performance of workers and adjusts work assignments to increase staff efficiency.	*Plastic Molding Machine Operator:* Monitors gauges and dials to ensure that the machine operates at the proper rate.
Technology	*Travel Agent:* Uses online search engines to retrieve information relating to the customer's request, plans the itinerary, and books the airline ticket.	*Accounting/ Financial Analyst:* Prepares the monthly debt schedule, including reviews of financial statements.	*Expeditor/ Purchasing Agent:* Accesses the computer to retrieve required forms used to request bids and to place purchase orders.	*Industry Training Specialist:* Uses available computer and video technology to enhance the realism of training and to conserve time.	*Order Filler:* Operates a forklift and ensures that it is in proper operating condition.

EXHIBIT 5.1 Tasks from Diverse Occupations Representative of Level of Performance in SCANS Know-How Skills Required for Entry into Jobs with a Career Ladder *CONTINUED*

	Position and Tasks				
Basic Skills	*Dental Hygienist:* Reads professional manuals to understand issues related to new techniques and equipment.	*Sales Representative, Hotel Services:* Assesses client accounts to determine adherence to company standards.	*Optician:* Measures a customer's facial features to calculate bifocal segment height.	*Law Enforcement Officer:* Prepares written reports of incidents and crimes.	*Contractor:* Prepares a letter to a subcontractor delineating responsibilities for completion of a contract.
Thinking Skills	*Expeditor/ Purchasing Agent:* Decides what supplier to use during a bid evaluation based on supplier information.	*Office supervisor:* Sets priorities for processing orders to resolve a conflict in scheduling.	*Salesperson/Outside Sales:* Collects money from delinquent customers and uses judgment on extending credit.	*Contractor:* Analyzes and corrects the problem when timber piles break before reaching specified bearing loads.	*Travel Agent:* Compensates a customer who is dissatisfied with a travel experience.
Personal Qualities	*Optician:* Responds to customer requests, demonstrates understanding of customer needs, and exhibits friendliness and politeness to customers.	*Quality Control Inspector:* Performs independent research to assess compliance.	*Computer Operator:* Assumes responsibility for the arrangement and completion of jobs run for several departments.	*Telemarketing Representative:* Displays a sense of concern and interest in customers' business and company.	*Sales Representative, Hotel Services:* Asserts self and networks with people at conventions.

Source: *School to Career Handbook* (California Community Colleges, Chancellor's office).

SUCCESS strategies The SCANS Report

Identifying the Basic Skills Required by Employers

In 1991, the U.S. Department of Labor issued the SCANS (Secretary's Commission on Achieving Necessary Skills) report. Its goal was to sum up the competencies and skills that form the basis of solid job performance. The results are based on the extensive questioning of employers and educators. The report has stood the test of time.

Review the core competencies, qualities, and skills identified by the SCANS report. These are considered essential skills that workers must possess to be competitive in the twenty-first-century job market. In how many of these areas do you currently feel you have adequate skill levels? If an employer asked you to prove your competencies, could you identify an area of accomplishment in which you demonstrated your use of these skills?

Workplace Know-How

The know-how identified by the SCANS report is made up of a three-part foundation of skills and personal qualities along with five competencies; both the foundation and the competencies are needed for solid job performance. For the foundation skills, first they are described and then you are given some ideas on applying them to your current level of proficiency.

The Foundation

Basic Skills. Reading, writing, arithmetic and mathematics, speaking, and listening. These are the *minimum* skills needed by today's workers. If you are unsure about your skills in these basic areas, now is the time to take steps to achieve a basic level of proficiency or improve them. Don't shy away from basic testing and coursework or assume that, as an adult, you naturally have these abilities. Begin thinking in terms of doing all of these basics *well*.

Thinking Skills. Thinking creatively, making decisions, solving problems, seeing things in the mind's eye, knowing how to learn, and reasoning. Thinking skills allow you to identify your strengths and weaknesses and take steps to remedy the latter. They allow you to acquire new skills, think creatively, and identify problems and solutions. If you are unsure of your abilities in these areas, talk to your career counselor or instructor about testing and coursework that can help.

Personal Qualities. Individual responsibility, self-esteem, sociability, self-management, and integrity. Included are the personality characteristics described in Chapter 2 and the adaptive skills described in this chapter.

The Competencies

Effective workers can productively use:

Resources. Allocating time, money, materials, space, and personnel.

Interpersonal Skills. Working on teams, teaching others, serving customers, leading, negotiating, and working well with people from culturally diverse backgrounds.

Information. Acquiring and evaluating data, organizing and maintaining files, interpreting and communicating, and using computers to process information.

Systems. Understanding social, organizational, and technological systems; monitoring and correcting performance; and designing or improving systems.

Technology. Selecting equipment and tools, applying technology to specific tasks, and maintaining and troubleshooting technologies.

Source: *SCANS (Secretary's Commission on Achieving Necessary Skills): What Work Requires of Schools: A SCANS Report for America 2000.* 1991, June. Washington, DC: U.S. Department of Labor.

TIPS FROM THE PROS

PEOPLE SKILLS

From the manager of the accounting department at Sony Technology Center:

> The number one thing that I look for when I am hiring someone is their people skills because it is very important that you have the skills to talk to people and find out what you need to know. I believe that everyone has the ability to learn anything in this world, but if you have the ability to find the answers to things you want, then you will succeed. . . . I spend 80 percent of my time or so dealing with people in other divisions within Sony . . . and my staff also deals with these people. (http://www.cord.org)

From Bill Gates, one of the founders of Microsoft, the world's largest software company:

> Today and in the future, many of the jobs with the greatest impact will be related to software, whether it is developing software working for a company like Microsoft or helping other organizations use information technology tools to be successful.
>
> Communication skills and the ability to work well with different types of people are very important too. A lot of people assume that creating software is purely a solitary activity where you sit in an office with the door closed all day and write lots of code.
>
> This isn't true at all.
>
> Software innovation . . . requires the ability to collaborate and share ideas with other people, and to sit down and talk with customers and get their feedback and understand their needs.

WHAT DO *YOU* THINK?

1. Why is it important to have people skills if you plan to be an accountant or a technician?
2. From this description, what do you think an accountant or technician does besides accounting and software development?
3. What is your conclusion about the importance of people skills to any career you choose?

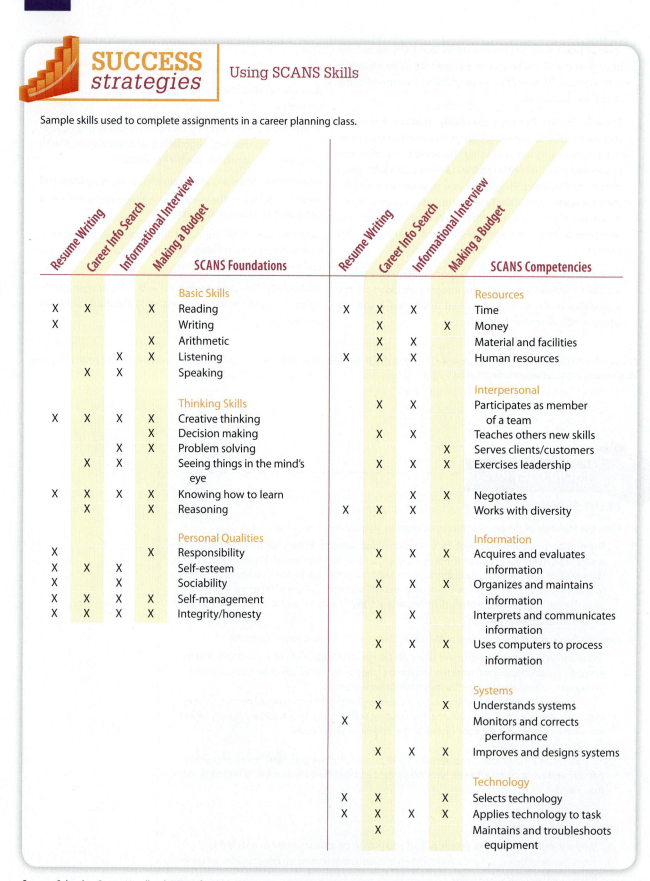

SUCCESS strategies — Using SCANS Skills

Sample skills used to complete assignments in a career planning class.

Resume Writing	Career Info Search	Informational Interview	Making a Budget	SCANS Foundations		Resume Writing	Career Info Search	Informational Interview	Making a Budget	SCANS Competencies
				Basic Skills						**Resources**
X	X		X	Reading		X	X	X		Time
X				Writing			X		X	Money
			X	Arithmetic			X	X		Material and facilities
		X	X	Listening		X	X	X		Human resources
	X	X		Speaking						
										Interpersonal
				Thinking Skills			X	X		Participates as member of a team
X	X	X	X	Creative thinking			X	X		Teaches others new skills
			X	Decision making					X	Serves clients/customers
		X	X	Problem solving			X	X	X	Exercises leadership
	X	X		Seeing things in the mind's eye						
X	X	X	X	Knowing how to learn			X	X		Negotiates
	X		X	Reasoning		X	X	X		Works with diversity
				Personal Qualities						**Information**
X			X	Responsibility			X	X	X	Acquires and evaluates information
X	X	X		Self-esteem						
X		X		Sociability			X	X	X	Organizes and maintains information
X	X	X	X	Self-management			X	X		Interprets and communicates information
X	X	X	X	Integrity/honesty						
							X	X	X	Uses computers to process information
										Systems
							X		X	Understands systems
							X			Monitors and corrects performance
							X	X	X	Improves and designs systems
										Technology
							X	X		X	Selects technology
							X	X	X	X	Applies technology to task
							X			Maintains and troubleshoots equipment

Source: *School to Career Handbook* (VTEA-funded project through the California Community Colleges, Chancellor's office).

TRANSFERABLE SKILLS DEVELOPED AS A RESULT OF COMPLETING A COLLEGE DEGREE

It is common to see a college degree required as part of the qualifications for many jobs. Of course, technical-, medical-, and science-related fields require completed courses that indicate a level of expertise in those specific majors, but even in nontechnical- or non-science-oriented majors, typically called "liberal arts majors," employers are looking for skills that are usually developed as a part of the college completion experience. The college degree is an indicator for the employer that the applicant has mastered certain higher-level transferable skills.

Let's examine the transferable skills that a liberal arts major should develop as a result of successfully completing college. A liberal arts degree is preparation for a variety of careers. In fact, the majority of those who graduate with a liberal arts degree do not find employment in fields related to their major (e.g., history majors do not necessarily become historians). As you read about the following clusters of skills, think about which skills you are developing as a student. Do you have research skills? Do you have organizational and time-management skills? Chances are, you do!

Examples of the skills acquired in a typical college liberal arts degree program include the following (note how these mirror the skills identified by the SCANS report):

Communication skills. Listening effectively, writing essays and reports, convincing individuals and groups of the importance of your ideas, negotiating disputes and differences, selling yourself and your product or idea.

Problem-solving or critical-thinking skills. Analytical thinking, thinking abstractly, connecting ideas or concepts in new or fresh ways, determining broader issues, defining an issue, identifying several solutions to the same problem, hypothesizing implications and future scenarios, creating new ways to handle an issue, persuading others to act in the best interests of the group, synthesizing ideas.

Human relations skills. Listening, communicating understanding verbally and nonverbally, compromising, speaking with colleagues, advising people, helping people resolve problems, communicating ideas effectively, cooperating with others to solve problems and to complete projects, working well with diverse groups of people, appreciating differences, teaching or coaching others.

Organizational skills. Assessing needs, planning or arranging presentations or social events, designing programs, coordinating events, delegating responsibility, evaluating programs, managing the implementation of projects, time management.

Research skills. Searching computerized databases and published reference materials, identifying themes, analyzing data, classifying data and/or handling detail work, investigating problems, recording data, writing reports and term papers.

You now know that you transfer many skills from one job to another. Once you understand what skills are required in a job, you can use these skills in your job application, in your resumes, and during job interviews to describe and reinforce the fact that you have what it takes to do the job, even if you have never had the exact job title. You make the connection between what you have and what the employer wants by claiming the same skills. Remember that in a nontechnical or nonscience career, your *natural abilities and attitudes and the skills learned at college* are perhaps your strongest assets—the most important set of skills you have for selling yourself. This is your competitive edge!

Identifying your skills

TIPS FROM THE PROS

SKILLS SETS FOR THE HEALTHCARE INDUSTRY

Although each career in the field of health care has its own unique requirements, you can be sure that there are common health-care career skills required of everyone in this rapidly expanding field. Most positions require excellent interpersonal and communication skills, some level of technical or quantitative thinking capacity, and a strong work ethic. Additionally, most positions entail a great deal of responsibility and maturity. Health-care workers must be willing to learn and to continue to learn, because constant updating and recertification are the norm in this constantly changing field with the development of new technology, advanced procedures, experimental treatments, and even new diseases.

WHAT DO *YOU* THINK?

1. From this description, what skills mentioned do you already possess?
2. What can you do now to develop any of the skills mentioned?

Your Most Valuable Assets: Your Personality Traits

We've talked about transferable skills that were learned or acquired at school, work, or home, or through leisure and volunteer activities. Many of your skills may have come to you naturally, without training or education. We call these skills *natural abilities*. We're referring here to aspects of your personality such as the ability to stay calm in a crisis, the ability to manage many things at once, a natural ability with math and numbers, and/or a natural ability with words. More important, we're referring to personal characteristics such as enthusiasm, a good attitude, persistence, confidence, a sense of humor, and many other qualities that contribute to success in the workplace.

These abilities will help you *sell yourself and your talents*. These personal characteristics, called *adaptive skills*, may in the end separate you from other qualified applicants and enable you to get the job, top evaluations, raises, and promotions. They may even help you keep your job in tough times.

We don't mean to imply that an employer will look at your enthusiastic, smiling face and say, "It doesn't matter that you have no experience—we want you because you're cheerful!" However, once you have learned to identify your job-specific skills and summarize your experience in such a way that it relates closely to the job being discussed, you will have a greater chance of succeeding if you are aware of and express your best self with interest, enthusiasm, and friendliness. Know and use your personal skills!

If you were to look at the skills listed at the bottom of the O*NET Exhibit 5.2, you might never come up with the job title of criminal investigator. However, this exhibit does include the tasks that are related to criminal investigation. Therefore, *skills* are very general abilities that relate to jobs, whereas *tasks* are usually specific requirements found in jobs. *The key to using your favorite skills to find a related job is to use O*NET.* Your local career center or One Stop Career Center has access to O*NET if you do not have access to its website (http://online.onetcenter.org) at home. This resource can help you discover the relationship between occupations and skills. O*NET is the acronym for the Occupational Information Network, and it was developed by the U.S. Department of Labor. The program is an easy-to-use, interactive computer database that collects, analyzes, and disseminates skill and occupational information in more than 1,100 occupational areas. Simply check off your desired skills and the O*NET program will list various occupations that use them. One especially useful feature in O*NET is the listing of related jobs. Exhibit 5.2 indicates the

---

EXHIBIT 5.2   O*NET Online

SUMMARY JOB DESCRIPTION REPORT FOR:
33–3021.03 – CRIMINAL INVESTIGATORS AND SPECIAL AGENTS

Investigate alleged or suspected criminal violations of federal, state, or local laws to determine if evidence is sufficient to recommend prosecution.

Sample of related job titles: Special Agent, Criminal Investigator, Investigator, FBI Special Agent (Federal Bureau of Investigation Special Agent)

TASKS

- Obtain and verify evidence by interviewing and observing suspects and witnesses, or by analyzing records.
- Record evidence and documents, using equipment such as cameras and photocopy machines.
- Examine records in order to locate links in chains of evidence or information.
- Prepare reports that detail investigation findings.
- Collaborate with other offices and agencies in order to exchange information and coordinate activities.
- Determine scope, timing, and direction of investigations.
- Testify before grand juries concerning criminal activity investigations.
- Analyze evidence in laboratories or in the field.
- Investigate organized crime, public corruption, financial crime, copyright infringement, civil rights violations, bank robbery, extortion, kidnapping, and other violations of federal or state statutes.
- Identify case issues and evidence needed, based on analysis of charges, complaints, or allegations of law violations.

Skills include writing, judgment and decision making, complex problem solving, coordination, instructing, social perceptiveness, speaking, active listening, service orientation, and persuasion.

Source: O*NET: **online.onetcenter.org**

related jobs for Criminal Investigator such as Special Agent. In this case there are only a few. However, for other occupations, there may be up to 10 examples. For example, if you searched for "counselor," you would find these related jobs: Supervisor, Special Services, Veterans Contact Representative, Counselor, Director of Counseling, Residence Counselor, Foreign-Student Advisor, and several others. When you click on any of these job titles, you will find the skills and job tasks describing these jobs.

 **SUCCESS** *strategies*   Describing Skills

Remember that skills are the currency of the job market. The more you have and the better you are at describing them, the greater your opportunities will be.

- Review the list of transferable skills of a college graduate (see p. 91).
- As you read each skill under each category, think of a specific time when you developed or demonstrated that skill in school, during your leisure activities, or during a past or present job.
- Create a skills folder on your computer as part of your career portfolio to remind yourself about your "self-motivated" skills and where you have used your skills.

- Review the skills folder the next time you are writing a resume or interviewing for a job so you can convincingly describe the skills you possess and how you demonstrated these skills.
- Your ability to communicate this critical information to employers will set you apart from the crowd in the interview process and help you to rise to the top of any employer's list of candidates for hire.

THE PORTFOLIO EMPLOYEE

As we have discussed, your skills are your most valuable asset in the job market because they are transferable. For example, the word processing and data management skills you use in your current job as administrative assistant or insurance claims processor will be equally valuable in other jobs that you seek in the future, such as journalist or lawyer. The more skills you develop, the more valuable and versatile you are in the job market. Such books as *You Majored in What?* by Katharine Brooks (2009), and *Free Agent Nation* (2002) and *A Whole New Mind* (2005) by Daniel Pink confirm that the number of portfolio workers will grow dramatically. Such workers will not be a full-time part of one organization but instead will sell their portfolio of skills to several employers on a freelance basis. Thus, the person who has graphic design and data management skills may work for more than one firm in various capacities. An ever-growing number of people will be self-employed, and their job security will come not from the traditional employer–employee relationship but from their ability to offer needed skills to many employers. This increased trend toward self-employed portfolio employees means that it is essential for each of us to identify our skills and determine which skills we want to use, improve, and develop to stay competitive in the job market.

SUCCESS strategies   Identifying the Transferable Skills of a Teacher

Do you think a teacher would have the skills necessary to find employment in the business world? If you know or have read about anyone working in sales, marketing, or management, you may notice that similar skills are involved in all of these jobs.

ASSESSMENT OF TEACHER SKILLS

Teaching. Training, coordinating, communicating, arbitrating, coaching, group facilitating, accessing the Internet, using computers.

Making Lesson Plans. Designing curricula, incorporating learning strategies, problem solving, creating visual aids.

Assigning Grades. Evaluating, examining, assessing performance, interpreting test results, determining potential of individuals, monitoring progress.

Writing Proposals. Assessing needs, identifying targets, setting priorities, designing evaluation models, identifying relevant information, making hypotheses about unknown phenomena, designing a process, estimating costs of a project, researching funding sources.

Advising the Yearbook Staff. Planning, promoting, fund-raising, group facilitating, handling detail work, meeting deadlines, assembling items of information into a coherent whole, classifying information, coordinating, creating, dealing with pressure, delegating tasks, displaying ideas in artistic form, editing, making layouts.

Supervising Interns. Training, evaluating, mentoring, monitoring progress, diagnosing problem areas, inspiring, counseling, guiding.

Interpreting Diagnostic Tests. Screening, placing, identifying needs, diagnosing.

Interacting with Students, Parents, and Administration. Confronting, resolving conflicts, establishing rapport, conveying warmth and caring, drawing people out, offering support, motivating, negotiating, persuading, handling complaints, mediating, organizing, questioning, troubleshooting.

Chairing a Committee or Department. Administering, anticipating needs or issues, arranging meetings, creating and implementing committee structures, coordinating, delegating tasks, guiding activities of a team, having responsibility for meeting objectives of a department, negotiating, organizing, promoting.

EXERCISE your options

By now you have noticed that you have developed skills while in school and throughout your life. Successful students have transferable skills that are useful in the workforce.

1. Identify three academic transferable skills:_____, _____, _____.
2. Write one goal toward developing workplace skills. (*Tip:* think about volunteer work, school projects, and church or community involvement.)
3. What have you learned about your skills that will help you in college and the workplace?

Summary

We all have our own special excellence, which is most likely to be demonstrated in experiences that each of us considers to be accomplishments or life satisfactions. Your most memorable accomplishments usually indicate where your greatest concentration of self-motivated skills exist. Now that you have analyzed several such achievements, you have discovered a pattern of skills.

The more you know about these motivated skills, the better you will be able to choose careers that require the use of these skills. Using these skills gives you a sense of mastery and satisfaction. You will be happier, more productive, and more successful if you can incorporate your motivated skills into your chosen work. You will also find that your skills transfer to many different jobs.

If you have started researching occupations online or in a library or college career center, you will find that occupational information sources list the skills related to the specific careers described. In addition to O*NET, there are also computer programs in career centers such as EUREKA in California, SIGI Plus (System of Interactive Guidance and Information), CIS (Career Information System), Bridges, and Career Cruising that include lists of skills correlated with job descriptions. To conclude this chapter, finish the final exercises to further flesh out your own talents.

PURPOSE OF EXERCISES

The following exercises will assist you in identifying and summarizing your personal constellation of skills. Exercise 5.5 will identify your cluster of favorite skills. Exercise 5.6 will help you recognize the extent of your experience related to the responsibilities of your ideal or fantasy jobs.

Exercises 5.7 and 5.8 review and summarize your preferred and most often used skills. Exercise 5.9, **WWWebwise**, is a web-based research exercise that will reinforce the learnings in this chapter. And lastly, **Rating Your Learning Outcomes**, will reinforce what you learned in this chapter.

EXERCISE
5.5 Your Favorite Skills

First Impression: Rank the following skills clusters as they reflect your favorite skills (1 = favorite; 6 = least favorite).

_____ **a.** Help people, be of service, be kind

_____ **b.** Write, read, talk, speak, teach

_____ **c.** Analyze, systemize, research

_____ **d.** Invent, create, develop, imagine

_____ **e.** Persuade, sell, influence, negotiate

_____ **f.** Build, plant crops, use hand–eye coordination, operate machinery

Now look back at Exercise 5.2. Do your accomplishments listed fall in the clusters you have ranked as your favorites?

EXERCISE

5.6   Ideal Jobs

Write five ideal job responsibilities using the examples from the clusters in Exercise 5.5. Next to each one, write two or more examples of your experience in each of these areas (e.g., "writing—I wrote a 10-page report that was used to support a grant application").

_____
_____
_____
_____
_____
_____
_____
_____
_____
_____
_____
_____
_____
_____
_____
_____

In areas where you have not developed extensive experience, you may want to create additional learning experiences to make yourself eligible for your ideal jobs. You can create learning experiences or gain experience by taking classes, volunteering for extra work in your present job, or finding another job closely related to your ideal jobs.

EXERCISE

5.7   SCANS

Review the SCANS skills description on pages 88–89. Identify up to eight volunteer, job, or homework activities to use on your own checklist that follows in the Exercise 5.7 worksheet.

1. _____
2. _____
3. _____
4. _____
5. _____
6. _____
7. _____
8. _____

On the following worksheet, check the skills you used in these activities. Use the grid on page 90 as an example. As a result of doing this exercise, you will realize all the skills you are using in various aspects of your life (e.g., volunteering, having a job, doing homework).

EXERCISE 5.7   WORKSHEET

Using the eight volunteer, job, or college homework activities, check off which skills were used in each activity.

1	2	3	4	5	6	7	8	SCANS FOUNDATION
								BASIC SKILLS
								Reading
								Writing
								Arithmetic
								Listening
								Speaking
								THINKING SKILLS
								Creative thinking
								Decision making
								Problem solving
								Seeing things in the mind's eye
								Knowing how to learn
								Reasoning
								PERSONAL QUALITIES
								Responsibility
								Self-esteem
								Sociability
								Self-management
								Integrity/honesty
								RESOURCES
								Time
								Money
								Material and facilities
								Human resources
								INTERPERSONAL
								Participates as member of a team
								Teaches others new skills
								Serves clients/customers
								Exercises leadership
								Negotiates
								Works with diversity
								INFORMATION
								Acquires and evaluates information
								Organizes and maintains information
								Interprets and communicates information
								Uses computers to process information

EXERCISE 5.7   SCANS *CONTINUED*

1	2	3	4	5	6	7	8	SCANS FOUNDATION
								SYSTEMS
								Understands systems
								Monitors and corrects performance
								Improves and designs systems
								TECHNOLOGY
								Selects technology
								Applies technology to task
								Maintains and troubleshoots equipment

Source: *School to Career Handbook* (VATEA-funded project through the California Community Colleges, Chancellor's office).

EXERCISE 5.8   Skills Review

WHAT SKILLS DO YOU USE AND WHAT WOULD YOU LIKE TO DEVELOP?

List the skills that you currently use as noted in Exercise 5.7.

_____

_____

_____

_____

_____

_____

Review your responses in the "Assessing Your Skills" activity on pp. 80–81. What skills would you most like to use in your future career?

_____

_____

_____

_____

_____

_____

_____

Which of the skills you just listed do you need to develop?

_____

_____

_____

_____

_____

_____

How will you develop these skills?

_____

_____

_____

_____

_____

_____

You have now identified your foundation, the areas in which you have been most effective and successful in your life. By examining these successes or achievements, you now know what you can do and what motivates you. It is especially important that you focus on skills you use and enjoy when you start to research which careers might be most satisfying to you in the next part of this book.

EXERCISE
5.9   WWWebwise

Go to **http://online.onetcenter.org/**. Click on Skills Search. Check off the skills you enjoy and would like to use in an ideal job. In one or two paragraphs, briefly identify the skills and the jobs related to those skills. (*Note:* Please be aware that websites can change without notice. If a link does not work, find a similar site to complete the activity.)

REINFORCING YOUR LEARNING OUTCOMES

Review and Rate Your Chapter Outcomes. Indicate in the right-hand column how well you do the following items (from 1 = very well, to 5 = not at all). If you rated yourself 4 or 5, review the material on the pages in parentheses to ensure your career success.

How Well Can You Do the Following?

- Discuss the importance of skills in your career search. (pp. 76–86)   1 2 3 4 5

- Define and identify your skills. (pp. 80–81)   1 2 3 4 5

- Recognize the power of the transferability of your skills. (pp. 85–93)   1 2 3 4 5

- Use the language of skills in writing your resume and preparing for an interview. (pp. 85–95)   1 2 3 4 5

Go to the Career Fitness Portfolio at the end of the book and complete this chapter summary to build and record your personal Career Fitness Portfolio.

Additional Opportunity: Your instructor may choose to assign the Career Fitness Portfolio for in class or online completion. If so, they will provide the handout or link for you to access.

PART 2

Harness Your Workplace Savvy

Scope Out the World of Work

Examining the World of Work

Broaden Your Outlook

Your assumptions, limitations, aspirations, dreams, and fantasies are all influenced by the spoken and unspoken rules and norms of the society in which you live.

In every society, even one as free as that of the United States, social and cultural traditions influence career choice. For example, it may still seem a little strange to us to hear the word *nurse* applied to a male health-care worker, even though both men and women are found in this profession. Old associations and stereotypes linger because of the many years during which societal limitations and expectations played a much greater role in determining career choices for men and women.

In this chapter you will explore the world of work and identify where you best fit. You will learn about some of the important and exciting changes that are occurring in the workplace. These changes will affect the kinds of occupations available to you. As you read about issues and trends in this chapter, think about your personal career profile and how it matches the opportunities that exist.

The first part of this chapter explores cultural norms, gender equity issues, cultural diversity, and ageism, as well as related factors that can constrict or expand your career options. The latter part of this chapter examines trends in the workforce as they relate to possible career choices. You will also explore careers for liberal arts and other nontechnical graduates and employer expectations of new hires, and you will complete some written exercises. The written exercises will help you identify your own barriers, attitudes, and biases to apply to your learnings. This self-knowledge will assist you in better planning your future.

> The illiterate of the 21st century will not be those who cannot read and write, but those who cannot learn, unlearn, and relearn.
>
> —*Alvin Toffler*

Societal Influences on Career Choices

Career planning does not happen in a vacuum. Your life situation influences the decisions you make and how you make them. The society in which you grow up, your background, your family, your peers, and the way you feel about yourself are all influences on the decisions you make. Sometimes these factors make it easier to choose and follow a career path. For instance, a friend or family member who encourages you in school and work efforts may help build your confidence and therefore improve your chances of success in whatever field you choose. Or family support may allow you to devote full-time effort to schooling and thus more quickly complete your chosen degree.

However, social and cultural considerations, family, peers, and feelings about yourself can also act as obstacles to making and following through on decisions. For example, your time available for school may be limited by family responsibilities, or you may feel that the career you would like to pursue requires an advanced degree, or that it would not pay enough to support your family. Consider the following statements:

> "I'm too old [or perhaps too far along in school] to start thinking about changing careers now."

> "What I would really like to be is an engineer, but I've given up on that because I can't go to school full time to get that kind of degree."

> "I don't know whether I'm going to apply for that job or not. Besides, they're not going to hire a Latino."

> "I'm not really qualified to do that kind of job, and my high school grades were weak. I was never good at schoolwork."

> "My family needs me to work to help out with expenses; there is no way that I could move away to go to college."

> "Sure, I'd like to go back to school, but how could I get all the housework done, and who would look after the kids? There's no money for child care."

Do any of the preceding statements sound like some you have heard people say, or maybe even some you yourself have said or felt? They represent some of the most common obstacles that people face when making academic and career decisions. An obstacle to a satisfactory decision is anything or anyone who prevents you from adequately considering all the possible alternatives. For example, the people who say, "I'm too old to start something new" when looking for a job will miss out by not even considering some positions for which they may be well qualified. Age stereotyping prevents these people from considering all the possible alternatives.

Exercise 6.1 helps you become aware of how you may react to roles and events that differ from those to which you are accustomed. Exercise 6.2 asks you to explore your own stereotypes. Be spontaneous with your answers; do not censor yourself because you fear your answer may be wrong.

EXERCISE
6.1   First Impressions

Think about each of the following situations. What are your first impressions? (You will share your impressions with a few classmates.)

1. You are applying for a job. A male receptionist ushers you into an office where you are greeted by a female vice president who will conduct the interview.

2. You are flying to Chicago. A male flight attendant welcomes you aboard the plane; later a female voice says, "This is your captain speaking."

3. You go to enroll your four-year-old in a nearby nursery school and discover all three teachers at the school are men.

4. You are African American and live in a neighborhood that is all white.

5. You have a conference with your child's teacher, who grew up in Taiwan.

6. You are in a class with many students who speak a different language.

7. You move into an apartment and learn your neighbors are gay.

8. You are temporarily disabled, must use a wheelchair, and have found a wonderful job opening. You haven't yet told the interviewer about your disability (and the room is on the second floor, with no elevator).

9. You arrive at your new dentist's office and find she has green-and-orange spiked hair.

10. You are referred to a hospital known for excellence in surgery, and your team of doctors is all Latino.

11. You go to court and find every jury member is African American.

12. You find yourself in a statistics class in which all the students are Asian American.

EXERCISE
6.2   Gender Roles Questionnaire

To explore your own stereotypes, complete these sentences with the first thought that comes to mind. Don't censor yourself. You will be sharing parts of this exercise in class.

1. Women are happiest in careers when
   _____

2. Men are happiest in careers when
   _____

3. The most difficult emotion for a man to display is
   _____

4. The most difficult emotion for a woman to display is
   _____

5. Women tend to be better than men at
   _____

6. Men tend to be better than women at
   _____

7. Men get depressed about
   _____

8. Women get depressed about
   _____

9. Men are most likely to compete over
   _____

10. Women are most likely to compete over
    _____

11. Men tend to get angry about
    _____

12. Women tend to get angry about
    _____

13. As a man/woman, I was always taught to
    _____

14. Men feel pressured on the job when
    _____

15. Women feel pressured on the job when
    _____

🌐 Striving for Equality in the Workforce

GENDER ROLES

As recently as 40 years ago, female students seeking career advice from school counselors were frequently encouraged to choose fields such as teaching and nursing. These choices were recommended both because they were "women's jobs" and because they fit best with the traditional female family role of mothering. It wasn't until the 1970s that newspapers no longer divided the classified employment ads into the categories of "men" and "women."

Within the past 35 years, school counselors began to recognize that female roles in society were expanding and that women could be doctors, engineers, and, in fact, members of any profession. Today, academic counselors are more aware of gender fairness issues (see the "Equity Definitions" feature) and more often attempt to treat men and women similarly, without making judgments or assumptions about marriage and family roles.

> We are what we repeatedly do. Excellence, then, is not an act, but a habit.
>
> —*Aristotle*

As suggested earlier, many of society's career and pay biases were based on the social norm of a so-called typical four-member family in which the husband was the principal wage earner and the wife was primarily responsible for raising the children. Societal changes have moved us away from these traditional roles and toward gender equity. Because many couples find it difficult, if not impossible, to manage a home and family on one income, both partners in today's "typical" marriage work outside the home. This major change has forced us (or permitted us) to rethink traditional male and female roles. For example, partners in a relationship are more likely to share home and child-rearing responsibilities.

Equity Definitions

Affirmative action: Programs, policies, or procedures that attempt to overcome the effects of past discrimination, bias, and/or stereotyping.

Ageism: Any action or policy that discriminates on the basis of age, affecting employment, advancement, privileges, or rewards.

Americans with Disabilities Act (ADA): Legislation first passed July 26, 1990, that prohibits discrimination on the basis of a disability. ADA Amendments Act of 2008 significantly expanded the definition of *disability*. As a result, more employers must offer reasonable accommodations to more workers with physical or mental impairments.

Barriers: Anything that prevents a person from equal access to the use of goods, services, facilities, and so on. There are physical and architectural barriers (such as stairs) and there are attitudinal barriers (such as stereotyping).

Discrimination: Practices, policies, or procedures that are specifically prohibited by law; any action that limits or denies a person or group of persons opportunities, privileges, roles, or rewards on such prohibited bases as their sex, race, age, and so on.

Gender bias: An attitude or behavior that reflects adversely on a person or group because of gender but may not be covered under present legislation; behavior resulting from the assumption that one sex is superior to the other.

Gender fair: Practices and behaviors that treat males and females similarly; may imply separate but equal.

Gender role: Social behavior that is prescribed and defined for males and females according to tradition, as contrasted with actual biological differences.

Gender stereotyping: Attributing behaviors, abilities, interests, values, and roles to a person or group of persons on the basis of gender.

The Genetic Information Nondiscrimination Act of 2008 (GINA): Prohibits discrimination based on genetic information

Nontraditional job: Working in a field or an occupation that typically employs 75 percent or more of the opposite gender (e.g., nursing employs only 8 percent males; construction work employs only 2.5 percent females).

Sexism: Any attitude, action, or institution that subordinates or assigns roles to a person or group of persons based on gender. Sexism may be individual, cultural, or institutional; intentional or unintentional; effected by omission or commission.

▲ Many must find a balance between family and career needs.

Just as women's roles have changed over the past few decades, so too have men's roles. For example, some men may choose careers that don't require extensive travel or long work hours because they want and expect to assume an equal parenting role. Many women now play the role of primary breadwinner in a family, while men are choosing to work or stay at home and take care of the children. Both traditional and nontraditional types of families face new challenges with each passing year; such challenges influence career decisions and directions.

In an ideally unbiased society composed of 50 percent men and 50 percent women, it can be expected that most occupations would employ approximately 50 percent of each gender and would pay them like salaries for like work. However, in our society such equity is being achieved gradually. Exhibit 6.1 illustrates ongoing inequities in the types of jobs held by women and men.

EXHIBIT 6.1 Quick Facts on Nontraditional Occupations for Women

A nontraditional occupation for women is one in which women comprise 25 percent or less of total employment.

This chart is important to you because, first, growth in the economy is projected to expand employment in many of these occupations, and second, there will be strong demand for workers in these fields due to projected retirements or transfers of current workers to other occupations. Even better, most of these jobs pay $20 to $30 per hour or more and are considered high-paying occupations!

Nontraditional Occupations for Women in 2007[1] (Numbers in Thousands)

Occupation	Employed Both Sexes	Employed Female	Percentage Female
Architects, except naval	240	59	24.7
Detectives and criminal investigators	135	31	23.2
Engineering technicians, except drafters	420	94	22.4
Chemical engineers	75	16	21.2
Computer software engineers	907	189	20.8
Chefs and head cooks	345	71	20.6
Drafters	187	38	20.6
Industrial engineers, including health and safety	161	28	17.5
Transportation, storage, and distribution managers	260	45	17.2
Chiropractors	62	10	16.8
Couriers and messengers	254	38	15.1
Network and computer systems administrators	214	31	14.7
Police and sheriff's patrol officers	669	92	13.7
Technicians and radio operators	89	10	11.6
Civil engineers	382	44	11.5
Construction and building inspectors	107	11	10.0
Computer hardware engineers	79	8	9.6
Engineering managers	114	9	8.0
Computer control programmers and operators	55	5	8.7
Electrical and electronics engineers	347	30	8.6
Broadcast and sound engineers, mechanical engineers	296	22	7.3
First-line supervisors/managers of landscaping, lawn service, and groundskeeping workers	330	18	5.4
Driver/sales workers and truck drivers	3,460	183	5.3
Firefighters	288	15	5.3
Machinists	422	22	5.2
Aircraft pilots and flight engineers	123	5	4.2
Tool and die makers	80	2	2.0
Aircraft mechanics and service technicians	126	3	2.1
Carpenters	1,824	35	1.9
Electricians	912	15	1.9
Automotive body and related repairers	155	2	1.6
Heating, air conditioning, refrigeration mechanics	403	4	0.9
Automotive service technicians and mechanics	879	6	0.7

[1]Nontraditional occupations are those in which women comprise 25 percent or less of total employed.

Source: U.S. Department of Labor, Bureau of Labor Statistics, Annual Averages 2007; Women's Bureau, May 2008.

Although you cannot predict the exact course of your life or your career, you can begin considering possible choices and how they relate to *you*. Take time now to anticipate challenges you may encounter in the future. Now is the time to plan. By setting objectives that lead toward accomplishment of a career goal, you may later avoid having to take a job just to pay the bills. It is now more important than ever to choose a career that truly reflects your interests and abilities, your values, your personality, and your life plan. The concept of gender equity means that everyone is free to explore a career of his or her choice.

FACTS & FIGURES

Women in the Workplace

- In 1970, 43 percent of women age 16 and over were in the labor force. Today, 60 percent of women age 16 and older work outside the home, 75 percent full time. Approximately 80 percent of women between ages 25 and 44 are in the workforce.
- In 1975, 47 percent of all mothers with children under 6 years old had paid employment. That figure has now increased to over 73 percent. Since 1970, households headed by women have increased 70 percent. Women are the sole earners in more than 18 percent of families.
- Currently, a woman earns, on average, 80 cents for every dollar earned by a man.
- Although percentages of women in nontraditional areas have increased, often the increase has occurred in the lower-paying jobs. About 39 percent of women work in what the U.S. Census labels "management, professional, and related jobs"; however, women are employed in only 8 of the 50 job titles that comprise that area. Two-thirds of employed women hold clerical, service, nursing, and education jobs; these are traditionally low-paying occupations. At least nursing and teaching salaries have improved because of demand.
- Women make up over 48 percent of managers and 53 percent of professionals, including teachers and registered nurses. In the professions, women have made gains in the last 10 years and now comprise 30 percent of doctors and over 25 percent of dentists. In such traditionally male jobs as pilots and navigators, women now make up 4.2 percent; among firefighters, women comprise 5.3 percent. Although women constitute 46 percent of the workforce, they fill only 13 percent of the top corporate positions, 24.7 percent of architects, and just over 13 percent of all engineers.
- Of the 15 jobs projected to have the greatest growth rate in the next decade, 12 are dominated by women (mostly in the Service and Education fields).
- Best-paying jobs for women include CEO, pharmacist, lawyer, computer software engineer, management

analyst, information systems analyst, and occupational therapist.
- Woman-owned businesses number approximately 10 million and employ more than 28 million people (35 percent more than all Fortune 500 companies employ worldwide). An estimated 40 to 50 percent of all woman-owned firms in this country are based in homes.
- Of the total of part-time workers, 25 percent are women.
- Approximately 20 percent of military personnel are women.

Women and Degrees

- In 1970, only 11 percent of women (ages 25 to 64) had completed college; by 2007, approximately 30 percent had a four-year college degree.
- Currently, women earn 62 percent of the associate degrees, 57 percent of the bachelor's degrees, and 60 percent of the master's degrees. In addition, approximately 50 percent of professional degrees and nearly 50 percent of PhD's are now given to women, but men earn more technical degrees.

WHAT DO *YOU* THINK?

1. Which of these statistics is surprising to you?
2. Why is it important to know these facts?
3. Why is it useful to know the best-paying jobs for women?
4. How does knowing this information influence how you make your decisions about your future career?
5. What challenges do women business owners face?
6. What suggestions would you give to help dual-income families handle the following: housework, meal planning and preparation, child care, and social activities?
7. Name three successful women and explain what makes or made them successful.

Source: U.S. Department of Labor, Women's Bureau, and Bureau of Labor Statistics, 2009.

FACTS & FIGURES

High Wages vs. Work-Life Balance Issues

Statistics show that, on average, women earn 80 cents for every dollar that men make and that many high-paying occupations have less than 25 percent females in their ranks. However, it is possible that these statistics don't tell the whole story. In *Why Men Earn More: The Startling Truth Behind the Pay Gap and What Women Can Do About It,* Warren Farrell (2005) writes that 25 differences are apparent in the nontraditional occupations for women listed in Exhibit 6.1. The authors don't endorse all of these recommendations but want readers to understand some of the reasons why women do not earn as much as men. For example, hazardous jobs (such as air conditioning and heating mechanic, garbage collector, construction, firefighting) receive few applications from women. Also, men are more willing to do certain things at work that put them into higher earning categories, such as working longer hours, relocating to undesirable places, traveling extensively, and working in poor conditions (hot, cold, cramped, isolated, outdoors, night shift, etc.). Companies that need workers to do these types of jobs often pay higher wages and benefits to make up for the demands of these jobs.

Additionally, young women often earn as much as or more than men until they have children and family responsibilities. It is typical at this point for men to take on more difficult work assignments with the hope of earning more (for the family), while women scale back to spend more time meeting the needs of their family and children. It may be a question of having more earnings versus having a more balanced life.

Farrell's book discusses six strategies anyone can use who is more interested in earning higher wages.

1. **Go for a job with bottom-line responsibility.** Operating (sales, finance, purchasing) jobs generate revenue, and companies are willing to pay more for people who take on the responsibility and risk of being held accountable for the bottom line.

2. **Find a field that entails financial or emotional risk taking.** Venture capitalists and entrepreneurs are handsomely paid for taking huge risks. Where the stakes are high, the personal rewards are often high as well.

3. **Work more hours, weeks, and years.** The U.S. Bureau of Labor Statistics (BLS) reports that the average person working 45 hours per week earns 44 percent more than someone working 40 hours. (The BLS indicates that men work an average of 41 hours per week; women average 35 hours per week.)

4. **Be willing to relocate anywhere.** Tough jobs in remote locations often lead to better-paying positions because employees have more responsibility to deal with and can gain the skills necessary to rise to the top more easily. These employees will also show that they can stand the pressure!

5. **Choose technology or hard sciences over the arts or social sciences.** In Exhibit 6.2, related to where women get the best pay, a majority of the jobs are management, engineering, and computer science jobs. Meanwhile, less than 15 percent of engineers are women.

6. **Select a field where you can't "check out" at the end of the day.** Farrell calls these jobs "7–11s" because they never close. Doctors, lawyers, and executives have trouble getting away from their work, work evenings and weekends, and even forgo vacations, but they are paid well for their commitment. These people are working a career, not a job.

These are the six strategies that many men (as well as women) have used to get ahead and to be paid better. We do not necessarily endorse these means to a higher paycheck. Ultimately, it would be best if companies could find ways to reduce the extreme hours required at work.

If the workplace doesn't change, employers may face a challenge finding young talent to take on the demanding jobs. Women who try some of these strategies eventually may revert toward finding balance in their lives, often sacrificing their high-paying careers. Several studies have shown that women are more likely to leave an intense high-paying career when company policies, practices, and attitudes at work result in their feeling underutilized and unappreciated. Studies from Boston College's Center for Work and Family are leading the research into how men are equally desiring work-life balance. Go to **http://wfnetwork.bc.edu/business.php** for further information.

It appears that workers from the Gen Y (Millennials) generation are influencing companies to address the need for work–life balance. With the Bureau of Labor Statistics indicating that there will be a shortage of qualified workers for high-level positions in the next decade and with more Millennials seeking to fill such positions, what are companies likely to do?

WHAT DO *YOU* THINK?

1. To what does Farrell attribute the gap in wages between men and women? Which of these strategies would work for you? Explain why or why not.

2. How do you think the demands on employees' personal time will continue to grow? Research *work–life* on the Internet. Then decide where you stand on the issue. Give at least three reasons to support your point of view. Here are two excellent online sources:

   - *Fast Company* (**www.fastcompany.com**) search for Work-life Balance.
   - *Wall Street Journal* (**http://online.wsj.com/**); search for "Work-life balance or Reinvent."

Source: Reprinted by permission of the publisher, from *Why Men Earn More*, by Warren Farrell © 2005 Warren Farrell, Ph.D., AMACOM, division of American Management Association, New York, NY. All rights reserved. **www.amacombooks.org**

EXHIBIT 6.2 Ten Careers Where Women Earn More Than Men

Field	Women's	Men's	Women's Pay as % of Men's
Sales engineers	$89,908	$62,660	143%
Statisticians	$49,140	$36,296	135%
Legislators	$43,316	$32,656	133%
Automotive service technicians and mechanics	$40,664	$31,460	129%
Library assistants, clerical	$23,608	$18,512	128%
Baggage porters, bellhops, and concierges	$26,468	$21,684	122%
Financial analysts	$69,004	$58,604	118%
Aerospace engineers	$78,416	$70,356	111%
Human resources assistants, except payroll and timekeeping	$30,420	$28,028	109%
Advertising and promotions managers	$42,068	$40,144	105%

Source: U.S. Department of Labor, Bureau of Labor Statistics, *Employment and Earnings*, 2007 Annual Averages and the *Monthly Labor Review*, November.

The ten occupations with the highest median weekly earnings among women who were full-time wage and salary workers were:

1. Computer software engineers, $1,553
2. Pharmacists, $1,475
3. Lawyers, $1,449
4. Computer and information systems managers, $1,411
5. Engineers $1,311
6. Physicians and surgeons $1,228
7. Psychologists, $1,152
8. Computer programmers $1,182
9. Management analysts, $1,177
10. Computer scientist/Systems analysts $1,167

Source: U.S. Department of Labor, Bureau of Labor Statistics, Women's Bureau, March 2009.

Other Barriers: Age, Race, and Disability

AGE AND OPPORTUNITY

Ten years ago, 20 million people over age 65 lived in the United States. By 2020, the over-65 population could be as high as 50 million. There will be more single people older than age 65, particularly women. Approximately 45 percent of all seniors are over 75 years old. In fact, workers age 55 and older are projected to increase from 15.6 percent in 2004 to 23 percent in 2016, according to the Bureau of Labor Statistics.

Note that the number of people retiring at age 65 continues to decrease. The Bureau of Labor Statistics projects that a majority of available jobs during the next decade will be related to retirement replacements; however, no one is sure how many people will actually be able to retire. Many victims of corporate downsizing and the economic recession have been "let go" before becoming eligible for retirement pensions. Because of no-fault divorce laws and lack of retirement plans in the traditionally female occupations, many divorced women must continue to work long after their male counterparts have retired.

If present trends continue, single women of retirement age will be the poorest segment of society.

Older workers competing in the workforce may face discrimination because they are perceived by employers as out of date or too old to learn. Although such ageism is illegal, it occurs. Young workers are valued for their energy, flexibility, technical savvy, social media involvement, and entry-level salaries. Some employers, however, may choose an older, more mature job candidate over a recent college graduate, in the belief that anyone, at any age, can display high energy and flexibility, because with age comes maturity, reliability, problem-solving abilities, and a wealth of experience. As a prospective employee, it is your responsibility to know your assets, whether those of youth, expertise, maturity, or other personal traits, and to highlight them at the right times with the right decision makers. The most effective way to deal with ageism (whether it's directed against your youth or lack of it) is to sell your present or prospective employer on how your age and particular experience are an asset to the job.

People who live long, healthy lives may change careers frequently during their lifetimes, and their most satisfying and perhaps most financially rewarding career may come later in life. Novelist James Michener was first published after the age of 40; Colonel Sanders started Kentucky Fried Chicken (now called KFC) after he was 50 years old; Dr. Ruth became a celebrity talk-show sex therapist when she was age 48; Sam Walton opened his first Wal-Mart at age 44; and Ted Turner started Cable News Network (CNN) at age 42. Don't forget Margaret Mitchell, who won her first Pulitzer Prize, for *Gone with the Wind*, when she was 37 years old; Shirley Temple Black, who was named ambassador to Ghana at age 47; and Jerry Brown, elected as Governor of California at age 72.

> Accentuate your assets no matter how old you are.

AFFIRMATIVE ACTION

Affirmative action has become a highly controversial and much-debated issue. Its advocates support policies and programs that increase opportunities for women, minorities, and other underrepresented groups. These policies involve special consideration or set-aside positions for candidates who would—if hired, admitted, or promoted—increase the percentage of diverse members in a professional, academic, social, or business group. Many people oppose preferences or quota selection criteria and would prefer to see impartial screening of all candidates, regardless of gender, ethnicity, or socioeconomic status. A wide range of feelings and opinions exists on this issue. Compounding the controversy is a high demand for scarce resources that is pervasive in the fields of education, health and welfare services, and employment opportunities. Immigration, both legal and illegal, also complicates affirmative action decision making.

Recent decisions by state and federal courts have narrowed the scope of affirmative action by rejecting quotas or preferential formulas in favor of open and competitive criteria. These courts, however, have reversed unjustified discrimination in hiring, firing, and admissions and have also rejected forced early retirements due to age. Affirmative action remains a challenge in the twenty-first century.

OTHER CULTURAL CONSIDERATIONS: VALUING DIVERSITY IN THE GLOBAL ECONOMY

Today's workforce is more culturally diverse than ever, and this diversity will increase as the next wave of workers joins the workforce. To remain globally competitive, companies in the United States must improve training and advancement opportunities and use each employee's talent to the fullest. Stereotypes about and prejudices against particular ethnic or racial groups must be diminished and opportunities expanded for all workers.

Hispanics, African Americans, and Asian Americans make up approximately 32 percent of the workforce, with whites declining to 68 percent. Moreover, projections for new workers entering the workplace indicate that in most urban centers, all minority group members together make up the majority of the entering workforce.

The Americans with Disabilities Act (ADA) prohibits discrimination on the basis of a disability and calls for the elimination of barriers—that is, anything that prevents a person or group of persons equal access to goods, services, and facilities. Employers with 15 or more employees must make reasonable accommodations for such otherwise qualified employees, including access to rooms and buildings, use of auxiliary aids, and services such as interpreters and hearing devices. Persons with disabilities should enjoy the same freedom of choice in making career decisions as those without disabilities, and this becomes more of a reality each year.

Companies are respecting diversity as an important component of the workplace. Just as many college campuses now require a course in diversity, firms are offering employee training in diversity to enable workers of differing backgrounds, educational levels, physical abilities, and cultures to accept and value people with differing sexual orientations, ideological and generational perspectives, and racial, religious, social class, or geographical backgrounds. Whether in a social, political, academic, or economic context, we have begun to realize that our society does benefit from the fullest use of all its citizens and their many diverse talents

Now that you have read and discussed issues related to diversity, in Exercise 6.3 list the advantages and disadvantages of belonging to one or more distinct groups.

EXERCISE

6.3   Famous People and Pros and Cons

Name two well-known people (past or present) in each category, and list a few of the advantages and disadvantages of belonging to any of the following categories:

1. Two well-known women _____

   advantage _____

   disadvantage _____

2. Two well-known men _____

   advantage _____

   disadvantage _____

3. Two well-known whites _____

   advantage _____

   disadvantage _____

4. Two well-known African Americans _____

   advantage _____

   disadvantage _____

5. Two well-known Latino/as _____

   advantage _____

   disadvantage _____

6. Two well-known Asian Americans _____

   advantage _____

   disadvantage _____

7. Two well-known Native Americans _____

   advantage _____

   disadvantage _____

EXERCISE 6.3 **Famous People and Pros and Cons** *CONTINUED*

Share your impressions with others in your class and find out others' impressions! Did you get any new impressions from reading this textbook or discussions in class? How do you think gender, race, age, sexual orientation, religion, or physical disability could affect your ability to get a job? Google Juan Williams, media commentator, and find out why he was fired for negative commentary related to Muslims. What do you think?

_____

_____

_____

The Changing Workplace

Twenty years ago, terms such as *offshoring, telecommuter, knowledge worker, global economy, computer literacy, learning organization, virtual workplace, small entrepreneurial business, woman-owned business, meeting customer needs,* and *temporary/leasing agencies* would have been irrelevant in a book on career planning. But these terms represent trends, and the trends affect a large percentage of new entrants to the workforce. Therefore, it is to your advantage to understand the shifting nature of the workplace. Also, even if you are a liberal arts major, at some point in your life, you might work for a corporation.

Manufacturing used to be the mainstay of the U.S. economy, but the country is now a service- and information-based economy, in which the majority of workers provide services (e.g., health care, education, retail, food preparation, financial planning) instead of producing a commodity. Manufacturing jobs are increasingly moving overseas to countries such as China, India, Indonesia, Viet Nam, and Thailand. This trend is called *offshoring* if the whole company is moved to another country and *outsourcing* if only part of the firm's work—for example, the accounting—is sent to workers in another country. One important reason that companies are hiring abroad is that it is where the largest proportion of cheap labor exists. Furthermore, companies such as Procter & Gamble, IBM, Caterpillar, and Coca-Cola get more than half of their sales and income from markets outside of the United States.

Globalization of the workplace affects you because many new workers will find that they need to work shifts other than 8 A.M. to 5 P.M. to reach and collaborate with "coworkers" in other countries at times when they are on duty. Global workplaces are expanding because of technology, which enables us to keep in touch with coworkers at all times of day and night. When someone sells an item in Detroit, the order is transmitted and the item can be immediately manufactured in China and available for sale. This is called *supply chaining*.

The United States is able to be a powerful economy because of constant innovation in products, services, and companies. However, we are competing with other nations, such as China and India, that are learning to be as enterprising as the United States. Product innovation depends to a great extent on engineers. Both China and India are graduating more engineers than the United States. In fact, China and India together have graduated approximately three times more engineers than the United States annually. Additionally, if China and India's engineers get training in the United States, they are now using their new skills in their own countries.

Many of today's jobs, such as diversity manager, digital librarian, health informatics specialist, and supply chain manager, did not exist 20 years ago. Owing to innovation and technology, there are more options for

▲ Learning more about our diverse world is an important part of today's global economy; people may work virtually anywhere in the world.

ways to perform your work, such as telecommuting or starting your own business or working anywhere in the world. Today's worker faces less stigma associated with changing jobs or changing careers. In fact, most workers will change their jobs up to 13 times in their career and will make three to five major career changes in their lifetime.

Just as there is less of a stigma related to changing jobs, there is also less stigma related to asking for flexible work schedules. A 2007 survey by the Society for Human Resource Management found that more than half of all companies offer some kind of flexible work schedule. Even the federal government passed the Telework Enhancement Act so that government employees could have this option. Telecommuting helps working parents and caregivers, the disabled, retirees, and people living in remote areas. About 30 percent of working women with school-age children have flexible schedules, according to the Bureau of Labor Statistics. You still work eight hours but have flexibility with your work schedule.

IMPLICATIONS FOR YOU

More job opportunities will be available at all hours of the day or night, any day of the week. Employees will have the option of working out of their homes or at the company workplace and will be expected to use technology to stay in touch with coworkers. Many workers will start as temporary employees and will need to prove their skills to be considered for long-term positions. More job opportunities will be available in the expanding service and information systems sectors, as well as in transportation, shipping, and logistics. The rapidly changing workplace requires that you understand the key trends shaping the workplace to find your niche.

THE NEED FOR KNOWLEDGE WORKERS

An employee becomes more valuable as he or she accumulates new skills. The challenge is to remain an outstanding contributor on the job (e.g., as a specialist) while learning new skills. As organizations downsize or flatten, employees must possess multiple skills, such as the ability to learn and use new technology or sell a product. These people have an edge. For example, they may be able to transfer from the training division, if it is reduced in size, to the sales division, and therefore remain employed.

> Research the fastest-growing careers.

There is still opportunity to move up. For example, Courtney got a job straight out of high school as a file clerk. Learning new skills on the job and while attending a community college, she began to manage the computer system and handle most payroll and personnel duties. Courtney is an example of a knowledge worker; when the company stopped needing file clerks, she still had a job and a job that was in demand! We are in the midst of a shift toward a knowledge-based economy in which employees like Courtney will be expected to manage technology and information itself. The Bureau of Labor Statistics forecasts that the fastest-growing careers by 2018 will be mostly in high-skill, high-wage professional, managerial,

FACTS & FIGURES   Jobs for 2018

Projected by 2018, the United States will need 22 million new workers with college degrees and a total of 101 million workers with some postsecondary education in the following areas:

- ▶ 28 million in Sales and Office Support
- ▶ 15 million in Managerial and Professional jobs
- ▶ 12 million in Food and Personal Services
- ▶ 10 million in Community Services and Arts
- ▶ 10 million in Education

- ▶ 8 million in STEM (Science, Technology, Engineering, and Math related fields)
- ▶ 8 million in Health Care

Source: Georgetown University Center on Education and the Workforce. (2010). "Help Wanted: Projections of Jobs and Education Requirements through 2018," Carnevale, P., Smith, N., and Strohl, Jeff. **http://cew.georgetown.edu/jobs2018**.

TIPS FROM THE PROS

- "If you want to succeed in America, you need to be educated, because people all over the world are willing to do low-wage work. Lack of an education is an economic death sentence." — Steven D. Levitt, Professor of Economics at the University of Chicago and author of *Freakonomics*

- "Postsecondary education or training has become the threshold requirement for access to middle-class status and earnings in good times and in bad. It is no longer the preferred pathway . . . it is, increasingly, the *only* pathway." — Georgetown University Center for Education and Workforce report, "Help Wanted 2018."

and technical areas. This does not mean that service jobs will disappear. Industrial and service jobs such as auto repair and retail clerk will still be available. The fastest job growth that pays the best, however, will be in those areas that involve the management and production of specialized knowledge. According to Georgetown University's Center on Education and the Workforce report (2010), approximately 63 percent of jobs available will require some college education. About 33 percent will require a bachelor's degree or better!

Sometimes it is necessary to spend time after work taking classes and studying job-related materials at home to get a head start. LaTricia was a public relations manager at a computer firm and had to spend as many as five hours a week on her own time becoming familiar with the company's new products. She also took a class in teaching English as a Second Language to become more sensitive to cultural diversity at a time when her business was becoming increasingly international. Exhibits 6.3 and 6.4 illustrate the correspondence of earnings to educational attainment.

Courtney and LaTricia are examples of workers continually learning new skills so they can be available for openings within their organizations and elsewhere. Remember, *luck is preparation meeting opportunity!*

> Prepare for lifelong learning.

EXHIBIT 6.3 A Median Weekly Salary by Degree Attained
B Unemployment According to Education Level

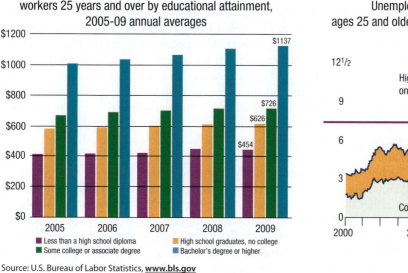

A. Median usual weekly earnings of full-time wage and salary workers 25 years and over by educational attainment, 2005-09 annual averages

Legend:
- Less than a high school diploma
- High school graduates, no college
- Some college or associate degree
- Bachelor's degree or higher

($1137, $726, $626, $454 labeled)

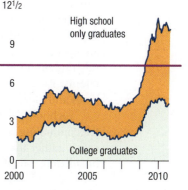

B. Widening Gap
Unemployment rate, ages 25 and older, by education level

High school only graduates

College graduates

Source: U.S. Bureau of Labor Statistics, www.bls.gov

EXHIBIT **6.4** **By 2018 Most New Jobs Will Require Some Postsecondary Education**

Community/technical college certificate: Six-month to two-year course of study at a postsecondary (after high school) college/technical school in an occupation/trade area.

Associate of Arts, Associate of Science degrees: (A.A./A.S.) Usually a two-year course of study that includes general education classes as well as a major: (1) occupation/trade area or (2) transfer studies that prepare students for transfer directly to four-year colleges.

Bachelor of Arts (B.A.), Bachelor of Science (B.S.) degrees: Usually a four-year course of study that includes general education classes as well as specialization in a subject area or major.

Master of Arts (M.A.), Master of Science (M.S.) degrees: Normally, two additional years of study beyond the bachelor's degree, specializing in a subject area or major.

Professional degree: Normally, one to three years of additional study beyond the bachelor's or master's degree depending on the subject area. Some professionals may decide to earn the doctorate degree also. Professional degrees are earned in medicine, dentistry, law, chiropractic, pharmacy, podiatry, theology, or veterinary medicine.

Doctorate degree: Normally, two additional years of study beyond the master's degree, specializing in a subject area.

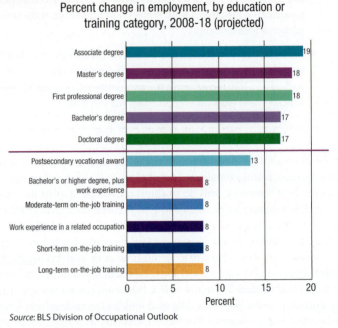

Percent change in employment, by education or training category, 2008-18 (projected)

Category	Percent
Associate degree	19
Master's degree	18
First professional degree	18
Bachelor's degree	17
Doctoral degree	17
Postsecondary vocational award	13
Bachelor's or higher degree, plus work experience	8
Moderate-term on-the-job training	8
Work experience in a related occupation	8
Short-term on-the-job training	8
Long-term on-the-job training	8

Source: BLS Division of Occupational Outlook

THE IMPORTANCE OF NEW TECHNOLOGY: WEB 2.0 AND STEM

Technology is so much a part of everyday life that most of us don't stop to think about how much we depend on it. Think about what you did today since you woke up, and you will probably be able to name many activities that depended on technology. Web 2.0 allows us to use the web on our phones and TVs and to play games online with friends. It is hard to remember when we couldn't "interact" with contacts on the Internet! Just as it has affected our personal lives, technology has revolutionized the kind of work we do, where we work, and how we complete our work; we can now collaborate online with anyone in the world who has access to the Web. One in eight jobs is directly related to the field of high technology. Software engineer, CAD operator, computer programmer, and network administrator are probably familiar job titles. The real impact of technology, however, is on jobs that are indirectly related to technology. For example, today's travel agents must learn a special computer program to access information for their clients; ironically, these agents are becoming less crucial as clients make their own online reservations. Graphic designers rely on computer-aided drawing programs to produce high-quality, low-cost materials for clients. Even journalists are finding a niche online with the advent of web-based magazines and blogs.

Technology has also affected where and how we do our work. As previously mentioned, telecommuting is on the rise. Telecommuting means that you work from a home or virtual office, rather than at the company site, using phones, fax machines, Web-based software, broadband, e-mail, and other mobile tools to stay in touch with your coworkers and clients. More small businesses known as SOHOs (small office/home office) are being created and operated with the aid of technology.

A variety of jobs are able to accommodate telecommuting such as nursing, marketing consultant, reporter, investment adviser, investment research firm manager, online tutor, and virtual assistant. Cybercommuters, as some telecommuters are called, are becoming more common in all industries. Working anywhere will become even easier as cell phones, wireless printers, and other handheld devices become more powerful and less expensive.

Job market projections show that more Science, Technology, Engineering, and Math (STEM) majors are needed to fill the high-demand, high-wage positions in such growing fields as nanotechnology, biotechnology, green technology, alternative fuel, and new vehicles. It takes STEM skills to use, produce, and maintain cell phones, music, videos, games, sports equipment, buildings, and cars—STEM is everywhere. As we move forward in our high-tech economy, almost every high-wage job will require some STEM knowledge and skills. In fact, of the 123 STEM occupations (**http://www.collegecampaign.org/assets/docs /stem/STEM-Executive-Summary_FINAL.pdf**) requiring a postsecondary education, nearly half will face labor shortages. Lack of STEM talent is not just a national problem; it is also a global challenge. Watch a related YouTube video clip by searching for the Director of Fast Future Research (**www.youtube.com/watch?v=4m7h2-H-Me4**) and STEM jobs. From the video you will agree that STEM jobs are so important because they are the industries of the future and will most likely drive innovation and economic growth.

Besides science, technology, engineering, and math, we will also need business majors to do the accounting and management of STEM-related companies. According to recent data from the National Association of Colleges and Employers, starting salaries for accounting, information systems, and engineering graduates are approximately 25 percent higher than those of liberal arts graduates, as noted in Exhibit 6.5. Also go to **http://cew.georgetown .edu/whatsitworth/** to find out what a college degree is worth.

Information technology (IT) employment also provides self-employed and independent contractors the flexibility and mobility to work outside of a traditional organization. Although these temporary workers often earn less in wages and benefits and have less security than permanent workers, many IT workers prefer to be independent because they can command comparably high salaries and move from one employment situation to another with relative ease.

EXHIBIT 6.5A Representative Starting Salaries for College Graduates

Associate Degree	Range
Maintenance Technician PC	$23,117–49,810
Registered Nurse	$40,000–52,000
Radiology Technician	$35,000–56,775
Respiratory Technician	$27,690–55,324
Engineering Technology	$28,722–55,436

Bachelor's Degree		2007–2010
Engineering	Electrical	$55,000–65,000
	Mechanical	$54,000–62,000
	Civil	$45,170–55,120
	Chemical	$60,000–70,000
	Computer Science	$55,000–68,000
Business	Business Administration	$33,280–52,000
	Accounting	$45,000–53,000
Other	History	$28,000–42,000
	Economics	$44,000–55,698

Sources: Payscale.com, Spring 2010; National Association of Colleges and Employers (NACE), Fall 2010 Salary Press Release.

EXHIBIT 6.5 B Median Earnings by Majors

Field	Bachelor's Degree	Graduate Degree
Engineering	$75,000	$99,000
Computers and Mathematics	$70,000	$89,000
Business	$60,000	$80,000
Health	$60,000	$80,000
Physical Sciences	$59,000	$90,000
Social Science	$55,000	$85,000
Agriculture and Natural Resources	$50,000	$70,000
Communications and Journalism	$50,000	$62,000
Industrial Arts and Consumer Services	$50,000	$65,000
Law and Public Policy	$50,000	$70,000
Biology and Life Science	$50,000	$85,000
Humanities and Liberal Arts	$47,000	$65,000
Arts	$44,000	$55,000
Education	$42,000	$57,000
Psychology and Social Work	$42,000	$60,000

see http://cew.georgetown.edu/whatsitworth/ to find out what other college degrees are worth (May 2011)

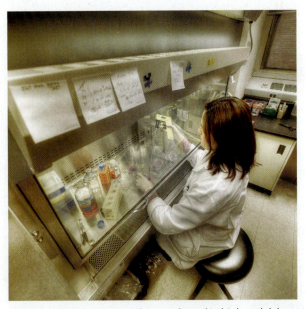

▲ High-technology research is conducted in high-tech labs.

Implications

When choosing the industry you wish to enter, the STEM careers provide both opportunities and challenges. For higher-skilled workers, such positions offer strong demand and high wages. Lower-skilled workers, however, are seeing skill requirements change often, which entails returning for training in new technologies. However, IT allows greater flexibility in working arrangements, letting employers quickly hire and release workers in response to changing market conditions and allowing workers to move more easily from job to job. Remember, such workers still need to know how to market themselves to move to new jobs or they will not be competitive when technology changes.

THE GLOBAL ECONOMY AND THE CHANGING CORPORATE STRUCTURE

A decade ago, the United States was generating most of the world's technology; today that figure has diminished. Global competition and multinational corporations will continue to influence the business world and our economy. Today it is not just the Fortune 500 companies, such as General Electric, IBM, and AT&T, that conduct business and have offices throughout the world. Employees wishing to advance in this new international economy must have the ability to speak more than one language and understand the cultural customs of other countries.

Today's global economy has created a need for multilingual talents. The twenty-first century has been predicted to see the acceleration of Asian enterprises. One example is that Asian investments in Latin America and Mexico are expanding. Many of the *maquiladora* (border) factories in Tijuana, for example, are run by Japanese, Chinese, and Korean corporations. The ability to converse in several languages is an asset in the marketplace.

Success in the global economy requires innovative, high-quality, timely, customized, and efficiently produced products and flatter, leaner organizations. Successful companies need to have the following traits to remain competitive:

> Today's organizations are flatter, leaner, more efficient.

1. Maintaining a flat management structure that has shifted away from management-directed systems toward team-directed systems that require knowledgeable workers in each team.

2. Using a virtual corporation by distributing design, marketing, and customer service operations across the globe through temporary partnerships that can focus on completing projects. One contract unit will handle product development and engineering, another will cover marketing needs, and the third will do the production work.

> Virtual organizations are increasing.

3. Creating even greater efficiencies. The production work is speeded up through robotics that cut assembly time by 80 percent!

4. Moving manufacturing plants to locations that offer availability of good educational institutions and low labor costs (e.g., China and India).

> Outsourcing is on the rise.

5. Purchasing product components from outside suppliers (outsourcing).

6. Maintaining low numbers of permanent employees and using specialized teams of temporary employees on short-term projects.

> Use of temps is on the increase.

7. Recruiting highly skilled workers worldwide who are knowledgeable about global issues.

8. Being able to evolve and adapt as a company. George Lucas's Industrial Light & Magic (ILM), one of the largest special effects film companies today, got its start in a converted airplane hangar where clay miniatures and models of battleships were built for the original *Star Wars* movie. It evolved to incorporate computers and technology in numerous office buildings and hundreds of ILM digital artists, modeling experts, and computer programmers working for months on *The Transformers* and *AVATAR*.

> Businesses need to be adaptable and flexible.

9. Pursuing e-commerce. As businesses use websites and social media to sell their goods and services, they are reaching broader markets.

> E-commerce is increasing.

10. Pursuing customization. Built-to-order products will proliferate. Web-based technology (Web 2.0) is contributing to customers shopping, reading, and playing games online. Just as *American Idol* gets your vote via text messaging, cell phone, or online immediately, Web 2.0 incorporates immediate feedback.

11. Managing a mega-corporation effectively. The need for managers with a master's degree in business administration will continue to expand owing to the complexity of today's businesses.

Implications

The main point for you to remember is that, in a global economy, the employee who helps the company remain competitive by being informed about technology, competition, cultural issues, and alternative/innovative ways to complete the job requirements will be the person who is most important to the company (see Exercise 6.4). Such employees will have the core jobs, whereas others will be hired as temporary portfolio employees. The more skills that you can demonstrate to the employer, the more valuable you will be. For example, a software engineer at a telecommunications company who can also market her product to customers around the world based on understanding their customs will be considered a most valuable employee and most likely will be able to evolve with the expansion or changes that occur in her industry. Watch for the growth of such jobs as "User Experience Designer" and "Data Miner."

EXERCISE

6.4   Globalization of the Work World

From your reading, list five impacts of globalization on the workplace:

1. _____
2. _____
3. _____
4. _____
5. _____

SMALL BUSINESSES

According to the U.S. Small Business Administration, small business is defined as any business that has fewer than 500 employees. Would it surprise you to know that small firms represent 99.7 percent of all employer firms and employ half of all private sector employees? There are approximately 25 million small businesses in comparison with 17,000 large corporations. During the past decade, small business accounted for 60 to 80 percent of net new jobs annually. Additionally, 41 percent of high-tech workers (such as scientists, engineers, and computer workers) and 97 percent of all identified exporters can be found in small businesses. If you want variety and responsibility and are results oriented, a small business might be the place for you.

It is estimated that about 35 million people have a home office. According to the Small Business Advocate website article by Jeff Zbar, about 33 percent of U.S. households support some home-working activities. These businesses include approximately 11.1 million full-time businesses, 4.1 million part-time home businesses, and 8 to 9 million more who telecommute from home

About 52 percent of all small businesses are home-based—representing a broad array of industries, from software development and mail-order sales to plumbing and general contracting—according to statistics from the Small Business Administration's Office of Advocacy (**www.sba.gov/advocacy**). However, not all home businesses are "income generating." Approximately half of all such businesses make a profit; it usually takes about two years to start earning anything but only 44 percent are in business by the fourth year.

> Small businesses strive to meet customer needs.

Every day, small businesses are created to serve consumer needs. Did you know that LinkedIn, a growing resume and networking social media company, started in a living room? Did you know that the Home Shopping Network was created when a company that could not pay its bills instead gave its inventory to a TV executive? The executive needed to get rid of the inventory and announced the availability of the materials on his network. Everything sold within two hours!

"Today, the most profound thing to me is the fact that a 14-year-old in Romania or Bangalore or the Soviet Union or Vietnam has all the information, all the tools, all the software easily available to apply knowledge however they want" (Marc Andreessen, cofounder of Netscape, in an interview with Thomas Friedman for his 2007 book *The World Is Flat* 3.0). Friedman also describes such a person in his book: Rajesh Rao, a young Indian entrepreneur who started an electronic-game company from Bangalore, which today owns the rights to Charlie Chaplin's image for mobile computer games. The latest 2.0 Web connection for small businesses: using social networks to create markets and build businesses!

WOMAN-OWNED BUSINESSES

It is estimated that at least 50 percent of the more than 10 million privately held firms in the United States are owned by women, and that one in seven American workers is employed in a woman-owned business (which accounts for approximately 19.1 million workers). Between 40 and 50 percent of these companies are home-based, according to a study by the National Foundation for Women Business Owners. More than 70 percent of these businesses are concentrated in the services and retail trade. A majority of woman-owned businesses got their start as home-based operations.

FACTS & FIGURES — Entrepreneurial Opportunities

The Kauffman Foundation completed a study in June 2009 to understand how jobs are created. The study, "The Economic Future Just Happened," found that more than half of the companies on the 2009 Fortune 500 list and just under half of the 2008 *Inc.* 500/5000 list were started during a recession. The following are a few of the specialties that are popular:

- Anti-aging spas and spa treatments
- Business/career coaching (aka consulting)
- College admissions consulting
- Garage organizer services
- Pet grooming/sitting
- Recycling/clean environment
- Smart clothes (performance apparel, sun protection, and aging-friendly clothing)
- Trash removal (now a franchise)
- Translation services
- Tutoring

WHAT DO *YOU* THINK?

1. Go to about.com and read about people who have started such companies.
2. Find and interview a person who has any of these kinds of jobs.
3. Given your interests and skills, what creative business opportunities might you consider for yourself?

Source: About.com, Small Business Information.

TEMPORARY AGENCIES/LEASING COMPANIES

Temporary employment agencies, in addition to their traditional business of providing secretarial and clerical professionals on a contract basis, now provide employees in such areas as accounting, health care, telemarketing, the paralegal field, and management. Technical services contracting firms place a range of engineering and computer

---

FACTS & FIGURES — Freelancers/Temps/Contingent Workforce

Today about 30 percent of the U.S. job market—roughly 42 million workers—is made up of independent contractors, part-time or temporary staffers, and the self-employed. Experts predict that by the end of the next decade, long after this recession is over, the "contingent" workforce will have grown to about 40 percent of the market. One contract employee website, Elance, saw 300,000 online professionals become their own boss in 2010 and embrace the independence of going freelance.

WHAT DO *YOU* THINK?

1. Do you agree or disagree with the following statements? Why?
   - Temporary workers are replacing permanent workers.
   - It may be useful to start as a temp to get your foot in the door.
   - There are more temporary job ads and fewer full-time job ads in your own community.
2. Do you know anyone who started at a job as a temp? What was his or her job?
3. How do you think that taking technology classes will improve your chances of getting hired?

professionals as well as technicians and drafters in temporary positions. If this trend toward growing numbers of temporary employees continues as predicted, many people will find themselves working for an employee-leasing/contingency worker firm. Kelly Services, one of the largest temporary service agencies, expanded 800 percent in one five-year period. Due to the growth of "smart phone applications developers," online companies such as Elance and Cha Cha have expanded to meet the demand for contract employees.

Trends: The Twenty-First Century

It helps to have a picture of tomorrow's opportunities when defining a future job target. For example, you might guess that now is not the time to prepare for a lifelong job in an automotive assembly plant. In fact, 80 percent of General Motors employees now work at jobs other than assembly. Production and assembly will be centered in other low-cost countries such as Korea, Italy, China, and Latin America.

The good news is that for the next two decades more people will be retiring than entering the job market. It is estimated that 76 million Baby Boomers (people born between 1943 and 1960) will retire in the next three decades and fewer than 41 million people in Generation X (children of Baby Boomers) are prepared to replace them. By 2018, the economy will create 46.8 million openings—13.8 million brand-new jobs and 33 million "replacement jobs," positions vacated by workers who have retired or permanently left their occupations. Nearly two-thirds of these 46.8 million jobs—some 63 percent—will require workers with at least some college education. About 33 percent will require a bachelor's degree or better, while 30 percent will require some college or a two-year associate degree. Only 36 percent will require workers with just a high school diploma. By 2018, **we will** need 22 million new workers with college degrees—but expect to fall short of that number by at least 3 million postsecondary degrees.

The not-so-good news is that during our recent recession, fewer college graduates secured college-level jobs after graduation, and those without a degree may have to get experience as temps before they can get hired permanently. As mentioned earlier in the chapter, many college graduates opt for graduate school, hoping the recession will be over by the time they are again ready for the job market. It is also assumed that some companies will be hiring back retired employees to fill vacancies. These options may slow the need for new permanent employees, but eventually, good temps will have a chance at securing these jobs.

> Graduate school may be an option.

However, if you are interested in these select fields, the United States is already experiencing shortages: nurses, pharmacists, health-care technicians, skilled contractors, electricians, plumbers, child-care workers, firefighters, and law enforcers. The fields of accounting, auditing, and financial planning are expected to expand some 20 percent in the next decade, and a large number of workers are due to retire from all levels of government work.

> Be aware of in-demand careers.

Finally, skilled laborers find themselves in demand often with higher hourly wages. Many of these trades have starting salaries around $35,000 plus overtime (e.g., installation, maintenance, and repair workers are expected to grow by 9 percent) according to the Bureau of Labor Statistics.

Be aware, jobs created in recent economic recoveries looked nothing like those that were lost, and the people hired for those new positions looked nothing like the people laid off from the old ones. In the past two recessions, the typical job loser was a high school–educated male in a blue-collar job, such as manufacturing or construction, working in the middle of the country. In the past two recoveries, the typical job gainer was a female with a postsecondary education who lived on either coast and worked in a service occupation—particularly health care, education, or business services. Again, you will be best positioned for the future if you know what you really want to do and how to get into the field.

LIBERAL ARTS MAJORS HAVE MARKETABLE SKILLS

Liberal arts refers to majors such as art, English, history, psychology, sociology, speech, or any bachelor of arts (B.A.) degree. Such majors provide preparation for a variety of careers. Pursuing a liberal arts degree enables you to develop skills such as problem solving, critical thinking, creative thinking, systems thinking, interpersonal savvy, resource management, communication, the ability to deal with ambiguity, teamwork, research, and how to learn! Employers will expect you to be able to scan information quickly and select what is relevant for your job. You will be expected to have a high level of reading comprehension and be able to prepare documents that are clear, concise, logical, and easy to understand. Such skills are necessary for this job market. You will be even better prepared for the twenty-first-century job market if you have also taken classes or developed skills related to business, computer software, or entrepreneurial thinking.

Although graduates with a degree in business, computer science, and engineering are often in greater demand because their curriculum has provided them with job-specific skills, there have always been employers who hire liberal arts graduates because their broad skills provide a strong foundation for job training in many fields. And such employers often find that liberal arts majors are excellent employees. One example is a political science major who graduated from a small liberal arts college. She had begun her education majoring in English, then switched to French before finally settling on political science. When she graduated she found a job with a financial services group. Vanguard provided her with six weeks of training, and she was able to continue to develop on the job (see "Meet Jessica").

Getting the right skills and education today will give you an advantage tomorrow. Over 80 percent of jobs require some postsecondary education or training. Computer literacy and familiarity with several software programs are a necessity in many jobs. Skills such as reading, writing, communication, the ability to reason, problem solving, and the ability to learn on the job make you competitive in today's job market. If you are a college student, take advantage of the computer access that is available at school and learn as much as possible about using computers. Familiarize yourself with the Internet and become proficient at researching online. When you get into the job market, you will find that companies value job candidates with these skills.

> Develop transferable skills.

LIFELONG LEARNING

More important than knowing what jobs will be available is being *flexible*, having the ability to adapt to this changing world of work. It is estimated that 40 percent of the jobs that will be available in the year 2018 have yet to be created. Thus, you cannot obtain training specifically for every career change you may encounter, but you can develop learning skills that will prepare you for training in new job skills and applications. It is also possible that, because of advancing technology and other factors, you may change careers many times during your life. Even if this is not the case and you move along one or two career paths throughout your life, you will need to continue educating yourself just to keep up with technological change in your chosen field. The trend toward lifelong learning is evidenced by the fact that

FACTS & FIGURES

Degrees Provide an Edge in Getting a Good Job

- ▶ A university degree has never been more essential for securing good employment.
- ▶ Graduates earn 54 percent more, on average, than those who never graduated, yet only a quarter of Americans between ages 25 and 34 have a bachelor's degree.
- ▶ Employers are increasingly using the bachelor's degree as a criteria for hiring employees.
- ▶ See a study on what a degree is worth at **cew.georgetown.edu/whatsitworth** as well as **http://cew.georgetown.edu/collegepayoff**.

REAL stories   Meet Jessica

Jessica was a political science major who graduated from a small liberal arts college in 2005. She had begun her education majoring in English, then switched to French before finally settling on political science. She loved learning everything and had a hard time narrowing her studies to one major. She finally settled on political science by using the College Career Planning Center, taking some career assessments, and doing some information interviews. While visiting Washington, DC, she visited with a French diplomat to the United States, and while visiting New York, she talked to a relative who worked for a big public relations firm. Additionally, Jessica was captivated by the excitement of touring Wall Street.

By graduation time, Jessica had used the College Career Planning Center and gained multiple job offers from firms ranging from public relations to financial services and marketing. Fortunately, the job market was expanding and she had choices. She had been counseled to consider graduate school and had taken the Graduate Record Exam (GRE) and scored well, but she was tired of college. She took a job with the Vanguard Group, an investment company, and now helps employees of the firms' corporate clients manage their 401(k) retirement accounts. Vanguard provided her with six weeks of training, and Jessica was able to develop her job her own way (just as she had learned to do in her class assignments when she was in college). However, by 2007, the job was not as exciting as she had envisioned. Her industry was very stressful, and people actually grew upset with *her* whenever the stock market went down.

Jessica went back to her college's Career Center for Alumni and discussed her concerns. The career counselor suggested that she see if she could focus on some specialty industries at Vanguard to learn about other industries that might be part of her future direction. She found that she could add a specialty and selected the health-care industry. When she met with clients in the health-care industry, she actually interviewed them, as well as provided them with assistance with their 401(k) retirement plans. She found that the issues facing hospitals interested her. Additionally, some of her clients told her there were great needs for her expertise in the human resources department, and if she had a master's degree in health-care administration she could work in industry or government or be a consultant.

Jessica is now going back to college for a master's degree and has her resume out to human resources departments at several hospitals and state and county health departments. She is also grateful that she has already scored well on the GRE and does not have to go back and study for it while she is under so much stress. Having taken the GRE made her more open to graduate school. She was happy to learn that she could attend graduate school after work, on weekends, and online. Having been out of college for three years and finding that her job was getting more stressful rather than more interesting, Jessica is now ready to exercise other options.

WHAT DO *YOU* THINK?

1. How is the major you have or are considering related to any job that you have had?
2. Could you imagine yourself in a job unrelated to your field of study and experience? What is an example of an unrelated job for you?
3. How could Jessica have done more investigation about the stresses related to her job?
4. What alternatives would you have explored that are not mentioned in this story?
5. What do you think about attending graduate school to expand your options?

---

several million people over age 40 were in college in 2000, compared with only 477,000 in 1970. Additionally, an increasing number of people are enrolled in corporate universities. Corporate universities and colleges range from company-run classes designed primarily for that company's employees to programs run by companies that confer credible degrees such as an associates degree or a bachelor's degree.

> **Explore distance learning.**

The days when formal education ended after college or graduate school have disappeared. Now that people work at all hours to keep in touch with colleagues all over the world, continuing education is available at all times via the Internet and it can fit into anyone's busy schedule. For example, one sales manager sometimes plugs in his laptop at midnight, whether he is in a hotel room when away from home on business or at his home office (also known as the family room at other times of the day). He downloads lectures, submits papers, joins in student discussions, and gets his grades online.

Just 23 million Americans were enrolled in continuing education programs in 1984; that figure is now over 100 million, according to the National Center for Educational Statistics. About 400 company-run universities operated in the United States in 1988, but there are now more than 3,700, according to the Corporate University Xchange, a New York research and consulting firm. Additionally, many adults are getting continuing education (also known as training classes) through their company's corporate university or training department. Motorola, for example, provides courses for 100,000 of its employees every year at 100 sites around the world.

Additionally, it is becoming the norm for those older than age 25 to attend college. According to the National Center for Educational Statistics, over 41 percent of those attending colleges and universities are age 25 or older. In fact, prestigious universities are offering reputable degrees online. Whereas 710,000 U.S. students were in distance education in 1998 (about 5 percent of the approximately 15 million higher-education students), 4.6 million were online by 2008. More and more colleges are offering hybrid classes that combine class attendance and Web-based instruction to reduce the amount of time students have to be on campus. How many in your class have tried a lecture or two on iTunes?

> Corporate universities offer options.

Implications

To maintain your currency in your career, you must get updated training throughout your life. Be sure that the training institution you choose is considered reputable by your employer before enrolling for a program of study. Also make sure that you have the time management skills and self-discipline to complete the required studying and research if you choose to take classes online.

As it gets easier to study anytime and anywhere and to earn college credit for such work, more people will be getting college degrees. The trend toward more people getting college degrees means that you will have to earn a college degree to remain competitive in the future job market. In fact, almost 30 percent of the U.S. population has achieved bachelor's degrees!

Many of the best job opportunities during the next decade will demand that applicants have cross-functional training to broaden their qualifications, which includes the following:

> If you think education is expensive, try ignorance.
>
> —*Derek Bok*

- Dual majors, interdisciplinary programs
- Foreign language proficiency
- People/Communications skills
- Technical skills and interest in Web 2.0 interaction

Even college graduates are finding that, to compete for the best jobs, they must commit to lifelong continuing education to bolster their job skills and prepare for career changes.

TIPS FROM THE PROS

Plan to explore the world now, before you have family and financial obligations. The experiences and learning will enrich your life, make you a more competitive job candidate and lead us one step closer to world peace through the powerful lens of cultural understanding and appreciation. If you can't afford to travel far, reach out to classmates or members of the community who represent a different culture and discuss the similarities and differences in lifestyle and philosophies

▲ Get education and experience to improve job opportunities.

JOB GROWTH TRENDS

If you aren't interested in a career that requires a four-year degree, there will always be a need in society for people selling merchandise, running businesses, maintaining homes, caring for children, working in restaurants, attending to health and fitness needs, and working in a variety of trades that may or may not require much training beyond high school. Many of these fields are experiencing greater demand owing to the important sociological changes mentioned previously in this chapter and the increase in the number of two-wage-earner households. Many of the jobs listed in Exhibits 6.6 and 6.7 do not require a bachelor's degree.

This final section of the chapter includes exhibits indicating the fastest-growing jobs and the largest job markets. Again, we emphasize that many of these jobs require only one or two years of postsecondary education, and many are in the fields of health, computers, law (e.g., prison guards, paralegals), and education. However, the number of new jobs open to college graduates will rise twice as fast as the number of jobs requiring short-term training. And jobs requiring master's degrees are predicted to grow 30 percent over the next decade!

For 12 of the 20 fastest-growing occupations, an associate degree or higher is the level of postsecondary education or training required: biomedical engineers, network systems and data communications analysts, financial examiners, medical scientists, physician assistants, biochemists and biophysicists, athletic trainers, computer software engineers and applications, dental hygienists, computer software engineers and systems software, and veterinary technologists and technicians as well as veterinarians. In contrast, only 6 of the 20 occupations with the largest numerical increases require an associate degree or higher as the most significant level of postsecondary education or training. In fact, health-care and computer-related occupations make up the majority of the fastest growing occupations.

The Occupational Outlook Handbook and the Bureau of Labor Statistics online updates its ten year predictions about the job market every other year. Exhibits 6.6 through 6.9 include two different categories of job growth: "fastest growing" and "largest job growth." The *fastest-growing occupations*, such as computer software engineer, are growing in terms of percentage of total number of current jobs (e.g., 175,100 new jobs in 2018 is 34 percent growth for this occupation). The *largest job growth* is stated in terms of how many people are currently in this occupation and how many more will be in this occupation by 2018 (e.g., registered nurses will grow by 581,500 jobs in 2018, so it is one of the largest job growth categories in terms of absolute numbers even though it is expanding only 22 percent).

> *The only place success comes before work is in the dictionary.*
>
> —*Vince Lombardi*

Fastest growing vs. largest growth.

EXHIBIT 6.6 Fastest-Growing Occupations and Occupations Projected to Have the Largest Numerical Increases in Employment between 2006 and 2016, by Level of Postsecondary Education or Training

	Fastest Growing Occupations	Occupations Having the Largest Numerical Job Growth
First professional degree	Veterinarians	Physicians and surgeons
	Pharmacists	Lawyers
	Chiropractors	Pharmacists
	Physicians and surgeons	Veterinarians
	Optometrists	Dentists
Doctoral degree	Postsecondary teachers	Postsecondary teachers
	Computer and information scientists, research	Clinical, counseling, and school psychologists
	Medical scientists, except epidemiologists	Medical scientists, except epidemiologists
	Biochemists and biophysicists	Computer and information scientists, research
	Clinical, counseling, and school psychologists	Biochemists and biophysicists
Master's degree	Mental health counselors	Clergy
	Mental health and substance abuse social workers	Physical therapists
	Marriage and family counselors	Mental health and substance abuse social workers
	Physical therapists	Educational, vocational, and school counselors
	Physician assistants	Rehabilitation counselors
Bachelor's or higher degree, plus work experience	Actuaries	Management analysts
	Education administrators, preschool and child-care center/program	Financial managers
	Management analysts	Computer and information systems managers
	Training and development specialists	Medical and health services managers
	Public relations managers	Training and development specialists
Bachelor's degree	Network systems and data communications analysts	Computer software engineers, applications
	Computer software engineers	Accountants and auditors
	Personal financial advisors	Business operations specialists
	Substance abuse and behavioral disorder counselors	Elementary school teachers, except special education
	Financial analysts	Computer systems analysts

EXHIBIT 6.6 Fastest-Growing Occupations and Occupations Projected to Have the Largest Numerical Increases in Employment between 2006 and 2016, by Level of Postsecondary Education or Training *CONTINUED*

	Fastest Growing Occupations	Occupations Having the Largest Numerical Job Growth
Associate degree	Veterinary technologists and technicians	Registered nurses
	Physical therapist assistant	Computer support specialists
	Dental hygienists	Paralegals and legal assistants
	Environmental science and protection technicians, including health	Dental hygienists
	Cardiovascular technicians	Legal secretaries
Postsecondary vocational award	Makeup artists, theatrical and performance	Nursing aides, orderlies, and attendants
	Skin care specialists	Preschool teachers, except special education
	Manicurists and pedicurists	Automotive service technicians and mechanics
	Fitness trainers	Licensed practical and licensed vocational nurses
	Preschool teachers, except special education	Cosmetologists
Work experience in a related occupation	Sales representatives, services, all other	Executive secretaries and administrative assistants
	Gaming managers	
	Gaming supervisors	Sales representatives, services
		Sales representatives, wholesale and manu-facturing, except technical and scientific products
	Aircraft cargo handling supervisors	
	Self-enrichment teachers	First-line supervisors/managers of food preparation and serving workers
		First-line supervisors/managers of office and administrative support workers
Long-term on-the-job training	Audio and video technicians	Carpenters
	Interpreters and translators	Cooks, restaurant
	Athletes and sports competitors	Police and sheriff's patrol officers
	Motorboat mechanics	Plumbers, pipefitters, and steamfitters
	Automotive glass installers and repairers	Electricians
Moderate-term on-the-job training	Medical assistants	Customer service representatives
	Social and human service assistants	Bookkeeping, accounting, and auditing clerks
	Gaming surveillance officers and gaming investigators	Truck drivers, heavy and tractor-trailer
	Pharmacy technicians	Medical assistants
	Dental assistants	Maintenance and repair workers, general

Source: U.S. Department of Labor, Bureau of Labor Statistics, Bulletin 2700, 2007.

EXHIBIT 6.7 Job Growth Throughout the Next Decade, by Major

ART/MULTIMEDIA: Writers, entertainers, party planners, artists, digital designers, animators, and graphic designers will have good prospects but must be entrepreneurial types.

BASIC SCIENCE: Biogenetic engineering will be an important field in the next decade, as will chemistry (especially food science) and fiber optics. Biotechnology uses living cells and materials produced by cells to create pharmaceutical, diagnostic, agricultural, environmental, and other products to benefit society. Clinical genomics will expand.

BUSINESS: Growing fields will be accounting, forensic accounting, statistical analysis, and payroll management, financial planning, and portfolio management. Main growth in retirement and estate planning is expected. Increased demand for temp employees. In management, managers of telecommunications, global business development, environmental protection, and security systems.

COMPUTER SCIENCE, INFORMATION SYSTEMS: Opportunities will continue to be strong in design, engineering, programming, networking, maintenance, data mining, and cyber-security.

CULINARY ARTS: Managers and chefs will be in demand for restaurants and hotel kitchens, as well as for food processing plants and labs. Specialty restaurants will continue to expand.

EDUCATION: Demand is growing in the school system, for both teachers and administrators to meet the changing needs of immigrants and new students. Corporate America will be hiring educators and trainers to teach literacy skills such as English. High-demand subjects include ESL, math, science, computer software, interactive learning modalities, and foreign languages such as Spanish, Japanese, Arabic, and Chinese. New interactive products are being introduced daily. Educational interactive "games" will grow as well as distance education.

ENGINEERING: Specializations in high demand will include robotics, aviation, biotechnology, manufacturing technology, nanotechnology, and civil engineering.

ENVIRONMENTAL SCIENCES: Specializations include hazardous waste management, environmental impact research, conservation and environmental preservation, and alternative fuels.

HEALTH SERVICES: Demand will be especially great for primary-care workers such as nurse practitioners, nurses and nurses aides, gerontologists (doctors) and social workers, radiology technicians, respiratory care technicians, home health-care aides, nutrition counselors, pharmacists, health informatics specialists, patient advocates, and health service administrators.

HOTEL MANAGEMENT/TOURISM: Tourism is a big and expanding business. This category includes restaurants, resorts, and travel services, as well as opportunities in conference planning.

HUMAN RESOURCES: The field of employee management continues to grow as a result of legislation concerning employee rights, payroll requirements, and compensation options. Specialists needed include job evaluation, hiring and firing, benefits planning, and training.

MAINTENANCE AND REPAIR MAJORS: These are the people who will take care of all the equipment that will keep tomorrow's world running (e.g., electricians; plumbers; heating, air conditioning and refrigeration experts; and network maintenance personnel).

SECURITY SYSTEMS RELATED: The protection of society from terrorism, including biological, chemical and nuclear attacks, is creating new jobs such as emergency planner, security guards, airport security, CIA and FBI analysts. Cyber-security is listed under computer science.

For specific predictions regarding growing job fields, see Exhibits 6.6 through 6.9. Because data are presented from several sources, figures may differ from exhibit to exhibit for the same profession and are meant to be representative.

EXHIBIT 6.8   Occupations With the Largest Numerical Growth to 2018

Occupations	New Jobs (in Thousands)	Percent Change	Wages (May 2008 Median)	Education/Training Category
Registered nurses	581.5	22	$62,450	Associate degree
Home health aides	460.9	50	20,460	Short-term on-the-job training
Customer service representatives	399.5	18	29,860	Moderate-term on-the-job training
Combined food preparation and serving workers, including fast food	394.3	15	16,430	Short-term on-the-job training
Personal and home care aides	375.8	46	19,180	Short-term on-the-job training
Retail salespersons	374.7	8	20,510	Short-term on-the-job training
Office clerks, general	358.7	12	25,320	Short-term on-the-job training
Accountants and auditors	279.4	22	59,430	Bachelor's degree
Nursing aides, orderlies, and attendants	276.0	19	23,850	Postsecondary vocational award
Postsecondary teachers	256.9	15	58,830	Doctoral degree
Construction laborers	255.9	20	28,520	Moderate-term on-the-job training
Elementary school teachers, except special education	244.2	16	49,330	Bachelor's degree
Truck drivers, heavy and tractor-trailer	232.9	13	37,270	Short-term on-the-job training
Landscaping and groundskeeping workers	217.1	18	23,150	Short-term on-the-job training
Bookkeeping, accounting, and auditing clerks	212.4	10	32,510	Moderate-term on-the-job training
Executive secretaries and administrative assistants	204.4	13	40,030	Work experience in a related occupation
Management analysts	178.3	24	73,570	Bachelor's or higher degree, plus work experience
Computer software engineers, applications	175.1	34	85,430	Bachelor's degree
Receptionists and information clerks	172.9	15	24,550	Short-term on-the-job training
Carpenters	165.4	13	38,940	Long-term on-the-job training

Source: Bureau of Labor Statistics Occupational Employment Statistics and Div: Outlook 2011–12.

EXERCISE your options

Identify in-Demand Jobs that Interest You

List five jobs found in this chapter that interest you and seem to fit your personality:

1. _____

2. _____

3. _____

4. _____

5. _____

EXHIBIT 6.9 Occupations With the Fastest Growth to 2018

Occupations	Percent Change	New Jobs (*in Thousands*)	Wages (May 2008 Median)	Education/Training Category
Biomedical engineers	72	11.6	$77,400	Bachelor's degree
Network systems and data communications analysts	53	155.8	71,100	Bachelor's degree
Home health aides	50	460.9	20,460	Short-on-the-job training
Personal and home care aides	46	375.8	19,180	Short-on-the-job training
Financial examiners	41	11.1	70,930	Bachelor's degree
Medical scientists, except epidemiologists	40	44.2	72,590	Doctoral degree
Physician assistants	39	29.2	81,230	Master's degree
Skin care specialists	38	14.7	28,730	Postsecondary vocational award
Biochemists and biophysicists	37	8.7	82,840	Doctoral degree
Athletic trainers	37	6.0	39,640	Bachelor's degree
Physical therapist aides	36	16.7	23,760	Short-on-the-job training
Dental hygienists	36	62.9	66,570	Associate degree
Veterinary technologists and technicians	36	28.5	28,900	Associate degree
Dental assistants	36	105.6	32,380	Moderate-on-the-job training
Computer software engineers, applications	34	175.1	85,430	Bachelor's degree
Medical assistants	34	163.9	28,300	Moderate-term on-the-job training
Physical therapist assistants	33	21.2	46,140	Associate degree
Veterinarians	33	19.7	79,050	First professional degree
Self-enrichment education teachers	32	81.3	35,720	Work experience in a related occupation
Compliance officers, except agriculture, construction, health and safety, and transportation	31	80.8	48,890	Long-term on-the-job training

Source: BLS Occupational Employment Statistics and Division of Occupational Outlook 2011–12.

Summary

How do all these social and cultural changes affect you? Your expectations about finding your place in a changing world are influenced by your early socialization and by the culture that surrounds you. Career opportunities can be discovered and pursued through family, childhood play, school experiences, volunteer work, and early work activities. *The degree of satisfaction you find in work and in life depends on your finding opportunities to develop and use your abilities, interests, values, and personality traits.*

Unfortunately, opportunity is not distributed equally throughout society. You may feel limited economically, academically, or by family responsibilities. Opportunities may be limited by gender stereotyping, by educational requirements, by discrimination, or by the changing economy. However, as perceptions change, as laws change, as the economy becomes more global and requires employers to appreciate and use diverse human talents, all women and men should feel free to choose and train for the type of career that best suits their interests and talents.

Although it is helpful to take growth trends into consideration as you explore your options, it is not necessary to choose a career path only in the areas most likely to have openings. In fact, the best direction to follow is most often *directly toward what you really want to do. The key is to believe in yourself and keep acquiring related experience and education.*

FACTS & FIGURES

Trend Exhibits

The exhibits in this chapter provide a cross-section of information about salaries, including pay equity across gender and race, and occupations projected to experience good job growth. The exhibits are intended to provide general information of interest to you as you consider various career options.

Although numerical data give the impression of being hard facts, remember that such information should be considered approximate. The future is only partially predictable, but it's a good idea to be informed!

PURPOSE OF EXERCISES

The Career Fitness Program encourages you to develop your own personal objectives, believe in yourself, acknowledge stereotypes pertaining to life and work, and develop a clear strategy for entering the career of your choice. Whether or not you have directly experienced bias or other barriers to employment, we would like you to use the written exercises in this chapter to reflect on your personal, social, and cultural opinions and biases. Exercise 6.1 helped you become aware of how you may react to roles and events that differ from those to which you are accustomed. Exercise 6.2 asked you to explore your own stereotypes. Exercise 6.3 asked you to list the advantages and disadvantages of belonging to one or more distinct groups and helped you to

become aware of your knowledge of various categories of people. The more difficult it was for you to identify names for this exercise, the more likely it is that you have led a life that excludes other cultures. Stereotypes and barriers tend to develop when we stick to our own groups. Exercise 6.4 asked you to list the possible impact of globalization on the workplace given what you have read and discussed in class. In Exercise 6.5, you will list jobs that did not exist a decade ago. Exercise 6.6, **WWWebwise**, is a Web-based research exercise that will reinforce the learnings in this chapter. Finally, **Reinforcing Your Learning Outcomes** will allow you to strengthen and reinforce your learning outcomes from this chapter.

EXERCISE

6.5 Changing Nature of Work

Think about jobs that you, your friends, and family have had. Name three jobs that did not exist 10 years ago:

1. _____

2. _____

3. _____

EXERCISE

6.6 WWWebwise

Go to **http://stats.bls.gov/oco** and report on what you learned about the careers you investigated. Include the following information: *the training and education needed, earnings, expected job prospects, what workers do on the job, and working conditions*. You may use national or your own state's information. (*Note*: Please be aware that websites can change without notice. If a link does not work, find a similar site in the Bureau of Labor Statistics website to complete the activity.)

REINFORCING YOUR LEARNING OUTCOMES

Review and Rate Your Chapter Outcomes. Indicate in the right-hand column how well you do the following items (from 1 = very well, to 5 = not at all). If you rated yourself 4 or 5, review the material on the pages in parentheses to ensure your career success.

How Well Can You Do the Following?

- Identify personal beliefs and assumptions that will affect your career. (pp.103–5) 1 2 3 4 5
- Recognize how social and cultural conditioning influences your career choice. (pp. 105–112) 1 2 3 4 5
- List and understand changes in the workplace. (pp. 113–119) 1 2 3 4 5
- Identify trends that will affect your career planning through the next decade. (pp.119–132) 1 2 3 4 5
- Recognize the skills employers expect in new employees. (pp. 114–122). 1 2 3 4 5
- Learn the value of a liberal arts degree. (p. 123) 1 2 3 4 5

Go to the Career Fitness Portfolio at the end of the book and complete this chapter summary to build and record your personal Career Fitness Portfolio.

Additional Opportunity: Your instructor may choose to assign the Career Fitness Portfolio for in class or online completion. If so, they will provide the handout or link for you to access.

Exploring Career Information

Expand Your Horizons

STUDENT LEARNING OUTCOMES

At the end of the chapter you will be able to . . .

- Brainstorm possible career options based on information you learned about your attitudes, beliefs, values, interests, personality, and skills.

- Adopt a strategy to approach occupational research that will enhance your efficiency and effectiveness.

- Research print and online sources of information to use in further clarifying your career choices.

- Develop your critical thinking skills to analyze information about specific occupations and career-related opportunities using library materials and online resources.

- Confirm or revise your first impressions about your top career choices.

By now, you may have one or several career areas in mind. This chapter will help you get more specific. It will enable you to review, clarify, and integrate the information you've collected about your needs, desires, values, interests, skills, and personal attributes. It is important to put these pieces together to identify some specific occupational areas that you can begin to research.

Sometimes the hardest part of making a career choice is knowing what kinds of jobs exist. The work world is changing so rapidly that it is difficult to stay current regarding all the jobs that are available. This can seem most complicated if you are looking for your first job, or are uncertain about how your academic background has prepared you for work, or if you have been out of the workplace for a period of time.

Discovery consists of seeing what everybody else has seen and thinking what no one else has thought.

Albert Szent-Györgyi

This chapter will introduce you to the printed and online resources available in libraries, in college career centers, and on computers when you are connected to the Internet. By using these references, you will have the information necessary to clarify and confirm your tentative career choices.

To assist you in visualizing specific occupations, try using the guided fantasy (Exercise 7.1). You might find it insightful to use Exercise 7.1 now and also after you have completed the exercises at the end of the chapter. Start by quickly reviewing all the written information that you've recorded at the end of the book in your Career Fitness Portfolio. Then close your eyes and visualize yourself in your perfect job.

EXERCISE

7.1 Guided Fantasy

Try this guided fantasy exercise now by recording it and listening to it or having a friend read this to you; if you are in a class, your instructor will read it to you:

Close your eyes, relax, and take a few deep breaths. Get comfortable and remove all feelings of tension from your body. Erase all previous thoughts and worries from your mind.

Imagine you are getting up on an ideal workday. You're sitting on the side of your bed deciding what to wear. Take a moment and look over your wardrobe. What type of clothing do you choose?

Imagine yourself getting ready for work. Do any thoughts about the day come to you while you're getting ready? What kind of feelings do you have as you prepare for your workday? Do you feel excited? Bored? Apprehensive? What gives you these feelings? It's time for your morning routine and breakfast now. Will you be sharing breakfast with someone, or will you be eating alone?

You've completed your breakfast and are headed out the door to go to work. Stop for a moment and look around your neighborhood. What does it look like? What does your home look like? What thoughts and feelings do you experience as you look around?

How are you getting to work? How far is it? What new feelings or thoughts are you experiencing?

You have arrived at work. Pause for a bit and try to get a mental picture of it. Think about where it is and what it looks like. Will you be spending most of your time indoors or outdoors? How many people will you be working with?

You are going to your specific job now. Who is the first person you encounter? What does this person look like? What is this person wearing? What do you say to this person?

Try to form an image of the particular tasks you perform on your job. Don't think about it as a specific job with a title, such as nurse or an accountant. Instead, think about what you are actually doing, such as working with your hands, adding figures, typing, talking to people, drawing, writing, calculating, designing, using the computer and other electronic technology, researching, strategizing, creating, connecting, imagining, or thinking.

In your job, do you work primarily by yourself or mostly with others? In your work with others, what do you do with them? How old are the other people? What do they look like? How do you feel toward them?

Where will you be going for lunch? Will you be going with someone else? Whom? What will you talk about?

How do the afternoon's activities differ from those of the morning? How are you feeling as the day progresses? Energized? Tired? Alert? Bored? Excited?

Your workday is coming to an end now. Has it been a satisfying day? If so, what made it satisfying? Was there anything about the day that made you less happy? Will you be doing some of your work at home in the evening? How do you feel about your work life at the end of the day?

Consider sharing some of your guided fantasy with a classmate and significant others in your life. How different is your vision from theirs?

Mental visualization can sometimes focus your thoughts on areas that suit you perfectly. This technique helps you tap into and integrate the wealth of information, intuition, and wisdom that you already have about yourself. It is common to feel hesitant and even fearful about committing yourself to a career decision. These feelings block you from getting specific. Mental visualization is a technique that can help your mind wander or lean into a career choice.

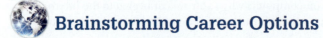

Brainstorming Career Options

Before you begin to narrow down and research the career options that best fit you, you need to broaden your knowledge about the job market. Many job searchers find this difficult because they simply do not know much about the kinds of jobs that are available. At this phase in your career decision making, you need to generate many different *possibilities*. In a later section of this chapter, you will learn how to research these possibilities with printed and online resources. This information will help you make the most satisfying decisions about your possible career choices.

TIPS FROM THE PROS

The more elements of your personal career profile that you can incorporate into your work, the more satisfied and happy you will be in your work. You are most likely to find an optimal career fit if you find the work interesting and you are using your most satisfying skills. Your personal preferences provide insight into your preferred work style. You want to find a job that is consistent with your values so that you are satisfied with your daily work and feel your work is worthwhile. Each of these areas needs to be satisfied regularly at work, not just once a month or once a year. Exploring a number of career options is the best way to ultimately find satisfying work.

One of the best ways to generate career options is to cultivate a brainstorming mind-set. *Brainstorming* is simply the process of generating and entertaining as many ideas on a particular topic as possible—career ideas, in this case. Start thinking beyond all of the obvious career options you have considered over and over again. Remember these two important rules for brainstorming:

> Brainstorm your way to a career choice.

- First, at this point, be more concerned with quantity than quality. Your goal is to come up with a long list of occupational ideas and pare it down later.
- Second, consider even the most outrageous ideas. Maybe being a lion tamer in the circus, or an astronaut, or a travel writer might not seem like a realistic occupational goal, but it might spark another idea that is possible. As you work through each section of this chapter you will be adding additional possibilities to your list.

As you begin this process, keep in mind your personal career profile. Your skills, interests, personality, beliefs, attitudes, and values all relate to the world of work. For example, think about one of your interests, such as tennis or the field of biotechnology. Assess your skills, values, and personality as related to this interest. Ask yourself the following questions:

- Could I teach people about this interest?
- Could I sell something related to this interest?
- Could I do research or write about this interest?
- What kind of service could I perform using my skills as related to this interest?

Suddenly, your interest has become a possible occupational consideration! The point of reviewing previous exercises is to help you identify and reaffirm the relationship between your personal career profile and optimal occupations.

Now that you understand how brainstorming works, the rest of this chapter will give you many ways to strategically generate your list of possible careers to further research so you can focus in on your best options.

Understanding Career Paths and Common Organizational Divisions

Sometimes you can gain a greater awareness of the job market by researching career paths or career ladders in a specific industry. Most career centers and libraries have books that outline career paths. Once you've assessed where you currently fit in, you can start preparing to move up the ladder. If you are presently working, your immediate supervisor and the human resources department can provide information about routes for advancement—for example, in-house workshops, institutes, on-the-job training, community college associate degrees and certificates, and bachelor's degrees.

Although the world of work includes a number of broad fields such as business, education, government (including the military), health care, and nonprofit agencies, all of these fields share certain common functional needs and have some common organizational units. As an example, many fields need the accounting functions of payroll and disbursement, budgeting, and servicing of accounts payable and receivable. Administration, finance, human resources, marketing, public relations, management information systems, and research and development are departmental functions common to almost all work fields. The upcoming list explains the general functions of these and other departments in typical businesses; however, you will find identical or very similar organizational units performing very similar functions in the fields of education, government, nonprofit agencies, and health care.

If you have been concentrating on specific industries in your search for job possibilities, you can gain a fresh perspective by selecting functions that may be interesting to you and then researching jobs within those functions, but among various industries. For example, if you have great communication skills and like to interact with people, *sales* might be a "function" to consider. You can then think about your interests in terms of what industry interests you. For instance, you can sell pharmaceuticals, iPhones, tennis rackets, travel, yachts, golf club memberships, microloans, wine—any product, service, or idea that interests you. The same applies to each function and every industry.

Common Organizational Functions

Administration: An organization's top executive officers and other managers, administrative assistants and word processing personnel, and human resources staff.

Corporate relations: Responsible for advertising, public relations, and community relations.

Distribution: Sometimes called the transportation and logistics department; oversees warehousing and shipping of the company's products.

Engineering: Product design and modification; often oversees manufacturing of products (process engineers).

Finance: Accounting functions, including payroll, budgets, and accounts payable and receivable.

Sales: Responsible for initiating and maintaining customer accounts, selling the company's product; sometimes includes marketing function.

Remember that some companies are restructuring so that jobs may not be part of career paths. Companies might hire a coordinator with cross-functional skills: That person develops and tracks the project, motivates the team, assists the team in marketing the project/product, and also keeps track of the budget. The project may last six months or so, and then the coordinator is assigned to a different project with either similar or different duties. This type of organization is called a *web*. Another type of web is a situation in which a specialist works for *several* companies, such as an accountant who does the books for a designer, publisher, educational consultant, and marketing specialist.

Generalist or specialist?

Your research should reflect the location of your chosen path(s). Do you hope to work somewhere as a *generalist* and be adept in many areas? Or do you prefer to be part of an organization as a *specialist*, such as an accountant? See Exhibit 7.1 for examples of career paths in business fields.

Now that you have a clearer idea of the jobs that best suit your personality, you are ready to research the actual requirements of the jobs. The two primary ways to obtain job information are searching through materials in the library or online and contacting people who already work in your area of interest. This chapter focuses on written and online materials. Your local library or college career center should be able to provide you with some or all of the resources discussed in this chapter.

Strategies for Researching Career Options

The best place to begin your research is not in the library but with a strategy. This will help you focus your efforts, know what to look for, and not waste time on dead-end research.

EXHIBIT 7.1 Sample Career Paths in Business: Typical Job Titles and Compensation Ranges of Marketing, Retailing, and International Professionals (Numbers in Thousands)

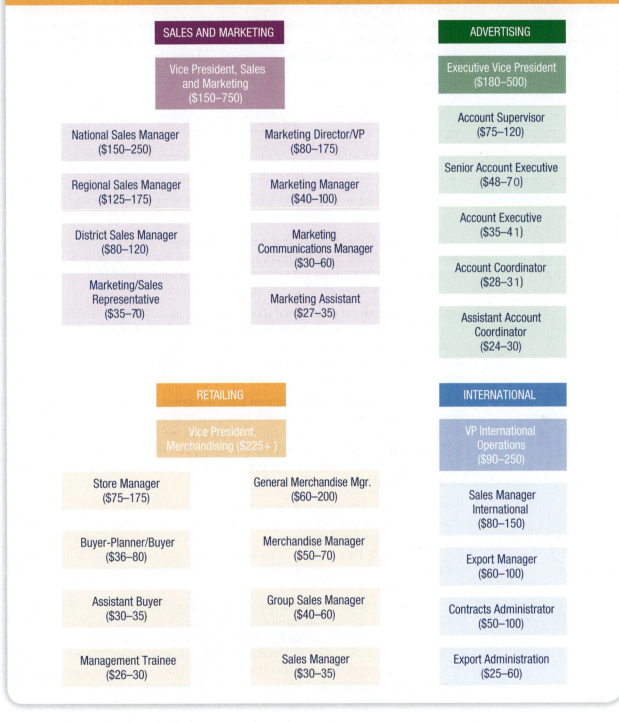

SALES AND MARKETING

Vice President, Sales and Marketing ($150–750)

National Sales Manager ($150–250)

Regional Sales Manager ($125–175)

District Sales Manager ($80–120)

Marketing/Sales Representative ($35–70)

Marketing Director/VP ($80–175)

Marketing Manager ($40–100)

Marketing Communications Manager ($30–60)

Marketing Assistant ($27–35)

ADVERTISING

Executive Vice President ($180–500)

Account Supervisor ($75–120)

Senior Account Executive ($48–70)

Account Executive ($35–41)

Account Coordinator ($28–31)

Assistant Account Coordinator ($24–30)

RETAILING

Vice President, Merchandising ($225+)

Store Manager ($75–175)

Buyer-Planner/Buyer ($36–80)

Assistant Buyer ($30–35)

Management Trainee ($26–30)

General Merchandise Mgr. ($60–200)

Merchandise Manager ($50–70)

Group Sales Manager ($40–60)

Sales Manager ($30–35)

INTERNATIONAL

VP International Operations ($90–250)

Sales Manager International ($80–150)

Export Manager ($60–100)

Contracts Administrator ($50–100)

Export Administration ($25–60)

1. **Decide which occupations you are going to research.** After completing Exercise 7.2, you should have a good list of occupational possibilities. It is unrealistic to suggest you should research every job you brainstormed. You can probably remove some jobs on your list right away. Review your list and prioritize your ideas. If you have a long list, try grouping

EXERCISE
7.2 A Tempting 10

Identify one industry that you find interesting, such as entertainment, business, health care, or education. In the space provided, write 10 different jobs related to that industry. When you have completed the list, prioritize the job titles in order of how interesting they sound to you, and list them. Repeat this exercise with two or three different industries if the jobs found at first are not "fitting" your personality. Use **www.yahoo.com** or **www.careerinfonet.org** website mentioned in this chapter.

1. _____   6. _____

2. _____   7. _____

3. _____   8. _____

4. _____   9. _____

5. _____   10. _____

your ideas according to industry or function. For example, if you have five occupational ideas related to writing and journalism, you might group them for purposes of research in a category called "communication careers." Identify a realistic number of occupations or occupational areas about which you would like to learn more.

2. **Research the industry and functional areas.** Once you have decided what you are going to research, your next step is to do broad research on the industry and field. It is best to start with resources that can give you concise information quickly to decide if a particular occupational area is interesting. The U.S. Department of Labor website, **www.careerinfonet.org**, is a good place to start.

3. **Learn about current events affecting your areas of interest.** Magazines and newspapers, especially publications that focus on business such as *Fortune*, *Bloomberg's Business Week*, or the *Wall Street Journal*, are rich resources for information about current industry trends, relevant new technology, key companies and organizations, and job growth. You can easily find the most current publications by completing a keyword search on most library databases or on Google.

4. **Identify relevant professional and trade associations.** Most industries have a professional organization. These associations bring together professionals in a particular industry for networking and continuing education. They exist to disseminate information about a particular industry. Professional and trade associations also publish journals and newsletters that can give you insight into the industry's current issues, types of employers, and common vocabulary.

   The Encyclopedia of Associations and Chamber of Commerce publications are the best resources for this information. As you research occupations, develop a list of relevant professional associations to contact for additional career information. If your college uses Career Cruising or Eureka, associations' websites are often listed in the occupational description area. A useful website for finding associations is **www.weddles .com/associations/index.cfm**. Additionally, later in this chapter is a list of associations connected to science-, technology-, engineering-, and math-related occupations.

5. **Locate useful websites on the Internet.** The Internet brings a wide range of information about different industries, professional associations, and employers literally to your fingertips. Colleges and libraries offer Internet access to their users. By using your industry as a keyword in any of the different Internet search engines, you can identify many useful websites that provide the most up-to-date information. As found in Exhibit 7.4 (later in this chapter), one comprehensive website for STEM (science, technology, engineering, and math) careers is *Sloan Career Cornerstone*, which specializes in careers related to science,

technology, engineering, and math and includes degrees, career paths, industry specifics, individual career profiles, and podcasts (**www.careercornerstone.org**; click on Industries).

A complete discussion of online and software-based job search resources begins on page 150.

6. **Identify key employers.** The last step is to compile a list of typical employers, noting all kinds of employers (e.g., nonprofit, government, or business) and actual organization names. Several of the directories listed in Exhibit 7.3 (found later in this chapter) can provide you with lists of companies that hire people for a particular industry. You may limit your research to employers in the local area or in geographic areas where you would like to live.

▲ These students work with a guidance counselor to learn more about career and education options.

SUCCESS strategies

Questions to Answer When Researching a Job

- What are the job duties and responsibilities?
- What qualifications are needed in terms of college degrees, skills, or work experience?
- Are you likely to receive on-the-job training in this field?
- What is a typical career path in this field?
- What is the employment outlook for this industry?
- What is the average salary for someone entering this field? What are the top salaries in this field?

- Who are typical employers in this field?
- What are the key professional and trade associations for this field?
- What is the work environment like for this field? Is traveling required?
- Is relocation to a specific geographic location required?
- Is this job/company interesting to you?

Government Employment Opportunities

State and local governments hire the majority of people in public work. Local government alone hires over 50 percent of all public employees. In addition, the federal government hires hundreds of people each day across the United States. When private industry is cutting back on hiring, government often seems like it is the best place to find a job. In fact, within five years, almost half of the federal government's current employees will be eligible to retire.

Federal, state, and local government employment information is often available on the Internet at colleges and One-Stop Career Centers. (For more information about surfing the Web, see the Internet section of this chapter and use your course website.) For those who don't have access to these locations, state personnel offices offer applications, tests, job descriptions, and occupational outlook data. For example, California publishes "A Guide to the Use of Labor Market Publications" to help prospective employees research job opportunities and it has an excellent website. Remember that it may take six to nine months to complete the application, test, interview, and conclude the hiring process for state government jobs. This is not a good option for someone who needs immediate employment; however, many people find it possible to complete the process while employed elsewhere. Also, many college students begin the application and testing process during their senior year in college, enabling them to interview for jobs before they graduate.

Excluding the postal service, the federal government employs almost 2 million workers. There may be 15,000 vacancies on any given day! No one in the federal government knows all the positions vacant on a particular day, week, or month. Contact the human resources office of each agency for a complete listing of vacancies in that agency. On the Internet, you may want to check out **www.usajobs.opm.gov/infocenter** (try searching by state). These services are updated daily and have links to many other employment options. At the end of this chapter, several other career information services available on the Internet are listed. These sources also link to federal and state employment information. One other website worth visiting is **www.careersingovernment.com**.

You can also find information about federal jobs in publications such as *Federal Careers Opportunities*, a biweekly publication containing more than 4,000 job listings representing vacancies in the executive branch or congressional and judicial staff as well as in the United Nations. Also check with the Government Printing Office or your nearest branch of the Office of Personnel Management (their website is **www.usajobs.opm.gov**). Exhibit 7.2 lists some of the many federal employment opportunities.

> Government listings offer opportunities.

Federal job information centers may also have access to a national job bank. This is especially useful for people who want to know about job opportunities located some distance away.

EXHIBIT 7.2 Sample Federal Employment Opportunities

Executive Departments

Agriculture	Health and Human Services	Labor
Commerce	Homeland Security	State
Defense	Housing and Urban	Transportation
Development	Interior	Treasury
Education	Justice	Veterans Affairs
Energy		

Sample Federal Employment Positions Covered by Announcements

Accountant	Forester	Occupational therapist
Architect	Geophysicist	Oceanographer
Astronomer	Hospital administrator	Patent examiner
Attorney	Hydrologist	Pest controller
Bacteriologist	Illustrator	Pharmacist
Biologist	Internal revenue agent	Prison administrator
Chemist	Librarian	Social worker
Dietitian	Mathematician	Soil conservationist
Education officer	Meteorologist	Special agent
Engineer	Nurse	Teacher

EXHIBIT 7.2 *CONTINUED*

Major Independent Agencies in the Federal Government

Central Intelligence Agency	Office of Personnel Management
Environmental Protection Agency	Small Business Administration
Equal Employment Opportunity Commission	Social Security Administration
Federal Deposit Insurance Corporation	Tennessee Valley Authority
General Services Administration	U.S. Information Agency
National Aeronautics and Space Administration	U.S. Agency for International Development
National Archives and Records Administration	U.S. Postal Service
Nuclear Regulatory Commission	

FACTS & FIGURES

Local Government

According to the Bureau of Labor Statistics, more than 18 million people are employed by states, counties, cities, and towns.

WHAT DO *YOU* THINK?

1. What kind of local government job might interest you?
2. If you know someone working for local or state government, what is the job and how did the person get the job?

U.S. Department of Labor Publications

Three government publications will be very helpful to you:

1. O*NET
2. Career InfoNet
3. Occupational Outlook Handbook

The Occupational Information Network (O*NET) is an interactive tool devised by the U.S. Department of Labor. The program is an easy-to-use database that collects, analyzes, and disseminates skill and job requirement information. It was designed to replace the *Dictionary of Occupational Titles (DOT)*.

O˚Net provides a summary report for approximately 1,000 occupations (including knowledge, skills, abilities, interests, and values, as well as examples of tasks in a job) and also identifies the physical, affective, and intellectual demands of a job. This information may help a person with a disability assess his or her potential for succeeding in a job. O*Net, as well as the next resource, CareerInfoNet, will also supply similar occupations to any job that is researched.

Another resource from the Department of Labor is America's Career Infonet (**www .careerinfonet.org**). This site provides information on fast-growing, high-demand occupations, including the skills and educational requirements needed for such jobs. It offers a link to apprenticeship training resources, state job banks, wage information, and industry trends.

Most libraries, college career and placement centers, One Stop Career Centers, and high school career centers have many career directories and online websites available to use (see Exhibit 7.3 for examples). You may use the online services or hard-copy publications.

The *Occupational Outlook Handbook (OOH)* (**www.bls.gov/oco**) includes information on job descriptions, skills, places of employment, training, educational requirements, personality traits, and values that might be important in a particular field, as well as salary ranges. It is updated every other year and presents a national survey of occupations, including a 10-year projection of the fastest-growing jobs. Also included is a review of industries and how they will change in the next decade. Compare salary information with local salaries and local cost-of-living factors. For example, Los Angeles employers tend to pay $1,000 to $2,000 more per year than many of the generalized estimates shown in the *OOH*.

Between editions of the *Occupational Outlook Handbook*, the *Occupational Outlook Quarterly* provides updates of occupational projections as well as compensation ranges and cost-of-living comparisons throughout the United States.

 **Employer Directories**

Employer directories provide information about specific companies, such as those in your field with current job openings (see Exhibit 7.3).

EXHIBIT 7.3   Sample Directories Useful to Career Explorers Often Found in College Career Centers

The Almanac of American Employers: About 500 companies are listed, with one page per firm, which includes the following information: recent financial performance, salaries and benefits, regional offices, brands, and divisions.

American Society of Association Executives: This list of directories may be found at **www.asanet.org**.

California Manufacturers Directory: Companies are listed by location and product, with an additional section on companies that have import/export business.

Directory of American Firms Operating in Foreign Countries: About 3,000 American corporations with factories and branch offices covering more than 36 countries are listed in this directory. It also lists key personnel, but because it is not published annually, such information may be out of date.

Dun's Employment Opportunities Directory: This directory lists over 10,000 companies throughout the United States. It includes information about educational specialties the company values, most promising areas of employment, and a brief description of the company's insurance plans. It is divided into geographic and industry sections.

Encyclopedia of Associations: Listed here are more than 15,000 associations in every field, with names of officers, telephone numbers, and brief descriptions of orientation and activities.

Gale Directory of Publications and Broadcast Media: Every newspaper, magazine, and radio station in the United States is listed. Information may be found by region or industry groups (e.g., retailing, restaurants). It is an excellent source of information about trade publications.

Guide to American Directories: This guide describes about 10,000 directories subdivided into hundreds of topical areas.

Hoover's Handbook of American Business: This industry master list has more than 300 industries and 4,000 detailed company profiles, including a very thorough overview of what each company owns, how it is structured, key personnel, and company performance. It shows how employment prospects compare (e.g., top 100 companies in employment opportunities). Go to **www.hoovers.com**.

Regional and Community Magazines: Published by most large cities and metropolitan areas, these magazines focus on business, industry, education, the arts, and politics; states and regions also have their own magazines.

Standard and Poor's Register of Corporations, Directors, and Executives. About 55,000 public and private companies are listed in three volumes. Volume 1 covers basic information; volume 2 includes summaries about key executives; and volume 3 indexes companies according to industry classification.

Standard Rate and Data Business Publications Directory: Names and addresses of thousands of trade publications are listed.

State Directories: Directories of trade and industry are published by each state. If one is not in your library, contact the local or state chamber of commerce, or write to U.S. Chamber of Commerce, 1615 H Street NW, Washington, DC 20006, or go to **www.uschamber.com**.

Thomas's Register of American Manufacturers: More than 100,000 manufacturers are listed by location and product.

Who's Who in Commerce and Industry. Names and biographical sketches of top executives are provided.

Information about a variety of enterprises, from foundations to corporations, can be found in directories. Directories list an employer's name and address, product, and geographic location, as well as other information including size in terms of volume of sales, number of employees, and names of top-level executives. Don't forget to use your local telephone directory. The white (or blue) pages list government agencies and departments, and the yellow pages list other places of employment.

The yellow pages are available on the Internet at **www.yellowpages.com**. A benefit of this resource is that small businesses are listed. If you are thinking about starting a landscape business, for example, determine the competition in a specific geographic area by typing "landscape" under "Business Category" and the city or zip code in the next box. Or, if you would like to work in a certain city to get experience before opening your own business, a phone call to the businesses listed in the yellow pages may provide you with information about a job or when one might be available.

> Let your fingers do the researching.

SUCCESS *strategies*   Research

Research can help you in the following ways:

- Locate high-level company information (such as names of executives)
- Obtain contact information
- Locate company websites
- Research company financial information
- Monitor company news and periodicals
- Review public opinion about a company
- Learn about an industry

- Learn to use business and financial websites
- Locate professional associations
- Find career-related conferences and seminars
- Research nonprofit organizations
- Identify international business resources
- Provide you with knowledge that can give you a strategic advantage in a job interview

As you review the directories listed in Exhibit 7.3, look for the following types of information:

- A geographic list of companies in a specified field
- Small growing companies
- A company with international positions
- Names and addresses of corporate officers

Note which directories give information about trade publications. These offer information about companies that are doing well, job openings in specific fields, and firms that may not be listed in any other directory. Again, a simple phone call or e-mail query can also provide you with valuable information.

Other Printed Sources of Information

NEWSPAPERS

Check out all the newspapers in the geographic area where you are interested in working. Read the Help Wanted section for openings as well as for local wage and fringe benefits information. There may be a separate business section that advertises professional jobs. Read

> Want ads = only 15% of job openings.

▲ Newspapers have classified ads sections.

Even the lonely woodpecker owes his success to the fact that he uses his head.

—Joe Marcucci

everything in terms of your own job target and keep a file, but be aware that only 15 percent of job openings are listed in newspaper want ads. Therefore, note other areas of the paper, such as articles that announce business expansions, personnel changes, and new ideas. Planning commission announcements usually mention new industrial parks and the expected number of employers to be located there. Marriage announcements usually list the bride's and groom's occupations and may give you the name of an important executive of a firm that interests you. Lifestyle sections may profile leaders in the community. Gossip columns may suggest where to find trendsetters.

TRADE JOURNALS

Almost every trade and profession has at least one regularly published journal. The business section of your library should have references. A book or pamphlet on your chosen career may list names of related associations and trade journals. Your library or career center may also have software retrieval systems (see "Career Information Resources Software" later in this chapter) to access trade journal information. The following resources are useful in tracking down particular trade journals: *Ulrich's International Periodical Directory*, *The Gale Directory of Publications and Broadcast Media*, and *The Encyclopedia of Associations*. Use these trade journals to locate job ads and to familiarize yourself with the people, products, current trends, and specific vocabulary of a field.

REAL stories   Meet Jackie

Jackie, a single mother with two children, is working as manager of the gift shop in the Los Angeles Hilton Hotel. Her days are long and her pay is not enough to support herself and her children. Her child support helps, but she is always short at the end of the month. Her boss is not the most understanding woman in the world, and Jackie knows she has to make a change. Her mother tries to tell her that having a job, any job, is important in this economy, but she can't imagine staying at this job for much longer.

Jackie attended community college several years ago and completed her general education classes. She wonders how long it will take her to obtain a degree, and decides to make an appointment with a counselor. When the counselor asks Jackie what she wants to do when she receives her AA degree, Jackie can't come up with one thing. Jackie worries that the counselor might feel she is wasting his time, but instead he asks, "Why don't you take a career planning class? It will help you learn about yourself and careers that might suit you." Because the class meets on Jackie's day off, she decides to do it.

Jackie likes the class and she learns a lot about herself. From the interest inventory she takes, she learns that she likes the helping professions and she is interested in physical fitness, science, and nutrition. She also learns that she values freedom, accomplishment, and creativity, prefers working with people, and has an organized, logical mind.

When Jackie looks over the occupations that match her assessment results, she discovers physical therapist, personal trainer, and occupational therapist. Jackie does not know much about each occupation, so she uses the Career Center's resources to do some research. She begins with the Chronicle Guides and the Vocational Biographies, and she also uses EUREKA, a computerized information system. Her research gives her information on education, training, job outlook, salary, and job search techniques. Jackie also interviews people working in those fields (who happen to be referrals from her former physical education instructor) to get a sense of what the daily routine of the job is like.

After all her research, Jackie decides to study physical therapy and sets about figuring out how she is going to do it. Jackie makes a plan. First she looks over the next semester's schedule and arranges all her classes in late afternoon and evening. Then she goes to her employer and asks if she may work part time. She asks her ex-husband if he can increase his child support. Then she applies for financial aid through the college. Finally, she asks her mother if she will watch her kids in the evening so she can save money on babysitting.

With a little luck, she can survive. The first year is a struggle, but her money management is not the biggest problem. Jackie passes only 12 of the 24 units she attempts. She hadn't realized how difficult the science classes would be, and she

REAL stories *CONTINUED*

also hadn't realized how rusty her English and math skills are. Discouraged, she makes an appointment with her adviser. He is sympathetic, but he feels that Jackie needs to be realistic about her career choice and about her chances of completing her program of study and transferring to the university in the time she has planned. After much discussion, Jackie decides to give herself two additional semesters, but after the first semester, she knows even with the extra time it will be impossible.

When Jackie sees the counselor again, he says he has a possible option: The college is planning to add a Recreation Fitness Certificate Program to the curriculum. Students with the certificate will be able to work in recreation programs for children and adults, and with a higher degree they can become supervisors. The counselor tells Jackie that she can speak with the department head for more specific information. Jackie makes an appointment and discovers that the field holds many opportunities, some of which she can take advantage of right now. With this news, Jackie feels better. She decides to talk again with her counselor and make a new plan of action.

WHAT DO *YOU* THINK?

1. What strategies would you use to overcome the situation that Jackie faced?
2. Was Jackie too optimistic in the beginning? What would you have done if you faced a similar situation?
3. Was Jackie too pessimistic at the end? How would you have reacted to the counselor's suggestion?
4. Give several reasons for quitting a job before you have another one.
5. Is college always the answer to a better life? Give examples of ways that you can improve your life or your career without attending college. Identify five jobs that pay well and don't require a college degree.

MAGAZINES

The *Reader's Guide to Periodicals Literature*, available at any library in either printed or electronic form, can be used both to locate names of magazines and to find titles of informative and useful articles about any field you wish to research. Do you want to learn the latest in animation careers, the outlook for engineers in the western United States, opportunities for liberal arts graduates? It's been covered in some magazine recently! Business magazines also provide profiles of both businesses and their executive officers, which is information you might use in comparing companies.

Ask the librarian for the *Business Periodicals Index*. It accesses trade journal articles and has citations for hundreds of publications. The articles are arranged according to subject;

Sample Useful Magazines for Business Information

Black Entrepreneur	*High Technology Careers*
Bloomberg's *Business Week*	*Inc.*
Entrepreneur	*Moneywatch*
Fast Company	*Success*
Forbes	*Wall Street Journal*
Fortune	*Working Mother*

Specialized Magazines for College Students and Graduates

Black Collegian

Business World (a career magazine for college students)

Equal Opportunity Magazine

Hispanic Times Magazine

Saludos Hispanos

broad subjects are divided into more specific categories. University business/management libraries are more likely to hold publications listed in the *Business Periodicals Index*; they are less likely to be found in local libraries.

IN-HOUSE BULLETINS AND ANNOUNCEMENTS

Human resources offices in virtually every business, agency, school, and hospital post jobs as they become available. Job posting best serves the people already employed at such places; however, some of the job listings may be open to anyone.

Large corporations such as Bank of America and General Electric publish in-house job announcement newsletters monthly or quarterly. Most of these newsletters are not intended for public use but are circulated among all employees to encourage internal job mobility. The job announcements list required skills, degrees, and relevant experience. Such in-house newsletters are an excellent way to explore current needs within large companies and to learn more about the types of job skills being sought. Check the company website to see if they have a newsletter.

Career Information Resources Software

Colleges subscribe to software programs that can often be more complete and current than those found in traditional sources. Many of the software subscriptions have been upgraded to website subscriptions. Contact your library or campus career center for assistance in locating the sources described here—and for others.

SAMPLE CAREER SOFTWARE

Probably the largest resource on occupational information is the Career Information System (CIS; also known as EUREKA in California). This software provides occupational information, including job descriptions, locations for training such as vocational schools and colleges, and financial aid information, specific to the state in which it is located. Another component of CIS, called QUEST, helps users identify the work characteristics that are common to certain occupations. A second program, SIGI 3 (System of Interactive Guidance and Information), is designed to clarify your values and to match your values, interests, and skills with occupations. A third program, GIS (Guidance Information System), acts as a source of national occupational information. The program DISCOVER identifies career sources and includes vital information on decision making.

A few other online subscriptions found in college career centers include Bridges, CareerCruising, CareerLocker, CHOICES, and GoldenPersonality. Most of these programs offer software to help students explore their personality and investigate occupations related to the students' interests. Often this software includes a file with information on all two- and four-year colleges in the United States, which can assist students in choosing a school, preparing for admission, and planning a course schedule.

Many college career planning and placement offices have online resources that provide employment information about some of the largest companies in the United States. Wetfeet.com provides company profiles in its "Career Research" section; Fortune.com has a company profiles section including descriptive information on the "Fortune 500," "Small Business 100," and 100 fastest-growing companies. Finally, online services such as America Online, Yahoo, Google, and MSN have company/job information on their business/financial sections and career sections. For more information, see the feature called "Job Market Research Sites" listed in the next section and see "Selected Online Employment Databases" in Chapter 9.

Exercise 7.3 requires that you investigate resources using the local library, college library, and a local newspaper.

EXERCISE 7.3 Job Research

1. Which directories could be most helpful to you now, and what do you need to know? Where are these directories found?

    _____
    _____
    _____

2. What are the names of three trade journals related to your field of interest? Where are they found?

    a. _____
    b. _____
    c. _____

3. What are two of the current trends reflected in these journals?

    _____
    _____

4. List one professional association related to your field with the following contact information:

    EXAMPLE:

    American Society of Women Accountants (ASWA)   Your field: _____

    Local contact: Joan Smith   Association: _____

    phone: 805–555–1213   Contact: _____

    Meeting time & location: 3ʳᵈ Thursday of each
    month, 7 P.M. (dinner), Colonial House, Ojai   Meeting: _____

5. Study a local daily newspaper for three weeks, and make a folder of articles that relate to your field of interest. (Include want ads, feature articles, meetings, networking groups, and names of executives in your field who were mentioned anywhere in the paper.)

The Internet

The Internet offers immediate access to unlimited sources for both job descriptions and company information. If you don't own a computer or haven't subscribed to an Internet service provider, access is possible through libraries, colleges, universities, quick-print centers, and even some coffeehouses.

LIBRARY RESOURCE CENTERS

Librarians, as information specialists, may be available to help you conduct your search and tro use the library's information-retrieval tools to access indexes, abstracts, and (in some cases) the full text of thousands of newspapers, magazines, and journals. The library's Internet connections are significantly faster than the typical online service, allowing users to search through hundreds of thousands of references very fast.

Libraries subscribe to powerful research index services such as Nexus, Dialog, and Infotrac and have access to databases containing hundreds of periodicals. Library Internet access can simplify the search for information and articles. (It may be possible to retrieve your college library documents at home or in the office, if your school has such an arrangement.)

▲ With laptops and wireless access, students today have unlimited access to research tools.

TIPS FROM THE PROS

If you have narrowed your interests to one or two majors, looking at a few college career centers' websites should provide you with a wide variety of jobs to start researching now.

Go to "What Can I Do With A Major In…" heading in **http://uncw.edu/stuaff/career/majors/** for finding jobs related to majors, or use other college career centers' websites found in your Weblinks.

CAREER SITES

To explore careers and the job market, online resources are available for every phase of the job search: identifying opportunities, researching specific industries and companies, posting resumes online, and making contacts with potential employers.

Blogs and podcasts. Blogs range in scope from individual diaries to arms of political campaigns, media outlets, special interests, and corporations insider information. They range in scale from the writings of one occasional author to the collaboration of a large community of writers. When using blogs, remember that they may be only one person's view or opinion. Therefore, you need to use multiple research sources to verify that what you learned on a blog is accurate.

You might be drawn to YouTube for short features about careers. Additionally, you may go to iTunes to download career or course podcasts. These podcasts can also be found on job boards, company career sites, as well as YouTube.com.

Finally, try Googling "JobsinPods" or go to YouTube and search for JobsinPods. These sites are blogs that are linked to many sites; you are bound to find one you like; just try a few out.

The following are two examples of "career blogs":

- *Science Magazine:* **http://nextwave.sciencemag.org**. Go to Career Development section or use the Search box to type in "Career Blog."
- *Monster's Career Center:* **http://monster.typepad.com**—what real people think about their jobs as well as referrals to experts' advice.

Websites. A few sample unique job blogs are located at the following websites:

- *Librarians:* **http://libraryjobpostings.org**
- *Videogame jobs:* **Gamasutra.com and Gamesindustry.biz**
- *Museum-related jobs:* **http://aam-us.org and MuseumJobs.com**
- *Environmental careers:* **ecojobs.com**
- *Affirmative action:* **www.aar-eeo.com**
- *Biotech, health care, and pharmaceuticals:* **MedZilla.com**
- *Government:* America's Job Bank (**www.careeronestop.org/**)
- *Students:* **www.studentjobs.gov** (if you type **studentjobs.com** you will get Canadian job information)

> Find out what you like doing best and get someone to pay you for doing it.
>
> —*Katherine Whitehorn*

EXHIBIT 7.4 STEM Associations Promoting Diversity

The following is a sampling of organizations that support underrepresented minorities; a full list is available on the Cornerstone association page (**www.careercornerstone.org/assoc.htm**):

- American Indian Science and Engineering Society
- Association for Women in Science
- Be an Actuary—Minority Site
- Caucus for Women in Statistics

EXHIBIT 7.4 *CONTINUED*

- Minority Scientists Network
- National Association for Blacks in Bio
- National Organization of Black Chemists and Chemical Engineers
- National Society of Black Engineers
- National Society of Black Physicists
- National Society of Hispanic Physicists
- National Society of Professional Engineers
- Society for the Advancement of Chicanos and Native Americans in Science (SACNAS)
- Society of Hispanic Professional Engineers
- Society of Mexican American Engineers and Scientists
- Society of Women Engineers
- Vietnamese Association for Computing, Engineering Technology, and Science

Source: **www.careercornerstone.org/diversity.htm**.

Job Market Research Sites

To begin your online search, consider some of the websites listed here as well as the U.S. Department of Labor website mentioned previously:

About: www.about.com. Its section titled "Jobs & Careers" provides helpful information on general job hunting and topics related to starting a business. Included is advice on developing effective resumes and cover letters.

Black Voices: www.blackvoices.com. This site includes job search and many other helpful features for African Americans. Another helpful site is **www.blackcollegian.com**, where many of the links lead to discussions of barriers to employment. This site also includes information about the best companies for African Americans.

Careerbuilder: www.careerbuilder.com. Classified ads from major newspapers can be found here. CareerBuilder also includes good career articles; many other websites (such as MSN and AOL) partner with Careerbuilder.

Glassdoor: www.glassdoor.com. This is a free career community that provides an inside look at jobs and companies. The information comes from current and former employees, interview candidates, and the companies themselves. Included are more than a million salaries, company reviews, interview questions, and office photos.

Hire the Deaf Network: www.hiredeaf.com. This is the number-one site for individuals who are hearing impaired to find jobs.

Hispanic Business: www.hispanicbusiness.com. This site offers up-to-date stories, links to business-related articles, and information about the top-500 Hispanic-owned companies in the United States.

Monster Board: www.monster.com. This is one of the largest sites on the Web, with an excellent career center. Its Resources section has information for new job seekers, career changers, and people making military transitions. Additionally, you can search for information on jobs, industries, franchises, salary statistics, resume writing, and interview techniques. Monster is also known as the largest database for job listings.

Quintessential Careers: www.quintcareers.com. This site offers thousands of pages of career tools to help you with your search, including expert advice, career articles, and thousands of "best" job sites on the Web. This site is very user-friendly.

Wetfeet: www.wetfeet.com. This popular website offers a wide range of job listings. Subscribe to the newsletter for weekly job-finding tips and interesting and different jobs. This website offers resources, including company research, stress management, personal finance, internship information, resume tips, and interview strategies. Especially useful at this stage in your exploration is the section titled "Career Research."

Industry searches. If you are interested in financial services such as investment banking and retail banking, use the following search method: In your browser's search box, type "financial services." Narrow your search by adding keywords, such as "banks," to the search box. From the results of this search you can investigate specific companies. To learn more about the banking business, visit several banking sites on the Web and return periodically to follow developments in each business. Firms often announce new departments, services, and products first on the web.

Trade journals online. Earlier in the chapter, we mentioned industry trade journals. Usually, these journals have websites. For example, *Advertising Age* is located at **www.adage .com**. Journals such as this provide the latest information about trends in an industry. You may be able to add your name to an e-mail list, which will allow you to receive information about current industry issues. Most magazines and trade journals print their e-mail and website addresses in the front of the publication. One website, **www.bizjournals.com**, allows you to search for articles from more than 40 local business journals across the United States. Also try **www.freetrademagazinesource.com**. Finally, don't forget to use a business magazine such as *Fortune* (**www.fortune.com**) that provides links to many businesses.

Be sure to check with your local library, college career center, and college career adviser to explore additional resources that can help you obtain information to aid in your career planning. *The sources mentioned in this chapter are all free resources, so don't be misled by advertisements on the Web!*

EXERCISE your options

Successful career planning requires flexibility. Technological advances, outsourcing, and a global economy can cause some careers to shrink in size or become obsolete. Strategic planning includes preparing to qualify for two or more closely related careers that require similar education, training, general capabilities, and skill sets. What are two related careers that you might equally enjoy and be qualified for, given the research you have done?

Summary

By completing this chapter you now have resources for broadening your list of possible careers and researching occupational information. You have learned how to use printed and online resources to further clarify your career choices. You now have developed critical thinking skills to analyze information about specific occupations and career-related opportunities using library or career center materials and online sources. Now you may confirm or revise your first impressions about your top career choices.

PURPOSE OF EXERCISES

The following exercises will help you digest the contents of this chapter. You can complete them by using your computer, local library, or college career center to explore some of the resources mentioned in this chapter. Exercise 7.1, Guided Fantasy, helped you visualize a future day in your worklife. Exercise 7.2 asked you earlier in the chapter to list 10 tempting jobs. From Exercise 7.3, you investigated resources using the local library, college library, and local newspaper. In Exercise 7.4, you will be asked to write about a job based on your interests. In Exercise 7.5, you will list five favorite jobs that people you know currently hold. Exercise 7.6 asks that you learn what kinds of information and assistance are available from your college career center, local state employment office, and other employment offices. Exercise 7.7 gives you a format for gathering facts about three jobs.

Exercise 7.8, Guided Fantasy Revisited, was used at the beginning of the chapter (see Exercise 7.1) and can be used at the end of the chapter to incorporate some of your research into your visualizations. Exercise 7.9, **WWWebwise**, is an online research exercise that will reinforce the learnings in this chapter. And finally, **Reinforce Your Learning Outcomes**, will strengthen your awareness of what you have learned that you can use in your career research.

EXERCISE

7.4   I'd Do This Even If I Didn't Get Paid

Pretend that you do not have to work for a living but instead can do whatever you enjoy all day. Write some ideas in the space provided. When you are finished, identify a likely job title for your activities and the relevant industry. For example, if you thought you would enjoy spending your time painting, you might give *portrait artist* or *graphic artist* as your job title and *art* as your industry.

_____

_____

_____

_____

EXERCISE

7.5   The Grass Is Always Greener

In the space provided, write the names of five friends or family members who hold jobs that interest you. Next to each name, write a key phrase to explain what interests you about the job. Prioritize the jobs and industries you find interesting.

1. _____
2. _____
3. _____
4. _____
5. _____

EXERCISE

7.6   Local and Internet Resources

1. Investigate local career and placement centers. Ask if they place people in your field or if they can refer you to others who do.

2. Visit the state employment office as well as private employment or temporary agencies to find out how they place people and how long it may take to get a job.

3. Find a local job opportunity on the Internet.

4. As you collect information, create a folder on your computer titled "Research." In this folder, create subfolders entitled "Associations/Conferences," "Company Profiles," "Job Search Strategy," "Industry Specific," "Labor Market Information," and "New Articles." Keep the information you gather organized in these folders.

EXERCISE

7.7 Gathering the Facts

Following the format provided, research three jobs in a library or career center. You may select either three different jobs (e.g., public relations specialist, social worker, manager), three jobs that are related (e.g., lawyer, paralegal, legal secretary), or three that represent the same field but vary in the nature of the work (e.g., marketing executive, graphic artist, display assistant).

Once you identify job titles of interest to you, gather the following information for each one:

Title of career: _____

Salary: _____

Hours: _____

Benefits: _____

Outlook (whether there will be jobs in the future): _____

_____

Educational requirements—minimum training necessary: _____

_____

If college is necessary, what types of programs are available locally? _____

_____

_____

Schools or colleges offering the training: _____

_____

Personal requirements: _____

_____

_____

Physical demands: _____

_____

Work description (attach a copy of the O*NET description): _____

Working conditions: _____

_____

Location: _____

_____

Opportunities for advancement: _____

_____

Related occupations with the following educational requirements:

No additional training needed: _____

Some college needed: _____

B.A. or B.S. degree needed: _____

Other training (e.g., master's degree or special license): _____

_____

Sources (may include resources in the career center and names of local people working in this field; include Internet addresses where you might find related information):

_____

_____

EXERCISE 7.7 *CONTINUED*

After researching the specifics, are you still interested? How well does this occupation mesh with your vision of a lifestyle?

_____

_____

_____

EXERCISE

7.8 Guided Fantasy Revisited

If, after reading about three different careers, you are still confused about how to choose one, try Exercise 7.1, Guided Fantasy, found at the beginning of this chapter.

Visualize yourself in each career you are considering. Which one feels most comfortable, most consistent with who you are? Has your vision changed since you first tried visualizing an ideal career? Consider sharing some of your guided fantasy with a classmate and significant others in your life.

_____

_____

EXERCISE

7.9 WWWebwise

Go to **http://online.onetcenter.org/**. Click on "Find Occupations." Scroll down to "High Growth Industries."

Choose one industry to explore: _____

List three jobs that interest you in this industry:

_____

_____

_____

What did you learn by using this website?_____

_____

_____

_____

(*Note:* Please be aware that websites can change without notice. If a link does not work, find a similar site to complete the activity.)

REINFORCING YOUR LEARNING OUTCOMES

Review and Rate Your Chapter Outcomes. Indicate in the right-hand column how well you do the following items (from 1 = very well, to 5 = not at all). If you rated yourself 4 or 5, review the material on the pages in parentheses to ensure your career success.

How Well Can You Do the Following?

- Brainstorm possible career options based on information you learned about your attitudes, beliefs, interests, personality, and skills. (pp. 136–137)   1 2 3 4 5

- Adopt a strategy to approach occupational research that will enhance your efficiency and effectiveness. (pp. 137–140)   1 2 3 4 5

- Research printed and online sources of information to use in further clarifying your career choices. (pp. 141–152)   1 2 3 4 5

- Develop your critical thinking skills to analyze information about specific occupations and career-related opportunities using library materials and online resources. (pp. 149–152)   1 2 3 4 5

- Confirm or revise your first impressions about your top career choices. (pp. 151–154)   1 2 3 4 5

Go to the Career Fitness Portfolio at the end of the book and complete this chapter summary to build and record your personal Career Fitness Portfolio.

Additional Opportunity: Your instructor may choose to assign the Career Fitness Portfolio for in class or online completion. If so, they will provide the handout or link for you to access.

Developing Your Decision Making

Strategize Your Game Plan

Career decisions are the Olympic trials of your career fitness program. They give you an opportunity to integrate and test out all the components of your career fitness program—your attitudes, values, skills, interests, and biases. For most of us, it is safe to assume that whatever decisions are made are the best, given the information, circumstances, and feelings of the moment. However, you can improve your decision-making performance by examining some of the assumptions and strategies that other people have used in the decision-making process. This chapter reviews decision-making strategies that are potentially limiting and those that are potentially empowering and success oriented. The primary focus of this chapter is to describe an effective decision-making model that involves setting realistic goals with specific time frames. They must be realistic for you, and you must affirm that you deserve and are capable of reaching these goals.

Complete the exercises as you read through this chapter. Doing so will help you test and develop your skill in using various aspects of the decision-making model as they are presented.

> Shoot for the moon. Even if you miss it, you'll land among the stars.
>
> —*Les Brown*

What Is Decision Making?

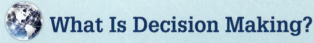

Decision making is the process of identifying and the selecting alternatives based largely on the preferences of the decision maker. There are always choices to be considered and your decision is one that best fits your goals, lifestyle, values, and past experiences.

Decisions are evaluated by their probability of success or effectiveness. You are constantly making decisions. Some are as mundane as selecting a movie or picking out a new pair of shoes. Others—like choosing a career, selecting a life partner, or deciding whether to have children—have much greater consequence.

Overcoming Barriers to Decision Making

Take time right now to think about recent decisions you have made. Even small decisions like when to get up, whether or not to exercise, what television programs to watch, what to eat, who to choose as friends and how to spend your free time count.
Write down at least five decisions you made *this week*:

1. _____
2. _____
3. _____
4. _____
5. _____

Essentially, your attitude shapes your behavior and your ability to make wise decisions. Attitudes are gut-level feelings and thoughts that guide our decision making. If you are aware of your attitudes and habits, you can enhance your daily effectiveness. If you believe you can, you can! And conversely, if you have a negative attitude, it will have an effect on your outcomes. Many people make decisions with limited knowledge or little sense of personal responsibility. They function on automatic pilot without considering the consequences. This stance may seem to simplify or accelerate the decision-making process but the results are often less than optimal. As you read the following sections, think about the process you followed in making the decisions you listed above.

Decision-Making Styles

The box below titled "Decision Making Styles" describes some of the ways people go about making decisions. Read it now, and then read "Meet Art" in the "Real Stories" feature on page 160. Try to determine what decision-making styles Art used.

Decision-Making Styles

Planning: "Weighing the facts." Considering values, objectives, necessary information, alternatives, and consequences; a rational approach with a balance between thinking and feeling.

Impulsive: "Don't look before you leap." Little thought or examination; taking the first available alternative.

Intuitive: "It feels right." Automatic, preconscious choice based on inner harmony.

Compliant: "Anything you say." Nonassertive; letting someone else decide; following someone else's plans.

Delaying: "Cross that bridge later." Procrastination, avoidance, hoping someone or something will happen to avoid making a decision, postponing thought and action.

Fatalistic: "It's all in the cards." What will be will be; letting the environment decide; leaving it up to fate.

Agonizing: "What if?" Worrying that a decision will be the wrong one; getting lost in all the data; overwhelmed by analyzing alternatives.

Paralytic: "Can't face up to it." One step further than "what if"—complete indecision and fear; accepting responsibility but being unable to act on it.

Defaulting: "Playing it safe." Choosing the alternative with the lowest level of risk.

We often use a combination of styles that can further complicate the decision-making process.

WHAT ABOUT YOU?

1. Which of these approaches to decision making do you use most and least often?
2. Which would you like to use more often? Which would you like to avoid? Why?
3. Consider a current decision in progress (e.g., one you wrote at the beginning of this chapter). Think it through using several of these approaches. Which prove to be most useful?

Choosing a career is a *life development process*. At various points during the process, different issues must be decided. Thus, planning (the first of the styles listed) is the key to reaching your goals. It implies gaining control of your life. Typically, the planning and intuitive styles are the most effective. The others contain a hint of fear: fear of failure, fear of imperfection, fear of rejection, fear of ridicule. Such fears are based on "internal factors" related to your attitudes and self-esteem.

When you feel stuck or unable to make a decision, try asking yourself the following questions:

1. What are my assumptions (attitudes) affecting my decisions?
2. What are my feelings regarding these decisions?
3. Why am I clinging to behavior that prevents me from making this decision?
4. What further information do I need in order to generate alternatives?

Complete Exercise 8.1 to explore factors that affect your current or future decisions.

EXERCISE

8.1 Factors Adversely Affecting Decisions

In this exercise you will investigate factors that may unfavorably influence decision making and determine whether any patterns are evident. On the list of five decisions you made on page 158, select your three most significant decisions. Then, using the chart that follows, indicate which of the factors influenced you in making each decision and to what extent they were present. To do this, use an X to represent decision 1, a Y for decision 2, and a Z for decision 3.

External Factors	Slightly Present	Moderately Present	Strongly Present
1. Family expectations			
2. Family responsibilities			
3. Cultural stereotypes			
4. Male/female stereotypes			
5. Survival needs			
6. Other (specify)			
Internal Factors	Slightly Present	Moderately Present	Strongly Present
1. Lack of self-confidence			
2. Fear of change			
3. Fear of making a wrong decision			
4. Fear of failure			
5. Fear of ridicule			
6. Other (specify)			

After filling in the chart, look for patterns:

1. Do you experience more internal or external obstacles when making decisions?

_____

_____

2. If a particular factor is "strongly present" only once, but another factor is "moderately present" in two or possibly all three of your decisions, which of the two factors do you think is more significant in affecting your decision making? Will this insight help you make a better decision?

_____

_____

What Are My Assumptions? Many people assume that if they could only make the one right decision about the matter at hand, everything else would fall into place. In fact, most decisions do not have such power over your life. Decisions are not typically black and white in terms of their consequences; rather, they simply move you in one direction or another. Decisions open up some options and close off others. If you assume that most decisions can be changed or altered—that most decisions do not, in fact, signify life or death—then you will not be so hesitant to make a decision, act on it, assess the implications as they occur, and make adjustments (or new decisions) as necessary.

What Are My Feelings? Some people create unnecessary stress about making decisions because they give themselves an either/or ultimatum. Neither option really feels right, but they panic and make impulsive decisions to ease the anxiety. You can become paralyzed without making any choice, allowing circumstances to decide an issue. When you are feeling pressured or paralyzed about making a decision, step back and take several deep breaths, and then begin to generate additional alternatives. A friend, counselor, or skilled listener can often help with this process. As you gain more information about your options, you will realize which decision is best for you. Other people cry over spilled milk; in other words, they think back over past decisions and lament not having decided differently. This wastes time and energy and can be destructive to the self-image. When you begin to feel self-doubt or regret about past decisions, remind yourself that you made the best decision you could, given the time, circumstances, and information available.

Why Am I Clinging to This Behavior? Acknowledging that you are causing this indecisiveness may generate a different point of view. For example, sometimes people cling to old nonproductive behaviors because they are the safe ways to act; they don't have to deal with the unknown or the possibility of making mistakes or taking risks. It is important to recognize when the old, comfortable ways of doing things no longer provide the payoffs they once did.

REAL stories   Meet Art

Art was born and raised in California. When he was a child he and his family loved to hike in the mountains, surf, and scuba dive. After graduating from high school, he attended state college, where he earned a degree in graphic design. After Art had spent several fruitless months' job hunting, a friend, Frank, from Ohio told him that he and his father were starting a new company, and they felt Art would fit right in. The company was going to specialize in designing packaging for educational materials and they needed someone to help with sales and develop new design concepts.

Art was very excited until he learned that they needed start-up money and wanted Art to put in a significant amount. They said that the cost of living in Ohio was less than in California, so Art could find affordable housing and insurance once he moved. Frank also promised that Art's investment would be repaid within the first two years. Art had a trust account from his grandmother that he was planning to use to return to school and get his master's degree. Without telling anyone, Art withdrew the money. The business did fairly well

the first year, and Art began to make a life in Ohio. He met a girl and soon they were married. Joan was in her last year of nursing school, working part time in a nursing home, and she had excellent prospects of work after she graduated.

Six months later, Art's friend declared bankruptcy. Depressed and embarrassed, Art didn't know what to do. The job market in Ohio was not strong in Art's field, so Art and Joan decided that Art would go back to California and Joan would finish nursing school and then join him.

With only phone calls and e-mails, Joan and Art found their relationship was in trouble. Art found work, but it was not what he wanted to do and the money was barely enough to support one person. Joan graduated and was offered a good job in Ohio. She encouraged Art to come back, but he knew he could not make a good living there and he didn't want Joan to be the primary wage earner. He tried to get Joan to come to California, but she felt comfortable in Ohio and was reluctant to make the move. After three months, Joan told Art that she didn't think the marriage was going to survive and she filed for divorce.

REAL stories *CONTINUED*

WHAT DO *YOU* THINK?

1. How would you evaluate Art's decision-making skills? What strategies did he use? What would you have done differently if you were Art?

2. How would you evaluate Joan's response to Art's request to move to California?

3. What assumptions did Art and Joan make in choosing to pursue careers in different geographic areas? Were there any issues they could have discussed before making their decision?

4. If you were Art, what research would you have done before you took the job in Ohio?

5. What strategies or resources could Joan and Art have used to save their marriage?

6. Would you use your savings on a new venture? Why or why not?

Everyone, to some degree, is a risk taker. Since there are always some unknowns to assess, risk is an essential element of the decision-making process. What has been your greatest risk? In its most basic sense, risk taking means moving from the safe and familiar to the unknown and scary. Most of us are fairly conservative risk takers in that we want the odds to be at least 50–50 before we jump in. Yet millions of people play the lottery, start businesses, and get married even when the odds are clearly not in their favor. Why? Because regardless of the probability of success (the odds), people sometimes take risks based on the *desirability* of the successful outcome.

In a lottery, the probabilities are a million to one against winning, yet people continue to gamble because of the high desirability of the positive outcome of winning. You are in the best position to take a calculated risk when you assess both the probability and desirability of an outcome and weigh it against other possible outcomes. Failure to consider outcomes in this fashion is the most common cause of unsuccessful risk taking. For example, many people are afraid to take the risk of changing their career direction. They immediately think of the worst possible outcome: "I'll fail" or "I will never find another job if I quit this one." They don't ask themselves how probable or desirable the best possible outcome would be. In many cases, the probability of their worries actually materializing (i.e., the likelihood of a highly negative outcome) is very low.

What Further Information Do I Need in Order to Generate Alternatives? Many people paralyze themselves with this "worst possible consequence" thinking, decide not to take the risk, and consequently feel trapped. What they haven't done is generate other possible outcomes that are more probable and more desirable. What are some of these? For the example just cited, there could be a new job that is more energizing and financially rewarding, a new career with an opportunity to grow and develop, or a chance to get retraining. The probability and desirability of these outcomes are positive; therefore the decision seems less risky. However, many people still miss opportunities because they fail to generate and assess all possible outcomes. This process often needs the assistance of another person who can help identify negative or limiting thinking, as well as some realistic and positive outcomes. Risk involves being committed to your decisions, but staying flexible in your approach, so, when choosing a college major, you might consider not only the ones listed in the catalog, but designing your own course of study (often called an individualized major.)

> You can't "try" to do things. You simply "must" do things.
>
> —*Ray Bradbury*

Conditions for Change

Decisions provide an opportunity to experience life in new ways, to learn and find out who you are and what you would like to do. Each path is filled with opportunities. Just imagine: By making good decisions, renewal and growth are within your reach. By engaging in affirming self-talk, positive change is possible.

It has been said that three conditions must be present to trigger change. *First, you must be dissatisfied with what is; second, you much have a concept of what would be better; and last, you must believe that there is a way to get there.* This whole process rests on the premise that the benefits of the change outweigh the costs of making the change. Affirmations help you believe that change is possible. The following questions relate to obstacles that may be interfering with the achievement of your desires:

- How much determination do you really have if your preferred job is not readily available? How willing are you to take a reduced salary, move to a new location, or consider a new career path?
- What identity would be threatened by achieving your goal? For example, would a better job make you too independent or enable you to earn more than your mate? Would it demand more time, giving you less time as mother, husband, or partner?
- Do you secretly feel you don't deserve to attain your desires?
- Are you proving to anyone else that you can change?
- Is the work, concentration, and time worth it to you?
- Are you following all the decision-making steps suggested?
- Is it what you really want?

A Decision-Making Model

Exhibit 8.1 offers a model for making informed decisions. The five steps necessary to make an informed and desirable decision are *defining your goal, assessing your alternatives, gathering information, assessing the consequences,* and *establishing your plan of action or the steps needed to achieve your goal.* Read through Exhibit 8.1 now.

EXHIBIT 8.1   Choice, Not Chance: Decisions Are in Our Power

Rational decision making uses the talents of the left brain, which is analytical and logical and deals with deductive thinking. It ideally follows the sequential, step-by-step procedure described here. Note that the arrows go in both directions to allow for new information and insights along the way.

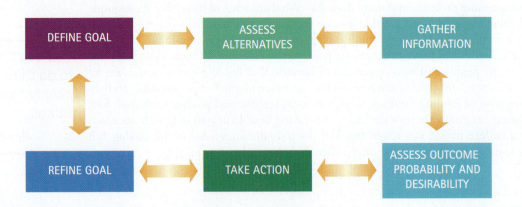

1. **Define your goal or objective.**
   - Can you change part of the problem into a definite goal?
   - What do you want to accomplish by what date?
   - Can you state your objective now?

EXHIBIT 8.1 *CONTINUED*

2. Assess the alternatives.
   - What are your alternatives or options?
   - Are your alternative choices consistent with your important values?
   - Can you summarize your important values in writing?
   - What is a reasonable amount of time in which to accomplish your alternatives?
3. Gather information.
   - What do you know about your alternatives?
   - What assumptions are you making that you should check out?
   - What more do you need to know about your alternatives?
   - What sources will help you gather more information about your alternatives?
   - What sources will help you discover further alternatives?
4. Assess the outcomes or consequences.
   - Probability:
     What is the probability of the success of each alternative?
     Are your highest values part of each alternative?
   - Desirability:
     Can you eliminate the least desirable alternatives first?
     When you consider the best possible alternative, how much do you want it?
     What are you willing to give up in order to get what you want?
5. Establish a plan of action.
   - Weighing everything you now know about your decision, what is your plan of action?
   - What dates will you start and complete your plan of action?
   - Does your plan of action state a clear objective?
   - Does your plan of action specify the steps necessary to achieve its objective?
   - Does your plan of action specify the conditions necessary to achieve its objective?

Until you start your plan of action, you haven't really made a decision. So start now. Make systematic decision making an adventure and a habit!

 # Rational/Linear Decision Making

Planning is also known as the rational, or linear, approach to decision making. Decisions involve prediction. Prediction involves uncertainty. And uncertainty makes most people uncomfortable. Planning is one approach that decreases the amount of uncertainty and discomfort, and increases your chances of achieving your designated goals. You reduce the degree of uncertainty by gathering more data. The more informed you are, the better able you are to make a satisfying decision. It is critical to consider the sources before acting on the information. It is easy to access data on the Internet; it is harder to determine its validity. It is easy to listen to others' opinions; it is harder to decide whom to believe. As you make decisions and evaluate the outcomes, you will develop confidence in your own ability to assess your data sources. As part of your fact finding, consult those who will be affected by, or may have to help implement your decisions. Input from others helps supply you with information in making a decision and often provides the support necessary in the implementation phase because others are part of the decision-making process. Since it is rarely possible to gather all of the facts, the lack of complete information must not paralyze your decision. As part of your data collection, consider your feelings, hunches, and intuition. Many decisions must ultimately rely on, or be influenced by, intuition because of the uncertainty involved in any situation.

Intuitive Decision Making

Most people use intuition as *part* of their decision-making process. Some people rely *primarily* on their intuition. Intuitive decision makers lean toward the direction that feels right. They use their right brain, which thrives on imagination and creativity and adapts to change spontaneously. These individuals feel confined when asked to write out a step-by-step process. When faced with career planning and a job search, they tend to engage in research until they have several alternatives that they believe would satisfy them equally. They like to get a feel for the overall global picture and then decide where they fit in. Once they have researched several options, talked to people in the field, and walked around the work environment, they tend to know if it's right for them. Call it intuition or a hunch, but it is based on the cumulative insight that fits their personality. Intuitive decision makers are most apt to say they were lucky in finding the right job, the right major, or the right college. However, their luck is actually "preparation meeting opportunity." Intuitive decision makers are highly adept at finding opportunities. They are familiar with their values, interests, skills, and personalities as they explore careers—this is why they will often say that the decision "feels right."

Sometimes, the best approach for the intuitive decision maker is to fantasize and describe an ideal occupation or to give examples of people who have appealing careers. Intuitive people tend to be able to fantasize, daydream, and create verbal or written pictures of what they think is appealing. A collage of images glued to poster board depicting elements of a career may be as useful as the written action plan created by a rational decision maker. Intuitive decision making works for some people as well as a logical, step-by-step approach works for others. But, in fact, upon reflection, both modalities are often involved in the most satisfying decisions.

FACTS & FIGURES

Decision Types

Personality/temperament studies have estimated that up to 75 percent of the population prefer and use the rational decision-making approach. These studies also suggest, therefore, that 25 percent of the population prefer to use the strategy known as intuitive. Your approach may also include aspects of negative thinking or procrastination previously discussed in this chapter. As you identify your style of decision making and your level of risk taking, it may be helpful to seek the assistance of a career counselor to help you clarify or move toward a desirable outcome.

WHAT DO *YOU* THINK?

1. If you are intuitive, do you feel that many people do not understand your decision-making style?

2. If you are intuitive, what is your biggest challenge or concern when making a decision?

3. If you feel confined when asked to write a step-by-step answer to questions in this book, what would be your alternative method to show that you understand the information you are reading?

4. If you are a rational thinker, what is your biggest challenge in making a decision?

5. If you are a rational thinker, do you prefer to make a decision and get it done, or do you find yourself procrastinating by thinking about everything over and over again?

SETTING YOUR GOALS AND OBJECTIVES

Your goals and objectives are the road signs that lead you to what you want to attain in life. Thus, it is important that a goal be distinguished from an objective.

Goals are broad statements of purpose. They also target the desired outcome, are specific, and are long range or short term. Goals refer to an ongoing process, a challenge that is meant to stretch your limits.

Objectives are the specific and practical steps used to accomplish goals. They are short-term, bite-sized steps. They are also visible and measurable signposts that indicate where you are in relation to reaching a goal. Objectives include a statement of intent, and what you are going to do. This helps you to be accountable and serves as a yardstick by which you can measure the results of your progress.

If your goal is to learn more about a career in the teaching profession, it will take a clear set of objectives to move ahead. If you want to stop smoking, lose weight, or find a job, these goals also require clear objectives to achieve the desired results.

The statement, "I want to learn to play the piano" is a goal. It may seem clear, but actually the statement lacks the detail to be more than just on your "wish list." It will take a series of clear objectives to accomplish, or even to begin the process of learning how to play the piano. A clear objective includes a statement of the action, conditions, and amount of time or effort—the more specific, the better. Here are some clear objectives related to this goal: "I will research piano teachers in a 5-mile radius of my home by next Friday." "I will check out recommendations and narrow down my choice by the following Tuesday." "I will attend a weekly one-hour piano class to begin at 6 P.M. on Wednesdays at Clara Smith's studio." "I will practice the piano one hour each day before dinner."

If you have trouble defining your goals, try listing the dissatisfactions and issues that capture your attention and spark your passion. Now ask yourself what you can do about them. In doing so, you have just identified some goals. For example, you may have determined that you are not currently working in a field that supports your values, interests, attitudes, and skills. The goal would be to find a career that is a better fit with your talents.

A career that meshes with your values, interests, attitudes, and skills but requires five or more years of training can be considered your long-range career goal. The entry-level jobs that can prepare you for this career can be considered your short-term career goals. Becoming a physical therapist would be a long-range career goal; becoming a physical therapy assistant or personal trainer would be the short-term goal.

Four points should be remembered in setting goals and objectives. First, ***consider what you are willing to give up*** to get what you want. When most people make career changes, life in general changes for them. You may need to give up free time to take special courses. You may need to take a cut in pay (temporarily or permanently) to obtain better fringe benefits, security, and a potential chance for growth in another field. Or you may need to give up being the expert and become the new kid on the block and need to prove yourself again as a competent worker.

Second, ***give yourself a realistic time line*** to reach your goal. If you've incorporated bite-sized steps (objectives) into your time line, you are more likely to achieve your goals. A time line is an effective way of listing in chronological order all the objectives needed to accomplish your goal.

Once you've developed a time line, it's a good idea to show it to a friend or counselor and to sign and date it as if it were a contract. In actuality, this is a contract with yourself. At best, you will achieve your goals; at worst, you will need to review and alter the time line or change your goal.

Third, ***set your goals high***. Of course, the goal must be realistic enough to be achievable. Remind yourself that you are deserving and capable; if your initial steps are specific, clear, and bite-sized, you will achieve them. The example provided in the "Success Strategies" box titled *Sample Goal and Objectives* illustrates that each objective must have importance in itself and must help lead to the overall (larger) goal.

Finally, the fourth point about setting goals is simple and significant: ***Reward yourself after completing each objective and after reaching each goal.*** Some say that the mere accomplishment of the goal should be reward enough. However, most of us tend to be more motivated toward success when we have both internal and external reward systems. The

SUCCESS *strategies*   Sample Goal and Objectives

Goal

To explore an alternative career to teaching by July of this year.

Objectives

1. By February 1st: I will start reading *The Career Fitness Program*.
2. By March 1st: I will begin work on each chapter exercise to advance my personal understanding and career awareness. By May, I will complete all exercises.

3. By April 1st: I will determine the strategies I will need to identify three jobs that use my talents.
4. By May 1st: I will attend a job search workshop at the college.
5. By June 1st: I will research three jobs by reading about them in the career center or library and by using the Internet to identify three or more people working in those jobs locally.
6. By July 1st: I will visit three of those people at their jobs and conduct informational interviews with them.

internal reward is the feeling of success; the external reward is something outside of ourselves (e.g., crossing the objective off the checklist, a grade on a paper, recognition from a group of friends, dinner at a special place, or splurging on those athletic shoes you wanted). How do you reward yourself when you attain an objective or reach a goal?

SUCCESS *strategies*   Time Management Strategies

1. Plan and set priorities each day.
2. Prioritize specific tasks.
3. Eliminate unnecessary work or distractions.
4. Have confidence in your judgment.
5. Work on your concentration.
6. Listen actively.
7. Focus on the present.

8. Accept the help of others.
9. Set firm deadlines.
10. Schedule relaxation time.
11. Build on successes.
12. Do something; get started!
13. Ask: What is the best use of my time now?

One way to jump-start your success is to hone your time management skills. Refer to the "Success Strategies" feature, *Time Management Strategies*, for hints on how to be more successful. Many recent high school graduates and reentry students face new unstructured situations in college and need to schedule their time strategically to allow for class attendance, study, work, leisure, and other responsibilities.

At this point, complete Exercises 8.2 through 8.6. Exercise 8.2 will help you identify and analyze three decisions. Exercises 8.3 through 8.6 will help you prioritize and evaluate decisions.

TIPS FROM THE PROS

People who reach their goals know how to manage their time. Notice how some of the busiest and most successful people always seem to have time. In fact, they make time because of their well-developed time management skills.

EXERCISE

8.2   Recent Decisions

List three significant decisions that you have made in the *past year*.

1. _____
2. _____
3. _____

EXERCISE

8.3   Priorities

Prioritize the decisions you listed in Exercise 8.2—number one (#1) being most important. What criteria did you use to prioritize them?

1. _____
2. _____
3. _____

EXERCISE

8.4   Irrevocable Decisions

Give an example of a decision you made or might make in the future that could be extremely difficult to change.

_____
_____
_____

EXERCISE

8.5   Harmful Decisions

Give an example of a future decision you could make that might keep you from doing something you want to do.

_____
_____
_____

EXERCISE

8.6   What If…

1. Suppose you have lost all financial aid plus all other sources of support. Perhaps you have been laid off or your family has withdrawn support of your education. List three things you could do to stay in school:

   a. _____
   b. _____
   c. _____

EXERCISE 8.6   What If... *CONTINUED*

2. Which of these alternatives would be acceptable to you?

_____

_____

3. Suppose you have one year before losing the support. With a year to prepare, what would you do?

   a. What alternatives would you choose? _____

   b. What information would you need about your chosen alternatives? _____

       _____

   c. What action would you take? _____

       _____

 # Managing Your Financial Resources

As you make career decisions, the goal of achieving financial independence is often one of the most important priorities. Learning how to budget money or earnings to meet your obligations is an important step toward being "career fit." Remember, *you* are the best investment that you will ever make as a result of your increased skills through education and career choice. Although it may require attention and effort, it is worth your time, energy, and determination to take advantage of the opportunities that become available as you earn income and make further decisions about your future. Consider each of the following categories as you plan for financial security.

▲ Planning and budgeting are essential to future savings. Easy-to-use software is available to help you track expenses and income and to fulfill savings goals.

SETTING FINANCIAL GOALS

Having a vision is powerful as you decide what you want to achieve financially. To begin with, knowing what your financial needs are every month is essential to meet the necessities of paying for rent, food, car, cell phone, utilities, and other personal expenses. Recognizing and budgeting for your short-term monthly survival goals for the entire year allows you to set medium-range goals for the next one to three years. Medium-range goals would include vacations, savings, electronics, new clothes, and other items that you want to own. Finally, set longer-term goals that your savings can help you reach over a five-year or longer period, such as a down payment on a new car, a home, or a special purchase.

SAVING MONEY

Planning is essential to future savings. This means you must have a clear vision and a positive affirmation to put money aside at the beginning of each month—well before you are tempted to spend it. Get used to saving money, and make it a habit just as you look for good deals and compare prices before making a purchase. The goal is to set aside at least *10 percent* of your income every month. By opening a bank savings account (if you have not done so already), you will see the dividends grow and will have money available for emergencies or special expenditures. When you save money, you will have a reserve to handle any financial setback. Most banks make it easier to save by setting up an automatic monthly transfer of funds from a checking account to a savings account so that you don't have to remember to do it.

CREDIT CARDS

Because very few people use cash to fund all of their expenses, at some stage you will find yourself borrowing money. Individuals borrow money for an education, a car, home furnishings, or a mortgage. Doing so carefully and responsibly builds your repayment history and a strong credit rating.

Credit cards are easily obtained, but they carry the most risk. Experts on debt management say the best way to use a credit card is to pay the entire balance at the end of each month. Remember, credit cards are like accepting a high-interest loan that can keep you in debt over a *long* period of time. The concept of buying it now and paying for it later is a risky trap. The plastic card should be viewed as a stop sign that continually blinks at you "Caution – Danger Ahead." Spend only what you can pay back this month to avoid the high-interest rate.

If you instead take the "easy" credit road, you will soon find yourself paying endless high-interest charges. Think critically about your priorities, what you really need now, and what you can put aside until your financial assets increase. One of the best methods to ensure financial independence is to learn how to manage your credit card.

INSURANCE AND HEALTH NEEDS

Insurance helps individuals meet unanticipated events and obtain necessary health services. Some companies may offer health benefits, including medical and dental, and may also include some retirement and insurance incentives. If you do not obtain all the insurance and health coverage you need when you are working, then these costs become part of your monthly budget (see Exhibit 8.2). Under a recent National Health Bill passed in 2010, all full-time students are covered by family health plans until the age of 25. Although

EXHIBIT 8.2 Monthly Money Management

Expenses	Jan	Feb	Mar	Apr	May	Jun	Jul	Aug	Sep	Oct	Nov	Dec	Total
Utilities/Telephone	175	175	175	175	175	175	175	175	175	175	175	175	2100
Rent	650	650	650	650	650	650	650	650	650	650	650	650	7800
Food	250	250	250	250	250	250	250	250	250	250	250	250	3000
Entertainment	200	200	200	200	200	200	200	200	200	200	200	200	2400
Clothing	125	125	125	125	125	125	125	125	125	125	125	125	1500
Medical/Insurance	120	120	120	120	120	120	120	120	120	120	120	120	1440
Car/Maintenance	300	300	300	300	300	300	300	300	300	300	300	300	3600
Laundry/Toiletries	40	40	40	40	40	40	40	40	40	40	40	40	480
Credit Card Payments	300	300	300	300	300	300	300	300	300	300	300	300	3600
TOTAL	2160	2160	2160	2160	2160	2160	2160	2160	2160	2160	2160	2160	25920

Net Income	Jan	Feb	Mar	Apr	May	Jun	Jul	Aug	Sep	Oct	Nov	Dec	Total
Net Salary	2400	2400	2400	2400	2400	2400	2400	2400	2400	2400	2400	2400	28800
Less Expenses	2160	2160	2160	2160	2160	2160	2160	2160	2160	2160	2160	2160	25920
SAVINGS	240	240	240	240	240	240	240	240	240	240	240	240	2880

it seems far into the future, it is wise to think ahead to retirement since you can no longer count on a pension from your employer. *You are your retirement plan,* so the earlier you begin, the more financially secure you will be. Paying for health, life, or car insurance or making a small retirement investment will take a portion of your money and add to your yearly costs.

TIPS FROM THE PROS

Most financial experts and self-made millionaires indicate that the fastest way to accumulate wealth is to live below your means. Stop comparing and competing for the newest, best, most expensive purchase. Make your goal to live lightly. Simplify and challenge yourself to downsize. Not only is this philosophy in fashion these days but this will ensure your financial security and resiliency in tough times.

BUDGETING

Living within your means often takes strong discipline and a willingness to establish limits to what you spend.

It takes a special effort to make a careful list of your monthly income and expense activities, but this is the most essential and useful action you can take to keep track of your spending habits. Budgeting feeds directly into financial independence and allows you to take that summer vacation and avoid high-interest payments. Use the monthly budget management example shown in Exhibit 8.2 to develop your own financial spreadsheet.

This preliminary budget includes typical cost-of-living categories. Some elements may be different for you based on geography, income level, or other factors. For example, if you live at home, share rent, get along without a car, or do not have personal debt, your expenses may be lower. After all monthly expenses are carefully examined and deducted from your earnings, what remains is savings. In addition to the categories where you budget and spend your money, there are also unexpected costs or emergencies that may arise. This is where your savings make a critical difference. If you dip into these savings for "fun" events or items, the money will no longer be available to you for any emergencies or future needs.

Suppose you want to purchase property in a few years. How could you best prepare for this possibility? Perhaps an additional 5 percent savings could make a vital difference? What else would you change in your budget?

A budget is a monetary plan to control your financial resources and prepare for the future. You will soon realize that budgeting is the first step toward financial freedom. Personal finance software such as Quicken or Microsoft Money will help you accurately monitor your accounts.

In the final analysis, the decisions that you make about education, career, and money all take careful attention and focus. The time you spend will pay huge dividends and lead to positive outcomes.

TIPS FROM THE PROS

FINANCIAL FREEDOM

1. Keep your financial reputation solid by establishing a healthy credit score. This is accomplished by avoiding debt and living within your means. Always ask yourself, "Do I really need this?" If it is a want, not a need, think twice.

2. Before spending money, ask yourself, "Is this in my best financial interest?"

3. Wait three days before making a large purchase (over $50). This will stop "impulse shopping" while you think carefully about how this impacts your overall budget.

4. To help pay for your education, check the opportunities for grants/work study before assuming loans.

5. When possible, live at home to save rental payments.

6. Consider the full costs of owning a car. Car-pooling, bicycling, and using public transportation amounts to huge savings for fuel, insurance, repairs/maintenance, and parking—and it is eco-friendly.

Stress Management

Sometimes the biggest obstacles that you will encounter in your job search and decision making are those you put in place yourself. Learn how to look out for one of those land mines that can explode and destroy your best efforts: stress.

One of the greatest sources of stress is change, even when it is positive and planned, such as the change associated with finding a new job. The College Undergraduate Stress Scale (CUSS) was developed by Renner and Mackin (1998) to help students assess events and the corresponding stress that is generated. Take this survey online to determine your current stress level (**http://home.cc.umanitoba.ca/~mdlee/Teaching/cuss.html**).

Some stress can be positive, associated with high motivation, high energy, and sharp perception. Negative stress, however, can reduce your effectiveness in your job search in many ways. Stress may produce psychological effects such as anxiety, frustration, apathy, lowered self-esteem, aggression, procrastination, and depression.

Recently, much research has been done studying the brain's role in stress management. Dr. Eric Jensen, author of the 2006 book *Enriching the Brain: How to Maximize Every Learner's Potential*, says, "Change the experience, change the brain." One of the most powerful ways to offset the negative emotions that cause stress is to develop a sense of control. You do this by developing time management and goal setting and rewarding your small achievements along the way.

You will need to activate coping strategies when you encounter obstacles to maintain your self-esteem and motivation to find work. To find work does not mean, however, that you need to give up your identity, sell out, or compromise on issues important to you. It is also not your responsibility to change the work world. Employers who want to hire successfully from a diverse worker pool also have an obligation to help eliminate obstacles for recruiting and retraining quality employees. You may offer a different background in terms of your language ability, culture, or ethnicity, or you may simply have some unique or practiced set of skills that will differentiate you and benefit the employer. In a competitive job environment, making that extra effort to effectively communicate your value will increase your chance of getting employed.

In a tight economic market, you will be wise to consider more options. Are you flexible and willing to change your job location? Can you manage with a lower starting salary than anticipated or previously experienced? Will you consider employment in fields that are not your first choice? Human resources experts suggest that expanding your choices reduces stress in a shrinking, highly competitive environment and will result in more job offers. In the face of adversity, persistence, flexibility, and creativity will sustain your efforts.

Strategies for maintaining a positive attitude and managing stress are essential. Some of these techniques are listed in this "Success Strategies" feature.

SUCCESS *strategies*   Stress Management Techniques

- **Take time for yourself.** Treat yourself well and pay attention to your personal needs and enjoyment.
- **Maintain or start a realistic exercise schedule.** Participate in activities you enjoy that will also get you moving. Exercise is one of the best remedies for stress.
- **Socialize with friends and family.** Your support network can help you keep your stressors in perspective.
- **Remind yourself about personal strengths.** Some people find it reassuring to have a list of things they do well to give themselves a motivational boost when life becomes overwhelming.
- **Encourage a sense of humor.** A good healthy laugh is a great way to keep perspective on all the changes in your life.
- **Keep your eye on the goal!** Remember why you are working so hard and how good it will feel when you finally reach your goals.

🌐 Deciding on a Major

Some students seem to have no trouble choosing a major. They select a major that is compatible with their skills or interests. Many students, however, remain undeclared until they are forced to choose. Often it is because they are unclear about their talents and preferences. If you are one of the undecided, you probably feel pressure and anxiety from peers, parents, and your college. Rather than choosing a specific major, start by choosing an area of general interest and just begin to lean slightly in that direction to imagine what that would be like. Think about your personal career profile—your values, personality, interests, and skills—to narrow down the choices of possible majors.

▲ If you require help making decisions about school or work, take advantage of campus resources such as counselors and advisers.

TIPS FROM THE PROS

Some of the best decisions are made effortlessly through the process of elimination. Once you have eliminated all the possible majors that do not fit, you will be left with a smaller number of potentially good choices.

Whenever you meet people who have interesting jobs, do your own research by asking them if they have a degree and in what major. Because many people have majored in subjects seemingly unrelated to their jobs, you will eventually have to decide whether you will choose a major closely related to an area of work that may be of interest (e.g., biology to become a biomedical technician) or if you should select a major that seems interesting to you at this time in your life (e.g., communications or psychology) without any specific job in mind. Research indicates that either strategy can lead you to a successful, satisfying career.

If all of your personal assessment does not help you identify a specific major, you might consider sampling some courses to see if they spark an interest. For example, you could take an introductory course in an area such as interior design, management, engineering, or film. It is better to sample courses in several areas during your initial semesters in college and research what those majors involve, than to choose one prematurely only to find out after several semesters and a great investment of time and money that you don't really like that field.

Remember, many occupations do not have a strong relationship to a specific college major. Employers are looking primarily for candidates who are well-rounded individuals and who have done well in college, no matter what their major. If you decide to choose a major not specifically related to your future career, identify a major that interests you and in which you can excel and enjoy the learning experience. Employers in the business world often focus more on knowledge and communication skills gained from extracurricular activities, internships, and work experience than on a student's specific major.

Choosing a Major

If you are still exploring possible majors, we will suggest an effective way to narrow your choices. First of all, historically, majors are simply a convenient way for colleges and universities to organize their courses of study. They were never primarily intended to help students make career choices. But most students assume that when they choose a major, they are also selecting a career. In some cases, a major such as engineering leads to a job as an engineer. In contrast, English or Sociology is an area of study that does not necessarily lead to a job as an English or Sociology teacher unless you are willing to continue on for a graduate degree. Here is one website that lists jobs related to a wide variety of college majors: **http://www .uncwil.edu/stuaff/career/majors/index.htm**.

TIPS FROM THE PROS

A report from the University of California–Irvine stated that "over 75% of students pursuing MBA degrees at top ranked schools completed undergraduate degrees in areas other than business."

Let's try to clarify and simplify the process for deciding on a major. We will focus on three popular clusters of majors to use as examples. As we describe them, think about yourself and your academic strengths, preferences, and interests, as well as your emerging career choices, and then decide what you can eliminate (see Exhibit 8.3).

First cluster: Liberal arts. Some of the most common majors in this grouping are psychology, sociology, art, music, communications, English, journalism, history, political science, and education. What they all have in common is less emphasis on math and sciences and more emphasis on a broad spectrum of courses in the other general education categories. In terms of careers, they have the furthest direct correlation between bachelor's degrees and entry-level job titles. So, with a bachelor's degree you will not get a job as a psychologist or

---

EXHIBIT 8.3   Quick Guide to Choosing a Major

LIBERAL ARTS (minimal requirements in science and mathematics)	BUSINESS/ ACCOUNTING/ FINANCE/ ECONOMICS/ MARKETING	SCIENCE TECHNOLOGY (maximum requirements in science and mathematics)
Anthropology	Lower division preparation classes for these majors include:	Anatomy
Archeology		Animal Science
Art	1 year of Economics	Architecture
Communications	1 year of Accounting	Astronomy
Criminal Justice	Calculus	Biology
Dance	Computer	Botany
Education	Information	Chemistry
English	Systems Courses	Chiropractic
Film	Introduction to	Dental Hygiene
Foreign Languages	Business	Engineering
History	Statistics	Environmental Science
Humanities	(Most people who	Geography
Interior Design	work in the	Geology
Journalism	business world	Health Sciences
Multimedia	do not have a	Kinesiology
Music	business major.)	Microbiology
Philosophy		Mathematics
Political Science		Nursing
Psychology		Nutrition
Radio/TV		Physics
Sociology		Physiology
Spanish		Pre-Dent.
Speech		Pre-Med
Theatre		Pre-Pharm
		Pre-Physical Therapy
		Pre-Vet
		Zoology

Choose a major based on your academic strengths and your interests/passion, not because you think it will be "good" for you.

a sociologist but you will be eligible for a variety of entry-level professional positions in the business and the not-for-profit sector. You can then decide to pursue your interest in a particular area in graduate school if you desire to be a professional in the speciality, or you may be able to progress in your career without additional graduate-level degrees through continued job experience. Some examples here would be in politics or as a para-professional employee or as a management trainee.

Second Cluster: Business/Economics. Some of the most common majors in this grouping are accounting, business management, finance, marketing, and economics. What they all have in common is a required core of courses in preparation for majors that include a year of economics, a year of accounting, math including some calculus, statistics, and information technology courses. Specific business classes are often not taken until the junior year in college. In terms of careers, these majors open doors to opportunities in the business world for accountants, financial analysts, and economists, to list a few. However, a common misconception is that a business degree is required for entry into the business world. In fact, the vast majority of people in most areas of business do not have a business degree. For instance, someone in marketing, sales, advertising, public relations, or corporate communications probably has a degree in one of the liberal arts majors and perhaps some coursework in business subjects related to their field.

Third Cluster: Science/Technology. Some of the most common majors in this grouping are biology, chemistry, physics, geology, environmental science, kinesiology, engineering, architecture, and computer science. What they all have in common is an emphasis on science and math courses, including calculus. In terms of careers, they have the closest one-to-one correlation to actual jobs. So, if you are a chemistry major, you become eligible to get employment as a chemist. A computer science major often leads to careers in that field as well.

Now that you have reviewed these three clusters, which ones can you eliminate, and why? Which ones seem most compatible with everything you know about yourself from the work you have completed in your career fitness profile? As you continue your career fitness program, you will have more opportunities to do further research and refine your career choices in moving toward career goals. For example, you may be thinking about becoming a doctor, lawyer, astronaut, author, webmaster, performer, or entrepreneur. None of these are bachelor's degree college majors. Some of them require a bachelor's degree, but it could be in any number of areas; others do not require an advanced degree, but you may want to earn a degree for the benefit of the knowledge acquired and as an added credential to make you more competitive in the job market. As you continue gathering ideas and completing research on some of your possible career choices, you will discover how a degree fits into your plan of moving toward your career goal.

Finally, deciding on graduate school is often another decision that occurs following the completion of a four-year degree. The sequential steps of lower division (the first two-year program at a community college or university), then a bachelor's degree can be a natural path toward additional specialized training toward higher degrees. The application process for law school, business, marketing, advertising, and management programs is available and can be easily researched. Preparation for a teaching career, counseling training, and a variety of other possible majors may later mesh with your interests and motivation. Because change is a part of the decision-making process, you can benefit from keeping all of your options open.

 **Deciding on Training**

If you are not interested in attending or completing four years of college but want to select a job that can best fulfill your career goals as soon as possible, you have at least two issues to address: job information and training requirements. Using your social network, contact

Tomorrow

She was going to be all she wanted to be…tomorrow.
None would be smarter or more successful than she…tomorrow.
There were friends who could help her—she knew,
Who'd be only too happy to see what they could do.
On them she would call and pay a visit or two…tomorrow.
Each morning she stacked up the letters she'd write…tomorrow,
And thought of the things that would give her delight…tomorrow.
But she hadn't one minute to stop on her way,
"More thought I must give to my future," she'd say…tomorrow.
The greatest of workers this woman would have been…tomorrow.
The world would have hailed her—had ever she seen…tomorrow.
But, in fact, she passed on, and she faded from view,
And all that was left here when living was through
Was a mountain of things she intended to do…tomorrow!

—Unknown

▲ Congratulations on making a decision!

people working in the field of your interest. Using your personal contacts, call people working in the field or the professional or trade association for that field to obtain information on training centers. Usually, people who work in a field know which schools have the best reputation. Public community colleges, technical junior colleges, and adult and proprietary schools also offer a variety of training programs. Be sure to compare the courses you will be required to take with the preparation and skills necessary to perform the job. Making informed decisions depends on accurate information.

If you are exploring career opportunities as a result of company downsizing or family changes, it is even more important that you make careful decisions. All that you have learned about yourself thus far should give you the incentive and confidence to apply the decision-making skills discussed in this chapter. The exercises that follow will give you additional decision-making practice.

EXERCISE your options

As you complete this chapter focusing on your decision-making process, you have heightened your awareness of all the variables that are involved in making satisfying decisions. You addressed your choices to deal with managing time, to live within a financial budget, to handle stress and learn to relax, and to narrow your focus toward selecting a college major.

What one decision can you make today to move forward on your future career plan?

Decision _____

 # Summary

Successful career planning involves two processes related to goals: defining your goals and knowing how to reach them. The more completely you plan out your objectives, the more likely you will be to achieve your goals. The key to the process is overcoming the hurdle of negative thinking. Block out the tendency to be self-critical. Put aside your anticipation of failure, your fears and excuses, and your past habits. Allow yourself the right to create goals that energize you and take you beyond your past efforts.

The following exercises are designed to help you become aware of steps in the decision-making process and to encourage you to set some career and life goals. For example, you will be asked to decide what you want to do by the end of the current year and then one year from now. This can mean acquiring new skills or improving current skills, moving toward career advancement or career change, or staying where you are. Remember to try to picture in your mind what you want in your work life (e.g., type of work, responsibility, surroundings, salary, management relationship), and then focus on the steps necessary to reach your goals. If you can't picture the necessary steps, you need to gather more information (e.g., from people who have been in similar positions or from written materials about the field) so you can move forward on career decisions.

PURPOSE OF EXERCISES

The exercises that follow will help increase your awareness about how you make decisions. *There are no right or wrong answers.*

Exercise 8.7 asks you to rank yourself on two dimensions of decision-making style. This helps you become aware of your personal style of decision making. Exercise 8.8 tests your ability to recognize and state clear objectives. In Exercise 8.9, you are encouraged to test your assumptions. Exercise 8.10, **WWWebwise**, is a Web-based exercise that enhances the learnings in this chapter. The last exercise, **Reinforcing Your Learning Outcomes**, will reinforce what you learned in this chapter.

EXERCISE

8.7 Ranking Yourself

Place a check (✓) on each of the scales here to indicate your style of decision making with number 1 being closer to words on left column and 10 being closer to words on right column:

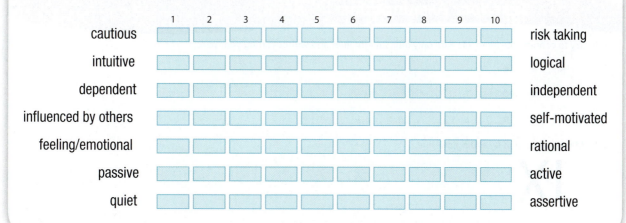

	1	2	3	4	5	6	7	8	9	10	
cautious											risk taking
intuitive											logical
dependent											independent
influenced by others											self-motivated
feeling/emotional											rational
passive											active
quiet											assertive

EXERCISE
8.8   Specific/Nonspecific Objectives

The following statements are objectives. Read each objective and decide whether the objective is specific or nonspecific. Imagine that a person will be clearly motivated to explore these objectives rather than merely think about them. These are statements anyone might make; they don't necessarily apply to you. Imagine that someone is standing in front of you making each of these statements. With that in mind, mark each objective as "S" (specific) or "N" (nonspecific) to the left of the statement.

_____ 1. I want to explore my interests.

_____ 2. I want to get a good job

_____ 3. I'd like to get an idea of the job I'm best suited for.

_____ 4. I'd like to take Spanish next semester and for at least two years more, so I'll have another skill to use as a teacher.

_____ 5. When I leave school, I want to get a job that pays at least $15 an hour.

_____ 6. Tomorrow I'm going to make a one-hour appointment to see Ms. Rogers in her office.

_____ 7. I want to get at least a B on every history exam and earn a B as my final grade this semester.

_____ 8. I'm going to ask Teresa to help me find some information about health careers in the Career Development and Placement Center right after class.

_____ 9. I plan to move to an area where there are lots of jobs.

_____ 10. I want to be accepted by the state university when I graduate.

_____ 11. I want to find out more about myself.

_____ 12. I want to get along better with other people at work.

_____ 13. Next week I'm going to spend more time with my friends.

_____ 14. I'm going to read one good book about social service careers tonight.

_____ 15. I want to get a good education.

Answers are located on page 180.

EXERCISE
8.9   Test Your Assumptions

1. Try to connect the nine dots with only four straight lines and without lifting your pen.

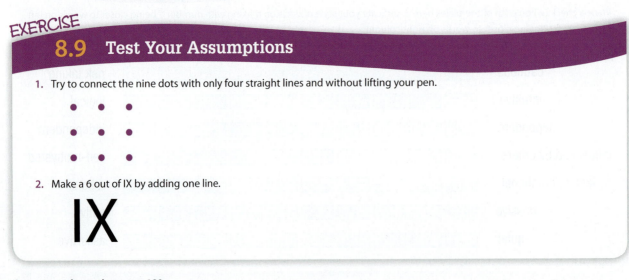

2. Make a 6 out of IX by adding one line.

IX

Answers are located on page 180.

EXERCISE
8.10 WWWebwise

Go to **http://www.coolworks.com/** Click on "Help Wanted Now." Indulge your fantasies! Choose a position that appeals to you. Which one would you select? What decision-making criteria went into your selection?

(*Note*: Please be aware that websites can change without notice. If a link does not work, find a similar site to complete the activity.)

REINFORCING YOUR LEARNING OUTCOMES

Review and Rate Your Chapter Outcomes. Indicate in the right-hand column how well you do the following items (from 1 = very well, to 5 = not at all). If you rated yourself 4 or 5, review the material on the pages in parentheses to ensure your career success.

How Well Can You Do the Following?

▪ Describe and explore your own decision-making process. (pp. 157–162)	1 2 3 4 5
▪ Apply the principles of decision making to your career search. (pp. 162–164)	1 2 3 4 5
▪ Write your goals and objectives. (pp. 164–168)	1 2 3 4 5
▪ Make tentative career/education training choices. (pp. 172–176)	1 2 3 4 5
▪ Define and use stress management techniques. (pp. 171–172)	1 2 3 4 5
▪ Set and manage financial goals. (pp. 168–171)	1 2 3 4 5

Go to the Career Fitness Portfolio at the end of the book and complete this chapter summary to build and record your personal Career Fitness Portfolio.

Additional Opportunity: Your instructor may choose to assign the Career Fitness Portfolio for in class or online completion. If so, they will provide the handout or link for you to access.

ANSWERS TO EXERCISE 8.8

1. N	4. S	7. N	10. N	13. N
2. N	5. N	8. S	11. N	14. S
3. N	6. S	9. N	12. N	15. N

ANSWERS TO EXERCISE 8.9

1.
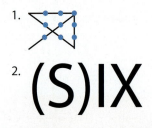

2. # (S)IX

(Note: The directions did not mandate a straight line.)

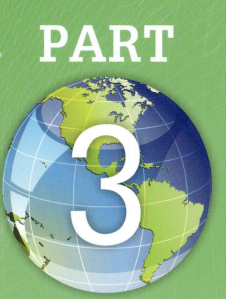

PART 3

Execute Your Game Plan

Job Search Strategy and Team Huddle

Targeting Your Job Search

Mobilize Your Network

STUDENT LEARNING OUTCOMES

At the end of the chapter you will be able to . . .

- Identify the components of a successful job search strategy.
- Begin the process of searching for a job.
- Explain how to find the hidden job market.
- Develop your network.
- Expand your network.

Congratulations! You have finished the personal assessment and world of work portions of your career fitness program. You have reviewed and analyzed your skills, your interests, your personality, and your values, and you have tentatively selected some career options. They are tentative because you may find reason to alter your decisions as you continue to gather information. Just as adjustments occur in a physical fitness program based on your body's responses, so must adjustments occur in your career fitness program based on your research and gut-level responses.

The next step is to begin to design your job search strategy, which represents the third part of the career-planning process. A job search strategy involves the long-term process of acquiring the training, background, and experience needed to be competitive in the job market associated with your anticipated career goal. Simultaneously, you need to begin to identify potential employers for your skills and to develop a resume that reflects your background and your particular career goal. Finally, you need to learn how to present yourself in the best light in job interviews.

> Experience is not what happens to you. It is what you do with what happens to you.
>
> —Aldous Huxley

Your job search must be conducted consistently over a period of time. Studies indicate that it can take many months of searching to land the job you are seeking. Regardless of how certain or tentative you are currently feeling about your career alternatives, you must have a specific occupation in mind to benefit from the remainder of this book. The goal of this chapter is for you to choose one of the occupations you have been considering. Then keep it in mind as you read and work through the following chapters. If you later identify another occupation, you will be able to apply the same strategies.

SUCCESS *strategies*

Your Comprehensive Job Search Strategy

1. Commit 100 percent to your job objective.
2. Compare the tasks and responsibilities required in your chosen job at different companies and organizations.
3. Get involved in volunteer and entry-level jobs related to your ultimate goal.
4. Identify the hidden job market through personal contacts and professional associations.
5. Use the Internet; maximize social media tools.
6. Utilize professional assistance, if necessary.
7. Network: Let everyone know you are looking for a job (friends, neighbors, dentist, etc.). Reconnect with people you have known; stay in touch online.
8. Conduct information interviews with people who are in jobs that interest you as well as people who may be in a position to hire you. Approach all contacts with enthusiasm and sincerity and send thank-you letters to all contacts.
9. Identify the needs of the organization. If the exact position you would like is not available, your task is to define a problem within the organization that you can help solve with your unique skills.
10. Convince an employer that you have the skills he or she needs.

▲ Brainstorm with others and surf the web for career possibilities.

The rest of this chapter will provide you with the information and skills to enable you to gain control in a competitive job market. In other words, you will learn many techniques to put yourself in the right place at the right time and to present yourself as the best candidate for your desired job. The underlying and most important concept, however, is focusing on what you want. Without this concentration, you run the risk of being swayed by random opportunities and jobs that don't live up to your expectations. *Focusing* means evaluating and comparing all new information with your personality, needs, values, interests, and skills. Remember, the first job you seek should not be considered an end in itself. It is one job on the way to several more that will compose your total career. As the dictionary defines *career*, it is a "pursuit of consecutive progressive achievement in public, professional, or business life." Career experts predict that the average worker can expect to make 3 to 5 major career changes and 9 to 13 job changes in a lifetime, which means that you will have many opportunities to arrive at your ideal career.

This approach assumes that you have identified a job objective for which you feel *100 percent enthusiasm,* that you will pursue with *100 percent determination,* and that you will interview for with *100 percent of your passion and commitment.* This approach charges you with the responsibility to make things happen!

Designing a Comprehensive Job Search Strategy

A comprehensive job search strategy involves much more than just researching to decide what your ideal job is, or simply identifying areas of employment in which you expect to find such jobs. It requires you, once having made these basic decisions, to be assertive in locating and actually becoming employed in your ideal job. A comprehensive job search strategy empowers you to consider many variables to attain your ideal goal, including education, training, experiences, as well as geographic and compensation issues. Equally important, your job search strategy enables you to select volunteer and entry-level activities that are the vital first steps toward your ultimate career goal.

> Go for the job you really want!

Assuming you have adequate skills and background and that you have identified a job for which you are 100 percent enthusiastic, the following approach will work for you:

> Identify your ideal job situation.

- First, you must make a contract with yourself to complete all the tasks necessary to get the job.
- Next, you must become totally informed about the tasks and responsibilities of the job you are seeking. Much of this information can be gained from the written and electronic materials previously cited.
- Additionally, you will need to augment any researched information by making personal contacts with insiders.
- Once you have identified your ideal job situation, investigate activities that may be indispensable first steps toward your goal. Such activities may be temporary, volunteer, or entry-level jobs in your chosen field. They can be critical in adding to your experience and connecting you with the right people to make you a better candidate for your preferred job. For example, a student who wanted to move into the advertising business took a job as a receptionist in the executive suite of an advertising agency in New York. Of course, he had brushed up on his office skills to get this entry-level job, but he didn't plan to remain at that level for long. He kept his eyes and ears open for ways that he could contribute to the efficiency of the business. Within six months he had learned enough about the advertising business to interview at a competing firm and become the assistant to an executive account manager.

One final suggestion before you conduct further research: You may find your ideal job is years of education and experience away from you, or you don't have the dedication or talent to make it in your ideal field. If so, you may be just as satisfied if you work in some job *related* to the career of your dreams. For example, behind every president of the United States are advisers, speech writers, guards, assistants, chefs, press representatives, and chauffeurs. Behind every rock musician are disc jockeys, public relations representatives, recording technicians, piano tuners, album cover designers, sound editors, cutting designers, concert coordinators, costume and makeup artists, and background musicians, business managers, accountants, personal assistants, and coaches. If you stay around the field, constantly adding to your experience, you may be at the right place at the right time and get the job you've dreamed of or one that is even better suited to your talents!

> Begin with an entry-level job related to your ideal.

TIPS FROM THE PROS

You can't always start right out in your ideal job, but guided by a job search strategy, you can start out in jobs and activities that will lead to your goals.

Your Job Search: Getting Started

To improve the chances of getting your ideal job, use a variety of strategies. *Using a wide variety of options will increase your chances of success.* Using only a few strategies—be it the Internet, a resume, job advertisements, or an employment agency search—is hardly enough in this competitive job environment. It takes a wide variety of strategies and creativity to get hired in your desired career. Typical resources include reading newspaper want ads and trade journals, using the Internet, sending resumes to potential employers through the mail and by e-mail, using permanent or temporary employment agencies, and volunteering, interning, or joining clubs and professional associations while in school. In addition, many hidden resources exist. The first section of this chapter focuses on the most commonly used job search resources; the latter part suggests ways to tap into those that are less apparent and often more effective.

UNDERSTANDING AND USING CLASSIFIED ADS

Although printed media has diminished in usage, employment and classified ads are still published in local newspapers, newspapers from your desired geographical area, trade journals, and supplements (such as the career section of the *Wall Street Journal*), as well as association magazines and related online resources that are listed at the end of this chapter. Other job listings are found in the state employment department, county and city human resources (HR) offices, college placement centers, private employment offices, and the HR offices of individual organizations and websites.

> Only 15 percent of jobs are found through ads.

Regularly reviewing the want ads, in print and online, especially in larger cities, over several months can result in potential employment leads. Although it has been estimated that only 15 percent of jobs are found through ads, thousands of ads are published in large newspapers and online. You can increase your chances of obtaining a job by looking at and applying for a variety of job titles. For example, people with accounting degrees may be eligible for junior accountant, management trainee, accounts payable, auditor, and securities broker, in addition to accountant.

Another way to increase your chances of finding a job involves combining a newsprint want ads search with your active accumulation of Internet information about companies. When you see a job opening at a firm you've already visited or reviewed online, try to establish a contact in that company to call and ask for more information about the opening. You may find that the ad is written with absolute qualifications but that the specific department will accept alternative experiences in lieu of some of the specific qualifications. Only people who have personal contacts inside the company can obtain such information.

PROMOTING YOURSELF THROUGH MAIL AND E-MAIL

Because postal mailings are not often used these days, you might want to consider a mail campaign, as it might differentiate you from the crowd of job seekers. Some career fields such as sales, marketing, advertising, and graphic design lend themselves to this type of self-promotion. If creative promotion would be a plus in your field, then a direct-mail campaign may be an important part of your job search. This approach will work best if you have researched specific, targeted names to contact.

No matter what your field, devote time and energy to coming up with your list of target employers. To encourage responses, include a stamped, self-addressed postcard for employers to use. Your postcard might include easy, check-off statements such as "No openings now, but contact me again in one month," and "Opening available; please contact _____ ," as well as blanks for the name, address, and telephone number of the organization.

In the case of e-mail, you will obviously be able to cover much more ground for less money. Additionally, online programs in Facebook, LinkedIn, Twitter, and YouTube can send your resume or other promotional material to unlimited specific groups and organizations.

Through social networks and other websites, you can gain access to e-mail lists, lists of interest groups and discussion forums, and other means for targeting your promotion. Refer to "Selected Online Career and Employment Websites" at the end of this chapter for additional methods to target possible employers electronically.

> Accentuate your assets.

Some Unwritten Rules for Job-Search E-Mail

Getting your e-mails read requires strategy. Remember to customize your cover-letter message and resume for the unique requirements for each job opportunity. A mass-mailed flyer is ignored among hundreds of others because recruiters do not have time to figure out which job you are seeking. Cookie-cutter messages are also ineffective, as they do not address a unique situation; they also look like spam and may be eliminated by an organization's e-mail system. Be sure your e-mail address appears professional rather than informal or humorous.

Following precise directions is crucial. Use the job requisition number or the exact job title from the online ad in the subject line of an e-mail. You will also increase attention by keeping your e-mails brief yet informative. Most of the words in the subject line should be visible when the recipient sees it in the in-box list. Use about four to six words, a maximum of 25 to 35 characters. This is a positive attention getter, similar to a headline for a news story.

Finally, keep people in the information loop and maintain your credibility by using the "cc" function appropriately. Sending a copy of the message to relevant people is a courtesy, especially to the person who may have referred you, the recruiter, or the appropriate HR manager.

UNDERSTANDING AND USING EMPLOYMENT AGENCIES

Before you register with an agency or website, check carefully on its fees, the types of positions it handles, and its reputation. Some agencies simply place you on a job with limited concern for your satisfaction. Good agencies, in contrast, are very concerned about matching people with jobs that suit them.

Temporary employment agencies provide excellent ways to get back into the workforce or to test the climate in a variety of companies. The jobs available are no longer limited to entry level. Many temporary employment agencies specialize in specific fields such as accounting or nursing. Some agencies place people part time; some place people for short-term assignments. Agencies often specialize in a field and are even placing chief executive officers and college presidents in temporary, as well as full-time, employment.

For energetic, industrious workers, part-time and temporary assignments may lead to full-time employment and the opportunity to move up to better positions. Any job you hold may be the first step in a career. Exhibit a positive attitude, and do your best no matter what the position. However, you will probably be under contract to the temporary agency for a specified period of time, and thus the employer cannot hire you until the contract expires.

PROFESSIONAL ASSOCIATIONS

Most industries have professional associations that bring together professionals in a particular industry for disseminating relevant information, networking, and continuing education. As mentioned in our "Real Stories" found later in this chapter, students can become "student members" and meet leaders in their field of interest. By attending meetings, workshops, and conferences and becoming a Facebook or LinkedIn friend, you will learn insider information about directions professions are taking and become informed about job openings.

Go to any association's website to find information about paid and unpaid positions. For example, the Association for Multimedia Communications at **www.amcomm.org** encourages you to join them on Facebook. (Their digital magazine also has good articles on creating a digital portfolio that could help you get an internship.) To find sites like this, use a search engine with the term "internship" and additional keywords to narrow the search, such as "multimedia internship." Since most associations have a presence on Facebook, it is also a good place to search for information.

REAL stories   Meet Xiao-Ying

As Xiao-Ying begins a master's degree program in anthropology, she realizes that studying native tribes in the wilds of Africa will not enable her to make the personal contribution to other people's lives that she feels necessary for her own job satisfaction. Although her undergraduate anthropology professors inspired her to go for the master's degree, she is feeling overwhelmed by the needs of people in Africa. She decides to use the Career Development Center to help her focus her future. The counselor asks her to identify her ideal workplace where she can make a personal contribution and encourages her to talk with people working in her ideal setting. After conducting some research, Xiao-Ying becomes aware that working in a family-planning clinic will best suit her personal needs. Xiao-Ying volunteers for one year in a clinic; in addition, she conducts some studies on pregnancy and childbirth. Within a year she has a full-time job in the education department of Planned Parenthood.

Once she has committed to a full-time job at Planned Parenthood, Xiao-Ying realizes that she enjoys researching people's needs and giving direct training and help to people. As luck would have it, she finds that, instead of remaining a student in anthropology, she can be accepted to an evening graduate program in counseling at the same university. This allows her to work full time and complete a master's degree in counseling within three years. Instead of becoming an anthropology professor or researcher, Xiao-Ying becomes a counselor for Planned Parenthood and begins a private practice on the side.

WHAT DO *YOU* THINK?

1. How did Xiao-Ying decide that her master's degree studies were not leading to her ultimate job satisfaction?
2. How did her volunteer experience help her?
3. What kind of volunteer experience, internship, or service learning assignment could help you choose, change, or confirm your career goals?

VOLUNTEERING

The importance of getting job-related experience cannot be overestimated. As can be seen in Xiao-Ying's story, her volunteer experience supplemented her previous training. Many people have negative images of volunteering. They think volunteering means doing paperwork or "go-fer" work. However, you can create meaningful volunteer positions for yourself rather than taking whatever is available. To optimize your chances for obtaining such useful experience, look online and or go through a community voluntary action center, a college volunteer services office (sometimes part of the college placement office), a college cooperative education office, or a college service learning office.

TIPS FROM THE PROS

Try out volunteering for a nonprofit to gain valuable work experience. Often called *service learning*, this type of volunteer experience is offered for credit in many colleges and is sometimes even required for graduation. In addition to direct service to the needy, you can learn transferable skills such as organizing, public relations, marketing tech support, and even accounting. These skills and your volunteer experience are important assets to include in your resume and interviews. If you can't find opportunities through your college, the following websites offer a variety of service experiences:

- Volunteermatch.com
- www.CreateTheGood.com
- www.compact.org/about/state/contact-your-state-office
- http://heartsandminds.org/member.htm
- www.Americorps.com

▲ Volunteer to get real-world experience.

An even more intense volunteer experience for those who have the time and resources may be through the U.S. Peace Corps, AmeriCorps, VISTA, or the United Nations Volunteers. Such volunteer work requires a commitment of one to three years and provides room, board, benefits (including government service experience), and a living allowance. More and more students are taking off one year between high school and college or after college and before a full time commitment to a job. This is often called "The Gap Year" and there is even a website with that name! Explore the variety of experiences you can acquire both at home and internationally to add to your personal and professional portfolio and make you a more competitive job candidate.

The Peace Corps recruits individuals with varied academic backgrounds; for example, regardless of your major, recruits may teach English in developing countries. Engineering, technology, and health science graduates are especially valuable in the Peace Corps, with their math and science expertise, and civil engineers are needed to build water purification plants and roads.

INTERNSHIPS

Your college or university may help to arrange *internships* in some fields of study. Internships may be paid or unpaid and are usually restricted to students who have studied in the subject area of the internship. For example, a history major or a political science major may be given the highest priority among applicants for an internship in local or state government; a graphic arts, English, or communications major may be given priority for an internship in an advertising agency.

Many colleges have career centers, internship offices, or experiential education offices that arrange internships of different types, including *fieldwork*, which involves work required as part of a major. (Prospective teachers usually must student teach, for example, to earn their degree or certificate.)

Internships can be used to build valuable experience and contacts. For example, at Keuka College in New York, one political science major had *three* government internships before graduation. At that campus, each political science major takes a four-week field

FACTS & FIGURES

Internships Result in Students' Jobs

On average, organizations who responded to a 2011 survey offered 66.7 percent of their interns full-time positions, up from 63.3 percent reported in the 2010 survey. An amazing 86.5 percent of those offers were accepted by the interns.

WHAT DO *YOU* THINK?

1. Do you have work or volunteer experience?
2. How can you get an internship or volunteer experience related to your career goals?
3. Who are the people and what are the resources you can use to find experience related to your goals?
4. Have you investigated cooperative education at your college? What is preventing you from enrolling in this program?

Source: The NACE survey was conducted January 5 through February 28, 2011; 266 organizations responded.

---

period either in January or during the summer. For instance, students have worked for state legislators, the lieutenant governor, and the Democratic Senatorial Campaign Committee in Washington.

At Concordia College in Minnesota, students alternate semesters of work and study or work part time while continuing classes in the school's cooperative education program. This arrangement gives them longer-term connections with an organization and allows them to learn more about workplace and professional environments. Ramapo College in New Jersey provided one of its students with overseas experience at a marketing firm in England. When she graduated, she got a job as an assistant account executive at the New York office of Lloyds Bank PLC, the British bank chain.

Interns are generally closely supervised by college professors to help ensure they gain educational experience and benefit from the internship personally while they provide services for the employer. Ideally, interns working as part of a college program enjoy a meaningful learning experience that provides them with skills that supplement book learning and make job contacts.

Cooperative education is used to gain experience that may lead to a full-time position. (At some schools, the terms *internship* and *cooperative education* are used synonymously, but others make distinctions between the two programs.) The Cooperative Education Association publishes a list of participating colleges and universities that have official co-op programs.

The *Princeton Review Online* site (**www.review.com**) is typical of many websites related to published materials, providing free registration to add you to their advertising database. Such sites are essentially advertisements for books and materials, but they also contain a variety of free career resources.

FACTS & FIGURES

Employers Rate Experience Important for Recruiting New College Hires (5 = extremely important; 1 = not important)

On-campus recruiting	4.2
Organization's internship program	4.2
Organization's cooperative education work	4.0
Career/job fairs	3.8

Source: Annual employer survey by NACE 2008 press release.

SUCCESS *strategies* | Find Internships Online

The Princeton Review Online: www.review.com

Would you like to intern with the Academy of Television Arts & Sciences? How about the White House? This website describes the positions, requirements, compensation (they're not all unpaid), duration, deadlines, and other important information.

The *Princeton Review Online* can be found at **www.review .com**. Search for "Career Center" or "College and Careers," and then click on "Career Internships."

The Idealist.org

The Idealist has focused internships related to making the world a better place or "action without borders." Included are children and youth, disability issues, housing and homelessness, human rights, legal aid, and peace and conflict resolution.

USING SOCIAL NETWORKS SUCH AS LINKEDIN, FACEBOOK, AND TWITTER

LinkedIn is a great place to put your resume and to join your college's alumni network as well as join "groups" related to your field of interest. LinkedIn is the new **Monster.com** (**Monster.com** is listed in the career websites at the end of the chapter). It has comprehensive job market information as well as CareerBuilder's job listings, but LinkedIn is a social network. It's where recruiters are spending a lot of time searching, because they can do it for low fees. A 2010 Jobvite survey indicated that recruiters are choosing LinkedIn as the number-one tool to publish jobs for free, get referrals, research candidates, and find direct-source candidates!

The following are a few features that make LinkedIn and Twitter very useful:

- In a section of LinkedIn's site, college students enter the name of their school, their major, and the industry in which they want to work. LinkedIn then lists relevant job openings based on jobs that similar LinkedIn users pursued.

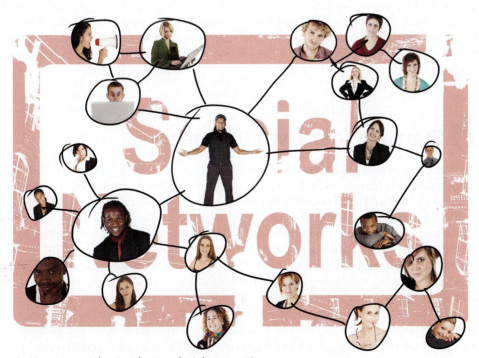

▲ Use your social networks to make job connections.

- Individual companies may include biographical videos of employees and tips on resume writing. For example, PwC (PricewaterhouseCoopers) launched its first Facebook and Twitter (@PwC) career pages in January 2010. Meanwhile, Ernst & Young has had a Facebook career page since 2006, where recruiters interact with students and answer questions about jobs. KPMG launched a Twitter account in 2009 managed by its recruiting team.
- Twitter has a search area that allows users to search in their local communities for jobs that may not be located on traditional career search engines such as CareerBuilder and Monster. Twitter is free to both users.

TIPS FROM THE PROS

1. Optimize your tweet pitch (or bio); make every character count (e.g., take out personal info); look for what key words others are using.
2. Find and follow the right community. People who have interest in your topics:
   a. Wefollow.com
   b. Advanced Twitter search
   c. Twellow.com (yellow pages for Twitter) (i.e., find your sociology professor)
   d. Search.twitter.com and search.twitter.com/advanced (can find local jobs)
3. When you use Twitter, you learn of others' interests that help you to connect with them; send out messages daily or several times a week to maximize your use of Twitter. You get to know and share some great tips about your professional as well as avocational interests.
4. Clean up your Facebook and Twitter biographies to ensure you look professional.

Examine your job-search strategies. Save time with a job-search engine or social network. Find new steps to take and conduct your search in a businesslike way, but don't ask basic questions on their websites. Look first at the company website for basic information. Review the FAQ sections of the companies as well as use the tutorials on the social network websites. Last, think twice before posting controversial comments on any social media website or blog. Hiring managers may find something you wrote that is inappropriate. You want only professional comments to be found to distinguish you positively from other candidates.

Starting Your Own Business

One more way to have a job is to start your own business. College students faced with limited job prospects have been starting businesses in record numbers—in essence, creating or inventing their careers. From franchise investments to short-term freelance assignments for specialists in accounting, marketing, management, and other traditional business functions, opportunities abound. Some independent contractor projects start part time and turn into full-time businesses. Entrepreneurial ventures are limited only by imagination and the marketplace. Examples run the gamut from Internet-related companies, organized walking tours in major cities with bilingual materials for foreign visitors, specialized photography to enhance pictorial magazines, networks for improved services for seniors, to green, eco-conscious pursuits. Additionally, due to the growth of "smart phone applications developers," online companies such as Elance and Cha Cha have expanded to meet the demand for contract employees. Go to www.Elance.com and http://chacha.myexacthire.com to see what they offer.

SUCCESS strategies — An Innovative Approach to the Job Search

Tommy Cates, director of online studies at the University of Tennessee at Martin, tells this story about one of UT's graduating senior's unique way of searching for a job. He wrote an ad stating, "If you have always wanted to leave your business to a son, but you do not have a son, I am the person you want to hire to run your business." He then gave his address and phone number. He chose 10 newspapers with nationwide circulation. Within a few days, the young man had received 40 responses. Instead of searching for a job like most grads, he had people calling him offering him a job. One offer stated, "Come and join our organization . . . anyone who is this creative can find a spot with us."

WHAT DO *YOU* THINK?

1. How might you separate yourself from the competition by creating a unique approach to your job search?
2. What are the advantages and disadvantages of an innovative approach?

HOME BUSINESS

The U.S. Bureau of Labor Statistics estimates that two-thirds of the more than 14 million full-time people who are self-employed work at home in a wide variety of careers. Approximately 25 percent of these home businesses are in the field of marketing and sales, with contracted services, professional jobs, and technical jobs accounting for another 25 percent. Among home business owners, 45 percent are college graduates and 85 percent are married, with half having dependent children. The average household income is approximately $55,000 annually. A relevant website is **www.usahomebusiness.com** and the National Association for the Self Employed can be found at **www.nase.org**.

GETTING HELP TO START YOUR OWN BUSINESS

Career centers, libraries, and the Internet have useful information on starting a business. The Small Business Administration (**www.sbaonline.sba.gov**) provides seminars and low-cost materials within local communities. A group called SCORE (Service Corps of Retired Executives) is composed of local retired businesspeople who lead low-cost workshops and offer free technical advice. Contact your local chamber of commerce for information about these resources. Also, a local community college or the extension/continuing education division of a local university may offer courses in small business administration or marketing. If colleges offer such courses, they may also have students available who get college credit by giving free technical assistance to newly formed small businesses. A healthy savings account will be needed to get you through many months until you can count on regular income from your enterprise. Better yet, begin building your new business while you are still employed (at least part time) to ensure some income.

> Become your own boss.

Related Websites:

- www.inc.com
- www.ideacafe.com
- www.entreworld.org
- www.kickstarter.com

The first is the site of *Inc.*, a magazine dealing with starting small businesses; the second specializes in helping small business owners with marketing, market research, starting businesses, legal information, operations, accounting, and more. The third site specializes in youth development and entrepreneurial leadership programs. A few other small business training programs are called "boot camps." The Kauffman Foundation's FastTrac, a 10-week boot camp offered throughout the country, trains aspiring entrepreneurs. A company called Y Combinator of Mountain View, California, and TechStars in Boulder, Colorado, offer cash and mentoring to young founders. Another group, Extreme Entrepreneurs, has been working with California Community Colleges to help students of all ages begin to see the possibilities available through creating your own business. The fourth site enables you to post your idea and get start up capital to fund your project.

SUCCESS strategies

A Creative Job Search

A business student from New York launched a website on which he promised a four-day cruise or $500 to anyone who provided him a successful lead for an upstate New York job not posted on a major job bank. He wanted a marketing or PR position following his graduation.

Although the contest drew widespread media coverage, 6,000 e-mails, and about 200 promising leads, he received only two face-to-face job interviews and one offer, which he declined partly because the job required very long hours. Incidentally, he did not have to pay anyone because he did not accept a job.

As it turned out, the 22-year-old instead pursued an opening he discovered on the website of his alma mater. In applying to be an admissions counselor, he cited his contest as evidence of his creativity as well as his sales and marketing skills.

Using Career Services

Check out the college career development and placement office at all stages of your career exploration. Ideally, you will start your career fitness program the minute you start college. Take a course in career exploration to explore academic alternatives, goal setting, and decision making. Career counselors can help you pursue internships, volunteer work, networking, and informational interviewing, assist you in finding part-time work, and advise you on creating new options such as joining and taking leadership positions in campus clubs.

College career centers offer job search workshops covering resume writing and interviewing techniques, and will also prepare you for interviews. In addition, they will help you contact alumni in your field of interest. Companies recruit for new hires on college campuses; many new college graduates find jobs this way. These interviews as well as job fairs are organized by the career center. Every college and many community organizations sponsor career fairs. During a career fair, you can make an impression on a company representative even if there are no current openings. Use your informational research skills, bring a polished resume, and dress professionally (yes, even on the college campus). Review the list of companies who will be at the fair by checking out the college career center's website prior to the date. At the career fair, ask the company representatives for names of people in their network of contacts who might be open to information interviewing related to your field of interest. If you have already graduated from a college, many alumni centers sponsor both on-campus career fairs and online career fairs. Finally, you might Google "career fair" and find future fairs close to home. Also, check with **Monster.com** and **CareerBuilder.com** because they often cosponsor career fairs.

FACTS & FIGURES

Job Hotlines

▶ Many companies and government agencies have job openings hotlines. Google "Job Hotlines" to find local and free phone numbers.

▶ U.S. Department of Labor's Jobs Helpline: 1-877-872-5627 or connect with a Career One Stop Center by calling 1-877-348-0502.

▶ In California, use **www.jobstar.org/socal/ index.cfm**.

Graduate School as an Alternative to a Full-Time Job

An error doesn't become a mistake until you refuse to correct it.

—*Orlando A. Battista*

Be prepared to be flexible when considering job offers. College graduates often find it difficult to land their ideal first job, and they often need to lower their expectations regarding starting salary.

Remember, a job that seems less than ideal may lead to one at which you can truly excel. For example, one university fine arts student became a recruiter at a large national life insurance company. Later, that art graduate's job involved purchasing art for regional headquarters. She traveled the world, purchasing art for her employer!

As a college graduate, you may decide that graduate school is a viable alternative. It is critical to use your finely honed decision-making skills to weigh the pros and cons. If your current job prospects are slim and your graduate degree would help you pursue your career goals, entering a graduate program might make great sense both economically and career wise. However, if you find you are considering graduate school simply to avoid the immediate realities of job hunting, consult a career counselor who can help you clarify all your options. For example, a Gap Year experience, Peace Corps, AmeriCorps, English language teaching in a foreign country, or other related programs might be a strategically wiser investment of your time and resources.

TIPS FROM THE PROS

Networking is the number-one most effective strategy in landing a job.

Networking

Networking refers to the activity of developing and maintaining contacts. Contacts, if cultivated and used wisely, can lead to or become potential employers.

Contacts make the strategic difference between being selected or passed by. This is true for several reasons. Because hiring someone new is always risky and costly, when considering two equally qualified candidates, most employers will choose someone who has been recommended. Often, jobs need to be filled quickly, before there is time to recruit, advertise, and review countless resumes. The majority of new jobs available each year are filled through business leads: They are offered to candidates who already have some connection, even if indirect, to the employer. Most people hear about jobs by word of mouth. You need to let people know you are looking. Internships, cooperative education, career fairs, and social networks provide you with a beginning network precisely because this is where you meet potential employers.

TIPS FROM THE PROS

Always remember, the purpose of networking is to mutually help each other toward your goals. First, it is to help you learn more about the field and company and about strategies or job-search efforts that would be useful in increasing your chances of becoming successful in that field. The second outcome should be that you will eventually return the favor.

TIPS FROM THE PROS

The secret of successful networking is reciprocity! Find a way to give back to the person who is helping you.

The best networking is a personal interaction. The meeting is not a hard sell or a sales transaction. It is all about gaining trust, building visibility, and listening carefully to the contact's wisdom, experience, and insight. The respect, attention, and appreciation you communicate for the valuable time provided to you are crucial to any further contact, referral, or consideration.

The term *network* is both a noun and verb. As a noun, a *network* is defined as a group of individuals who are connected to and cooperate with each other. As a verb, *to network* is to develop contacts and exchange information with other people for purposes of developing personal or business opportunities. The people you meet can become a lifelong mutual support network as you build your career!

> **Secret of successful networking is reciprocity.**

Reciprocity is as basic as a genuine thank you in person and via regular and email. It also includes the courtesy to get back in touch and keep your contacts informed of your progress. Dr. Beverly Kaye, internationally recognized career consultant and author, calls it "elegant currency." She is most impressed when someone actually asks her what they can do for her in exchange for her help. This genuine gesture of gratitude sets them apart and she is likely to remember and continue to help. Don't hesitate to ask, and even if there is no immediate way to give back, keep this person in mind. When you find an interesting article related to the field or an area of their interest, send it on with a brief note and another thank you. This extra gesture of gratitude will take you to the top of world-class networking!

Develop your network each day. Although the social networking sites on the Internet are a powerful tool, remember that your real-life encounters will likely be most useful in your job search. Friends and contacts can make a difference in helping you secure an information interview or a job lead. Think about it: The more people you get to know, the more information you gather. The more visible and proactive you are, the greater your chances will be of finding the right job. It may be a relative or neighbor or classmate or friend who points you to a job opening or provides you with valuable strategies. Millions of people throughout the world find jobs every day through the power of networking; it's as simple as telling everyone you encounter that you are looking.

> **Use all available sources for contacts.**

You probably have many acquaintances willing to provide names and ideas to help you be successful in finding your preferred career. These acquaintances may come from any of the following groups: clubs, organizations, health and sports team affiliations, teachers and professors (past and present), religious groups, coworkers, and previous employers. Exercise 9.1 suggests people to contact who are part of your network.

EXERCISE

9.1   Support Network Checklist

Fill in the names of people who might help you. Specifically ask yourself: How can this person help (provide information, introduce me to someone, offer advice, write a reference, etc.)?

Former employers: _____

Former coworkers: _____

Present employer: _____

Friends: _____

Relatives: _____

Civic group members: _____

Professional association members: _____

Alumni group members: _____

Religious group members: _____

Clients: _____

Counselors: _____

Teachers: _____

Clergy: _____

Neighbors: _____

Classmates: _____

Salespeople: _____

Medical professionals: _____

Others, such as online social networks (Facebook, LinkedIn), your accountant, bankers, financial planners, real estate agents:

_____

"Friends":_____

_____

One easy and natural way to network is to meet professionals where they gather. Note that "Professional association members" is listed above; and in this next "Real Stories," Felipe used his association contacts. For example, if you are interested in human resources management (HRM), you will find HRM personnel at association meetings such as the American Society for Training and Development (ASTD); if you are interested in personal communications services, read the trade journal *Radio Communications Report* to find out about local meetings or national conventions.

Many professional associations have related student groups or student sections. Find out whether there are groups or clubs on campus related to the field you want to pursue. Make this your first step in networking. Another resource is *The Encyclopedia of Associations*, and the *Occupational Outlook Handbook* which lists names and addresses related to each occupation. You can always go to **Google.com** or **Ask.com** to find an association. Consider writing an association to inquire about local meetings and the possibility of becoming a student member.

> Join professional associations.

REAL stories ⟨ Meet Felipe

As a business student, Felipe wanted to focus on human resources development and training in industry. So he joined the American Society for Training and Development (ASTD). He volunteered to chair the student recruitment subcommittee and joined the Career Development Special Interest Group (SIG). One year later, Felipe asked a SIG contact for an internship in a Human Resources Office and got it; two years later, he got a job with the firm as a trainer. When interviewing for the training job, he found he knew people who had worked with the director and knew about the needs of the Training Department. Felipe aced the interview!

Attend conferences.

Additionally, check the business section of the local newspaper or website to keep up on what's happening in your community. Review the list of groups using your city's convention center, and plan on attending conventions related to your interests. For example, one trade show related to theme parks had 20,000 registrants and 800 exhibitors occupying 2,600 booths; it lasted four days. Students majoring in communications, radio and TV, theater arts, business, and computer science would all find experts related to their majors at such a conference. Such conventions usually offer reduced fees for attending only one day or only entering the exhibit area.

These are all ways of meeting professionals in your field of interest, a key factor in finding the job you want. A survey of 1,500 successful job applicants by *National Business Employment Weekly* found that 67 percent got their jobs through networking, 11 percent by answering an ad, and only 2 percent by sending out resumes and filling out applications.

MOVING BEYOND THE FEAR OF NETWORKING

If people believe in themselves, it's amazing what they can accomplish.

—Sam Walton

Many people are reluctant to develop contacts by networking. They may feel they are imposing on busy individuals whose time is precious. This hesitation can be overcome, however, by realizing that many people truly enjoy talking about themselves and their profession. Many remember their own difficulties in connecting to a new career, and therefore they are very receptive to others' requests.

Keep in mind that as you meet people, you are finding out about the work they do and discovering if you feel comfortable and if you fit into their environment. You will also discover how your skills can address needs in each workplace you visit while networking. Let the contacts know what you can do for them—you may be just the person they need! One graphic design student visited the company of a graphic designer who had spoken in her art class. When asked if she had used Adobe Photoshop (software for modifying photographs), she was very enthusiastic in her answer about using the program in one of her classes. She was hired for a summer job on the spot!

Some job seekers find it difficult to network because they are uncomfortable approaching strangers and asking for what seems like a favor. If this is the case for you, consider writing an introductory note to ask for a brief meeting. List the questions you want to discuss and explain that you would like to meet in person to get a sense of the job environment. When you get a positive response, confirm the meeting details, be on time, and stick to the agreed-on time. Having already established your questions beforehand, you will be more able to relax, listen, and take notes. It will make the in-person meeting more predictable and comfortable. Practicing general conversational techniques may help. For instance, discuss mutual professional interests, such as, "I'm so glad to meet someone who shares my passion for fitness," as a conversation opener before starting to ask questions. This technique develops rapport and sets you both at ease. Extroverts tend to be good at spontaneous conversation, but introverts are often good at first meeting people on Twitter and finding out what they have in common. In person, introverts tend to be good listeners. Use your listening skills to develop rapport and show genuine interest in your contact. Engage in networking activities when your energy level is at its highest. For example, if you are a morning person, do your networking in the morning.

You might feel reluctant to start the process. Sometimes it is necessary to do what you must, even though it's the last thing you want to do. Each time you push yourself to meet with someone new, you are a step closer to feeling more confident and believing in your ability to learn and grow from this networking experience. Think of how good you feel after you've exercised, even when you didn't feel like it at first! Until you have tried, you will never know!

Last, if you are a student, you have access to professors in many fields. Make an appointment with a faculty member. Most faculty members have connections in their fields that they are happy to share with interested students. Finally, be sure that you exercise courtesy and tact with every contact, and be prepared with specific questions that go beyond the general information found on websites (you will have already researched that information before the interview). Write a thank-you note to be e-mailed, followed up by a mailed note. The best networking is not simply a one-time meeting but a continuing connection. Networking will positively affect your job search and every aspect of your life.

Interviewing for Information

Survey after survey on job hunting confirms a basic fact about job-search strategy: Namely, the one best way to find out about a job and to get a job is through *people*. Once you have a job identified, you are now better able to make the most of using *informational interviews*. These interviews help you develop contacts in your field of interest, give you insider sources of knowledge, and present opportunities for referrals to meet other people in the field. This network of people will keep you informed and connected to possible job openings. The experience you gain through information interviewing and networking will help you master the techniques involved in interviewing for a job.

INFORMATION INTERVIEWING: THE PURPOSE

Information interviewing involves identifying people who are doing what you want to be doing and asking them questions related to their current job. This type of interview serves several purposes. It helps you further refine your knowledge and understanding of the field you are exploring. It enables you to develop social skills related to feeling comfortable and knowledgeable while you are being interviewed. Also, information interviewing creates the setting to develop contacts. These contacts are often helpful to your specific job search. The people you interview may themselves be in a position to hire someone like you for a job, or they may simply hear about a job opening and pass the information on to you. *Remember that your specific purpose in information interviewing is not to look for a job but to confirm your research about the field and to develop contacts that may be helpful in the future.* When involved in an information interview, *you are asking* the questions. When on a job interview, *you are being asked* most of the questions.

Other information you can gain from an information interview involves much more than simply confirming the skills needed and the salary range. On one hand, you can find out if you like the people and the environment, if the atmosphere feels comfortable, and if the people are friendly and helpful. Is this a good fit? On the other hand, you may find that no one has time to talk to you, they keep you waiting, they are interrupted and/or distracted during your interview, and they work in noisy cubicles. This information is available only through an on-site visit. Thus, the overt goal of information interviewing is to collect information, but an additional goal is to make contacts and determine whether you have made an appropriate match between your personal needs and your career goal.

INFORMATION INTERVIEWING: THE PROCESS

The first step in the process of information interviewing is to identify people who are working in the fields that are interesting to you. It's especially helpful if you know a relative, friend, or neighbor involved in the field or at least someone who can refer you to a potential contact; it's always easier to get a meeting if you can use a familiar name as a referral. The hardest step is making the first contact with a stranger or, worse, a strange firm and asking for the name of a person doing that interesting job! Luckily, you will only have to contact a stranger if you have not identified, through your networking, someone who is working in your preferred area of interest. Alert everyone you know—and especially

▲ Arrange for interviews with people who work in a field that interests you. You may gain information as well as contacts for your job search later.

those in your social network—that you are actively "researching" and "searching" for a job. Social networks are most effective when you have regular, continuous communication with your contacts. (You might even attend a workshop on maximizing social networks for a job search.) If you have not found someone in your preferred career, often someone in your social network will be able to refer you. If you are in a class, someone in your class may be your best source. This is called the law of *six degrees of separation*. It means that there are 6 or fewer layers of people separating you and virtually anyone you want to meet. Think of someone you'd like to meet—someone such as a social director on a cruise line. Then ask everyone you know who is in your social network. See how many people it takes before someone can refer you to someone who knows or can refer you to this individual. The web and social networking has made this process effortless and fun. Test it out for yourself.

Strangers, as well as acquaintances, will be more receptive to talking with you if you do the following when reaching them by phone:

1. Confirm the person's job title by saying, "Hi, my name is _____. I was referred by _____. I believe your job is _____. Is that right?"
2. Sound enthusiastic and delighted to have reached this person (e.g., the underlying feeling your voice should convey is "I'm really thrilled to have a moment to speak with you!").
3. Indicate why you want to talk to the person (e.g., "I'm interested in your field as a possible career and I'd like your help in making my decision and in planning my next career steps. Would you be willing to give me 20 minutes of your time, ideally at your workplace, so I can ask some specific questions?")
4. Refer to the research you've already completed about this field or company (e.g., "As I understand from my research, you work for one of the best companies in the field").
5. Ask for a specific meeting time and place and be sure you honor the agreed-on time frame unless the interviewee suggests talking longer. Get his or her e-mail address. Send an e-mail confirming your appointment and include some sample specific questions.
6. Thank your interviewee, and follow up with a thank-you note.

Here are some examples of lead-ins to help you get started either by phone or e-mail. Remember to identify yourself, state your purpose, and ask for an appointment with the appropriate person. This straightforward approach is generally effective.

Example:

Hello, Mr. Jones, I am Diane Smith from Moorpark College. I'm doing some research in the field of houseplant maintenance services, and I'd like to stop by at your convenience to ask you a few questions. I'd appreciate about 15 to 20 minutes of your time. When might that be possible? Is Thursday at 2 P.M. all right?

or:

Hello, Ms. Smith, this is George Brown. This morning I talked to Dr. Green about the opportunities in food supplement marketing, and he spoke very highly of you. I'm calling to find out when you might have a few minutes to talk to me. Would it be convenient to meet with you in the morning or afternoon?

TIPS FROM THE PROS

If the person you contact is not receptive, express your understanding and ask if there is someone else with whom you might speak or any other suggestion to help make your decision. Use every contact as a stepping stone to another networking opportunity.

INFORMATION INTERVIEWING OUTLINE

After you have made definite appointments to interview your target people, then you need to consider in specific detail the best questions to ask to gain the maximum useful information as quickly and pleasantly as possible. Remember, you will be talking to busy people with many demands on their time; they will expect you to be, and it's to your advantage to be, as business-like as possible.

Here is a framework to help you design your information interview. You may think you already have answers to some of the questions, but personal interviews should help flesh out details and possibly fill in some gaps in your knowledge that you don't realize are there. Choose your questions from the general categories of type of business, position classifications, position descriptions, work environment, benefits, and entrance requirements, as follows.

Ask about details that are not evident from your Internet research that you will do prior to your visit. Do not ask the obvious questions that are readily addressed on the company's website unless you need further detail or clarification.

Create your questions from the general categories of type of business, position classifications, position descriptions, work environment, benefits, and entrance requirements, as follows:

Type of Business

What are the services, products, or functions of the organization?

Who uses the organization's services or products?

Who are the competitors in this field?

What sets the company apart or distinguishes it from others in the same industry?

What are the projections for future development or new directions?

Position Classifications

In each major corporate division, what types of positions are available?

What are the qualifications for entry-level and experienced positions? (Consider education, skills, abilities, etc.)

Position Descriptions

What duties and responsibilities are performed in the area in which you are interested?

What are some examples of projects currently under way and problems currently being solved?

What is a typical day like?

What contacts would there be (e.g., personal, telephone, e-mail) with other organizations?

Work Environment

What type of physical localities are involved: outdoors, indoors, travel? How much pressure? Routine? Variety? How much supervision is there? Do flexible work schedules exist? Is overtime typical or atypical?

Benefits

How does compensation compare to other companies in the field?

What are the opportunities for advancement, promotions, or lateral mobility?

What opportunities are available for advanced training, on-the-job training, or academic course work? Is there a tuition reimbursement plan?

What other benefits are available? Possible benefits might include:

Medical/dental insurance	Child-care facilities
Life, disability insurance	Profit sharing
Vacations, holidays	Retirement
Expenses for moving, travel	Preretirement planning
Outplacement	Employee assistance programs (counseling for work-related problems)
Recreation, personal health services	

Entrance Requirements

What suggestions do you have for an individual wishing to enter this field of employment?

What other companies might employ individuals to perform this type of work?

Could you refer me to someone else for more information about opportunities in this field?

INFORMATION INTERVIEWING SAMPLE QUESTIONS

Moving from a general categorical framework to more specific detail, here is a list of typical questions you might ask in your information interviews.

1. What do you like most about your job and why?
2. What do you like least about your job and why?
3. How did you decide to get into this field, and what steps did you take to enter the field? What alternative ways can one enter this field?
4. What training would you recommend for someone who wanted to enter this field now? What skills and background are needed to get into this field now?
5. What is the salary range for a person in this field? Entry level to top salary?
6. What personal qualities do you feel are most important in your work and why?
7. What are the tasks you do in a typical workday? Would you describe them?
8. What types of stress do you experience on the job?
9. What types of people survive and do well in this field?
10. Are resumes important in getting a job here?
11. What are the opportunities for promotion?
12. Is this field expanding? Taking any new directions?
13. What related occupations might I investigate?
14. Can you give me the names of three other people who share your enthusiasm for this kind of work? How can I contact them?
15. Is there anything else about this field that would be helpful for me to know?

When you approach professionals in your field of interest from a research point of view and *not* as if you want a job, they will usually be happy to talk with you. Even the busiest executives will often find time for you. If one person doesn't have time, ask to be referred to another professional in the field. It is the assistant's job to protect the boss from distractions. When asked, "What is this call regarding?" you might respond, "I was referred to Ms. Smith by her associate Don Reid." Be certain to sound confident and friendly. It's best to call on a Tuesday, Wednesday, or Thursday between 8 A.M. and 11 A.M. If the person isn't in and you must leave a message, leave just your name and phone number.

Interviewing people who work in a field that interests you will provide you invaluable information, either confirming or revising your views. But even better, you will make contacts with people who may be able to help you actually find a job in the future. These contacts can suggest groups or associations to join, colleges to attend, and classes to take, as well as the current status of employment activity in their field. It's never too early to start. If you would like to read some sample interviews on the Web, go to **www.ideacafe.com** and click on Profiles of Fun Entrepreneurs. If your college career center subscribes to "Career Cruising" (**www.careercruising.com**), you will find excellent information interviews under the category of "interview" within each job description.

TIPS FROM THE PROS

Review the "people" aspect of your life. Are you staying connected with people? Meeting new ones? Consider going out to lunch or meeting for fun or exercise with old contacts and friends. If you attend a community organization (e.g., a 12-step program, Women in Business Club, Rotary, church, etc.), ask everyone for leads and to keep you in mind for job openings, internships, or contract work. Volunteer with organizations to maintain contacts as well as currency in your field. Try making new Twitter friends!

PRACTICING INFORMATION INTERVIEWS

Some people prefer to practice information interviews until they become confident in approaching people about their career. If you need to practice, you might try one of the following approaches. You can interview someone you already know about a hobby that sounds interesting or you can ask people about their hobbies and careers at any informal gathering you attend (e.g., clubs, parties, classes). These informal activities tend to build your self-confidence in asking questions. Once you get started, you might find you enjoy interviewing people!

Two interesting success stories may help you get started. Thomas Shanks, a college assistant professor of communications, tells how one of his students moved from California to New York to pursue a job in television broadcasting. For three months, the student sent his resume everywhere and knocked on the door of every friend, relative, and remote acquaintance he could find. He researched which after-hours spots the television crowd preferred, and he frequented those places. He eventually got offers from three networks.

Another student, a freshman, was a business major with an interest in art. In November, the vice president of industrial relations at an engineering firm gave a talk in the student's leadership class. After class, the student asked the guest speaker about summer jobs with his firm (notice how early she did so). By January, he had arranged for her to interview in the graphic arts department of his firm. She got the summer job—a job that many graduates of art programs would have coveted.

Exercise 9.2 asks you to use some of the networking/information interviewing suggestions from this chapter.

EXERCISE

9.2   Information Interviews

Select three individuals who work in fields that are interesting to you, and conduct brief information interviews using the list of sample information interview questions given in this chapter as your guide. Write a brief report of each interview and share with classmates what you learned and how it felt to contact these people compared to how you felt talking with a faculty member. Is it easier to talk to strangers now?

Job Search While Unemployed

Although experts agree that it is best to look for a job while you are still employed, not everyone is in that position. If you are unemployed and seeking employment, you will benefit by disciplining yourself to stick to a daily job search schedule. Otherwise, your best intentions may be thwarted by procrastination, which can then turn into paralysis and even depression about being unemployed.

Let's consider that you graduated from college but have not found a full-time job related to your career goal and you are not planning to take postgraduate courses full time. Some of you will be tempted to take a vacation. If you have the resources and can afford not to work for a while, that is fine. Consider googling Gap Year to gather some ideas for interesting projects that will enhance your employability. However, at some point you will need to create a disciplined job search to replace the work schedule missing from your life. You will be more productive if you begin the day as if you were going to work. Get dressed, have breakfast, and begin the day with a few hours of contact work. Identify employers who can use your skills. Be aware that successful phone and e-mail contacts rely on sheer numbers. *The greater the number of contacts you make, the greater are your chances of getting an interview.*

Here is an outline/review of the points we have discussed about information interviewing. Use this form as a guide in preparing for each interview.

1. **Find someone with whom to start the interview process.** Make sure you get the person's name. Call the person directly.

    What is the name of the person you're going to call?

    _____

2. **Make a specific appointment, for a specific length of time.**

    When is your appointment and for how long?

    _____

3. **Make a list of specific questions, things you want to know about the job.**

    Your questions for this interview. (See list on page 202.)

    _____

    _____

    _____

    _____

    _____

    _____

    _____

    _____

    _____

    _____

4. **Explain why you're calling for the interview.** Some explanations:

    a. You want to know more about this kind of work before you decide you're interested or before you decide you should choose it as a career.

    b. You are getting ready for a job interview and would like to get some advice from someone in the field before the interview.

    c. You are interested in the field but haven't found much information on it and would appreciate someone filling you in on it.

    d. You are doing some research for a career class and would like some specific information in this field.

    Which explanation will you give when you call? *(Create your own if you wish.)*

    _____

    _____

5. **Give the employer the name of the person who recommended that you call, or mention how you found the employer's name and number.** (A reference helps.)

    Who is your reference for this interview? _____

6. **After the interview, send a note thanking the person for her or his time and help.**

    Date sent: _____

Plan to spend a portion of your day online, researching job information, a portion looking for leads, and a portion filling out job applications. Another important part of the day should include being with supportive people—for example, attending networking and association meetings (remember, local newspapers have business sections that announce weekly association meetings), going to job club meetings, joining friends for lunch, and enjoying recreation.

- Keep active and in touch with people. It will reenergize you and keep you visible to those who might be able to refer you to a job.
- Reserve the final part of your day for returning phone calls and e-mails, redrafting letters, revising your resume and cover letter, and writing specific thank-you letters to people you have met. Planning and preparation can make the critical difference in turning contacts into interviews and interviews into job offers.

Many college graduates use their college or university career center. Those who have been out of college for a while often use the services of their state "One Stop Center." (The unemployment office usually requires you to contact a minimum number of employers each week or month to remain eligible to collect unemployment insurance.) The One Stop Center offers workshops on job-search strategy, assistance in writing a resume, and a job bank. Some offices also conduct targeted group meetings for workers in designated fields (e.g., aerospace, automotive, banking, executive, and manufacturing). Use support groups; they offer both encouragement and job leads.

▲ While unemployed, maintain a job-search routine and make phone calls every day.

Planning for Action

Effective job search strategy requires you to master the skills of goal setting and action planning. This means you set objectives such as those indicated in the following nine suggestions and designate specific times to complete each one:

1. Schedule planning time.
2. Maintain a list of activities to get done; for example, develop a weekly calendar and enter each item per day or hour.

> He who asks is a fool for five minutes; he who does not ask a question remains a fool forever.
>
> —*Chinese Proverb*

EXHIBIT **9.1** **Sample Contact File Format**

1. Company: **Phone No.:**   **Contact Person & Title:**   **Type of Contact & Date:**

Referred By: **E-mail:**   Letter _____

Address: Phone _____

Job Target: Resume _____

Application _____

Conclusions: Interview _____

Follow-up:

2. Company: **Phone No.:**   **Contact Person & Title:**   **Type of Contact & Date:**

Referred By: **E-mail:**   Letter _____

Address: Phone _____

Job Target: Resume _____

Application _____

Follow-up: **Conclusions:**   Interview _____

EXHIBIT 9.1 Sample Contact File Format   *CONTINUED*

3. Company: Phone No.:   Contact Person & Title: Type of Contact & Date:

Letter   _____

Referred By: E-mail: Phone   _____

Resume   _____

Address: Application   _____

Job Target: Interview   _____

Follow-up: Conclusions:

4. Company: Phone No.:   Contact Person & Title: Type of Contact & Date:

Letter   _____

Referred By: E-mail: Phone   _____

Resume   _____

Address: Application   _____

Job Target: Interview   _____

Follow-up: Conclusions:

5. Company: Phone No.:   Contact Person & Title: Type of Contact & Date:

Letter   _____

Referred By: E-mail: Phone   _____

Resume   _____

Address: Application   _____

Job Target: Interview   _____

Follow-up: Conclusions:

3. Start a notebook or online/file with one section for contacts' names, addresses, and phone numbers and another section for notes about different companies (see Exhibit 9.1).

4. Conduct information interviews and attend networking events to create possible contacts.

5. Have a one-minute "Elevator Speech" ready in case you happen to be at a conference or a impromptu meeting and want to make a quick impression. In one minute you could say the following:

> "I have a bachelor's degree in communication with a minor in marketing from the University of Madison at Wisconsin. I interned at the Mustard Museum and increased the percentage of visitors by 25% in two months by creating a Facebook page and being the Twitter contact. I have always created blogs and travel photos online for my family and could do the same for your company. I also have a background in technical art, writing, and design, which I could combine to tell your story in a special, get-their-attention way. Here is my business card for future reference. Could I meet with you at a future date?"

This is also called an "elevator pitch"; if you want more ideas, just google "Elevator Speech." Note that an Elevator Speech always includes your relevant skills and a unique story that someone would remember about you.

EXHIBIT 9.2 Branding or Business Card

ALICIA SMITH

B. A. Communications & Marketing

University of Wisconsin at Madison

E-mail: asmith@aol.com Phone: 555-444-8888 Fax: 555-444-8889

Blog: **www.wordpress/asmith**

Skills and Competencies

Graphic Designer

Web Developer (see **www.mustardmuseum com** and **www.surfshop.org**)

Bilingual: Spanish and English "Se Habla Espanol"

Marketing minor

Can design social media campaigns on Facebook and Twitter

Available for full time or for contract services

---

6. If you can't leave a resume, have a business card (list years of experience and skills) or a "branding card" (list skills) that you can hand out when networking (see Exhibit 9.2)

7. Use Internet bookmarks/favorites for often-used addresses.

8. Stay current in your field:

   - Sign up for news alerts at **www.google.com/alerts** to receive email updates of the latest news relevant about your profession.

   - Read relevant blogs to stay updated in your field; google "blog + industry name" and use Google's search feature at **http://blogsearch.google.com**.

   - Use LinkedIn and relevant groups on LinkedIn regularly.

9. Review your progress by checking off completed activities.

An effective job search requires clerical and organizational skills. Every week you will need to update names, obtain more exact titles, and confirm addresses. You can keep this information in a notebook or in your computer. Being able to retrieve at a moment's notice the information you have been collecting can make the difference between getting your resume to the potential employer today or tomorrow (which may be a day too late). The fastest way to update a resume is to have it stored in your computer or flash drive for use in a computer at school, at a local copy center, or at a friend's home.

Software packages and mobile applications can help you create a tracking system for all your contacts and activities. One software program, for example, leads you through planning, analysis, targeted markets, and commitment to a schedule of tasks. After working through the program, you will have created a list of potential employers, a resume, and a cover letter, and you will have prepared for the interview.

If you do not already have Internet access, consider investing in a service such as America Online or MSN that provides access. If you can not afford a service, a library, the One Stop Center, or the college career center will provide you with most of the tools you need. Most companies are advertising job openings first on the Web and requiring electronic transmission of resumes and applications. Also, company insiders may provide information about job openings via company websites, blogs, and discussion forums. Discussion forums may be available through Google groups (**http://groups.google.com**), LinkedIn, Facebook, and **Yahoo.com**.

Implementing Your Job Search: A Lifelong Venture

The comprehensive approach to job hunting involves putting yourself in the right place at the right time again and again throughout your lifetime. It involves strategies that assist you in finding openings in your target area before the openings are publicly announced. In situations when you do not appear to be the ideal candidate, this approach will assist you in getting noticed and getting an interview.

Many times, this approach works best while you are still employed because potential employers tend to defer unemployed inquirers to the HR office. Ideally, before starting a job search, you will have a specific field and job objective in mind. Let's say you have selected business administration and want to specialize in real estate finance. Your first decision is whether you want to work for a commercial bank, a private developer, the government (such as an appraisal office or bureau of land development), or a related association that employs people to interact with the government. The "Real Stories" feature in which you meet Susan offers an example.

REAL stories ‹ Meet Susan

As an assistant to a county supervisor, Susan finds many of her assignments relate to land development. While finishing work toward her bachelor's degree in business (attending college after work hours), she increasingly represents her supervisor when land developers appeal to the board of supervisors for zoning and code changes. When her supervisor decides not to run for reelection, Susan is hired as a director for the business-industry association to lobby the county for the industrialization of farmland. Within a few years, she becomes a consultant to land developers and interacts with her present boss, who hires her into his prospering real estate development firm as vice president of government relations.

Even while working in an entry-level job, Susan met people working in real estate, the field of her interest. As an assistant to the county supervisor, she met people in government, nonprofit associations, and private industry. She maintained high visibility by speaking at community events, representing her supervisor when necessary, and joining relevant organizations and community clubs. When Susan wanted to make a job change, she had already identified and made contact with the types of places and people with whom she wanted to work.

Susan had contacts who were insiders and could recommend her for jobs even before they were announced. But even more important, she had discovered the hidden job market. She knew the needs of the business-industry association and could tell its people how her skills and contacts could benefit them. She was able to sell herself. She knew she had skills and contacts with government that could enhance her present employer's expansive plans. She was hired because she was able to describe the job she wanted to do in the firm and because her ideal job meshed with the vision of the president of the company. She actually created her current position.

WHAT DO *YOU* THINK?

1. What job strategy did Susan use to great advantage?
2. How did Susan develop visibility while working on the job?
3. How did Susan use her knowledge and contacts to create the job of her dreams?
4. How can you develop your network through your job, internship, volunteer, or service learning experience?

EXERCISE your options

Do This in the Next Week: Try out a few of the networking/information interviewing questions in this chapter with a faculty member at your local college or a friend of your family. Afterward, write a note to yourself about how it felt to approach someone as a networking contact. Save your first impressions on your computer or in a notebook; you can use this impression in Exercise 9.2

 **Summary**

This chapter has discussed the comprehensive job search. Your goal is to confirm your impressions about your ideal career. You won't know the accuracy of your researched information until you volunteer in the field, do part-time work in the field, or find a job that will put you around the people doing the type of work you desire. Only then will you know how you feel about the real job environment. It also takes practice to remember to ask everyone you meet about his or her job. The more jobs you learn about, the more alternatives you will have.

You will uncover the hidden job market through the people you meet in the process of networking and information interviewing. They can help you uncover potential jobs before they are advertised. Your ability to develop and maintain your contacts will help you when you need one!

Selected Online Career and Employment Websites

Searching online can be overwhelming. Thousands of websites are available for job searching. Find a service suited to you and remember, the more you target your search, the more efficient it will be. Rather than typing "job search," use terms such as "entry-level job" or "job in advertising." Here are a few sites to get you started.

California Career Café (www.Cacareercafe.com) Go to the "Get Experience Section" to find resources related to volunteering, internships, professional associations, and information interviews. Use the links to Road Trip Nation and to several university career centers' websites.

Career One Stop Center (www.careeronestop .org) This Department of Labor website will help you find the online labor market information for your state. Your state's website (e.g., in California, **www.caljobs.ca.gov**) provides resume writing, networking, and job services for job candidates, employers, and recruitment firms. This is a free service to job hunters.

CareerBuilder (www.careerbuilder.com) The CareerBuilder site has its own database of job opportunities; it lists thousands of jobs and directs the user to online job fairs, employer profiles, and special resources for students. Instructions and tips about electronic resumes are provided. You may search by job type, industry, or company. There is an application with full website functionality and built-in geolocation technology.

INDEED (www.indeed.com) Search for postings on thousands of job boards and company websites at once, using their Job Search tool. Also look at salaries, trends, and forums (people reporting back what they found).

The Monster Board (www.monster.com) This is one of the largest databases for job listings on the Web and it has an excellent "career center." Its resources section has information for new job seekers, career changers, and people making military transitions. Additionally, you can search for information on jobs, industries, internships, franchises, salary statistics, resume writing, and interview techniques.

Nation Job Network (www.nationjob.com) In addition to the standard search by job title or company name, this site features Personal Job Scout, which keeps an eye on listing updates and notifies you via e-mail about related jobs. This service is free, but it also offers for-fee services. The site is a good resource for government jobs and trade magazines and has an excellent link to a sample resume website (**www.greatsampleresume.com**).

National Resources for People with Disabilities (www.pacdbtac.org/resources/resources-federal .htm) This is a national site with more than job and ADA (Americans with Disabilities Act) resources. For sources related to job accommodations, go to **www.jan.wvu.edu**. Also, for those who are blind, go to National Federation of the Blind, **www.nfb.org**.

Online Job Search Guide and Career Resource Center (www.Job-Hunt.org) Rated highly by *PC Magazine*, this site includes basics on job searching, good career articles, state-by-state job resources, and international job information. It also offers a comprehensive industry database and excellent links to employment supersites, job fairs, classified ads, and recruiting guides and links to the *Wall Street Journal* career articles. For social networks, go to **www.job-hunt.org/ job-search-networking/social-networks.shtml**.

The Richard Bolles Parachute Site (www.JobHunters Bible.com) The author of *What Color Is Your Parachute?* has an abundance of career information and resources on his site, including job-search information, resume writing tips, and company information. Bolles also provides tips for using the Internet to conduct your search effectively.

The Riley Guide (www.rileyguide.com). *Riley's Job Guide* provides a wealth of information with many good links regarding job listings, resume postings, employer profiles, and current articles. It also contains articles from job searchers who have tried online job searches and can tell you how it really works. The site gives very detailed information. Get it on Facebook: **www.facebook.com/ TheRileyGuide**.

USA Today News (www.usatoday.com). Go to Money and click on Company News to get to Company Research. This website links to Vault company research.

Vault (www.vault.com). This is an excellent source for information on internships and company research and to try a Career Advice Blog. (You may need to check with your college career center for a password.)

Online Services with Good Career Sections
America Online: www.aol.com
Microsoft Network: www.msn.com
Yahoo!: www.yahoo.com

Check with your local university or 800 directory for more online services.

Search Engines and Browsers

Here is a list of the most used search engines as well as some unusual ones. Following the name is a description of how it catalogs various sites. Start with Google, Yahoo!, or Bing— all of which target mainstream users and are considered user-friendly.

- **AltaVista (www.altavista.com)** This is one of the most comprehensive indexes of documents on the Web. Unless you're very specific about your search criteria, it often turns up so many matches that you will have more than enough to meet your needs. This engine will locate the most obscure topics.

- **Google (www.google.com)** Google rates sites by how many pages link to the site. This search engine is constantly expanding. If your search is too broad, try searching by "group."

- **Search (www.search.com)** This is an excellent reference site.

- **Yahoo! (www.yahoo.com)** Yahoo! organizes sites by category. When it finds a site that matches your request, it displays a summary of the site and a link to the site's category. Look for free information because some links may be fee based.

- **Ask.com** is similar to Yahoo! but you can ask a question or search by topic.

Search Engine Watch (www.searchenginewatch .com) This site provides a tutorial on using search engines and also rates them for a variety of subject areas.

PURPOSE OF EXERCISES

These exercises serve to increase your ability to network effectively. Exercise 9.1 asked you to identify specific people who are part of your network. Exercise 9.2 directed you to conduct information interviews. Exercise 9.3 helps you expand information about your job target by using practice information gathering, expert information gathering, and interviewing for employment strategies. Exercise 9.4 suggests what you can add to your career portfolio folder. Exercise 9.5, WWWebwise, is a Web-based exercise that reinforces the learnings in this chapter. Finally, Reinforce Your Learning Outcomes, strengthens your learning in this chapter.

9.3 Personal Contact Log

Prepare a log of personal contacts (at least five) using the approaches described in this chapter under "Interviewing for Information." Focusing on your own job target, see how much information and how many new contacts you acquire. Use the appropriate format provided for each type of contact you make.

Name: _____ Job Target: _____

Practice Information Gathering

Hobby or interest: _____ Contact: _____

Information gathered as a result of the interview: _____

_____

_____

_____

Other possible contacts: _____

_____

_____

Expert Information Gathering

Occupational interest: _____

Contact (who, where employed, how you found this person): _____

_____

_____

Information gathered: _____

_____

_____

New contacts: _____

_____

Any contradictions: _____

_____

_____

Conclusions: _____

_____

_____

Interviewing for Employment, Apprenticeship, or Volunteer Experience

Choice of possible work site: _____

_____

What do you want (job, apprenticeship, volunteer experience)? _____

_____

Who is in a position to hire you? _____

Your approach (telephone, letter, in person): _____

Outcomes and follow-up: _____

_____

_____

EXERCISE

9.4   Expand Your Career Portfolio

Add to the Career Portfolio that you started with the chapter summaries found at the end of the book, and keep the responses to the questions below with your other summaries so that you can retrieve and add to your portfolio as you complete the remaining chapters.

Identify your ideal job situation and then list an entry-level job related to your ideal:

_____

_____

_____

Identify volunteer, freelance opportunities or part-time opportunities:

_____

_____

_____

Identify people who are doing what you would like to do:

_____

_____

_____

List your information interview questions and what you learned from interviewing someone:

_____

_____

_____

List your contacts and professional associations for this ideal job:

_____

_____

_____

EXERCISE

9.5   WWWebwise

Go to **http://www.careerbuilder.com**. Search by category and location. Explore job market opportunities within a career field of your choice. Report on job market opportunities within a career field of your choice in writing or to the class. Be sure to list three jobs and include the following (or cut and paste the information): Company, Location, Job description, Salary, and Minimum requirements to apply,

Go to **RoadtripNation.com**. Find an interview that has been done by others and write what you learned: _____

_____

Go to **http://heartsandminds.org/member.htm** and list one volunteer activity that would help you in expanding your career network: _____

(*Note:* Be aware that websites can change without notice. If a link does not work, find a similar site to complete the activity.)

REINFORCING YOUR LEARNING OUTCOMES

Review and Rate Your Chapter Outcomes. Indicate in the right-hand column how well you do the following items (from 1 = very well, to 5 = not at all). If you rated yourself 4 or 5, review the material on the pages in parentheses to ensure your career success.

How Well Can You Do the Following?

- Identify the components of a successful job search strategy. (pp. 183–185)   1 2 3 4 5

- Begin the process of searching for a job. (pp. 186–195)   1 2 3 4 5

- Explain how to find the hidden job market. (pp. 188–195)   1 2 3 4 5

- Develop your network. (pp.195–205)   1 2 3 4 5

- Expand your network. (pp. 205–208)   1 2 3 4 5

Go to the Career Fitness Portfolio at the end of the book and complete this chapter summary to build and record your personal Career Fitness Portfolio.

Additional Opportunity: Your instructor may choose to assign the Career Fitness Portfolio for in class or online completion. If so, they will provide the handout or link for you to access.

Crafting a Winning Resume and Portfolio

Market Your Unique Brand

STUDENT LEARNING OUTCOMES

At the end of the chapter you will be able to . . .

- Differentiate between types of resumes.
- Recognize the value of a professional portfolio.
- Prepare a winning resume.
- Write a cover letter.

Every successful fitness program includes a chart that indicates visually where you started, where you are at the present time, and where you are headed in the future. In a career fitness program, this chart is called a *resume*. Eventually, in the course of job hunting, you will be asked to present a resume to a prospective employer. Most career counselors caution that the resume alone is not going to get you an interview without an active social network, strong contacts, or an introduction inside a company. At the same time, a strategic resume can lead to an interview. Most resumes are transmitted electronically and scanned by computer programs. This approach is useful to employers who receive hundreds of resumes daily; however, it is much easier for your resume to be rejected if it is not strategically composed and formatted. This chapter will help you gain a competitive edge in developing a winning resume and portfolio, which can potentially reach countless employers.

A resume is a document that you compose to communicate your background and value to an employer. At best, it is a marketing tool used to gain an interview. It is also a strategic review of your skills in terms of a specific job objective as well as a useful memory jogger in an interview to respond to such common questions as "Tell me about yourself," "Why should I hire you?" and "What skills do you bring to this job?"

In this chapter, you will become familiar with three resume formats: functional, chronological, and a creative combination. You will understand the value of a portfolio that presents concrete samples of your work products to further highlight your past performance. In addition, you will understand the importance of cover letters and application forms as part of your job-search strategy. Once you have completed this chapter, you will be prepared to craft your own winning resume.

> Life is 10 percent what you make of it, and 90 percent how you take it.
>
> —*Irving Berlin*

Your Resume as a Marketing Tool

You are creating your marketing program to sell the brand: YOU. The appearance of this document is critical. It is a reflection of you as a potential employee. It is equivalent to your unique photo or thumbprint. You are in control of its look and content so take care in creating this document. Spend as much time preparing and crafting it as you would when preparing for an important date. Your advertisement—the resume—must be concise and interesting enough to attract your potential employer. As you read a job description, look for the skills that are required to perform the job. Strategically, because of the widespread use of computerized scanning software, your resume must incorporate the exact words found in the job description for which you are applying or you risk being eliminated from the running. You must get past the computerized selection process before a potential employer ever sees your resume. Then, the human screener will quickly review your document, often no more than 10 seconds before deciding to put your document on the reject or further consideration pile. Your challenge is to make it easy for the reader to see the connection, the fit between you and the job.

In addition to job-specific skills, there are critical skills that all employers want regardless of the specific job. Employer surveys always cite communication skills (the ability to listen, write, and speak effectively) at the top of the list of essential skills. Strategically, through your resume, you must indicate that you have these skills and show how you have demonstrated them. If your resume is clearly composed, without spelling or grammatical errors, it will make a positive first impression about your communication skills. Check it carefully to avoid being eliminated for careless errors.

You will then highlight these skills by providing a brief description of an achievement, plan, or event that you conceived and implemented. These brief descriptions will demonstrate how effectively you communicate. Other skills you might include would be examples of your flexible learning style, computer/technical literacy, multicultural or foreign language experience, and teamwork capabilities. Such talents are always high on the list of skills that employers find desirable in a candidate.

THE CHALLENGE OF YOUR RESUME

Assuming you pass the scanning screening, who will be reading your resume and why would she or he care enough to have you proceed to an interview? Will your resume be compelling and credible? Did you carefully present your resume as a polished and professional product?

Employers receive hundreds of resumes and cover letters for any open position. Every resume must be reviewed and only the top 8 or 10 candidates are invited to an interview. Given the precious seconds that you have to

▲ A resume customized for the job for which you are applying, accompanied by a well-written cover letter, will be much more effective than a general resume.

TIPS FROM THE PROS

Creating the connection between you and the job—that is, the "fit" in terms of the position and work environment—immediately enhances your chances of making it to the interview and getting the job. Here's how to do it:

- Focus on accomplishments as well as job duties.
- Think about your target audience and the specific job description. Remember you are selling yourself.
- Use hard data to back up your statements—for example, "I increased retail sales by 25%, which resulted in $10,000 in quarterly revenue."
- Ask associates and friends to review your resume for content and appearance.
- *Always* include a cover letter with your resume.

present yourself as one of the best possible job candidates, your resume needs to sell your "value" to the company so the reviewer *wants* to read more. After listing your specific job objective, which will be custom tailored for each opening, you will exercise your competitive edge by strategically emphasizing how your skills and experiences match the job description.

Your advertising message starts at the very beginning of your resume. Your special skills, experiences, and strengths must focus on how these will be of benefit to the employer. A valuable addition to your first page (of no more than a two-page resume) is to define the value that you will add that will directly benefit the company. For example, if you helped a program get started, raised sales or profits, added a new procedure, or helped design a marketing campaign, that achievement should be mentioned. Facts and activities that highlight your accomplishments, professionalism, and knowledge will impress a reviewer.

TYPES OF RESUMES

The most widely used types of resumes include the following:

- **Scannable paper.** A specially formatted hard copy resume used by employers to scan into a computer database. The database can then be searched for keywords to help identify applicants with qualifications or job openings.
- **Electronic.** An ASCII text-only resume stripped of formatting to ensure the file will transmit correctly from any e-mail, Internet, or electronic interface to an employer's resume-tracking software.
- **Online/Web-based.** A resume in HTML format published to a web server for viewing over the Internet with a web browser program. This format adds flexibility in that it supports incorporation of more sophisticated elements such as animated graphics as well as sound and video clips.

The use of online resumes is most common in high-tech industries and is effective as a link from a personal to a business website. Also note that an online resume should be used in addition to standard paper and electronic resumes.

BENEFITS OF ONLINE RESUMES

The benefits of developing and posting a well-designed online resume are numerous:

- A well-developed online resume is a powerful tool for displaying your expertise in computer technology (e.g., HTML, website and graphic design).
- Listing the URL to your online resume is effective in a networking e-mail.

- Listing the URL for your resume in your paper and electronic resumes can also expand your job-search marketing effectiveness.
- An online resume can be a useful meeting or interview follow-up tool. It may provide an important opportunity to initiate further communication with your contacts.
- Having business cards available with your website URL may be more appropriate or convenient to give to contacts or potential employers in some networking situations than offering your printed resume.
- Employers and recruiters constantly search the Internet for candidates with specific job skills.

SUCCESS strategies   Winning Online Resumes

- Use key action words and skill words that fit the job (e.g., *creative, team player, organized, and technology savvy with Adobe software, blogs, and wikis*).
- Use key words related to the job description and the employer's industry.
- Highlight relevant accomplishments that are closely related to the job.

- Emphasize nouns for industry-specific terms (e.g., *accountant* instead of *accounting*).
- In email attachments, use MS Word and Plain Text.
- Emphasize measurable skills and other accomplishments under the heading of Work Experience.

Portfolio and Digital Resume Alternatives

An electronic portfolio is becoming an essential addition to a resume for the strategic job hunter. Your portfolio is a summary of your work products that you create and showcase in your unique way on a webpage.

▲ For many jobs, an electronic resume will be required.

With an electronic portfolio, information can be easily stored. A portfolio provides a personal and vivid picture of your work qualities; it differentiates you as a unique brand. *Branding* is best defined as broadcasting your distinctive product or message. *The challenge and appeal is to creatively capture the attention of your audience.*

Once the work is organized, you can enhance an electronic portfolio by adding sound, music, pictures, graphics, and video to highlight your authentic brand. In summary, electronic portfolios are both practical and effective. The benefits include quick access, easy storage, and immediate updating. The following template is a way to organize the contents of the portfolio. View the potential power of a personal portfolio from the example shown below.

Electronic Portfolio Sections

Name: John Smith
Branding Title: "Motivating Every Student Toward Full Potential"

Site Navigation

- Home
- Career Objective
- Professional Portfolio
- Field Experiences
- Teaching Samples
- Education
- Honors and Awards
- References and Testimonials

(Sample Cover Letter or inserted video introduction for the Electronic Portfolio):

Hello, I am John Smith. Welcome to my personal portfolio. As an elementary teacher for your announced opening beginning in the spring of 2012, I believe you will find me to be an exceptional candidate. I have recently completed all of my field work and teaching credentials at the State University of New York. My youth volunteer experiences, working with children to increase their self-esteem, and my personal commitment that every child deserves a bright future are values that I put into practice. I have a passion for students' success as evidenced by the videos in my teaching samples.

Please view my site for more in-depth information on my qualifications. I look forward to meeting with you for a personal interview.

Sincerely,

John Smith

VIDEO AND SOCIAL MEDIA RESUMES

A video resume could be part of an overall portfolio management strategy and would have the potential of enhancing your online presence across the Web. Imagine a company advertising an exciting new venture and requesting that candidates provide a two-minute video resume in order to proceed to the next stage of a personal interview. You would be challenged to present your skills, accomplishments, and personality through this medium.

A visual *CV (Curriculum Vitae)* is essentially defined as an expanded online portfolio. This format allows all types of interactive content to be restructured into a traditional resume format with additional links to blog posts. You can change colors as well as add video, photos, and downloads. Using a visual CV makes it possible not only to tell but to actually show someone what makes you a great candidate for a position.

Similar to a visual CV, the content in social media resumes as found in Facebook and LinkedIn focuses more on the present compared to a traditional resume that often tells people what you have done in the past. Facebook has become the "it" company of the technical world with a user base in the hundreds of millions. With permission from the Facebook page owner (you), employers have access to information about you! Facebook now links employers and corporate recruiters. It is important to ensure that the security settings on your Facebook page allows potential employers to see only what you want them to see.

FACTS & FIGURES

LinkedIn

What do Microsoft, Netflix, IBM and Target have in common? The answer is that they all use LinkedIn to recruit candidates for employment! Recruiters search for people with relevant skill sets and experiences that match a list of company requirements.

LinkedIn is the Internet location for professional visibility. There are members from all 500 of the Fortune 500 companies comprising 130 different industries and as well as more than 2 million companies with LinkedIn Company Pages.

Source: Alison Doyle, About.com Guide, retrieved on August 19, 2011 from **http://jobsearch.about.com/od/networking/a/linkedin.html** and **http://press.linkedin.com/about**

LinkedIn is viewed as the branding and professional network. Millions of users are utilizing LinkedIn as their digital resume website in order to attract job offers. In today's competitive market where brand is a key element of survival, LinkedIn is a magnet for self-promotion.

CREATING YOUR RESUME

As you now move closer to producing your own resume, visualize a pyramid or triangle with the job objective at the top and everything beneath it supporting that objective. In actuality, you will design a fresh, distinct resume for each job objective. You will craft your basic resume by the end of this chapter and then, as specific jobs become available, you will tailor your basic resume so that it reflects the specific language and skill sets of the job description. Remember, there are no jobs titled "anything." The job objective is a concise and precise statement about the position you are seeking. This may include the type of firm in which you hope to work (e.g., a small growing company, a local artisan bakery). A clear objective gives focus to your job search and indicates to an employer that you've given serious thought to your career goals. A job objective is sometimes referred to as a goal, professional objective, position desired, or simply objective. It can be as specific as "Parole Officer in L.A. County", "Human Resources assistant in an accounting firm," or "junior programmer"; it can be as general as "management position" or "administrative assistant." The more specific the objective statement, the better, because a clear objective enables you to focus your resume more directly on that target. The effect is pointed, dramatic, and convincing. In choosing information to include in your resume, avoid anything that may not be considered in a positive light or that has no relationship to your ability to do the job (e.g., marital status, number of children, political or religious affiliation, age, photos). When in doubt, leave it out.

To begin the rough draft of your resume, prepare a hard copy or word document version of 5 × 8 index card for each job you've held (see Exhibit 10.1). The index card will contain the following items:

1. Name, address, phone number of employer, and immediate supervisor at work site
2. Dates employed (month/year to month/year)
3. Job title
4. Skills used

Once you have clear descriptions of your past jobs and skills, you can begin to develop the background for your resume and/or portfolio by completing Exercise 10.1, "Resume/Portfolio Review." From your research, integrate your answers with the categories.

EXHIBIT 10.1   **Resume Index Card** *(The Format Can Easily Be Adapted for Use in Creating a Computer File)*

Elaine's House of Coffee
555 Stevens Circle
Roanoke, VA 23640
(540) 555-1211

April 2010 - Present

Skills Used:
Related well with continuous flow of people.
Attentive to detail; organized; energetic.
Bilingual—Spanish/English

Supervisor:
Joe Smith

Position:
Bookkeeper & Shift Supervisor

Functions:

Management
—Coordinated service with customer needs, documented payroll, interviewed and scheduled employees.

Communications
—Welcomed guests. Directed staff in performing courteous and rapid service. Responded to and resolved complaints.

Bookkeeping
—Maintained records of financial transactions. Balanced books. Compiled statistical reports.

EXERCISE 10.1   **Resume/Portfolio Review**

A. PERSONAL DATA

   1. Name _____

   2. Address _____

   3. Phone _____

   4. Email/website _____

B. CURRENT JOB OBJECTIVE _____

C. EDUCATION

   1. High school and college _____

     a. Favorite subjects _____

     b. Samples of best work in classes related to job objective _____

     c. Extracurricular interests _____

     d. Offices held _____

     e. Athletic achievements _____

     f. Other significant facts (e.g., honors, awards) _____

   2. Other (military service, volunteer work that provided training, correspondence courses, summer activities, languages, technical skills, licenses, and/or credentials)

D. WORK EXPERIENCE

   Employer _____

   Length of employment _____

   Position _____

   Skills and accomplishments (These may be featured in a bulleted list following Current Job Objective.) _____

   Samples of best work if relevant _____

EXERCISE 10.1 Resume/Portfolio Review *CONTINUED*

E. ASSOCIATIONS, VOLUNTEER WORK, AND COMMUNITY INVOLVEMENT

_____

_____

F. SPECIAL SKILLS (e.g., language proficiency, computer skills)

_____

_____

TIPS FROM THE PROS

Resume templates can be found by googling "Resume Templates" or using templates from a college career center or a library's career resources, such as Peterson's Guides, Career Cruising, or Eureka.

USING ACTION WORDS

Your writing style communicates the work activity in which you have been involved. Use phrases and document experiences that both involve the reader and make your resume outstanding and active. Following are basic guidelines for selecting your "power" words:

- Choose short, clear phrases.
- If you use complete sentences throughout, keep them concise and direct.
- Use the acceptable jargon of the work for which you are applying. Remember: You want your prospective employer to *read* your resume.

 **SUCCESS strategies**   Action Words

Here are some examples of action words to include in a strategic resume:

accomplished	evaluated	negotiated
achieved	expanded	organized
analyzed	facilitated	oriented
arranged	guided	planned
built	identified	processed
controlled	implemented	produced
coordinated	improved	proved
created	increased	provided
demonstrated	initiated	raised profits
designed	inspired	reduced costs
developed	interpreted	researched
directed	invented	sold
effected	led	supervised
encouraged	managed	supported
established	motivated	wrote

- Avoid general comments such as "My duties were..." or "I worked for...." Begin with action words that concisely describe what your tasks were—for example:

     Implemented new employee database.
     Developed more effective interviewing procedure.
     Evaluated and revised training program for new employees.

- List the results of your activities—for example:

     Reduced office filing by 25 percent.
     Designed interview evaluation form.
     Increased efficiency in delivering services by 10%.

- Don't dilute your action words with too many extraneous activities. Be *selective* and sell your *best* experiences.

- Target your words to the employer's needs.

Resume Formats

The three general resume formats are functional, chronological, and combination. The next part of this chapter discusses all three in detail. The combination or hybrid resume, as the name implies, is a combination of the functional and chronological. Exhibit 10.2 provides you with a resume template that describes the categories that can be included in either format.

EXHIBIT 10.2 Resume Template

Name
Address
Phone Number/E-mail Address

Job Objective	State and describe your objective as specifically as possible.
Special Skills	Put this category directly after Job Objective if your professional experience does not adequately reflect the skills that best support this job objective. *Examples*: Facility with numbers or technology, social media experience, patience, writing ability, self-taught skills, language fluency.
Education	Depending on your job objective and the amount of education you have had, you may want to place this category directly after Job Objective. (However, if your job experience is more relevant to the position or if your education is not recent, you will want to list job experience *prior* to Education.) The most recent education should be listed first. Include relevant credentials and licenses. As employers, educational institutions are usually more concerned with appropriate degrees than are other employers. Include special workshops courses and self-taught skills when they are appropriate to your job objective.
Work Experience	Describe *functionally* (by activities performed) your experience relevant to the particular job for which you are applying; start with the most relevant and go to the least relevant. Include without distinction actual job experience, volunteer experience, your work on class projects, and school and class offices held. Alternatively, if you have no breaks in employment, show your experience *chronologically*, listing your most recent professional experience first. *(See samples on next page.)* Use action verbs; do not use full sentences, unless you decide to write your resume as a narrative. Use the *Dictionary of Occupational Titles* or O*NET to help you describe accurately what you have done, always keeping in mind how your experience relates to your job objective and job description.
References	Include "References Available Upon Request" only if you have space.

If references are requested, you will need to submit their names and contact information on a separate form. Although you don't have to list specific names on the resume, have at least three people in mind who are willing to endorse your work habits, your skills, and your accomplishments. When you are job hunting, ask these people in advance if you may use them as references. Keep your references updated on your job search and inform them of your job objective so they will be prepared if a prospective employer calls. Many college placement centers act as a clearinghouse for the collection of resumes and letters of recommendation. You establish a file, and the center sends out your resume and references when you make a request. The placement center often makes this service available for alumni, and it may have reciprocal agreements with other colleges across the country.

Sample Functional Entry under Professional Experience	Sample Chronological Entry under Professional Experience
Budgeting/Financial	**Sales Associate**
Analyzed and coordinated payroll record keeping, budgeted expenditures, and requisitioned supplies; prepared attendance accounting reports; and initiated budget system for $10,000 of instructional monies allocated to the school.	Builders Emporium, Wadsworth, TX 2008–Present Operated cash register and made change, worked well with public, motivated fellow employees, excellent customer relations skills, increased sales 25% in two months.

THE FUNCTIONAL RESUME

A functional resume presents your experience, skills, and job history in terms of the functions you have actually performed rather than as a simple chronological listing of the titles of jobs you have held. Like any resume, tailor it to fit the main tasks and competencies required for the job you are seeking. Select and emphasize activities from previous employment that relate to the specific job sought, and deemphasize or omit irrelevant background.

The functional resume is especially useful if you have limited work experience, breaks in your employment record, or you are changing fields. You need not include dates or distinguish paid activities from nonpaid volunteer activities. By omitting previous employers' names, you downplay any stereotyped assumptions that a prospective employer may make about previous employers (McDonald's, the PTA, a school district). Similarly, highlighting skills and deemphasizing job titles help direct the future employer to the fact that you are someone with specific abilities that closely fit the present job opening. This format also can emphasize your growth and development.

To use this format effectively, you must be able to identify and write about your achievements. Samples for effectively written job functions can be found at O*NET (**http://online .onetcenter.org**; type in any job title in the search area). Be aware that some employers may prefer resumes that include exact dates and job titles.

Suggestions for Job Descriptions

Descriptions in the *Dictionary of Occupational Titles*, in O*NET, and in some Human Resources manuals provide helpful phrases and statements to use in describing your own job history and experience. The following two descriptions, for example, would be useful to you in composing a functional resume for a job in business. *However, you would use only relevant sentences, adapting them to your personal background.*

Office Manager

Coordinates activities of clerical personnel in the organization. Analyzes and organizes office operations and procedures such as word processing, bookkeeping, preparation of payrolls, flow of correspondence, filing, requisitioning of supplies, and other clerical services.

Evaluates office production, revises procedures, or devises new forms to improve efficiency of work flow. Formulates procedures for systematic retention, protection, retrieval, transfer, and disposal of records. Plans office layouts and initiates cost-reduction programs. Reviews clerical and personnel records to ensure completeness, accuracy, and timeliness. Prepares activity reports for guidance of management. Prepares employee ratings and conducts employee benefits and insurance programs. Coordinates activities of various clerical departments or workers within department.

Administrative Assistant

Aids executive in staff capacity by coordinating office services such as personnel, budget preparation and control, housekeeping, records control, and special management studies. Studies management methods to improve work flow, simplify reporting procedures, and implement cost reductions. Analyzes unit operating practices, such as database management, office layout, suggestion systems, personnel and budgetary requirements, and performance standards, to create new systems or revise established procedures. Analyzes jobs to delineate position responsibilities for use in wage and salary adjustments, promotions, and evaluation of work flow. Studies methods of improving work measurements or performance standards.

If you are applying for a specific job, ask the HR department for a copy of the job description; then tailor your resume to the skills listed in that description. See Exhibit 10.3 as an example of a functional resume.

EXHIBIT 10.3 Functional Resume for a College Undergraduate

ABDUL MUHAMMED

66 Cheyenne Dr.
Billings, MT 46060
(712) 555-1212
abdulm@earthlink.net

Professional Objective: Administrative Assistant

Summary of Skills

Administrative	Answered phones, scheduled appointments, sorted mail, filed
	Implemented new database management system
	Software programs used include Windows 7 and Office Professional
	Maintained appearance of office
	Created and maintained Facebook and Twitter
Bookkeeping	Handled cash register
	Closed cash register at the end of the evening
	Recorded cash transactions
	Balanced books
Communications	Served as peer counselor for 2 years
	Assisted in dental office
	Demonstrated proper dental hygiene to children
	Created games for children
Education	Billings Community College, Transfer Program, 2010 to present, Dean's List
	Billings High School, graduated 2010
Experience	Lombard Medical Group, Billings, MT, October 2010–present
	Sandy's Office Supplies, Billings, MT, February 2009–October 2010
	Oakbrook Dental, Billings, MT, September 2008–October 2009
	Fantastic Sam's, Billings, MT, June 2007–August 2008

THE CHRONOLOGICAL RESUME

The chronological resume is the traditional and most frequently used resume style. It lists your work history in reverse chronological order, meaning the most recent position or occupation is listed first. The work history should include dates employed, job title, job duties, and employer's name, address, and telephone number.

This type of resume is most useful for people with no breaks in their employment record and for whom each new position indicates continuous advancement or growth. Recent high school and college graduates also find this approach simpler than creating a functional resume.

Because dates tend to dominate the presentation, any breaks or undocumented years of work may stand out. If your present position is not related to the job you desire, you may be eliminated from the competition by employers who feel that current experience is the most important consideration in reviewing resumes. However, if you emphasize skills in your present job that will be important to the new position, this will be less of a problem. See Exhibit 10.4 as an example of a chronological resume.

EXHIBIT 10.4 **Chronological Resume for a College Undergraduate with Limited Experience**

JOHN JONES
1050 Baez Street
Mesa, AZ 85201
(480) 555-1221
jj123@aol.com

OBJECTIVE: Sales

SUMMARY: Three years of part-time and summer employment related to sales, public contact, and accounting while attending high school.

EDUCATION: Mesa Community College 2010–Present. Resumed studies for an AA Transfer Track to the University of Arizona, majoring in accounting.
2006 Red Mountain High School, Mesa, Arizona. Graduated with emphasis in mathematics and business.

Courses included:

Computer Information Systems	Office Professional
Excel	PreCalculus
English	Business math
Journalism	Accounting principles
Algebra	Marketing

EXPERIENCE: 2009–Present: Mesa General Store, Mesa, Arizona
Salesperson. Sold apparel in men's and children's departments.

2008–2009: Tower Records & Video, Mesa, Arizona
Counterperson. Assisted customers. Handled monetary transactions.

2006–2008: Miscellaneous employment: babysat for four families with one to four children. Stayed with children weekends and while parents were on vacation, and assumed full responsibility for normal household routines.

HONORS: Vice President, Future Business Managers Association, 2009–2010

ACTIVITIES: Future Business Managers Association, Journalism Club, Student Tutoring Association, Young Republicans Club

THE COMBINATION/ HYBRID RESUME

If you have major skills important for success in your desired job in addition to an impressive record of continuous job experience with reputable employers, you can best highlight this double advantage with a *combination* of the functional and chronological styles of resume. This combination style usually lists functions followed by years employed with a list of employers. The combination style also satisfies the employer who wants to see the dates that you were actually employed. See Exhibit 10.5 as an example of a combination resume.

> Obstacles are things a person sees when he takes his eyes off his goal.
>
> —*E. Joseph Cossman*

EXHIBIT 10.5 Combination Resume for a Sales Executive Position

JOHN BENNETT	(803) 555-3692 (w)
304 Amen Street	(803) 555-1126 (h)
Columbia, SC 29260	E-mail: jben@msn.com

OBJECTIVE
Regional Advertising Account Executive

SALES PROMOTION
Designed and supervised sales promotion projects for large business firms and manufacturers, mostly in the electronics field. Originated newspaper, radio, and television advertising. Coordinated sales promotion with public relations and sales management. Analyzed market potentials, and developed new techniques to increase sales effectiveness and reduce sales costs. Created sales training program.

As sales executive and promotion consultant, handled a great variety of accounts. Sales potentials in these firms varied from $100,000 to $5 million per annum. Raised the volume of sales in many of these firms 25 percent within the first year.

SALES MANAGEMENT
Hired and supervised sales staff on local, area, and national bases. Established branch offices throughout the United States. Developed uniform systems of processing orders and maintaining sales records. Promoted new products, as well as improved sales of old ones. Designed sales training program. Devised a catalog system involving inventory control to facilitate movement of scarce stock between branches.

MARKET RESEARCH
Originated and supervised market research projects to determine sales potential, as well as need for advertising. Wrote detailed reports and recommendations describing each step in distribution, areas for development, and plans for sales improvement.

SALES
Retail and wholesale. Direct sales to consumer, jobber, and manufacturer. Hard goods, small metals, and electrical appliances.

EMPLOYERS
2007–Present	B. B. Bowen Sales Development Co., Columbia, South Carolina	Sales Executive
2004–2007	James Bresher Commercial and Industrial Sales	Senior Sales Promotion
2001–2004	Research Corp., Oakland, California	Manager
1998–2001	Dunnock Brothers Electronics Co., San Francisco, California	Sales Manager, Sales Rep

EDUCATION
University of California, Berkeley, B.S.; Major: Business Administration

ASSOCIATIONS
American Advertising Federation, Leadership Forum, Chair; Columbia Chamber of Commerce; Columbia Kiwanis Club, liaison with local colleges

If you use a specialized resume preparation service, make sure to customize the resume to fit your personality and situation. An employer can usually spot a canned resume and might assume that the applicant lacks initiative or self-confidence. The time you spend writing your resume will be time well spent. It gives you the opportunity to summarize what you have to offer to an employer.

The look of your resume matters. Use an attractive bond paper for copies of your resume; usually a neutral color such as ivory or white is best. Copy centers typically have a wide selection of stationery available. It is advisable to have a career counselor, potential employer, family member, or friend review a draft of your resume before you complete and duplicate or send your final copy. Ask them to assist you in a careful check of content, format, grammar, spelling, and appearance. Your goal is to produce a document that is strategic and free of error.

RESUMES FOR INTERNATIONAL JOBS

If you want to increase your success rate, double your failure rate.

—Thomas J. Watson, Sr.

Resume and curriculum vitae guidelines vary from country to country. However, some rules apply in most cases. For example, letters that accompany a resume or CV, known as cover letters in the United States, are called letters of interest in some countries and motivation letters in others. The best advice is to find out what's appropriate according to the corporation, the country culture, and the culture of the person making the hiring decision. Ask employers or recruiters for examples of resumes or CVs that they think are particularly good. One good source for examples is *The College Journal: Global Careers Section*. Otherwise, your university career center should have some good resources to use to adjust your resume or CV. Additionally, whenever you happen to be traveling in a country in which you think you might like to work someday, drop into the local college career center and inquire and collect job search information before you really need it!

REAL stories — Meet Eduardo

It is almost one o'clock in the morning and Eduardo Garza is just finishing his shift at Elaine's House of Coffee. On Friday and Saturday nights, a small band plays at Elaine's until midnight. Eduardo has been working these weekend shifts ever since his mother's illness. Mrs. Garza, a single mother of five children, recently underwent surgery, and she will not be able to work for approximately six months. Eduardo is the oldest child and he takes much of the responsibility for his family. Until his mother is well again, he must bring in as much of the income as possible.

Eduardo graduated from high school and attended community college for one year but he dropped out because of his family situation and because he was having trouble in some of his classes. He is a very quiet young man and likes to spend his spare time reading and listening to music. In high school, his favorite subject was math. Eduardo has a strong work ethic, and his supervisor at Elaine's promoted him to manager. He is not comfortable managing other employees, but he does enjoy his bookkeeping responsibilities. Eduardo looks in the want ads daily for better-paying jobs with hours that will let him be home in the evenings, but many of the positions require a resume. Eduardo does not feel he has enough skills to put together a resume, and he is very concerned about his ability to compete for a better job.

WHAT DO *YOU* THINK?

1. Based on the information you have read about Eduardo, what kind of resume—functional, chronological, or combination—would be best for him? Why?
2. Where could Eduardo go for help in preparing a resume?
3. What other resources could Eduardo use to look for a job?
4. What might help Eduardo strengthen his self-esteem?

FACTS & FIGURES

Resume Problems

When scanning a resume, the HR manager looks for key "knockout" factors. Survey results from HR managers indicate that the following items help them decide that the candidate has *not* matched his or her resume with the needs of the company:

- ▶ Job objective incompatible with job requirements
- ▶ Insufficient educational credentials
- ▶ Geographic restrictions incompatible with current openings
- ▶ Lack of U.S. citizenship or permanent resident status
- ▶ Resume poorly organized, sloppy, or hard to read
- ▶ Resume is too long

Review your resume in light of these potential problems and correct as needed.

WHAT DO *YOU* THINK?

1. Have you ever created or submitted an electronic resume?
2. Do you know anyone who has gotten an interview by sending an electronic resume?
3. What is the advantage of sending your resume by e-mail?
4. See Exhibit 10.2 for suggestions for composing your resume. Which points seem to be most relevant for you?
5. In addition to a resume, what other strategies would you use to get an interview?

Cover Letter Guidelines

Want to turn off a prospective employer? Send a resume without a cover letter. Or send a form letter addressed to Personnel Manager. Or address your letter "Dear Sir," only to have it received by a female manager. There is no one with the name "To Whom It May Concern." It may not concern anyone! So, when you do not have a specific name, it is best to address your letter to "Dear Interviewer."

A cover letter announces your availability and introduces the resume. It is probably one of the most important self-advertisements you will write. The cover letter indicates you have researched the organization—its products, reputation, and quality, and how this would directly relate to your background. State this in the first paragraph to clearly show how your abilities, experience, and motivation fit their needs.

You may have heard people say, "It's not *what* you know but *who* you know that counts." This is only partly true, but nonetheless important. You can often get to know someone with only a little effort. Call or, better yet, visit the organization and talk to people who already hold the job you want. Be tactful and discreet, of course. Then, in your cover letter, mention that you talked with some of the firm's employees, and these discussions increased your interest. You thereby show the reviewer you took the initiative to visit the company. Always request an interview or an opportunity to discuss the position in greater detail near the conclusion of your one-page cover letter.

Basic principles of letter and resume writing include being self-confident when listing your positive qualities and attributes, writing as one professional to another, and having your materials properly prepared. A cover letter template appears nearby.

▲ An accurate, well-written, and personalized cover letter can help your resume stand out from the many others a manager will review.

Resume Cover Letter Template

- Keep your cover letter to one page and to the point.
- Refer to your resume, highlighting relevant experiences and accomplishments that match the firm's stated needs.
- When you ask for an interview, indicate when you will be calling to confirm a convenient time.

- Always review both the cover letter and resume for accuracy. Appearance does count!
- Prepare a cover letter individually for each job. It may be included in the body of an email with the resume attached.
- See Exhibit 10.6 which is a sample cover letter.

Whenever possible, address your letter to a specific person, with the name spelled correctly and the proper title. These details count. The opening paragraph must contain a clear link to the job announcement. Summarize what you have to offer. Details of your background can show why you should be considered as a top-notch candidate. The self-appraisal that went into the preparation of your resume tells what you *can* and *like* to do and where your strengths and interests lie. Your research on the prospective employer should have uncovered the qualifications needed. If your letter promises a good match—meaning your abilities match the company's needs—you've attracted attention and interest.

EXHIBIT 10.6 **Cover Letter for a Community Health Worker Position**

March 4, 2012

Mr. Harvey J. Finder
Executive Director
Lung Association of Alma County
1717 Opportunity Way
Santa Ana, CA 92706

Dear Mr. Finder:

I am interested in the position of community health education program coordinator with the Lung Association of Alma County. I feel that my education, skills, and desire to work in this area make me a strong candidate for this position.

My education has helped me develop sound analytical abilities and has exposed me to the health-care field. My involvement with health-care and community organizations has provided me with a working knowledge of various public and private health institutions, which has increased my ability to communicate effectively with health-care professionals, patients, and the community at large. This combination of education and exposure has stimulated my interest in seeking a career in the health-care field.

Please review the enclosed resume and contact me at your convenience regarding a personal interview. If I do not hear from you in the next week, I will contact you. I look forward to talking with you.

Sincerely yours,

Denise M. Hunter
18411 Anticipation Drive
Northridge, CA 91330
(213) 555–0217
DMH@hotmail.com

Enclosures

Application Forms

A final type of form, accepted sometimes as a substitute for a resume, is an *application form*. The employment application form is used by most companies to gain necessary information and to screen applicants for work (see Exhibit 10.7). This information becomes a guide to determine a person's suitability for both the company and the job that needs filling. Observe carefully the guidelines for completing an application form in the feature titled "Success Strategies."

▲ Completing the employment application neatly and thoroughly is important.

You will probably be asked to fill out an employment application form before any interview takes place. Therefore, it is good practice to arrive at the employment office at least 15 minutes ahead of the time of your interview. Bring along a pen and your resume or a personal data sheet. You will be asked to provide your name, address, training or education, experience, special abilities, and possibly even your hobbies and interests. Practically all application forms request that you state the job you are seeking and the salary you have received in the past. Most firms require an applicant to complete an application form.

Many times the employer wants to make certain rapid comparisons, which she or he can do simply by reviewing the completed company employment application forms on file. For example, Ms. Ford needed an administrative assistant with current computer skills. She examined many application forms of people who had word-processing skills. By referring to the same section each time, she quickly thumbed through dozens of applications, eliminating all candidates who had only minimum computer skills. Remember, a close reading of the job description will give you an indication of what to highlight in your application, resume, and cover letter so that you will get an interview.

NEATNESS COUNTS

The way in which an application form has been filled out indicates the applicant's level of neatness, thoroughness, and accuracy. If two applicants seem to have equal qualifications but one's form is filled out carelessly, the application itself might tilt the balance in favor of the other applicant. Unless your handwriting is especially clear, print or type all answers. Look for "please print" instructions on the form.

EXHIBIT 10.7 **Sample Employment Application**

PERSONAL INFORMATION:

Date _____

Name _____
Last   First   Middle

Address _____
Street   City   State   Zip

Telephone Number (_____) _____   Are you over 17 years of age? ☐ Yes ☐ No

POSITION WANTED:

Job Title _____ Date Available _____ Salary Desired _____

Check any that apply: ☐ Full Time   ☐ Part Time   ☐ Day Shift   ☐ Night Shift

EDUCATION:

Begin with high school; include any military school you may have attended:

NAME OF SCHOOL   LOCATION OF SCHOOL   DEGREE OR COURSE OF STUDY

_____

_____

List any academic honors or professional associations:

_____

WORK EXPERIENCE:

List last three employers. Start with the current or most recent.

Name and Address of Employer _____

Dates Worked _____ Pay _____ Reason for Leaving _____

Job Title _____ Job Description _____

Name and Address of Employer _____

Dates Worked _____ Pay _____ Reason for Leaving _____

Job Title _____ Job Description _____

Name and Address of Employer _____

Dates Worked _____ Pay _____ Reason for Leaving _____

Job Title _____ Job Description _____

Computer Skills (describe)   Typing Speed _____ *wpm*
   (if applicable)   (if applicable)

Do you have any physical condition or handicap that may limit your ability to perform the job applied for? ☐ Yes ☐ No

If yes, what can be done to accommodate your limitation?

Have you ever been convicted of a felony? ☐ Yes ☐ No If yes, give kind and date.

A conviction will not necessarily disqualify you from employment.

Are you legally entitled to work in the U.S.? ☐ Yes ☐ No Can you provide proof of citizenship after employment? ☐ Yes ☐ No

Are you a veteran? ☐ Yes ☐ No If yes, give dates:

List the names of three references whom we may contact who have knowledge of your skills, talents, or technical knowledge:

(1) _____ (2) _____ (3) _____

Name and Relationship
(Supervisor, Teacher, etc.) _____

Address _____

Telephone _____

I certify, by my signature below, that any false or omitted important facts in my answers on this application may be cause for dismissal.

_____
Applicant's Signature   *Date*

SUCCESS strategies — Filling Out Application Forms

(See Exhibit 10.7 for a sample form.)

1. Fill out the application form in ink or use a word-processing program if feasible.

2. Answer every question that applies to you. If a question does not apply or is illegal, you may write *N/A*, meaning *not applicable*, or draw a line through the space to show you did not overlook the question.

3. Give your complete address, including zip code.

4. Spell correctly. If you aren't sure how to spell a word, use another word with the same meaning.

5. Answer a question on job preference or "job for which you are applying" with a specific job title or type of work. Do not write "anything." Employers expect you to state clearly what kind of work you can do.

6. Have a prepared list of schools attended and previous employers. Include addresses and dates of employment.

7. Be prepared to provide several good references. It is advisable to ask permission of those you plan to list. Good references can include a recognized community leader, a former employer or teacher who knows you well, and friends who are established in business.

8. When you write or sign your name on the application, use your formal name, not a nickname. Your first name, middle initial, and last name are usually preferred.

9. Be as neat as possible. Employers expect that your application will be an example of your best work.

EXERCISE your options

You now have the knowledge and strategy to develop a winning resume, portfolio, and cover letter. In addition, you must be aware of the impact of your digital presence online. Most prospective employers will google your name to see what comes up. They will also check common social networking sites. Make sure you google yourself first to determine if your public online image reflects the kind of person you are portraying in your resume. If you are in doubt, ask others who might be in a position to employ you (e.g., family friends, neighbors, teachers, and counselors) to google you and give you feedback related to your online profile and the impression it leaves. Investigate how to remove anything online that might interfere with your image as a responsible employee.

Summary

This chapter has provided discussion and examples of resumes, cover letters, and application forms, as well as highlighted the benefits of electronic resumes and portfolios. In the digital age, creativity in social networking provides new avenues for presenting your skills and getting interviews.

Your challenge is to develop a winning resume. Use the exhibits and ideas in the following written exercises as well as the tips throughout the chapter to assist you in getting your resume into strategic shape.

PURPOSE OF EXERCISES

These exercises will enable you to prepare a resume as well as critique it. Exercise 10.1 had you prepare and complete a resume/portfolio review. Exercise 10.2 will help you organize pertinent information about yourself. In Exercise 10.3, you are asked to draft a resume. Exercise 10.4 reminds you to save copies of your work for a portfolio. Exercises 10.5 and 10.6 provide guidelines for critiquing your own resume and obtaining valuable feedback from others. In Exercise 10.7, you are asked to write a cover letter and get feedback on its merits. Exercise 10.8, WWWebwise, is a Web-based exercise that reinforces the learnings in this chapter. Finally, in the last exercise, you will rate your Student Learning Outcomes.

EXPAND YOUR CAREER PORTFOLIO

Complete Exercises 10.2 through 10.7 to add to the Career Portfolio that you started with the chapter summaries found at the end of this book. Keep your responses to Exercises 10.2 through 10.7 with your other entries so that you can retrieve and add to your portfolio as you complete the remaining chapters.

EXERCISE

10.2 Create a Card File

Create a card file (or an electronic file) describing your work experiences, using Exhibit 10.2 as a guide. This enables you to write your job tasks in functional terms.

EXERCISE

10.3 Write Your Resume

Choose the format desired and write your own resume, referring to Exercises 10.1 and 10.2 for data. Refer to the suggestions in the chapter and the exhibits that follow these exercises.

EXERCISE

10.4 Save Sample Work for a Portfolio

Start now to keep a folder of the best work you have done in work-related classes and jobs, internships, and volunteer positions.

EXERCISE

10.5 Critique Your Resume

Use the resume checklist and critique form (Exhibit 10.9) to evaluate your resume.

EXERCISE
10.6   Ask Others to Critique Your Resume

Ask other people (e.g., career counselors, those who have been receptive to you during informational interviews, teachers, friends) to give you feedback about your resume. Use the checklist of Dos and Don'ts in Exhibit 10.10 to help others give you feedback.

EXERCISE
10.7   Write a Cover Letter

Referring to Exhibits 10.11 through 10.21, write a cover letter to accompany your resume. Ask others to critique it, as you did in Exercise 10.6 with your resume.

EXERCISE
10.8   WWWebwise

Go to **http://www.careerlab.com/letters**. Click on any of the topics and select a free cover letter to read. Report on how the letter might give you a creative idea about getting a job.

(*Note*: Please be aware that websites can change without notice. If a link does not work, find a similar site to complete the activity.)

REINFORCING YOUR LEARNING OUTCOMES

Review and Rate Your Chapter Outcomes. Indicate in the right-hand column how well you do the following items (from 1 = very well, to 5 = not at all). If you rated yourself 4 or 5, review the material on the pages in parentheses to ensure your career success.

How Well Can You Do the Following?

- Differentiate between types of resumes. (pp. 215–229)   1 2 3 4 5
- Recognize the value of a personal portfolio. (pp. 218–220)   1 2 3 4 5
- Utilize digital alternatives and web resumes. (pp. 217–220)   1 2 3 4 5
- Write a cover letter. (pp. 229–230)   1 2 3 4 5
- Prepare a strategic resume. (pp. 215–247)   1 2 3 4 5

Go to the Career Fitness Portfolio at the end of the book and complete this chapter summary to build and record your personal Career Fitness Portfolio.

Additional Opportunity: Your instructor may choose to assign the Career Fitness Portfolio for in class or online completion. If so, they will provide the handout or link for you to access.

EXHIBIT 10.8   Resume Checklist and Critique Form

	Strong	Average	Weak	Plans for Improvement
1. **Resume format.** Does it say "READ ME"?				
2. **Appearance.** Is it brief? Did you use a clear, engaging layout? Type clearly? Use a correct format?				
3. **Length.** Are the key points concise?				
4. **Significance.** Did you select your most relevant experiences?				
5. **Communication.** Do your words give the "visual" impression you want? Is the job objective clearly stated?				
6. **Conciseness.** Does your information focus on the experiences that qualify you for the position?				
7. **Completeness.** Did you include all important information? Have you made a connection between the job desired and your experience?				
8. **Accuracy.** Does the resume represent you well enough to get you an interview?				
9. **Skills.** Does your resume reflect the skills necessary for the job?				

EXHIBIT 10.9   Resume DOs and DON'Ts

DO

- Focus your job objective to illustrate specific skills and responsibilities.
- Interest your reader with significant employment, education, accomplishments, and skills.
- Present yourself positively, honestly, and assertively.
- Keep the resume to no more than two pages.
- Use an attractive and readable layout, including top-quality paper, for a professional appearance.
- Have your resume carefully proofread prior to its final printing.

DON'T

- Be too wordy or use buzzwords and unnecessary verbiage.
- Provide personal data on your age, race, marital status, religion, or other private matters.
- Suggest abilities or objectives beyond your reach or qualifications.
- Make reference to a desired salary or income.
- State a reason for leaving a previous job.
- Provide names of references in the resume.

EXHIBIT 10.10   Functional Resume for an Administrative Assistant Position

OLIVIA MARTINEZ

P.O. Box 1111
Cincinnati, OH 14528

Day Phone: (513) 555-1212
E-mail: omartinez@aol.com

OBJECTIVE
Administrative Assistant

SUMMARY OF EXPERIENCE

Ten years of increasing responsibility in the area of office management involving organization, problem solving, finances, and public relations.

MANAGEMENT

Initiated and organized procedures used in the office, coordinated activities of clerical personnel, and formulated procedures for systematic retention, protection, transfer, and disposal of records. Coordinated preparation of operating reports, such as time and attendance records, and of performance data. Reviewed, composed, and answered correspondence. Directed services such as maintenance, repair, supplies, mail, and files. Aided executive by coordinating office services, such as personnel, budget preparation and control, housekeeping, records control, and special management studies.

PUBLIC RELATIONS

Coordinated communications with state, county, and district officials as well as district and local employees, student body, staff members, and parents in our community. Planned and coordinated social functions for school, staff, and two social clubs. Promoted sales of jewelry, gourmet foods, and liquors in sales-related jobs.

PROBLEM SOLVING

Made decisions according to district policy in the absence of the principal. Worked under constant pressure and interruption while attending to student problems regarding their health and welfare. Served as liaison between school and community, resolving as many problems as possible before referring them to superior.

BUDGETING/FINANCIAL

Analyzed and coordinated payroll record keeping, budgeted expenditures, requisitioned supplies, prepared attendance accounting reports, and initiated budget system for $25,000 instructional equipment monies.

CREATIVE

Created social media website, as well as news copy and layouts using Adobe Premier. Designed fliers, posters, calendars, and bulletins. Personal hobbies include ceramics, oil painting, sculpting, and interior design.

EMPLOYERS

Cincinnati Unified School District
1115 Old School Road
Cincinnati, OH 14528
(513) 555-2345

Cincinnati Blue Cross
5900 Erwin Road
Cincinnati, OH 14526
(513) 555-3698

EXHIBIT 10.11   Functional Resume for a Teacher Changing Careers

STACY L. MOLLARD

1001 Gainsborough Street   312-555-3581 (cell)
Chicago, IL 60664   stacymollard@cox.net   312-555-4343 (work)

POSITION OBJECTIVE:

Training Specialist

QUALIFICATIONS IN BRIEF:

B.A. in English, Mundelein College, Chicago.
Six years' elementary teaching with experience in English as a Second Language,
communications, human relations, instruction, and supervision.
Bilingual (English, Spanish).

EXPERIENCE SUMMARY:

COMMUNICATIONS:

Conducted staff development workshops; presented new curriculum plans to parent groups, sent periodic progress reports to parents, and developed class newsletter; presented workshops in parent effectiveness training at state and local conferences.

HUMAN RELATIONS:

Directed effective problem solving/conflict resolution between individual students and student groups; initiated program of student self-governance; acted as liaison between families of diverse cultural, ethnic, and economic backgrounds and school personnel/services; conducted individual and group conferences to establish rapport with parents and discuss student progress.

INSTRUCTION:

Developed instructional modules to solve specific learning problems; developed instructional materials; used whiteboard and created online modules; researched learning styles compatible with cultural diversity in various curricula; chaired curriculum development committee; introduced new motivational techniques for students.

CURRENTLY EMPLOYED:

Austin Elementary School, Chicago, Illinois

COMMUNITY INVOLVEMENT:

American Society for Training and Development, member
Chicago Community Services Center, Board Member
Chicago United Way, Allocations Committee

EXHIBIT 10.12 Chronological Resume for an Office Management Position

THUY NGUYEN

532 Castilian Court
Seattle, WA 98102

(206) 799-1212 (Home)
(206) 555-1212 (Work)
thuynguyen@netstar.net

OCCUPATIONAL OBJECTIVE:

Office Manager

SUMMARY OF QUALIFICATIONS:

Three years of increasingly responsible experience in different positions.

BOOKKEEPER

Hungry Hunter and El Torito Restaurants
Seattle, WA 2010 to present

Recorded financial transactions on Access. Balanced books and compiled reports to show statistics, such as cash receipts and expenditures, accounts payable and receivable, and other items pertinent to operation of business. Calculated employee wages from time cards and updated to accounting system.

RESTAURANT GREETER

Hungry Hunter Restaurant
*Thou*sand Oaks, CA 2008–2010

Welcomed guests, seated them in dining area, maintained quality of facilities. Directed others in performing courteous and rapid service; assisted in settling complaints. Related well with the continuous flow of people, coordinated the service with customers' needs.

SPECIAL ACCOMPLISHMENTS:

National Forensic League, vice president (third place, statewide oratory competition); Athletic Association (gymnastic team); Honor Roll and Dean's List; Alpha Gamma Sigma; *Who's Who Among American High School Students*, 2007–2008

EDUCATION:

Seattle Pacific University, Seattle, WA
Majoring in Business Administration
GPA: 3.5 on a 4.0 scale

ASSOCIATIONS

American Management Association, Student Delegate
American Association of University Women
American Association of Administrative Professionals

EXHIBIT 10.13 **Chronological Resume for a Community Service Worker Position**

SARITA SANDHA
980 Victory Blvd.
Brooklyn, NY 11321
(405) 555-4150
ssandha@aol.com

JOB OBJECTIVE:	Community Service Worker
SUMMARY OF QUALIFICATIONS:	Six years' experience in public relations, media work, and writing press releases and newsletters. Organized concerts, rallies, walk-a-thons, and volunteer-a-thons. Basic qualifications in office procedures: phone networking, word processing, mailing, leafletting, outreach, and public speaking.
EDUCATION:	2010 to present: Brooklyn College, currently attending.
	Sociology major. Additional specialized institute training at Loyola Marymount University in social organizing.
	Two years as teacher's aide in New York City school system. Interrelated with a variety of cultural groups.
	2010: Alemany High School, graduated.
EXPERIENCE:	2009 to present: Community Service Organization, New York
	Organized, educated, persuaded, created social change via social media, raised over $25,000 and performed administrative duties.
	2007–2009: Receptionist and secretary
	Maintained records, answered phones, and performed light clerical work.
SPECIAL SKILLS:	Interact easily with diverse people while under pressure. Knowledge of fund-raising practices. Self-motivated. Experienced in analyzing and working with issues and strategies underlying a particular campaign. Computer and Social Media Proficiency.

References Available Upon Request

EXHIBIT 10.14   Combination Resume for a Programmer Trainee Position

ALBERT CHAN
111 East Maple
Minneapolis, MN
(508) 866–1592 • albertchan34@aol.com

JOB OBJECTIVE	Programmer Trainee
QUALIFICATIONS BY EXPERIENCE	Flowcharted, coded, tested, and debugged interactive programs for the HP6000. Created a system of five programs from a system problem statement and flowchart. Designed and wrote other documentation for improved payroll system for previous employer, as System Analysis course project.
	Tutored students in Visual BASIC, C+ and C++, working with Hispanics, Vietnamese, and reentering adults, as well as other diverse students.
	Currently creating a bibliographic database as a volunteer at Minneapolis Public Library and designed library's Web page.
EDUCATION	2012: Bachelor of Science Degree in Computer Science, Minneapolis Central College. Courses included UNIX and C++.
	3.6 GPA in computer science classes.
	2009: Associate of Arts in English, Tri-County Community College.
	Minored in computer science.
	Supported self through college by security work at various firms. Gained secret clearance while at IBM Federal System Division.
SPECIAL SKILLS	Attentive to detail, organized, work well with little supervision, enterprising, enjoy problem solving and interacting with others to plan projects, work well under pressure, able to see relationships between abstract ideas, excellent communications skills.
COMMUNITY SERVICE EXPERIENCE	Organized CROP Walks (fund-raisers for Church World Service), which resulted in raising $6,000 in 2008 and $10,000 in 2011.
	Chaired the planning committee, recruited members, mapped walk route.
	Obtained parade permits and business tax exemptions.
	Wrote press releases.

EXHIBIT 10.15　A Poorly Constructed Resume (See Corrected Version in Exhibit 10.16 on the Following Page)

Omit entirely

① PROFESSIONAL EXPERIENCE AND TRAINING OF SARA CRANE: SOCIAL CASE WORKER

Place name, address, phone on top of page in correct format; include e-mail address

② 4234 S. Platt Avenue, Salt Lake City, Utah 84100 (801) 765–4321

List as job objective, with more specific summary

③ Social case worker with RN degree wants a responsible position with a large medical firm that could benefit from my experience in both nursing and social work.

EXPERIENCE

Edit and highlight key responsibilities

④ 2010–present . . . Family caseworker. Working through Parker General Hospital Services in Salt Lake. Worked directly with families at their homesites. Met with family and formulated a plan after consultation and comprehensive investigation of needs. Developed assistance and support as appropriate with follow-up services.

Same as #4

⑤ 2006–2010 . . . RN and convalescent services. Grand Junction, Utah. Treated patients with disabilities. Reviewed financial aspects and fee payments, all inpatient and outpatient services, and full family participation in health program to ensure cooperation and support.

EDUCATION

Omit years (if over 10) and reduce excess words

⑥ 2000–2006 . . . Bachelor of Science. Social Work. Brigham Young School of Social Work. Training in all areas of social work including internships in pediatrics, psychiatric, rehabilitation, and gerontology sections.

1996–2000 . . . Registered Nurse. Baker College, Salt Lake City, Utah General nursing curriculum including family health concerns. Took additional courses in specialized nursing for retired patients and also advanced psychiatric techniques. I realized that my experience and interests were becoming directed into social work.

PROFESSIONAL AFFILIATIONS

The National Association of Case and Social Workers

INTERESTS

Too wordy and unrelated to job objective. Edit to highlight language ability.

⑦ Travel and reading. Conversational abilities in Spanish and French, including reading knowledge. Good cook and enjoy theater productions. Any references regarding my education or work experience

Separate and edit

⑧ may be requested at any time.

EXHIBIT 10.16   A Corrected Resume

SARA CRANE
4234 S. Platt Avenue
Salt Lake City, UT 84100
(801) 765-4321
scrane@earthlink.net

JOB OBJECTIVE

Bilingual nurse

EXPERIENCE

Family Caseworker. Parker General Hospital, Salt Lake City, Utah, 2010–Present.

Report to Social Services Director of largest family assistance program in Salt Lake City, attached to hospital intake services. Duties include:

- Interviewing family members at the hospital and in their homes to determine needs.
- Investigating claims and proposing plans for assistance.
- Counseling and guiding families in special circumstances, including personal and health issues.
- Providing follow-up treatment and reports.

Convalescent Service as an RN. Grand Junction Hospital, Grand Junction, Utah, 2005–2010. Reported to Health Services Center with following responsibilities:

- Interviewed patients' families to determine financial capabilities.
- Arranged fee structures.
- Planned outpatient plan and referral services.
- Counseled families for inpatient and/or convalescent needs.

EDUCATION

Bachelor of Science, Social Work, Brigham Young University, School of Social Work, Provo, Utah.

Internships in pediatric, psychiatric, rehabilitation, and gerontology sections.
Additional courses in Financial Planning.

Registered Nurse, Baker College, Salt Lake City, Utah.

Full training in general nursing with specialization in psychiatric nursing. Workshops in family health led to social work career path.

SPECIAL SKILLS

Fluency in Spanish and French. Psychological specialty in Cognitive Behavioral Therapy.

PROFESSIONAL AFFILIATIONS

National Association of Case and Social Workers.

EXHIBIT 10.17   **Cover Letter for an Electronics Technician Position**

412 Melbrook Avenue
Omaha, NE 77050

June 17, 2012

Mr. Lloyd Johnson
Sonat Technical Supervisor
Lear Electronic Company
1229 Van Owen
Knoxville, TN 37917

Dear Mr. Johnson:

I am interested in working for your company as an electronics technician in the field of systems installation and calibration.

During my tour of duty in the service, I became acquainted with many of your electronic systems aboard ship and was extremely impressed with their design and documentation. I have since pursued a course of studies at Hastings College to increase my competence in the field of electronics. For these reasons, I feel I would be an asset to your company.

Enclosed a copy of my resume for your consideration. I will contact you by telephone next week to set up a meeting to discuss employment opportunities with your company.

Sincerely yours,

Emilio Reyna

Enclosure

EXHIBIT 10.18 **Cover Letter for a Public Relations Position**

1234 Evanston Avenue
Cambridge, IL 61238

May 16, 2012

Mr. Harrison MacBuren
Director of Personnel
North Hills Mall
Cambridge, IL 61238

Dear Mr. MacBuren:

I am very interested in the position currently available in your public relations department for an assistant to the director of public relations.

As you can see by my resume, my previous administrative experience would be a definite asset to your company. I feel that a vital part of any public relations job is the ability to deal with people. This is a skill I have acquired through many years of volunteer work.

I would like to meet with you to discuss how we might work together for our mutual benefit. I will be contacting you within the week to arrange a convenient meeting time.

Sincerely,

George Herounian

Enclosure

EXHIBIT 10.19 **Cover Letter for a Marketing Manager Position**

1736 D Street NW
Washington, DC 20006
(202) 555-8192
May 3, 2012

Ms. Emma Major, President
Vendo Corporation
1742 Surf Drive
Fort Lauderdale, FL 33301

Dear Ms. Major:

I was intrigued by the write-up about your new portable vending centers in *Sales Management* magazine. I think it is an extremely good idea.

As you will note from the enclosed resume, my marketing, planning, and sales management experience could be of great assistance to you at this early stage in your project. Enclosed are some specific marketing ideas you might like to review. I would like to make arrangements to meet with you in Florida during the week of May 17 to discuss some of these ideas.

Because of my familiarity with the types of locations and clients you are seeking, I am sure that if we were able to work together in this new venture, the results would reflect my contribution.

I am looking forward to meeting with you and will call next week to arrange for an appointment.

Very truly yours,

Janet Perrill

Enclosure

EXHIBIT 10.20　Letter of Introduction

This will introduce Mary Smith, a trusted and valued member of my staff for the past two and a half years.

During this time Mary has held a key position, performing a variety of secretarial tasks, as well as having full charge of the ordering procedures, maintenance work, and updating in our career resources library. She is keen at spotting deficiencies and was instrumental in developing a more efficient system of updating our materials.

Mary has been recognized by other members of the staff, including the counselors and our program director, the dean of student personnel, as being outstanding in poise, appearance, and reliability. Additionally, and probably most important, she has been exceptionally effective in working with the students, faculty, and professionals who use the resources of our center.

Mary is a good organizer, capable of dealing with concepts and goals and devising systems approaches to problem solving. She is loyal and discreet in dealing with unusual situations and those calling for confidentiality.

If there is anything more you feel you would like to discuss regarding Mary's qualifications, please feel free to contact me.

Very truly yours,

W. T. Jones
Philo Corp.

Interviewing Strategically

Become Your Own Coach

11

STUDENT LEARNING OUTCOMES

At the end of the chapter you will be able to . . .

- Describe the art of interviewing.
- Recognize essential steps in preparing for an interview.
- Use guidelines and techniques for effective interviewing.

Once you begin to feel comfortable with networking and practice interviewing, you are ready to begin preparing for the "Olympic Finals"—the interview. In fact, the time you spend networking and informational interviewing, in person and online, will be some of the most valuable preparation you can do for a successful interview. You will develop ease and confidence by discussing your skills and job-related topics. This confidence will transfer to the formal interview process.

The trouble is, if you do not risk anything, you risk even more.

—Erica Jong

Before the Interview

Here are the three most important tips to consider as you approach your first interview or refine your current interviewing style: *prepare, prepare, prepare.*

Besides your ongoing networking and informational interviews, some of the best preparation for the interview occurs when you research the prospective employer. Your goal is to show the employer why you will be the best person for the job, relating your personal strengths, skills, and accomplishments to this particular enterprise. Specifically, you want to tell the employer how you can help with current challenges and contribute to the organization. To find out more about a prospective employer and the job you're interviewing for, research the organization's website and look for articles about the organization.

Before the interview, research the essential responsibilities of the job, which should be found in the job description. Make a mental note of them, and throughout the interview, feed back the kind of information from your background that shows you can handle these responsibilities. If you need further clarity about the job, be prepared to ask when given a chance during the interview.

Interviewing becomes easier as you gain practice. Don't be overly discouraged if you don't get the first job for which you interview. Interviews and even rejections are actually invaluable opportunities to reassess and reaffirm your qualifications, strengths, weaknesses, and areas for development.

TIPS FROM THE PROS

If you've already scripted your 60-second Elevator Speech as part of your networking effort, you can use it to answer this commonly asked interview question (Tell me about yourself). If you are preparing an "elevator pitch" for the first time, be sure it includes a summary of your educational background, special skills as related to the job, work/volunteer experiences, and your interest in working with this company. Time yourself as you practice delivering the script in front of the mirror, on video, or to a group of friends until you feel comfortable and confident with your presentation. Be sure not to quickly rattle it off as a memorized speech; rather, it should come off as somewhat relaxed and spontaneous.

The **seven** sample questions discussed here are representative of the types of questions commonly asked in an employment interview. Review these, and be prepared beforehand to answer such questions.

1. **Tell me about yourself.** Refer mentally to your resume; do not assume that the interviewer has even read it or remembers it! Briefly recap your skills and experiences as they relate to this particular job. Include a clear demonstration of the ways your education, training, skills, and experiences match the needs of the company. Prepare a 60-second Elevator Speech that will summarize the above points clearly and succinctly. If the interviewer wants more detail, she or he will ask additional questions.

2. **Why do you want this job? Why did you apply here?** Refer to information about *this job* and *this company* or institution that makes it particularly appealing to you. Do not give the impression that you're here just because the firm has a job opening. Refer to the company's history, products, services, corporate culture, and mission statement. Let your interviewer know that you have researched the organization and that you want to work here.

SUCCESS strategies   Job Interview Tips

- Your ability to express what your skills are, how you can contribute to the company, and your willingness to learn new skills is as important as being able to do each task listed in the job description. In fact, if you can already do each task described, you might be labeled as overqualified and not get the job!

- Your resume and cover letter become the written and mental outline on which you elaborate to translate your skills into potential benefits to the employer. Use your resume as a point of reference; write on index cards the key points you want to remember and convey during the interview. It's fine to bring these cards with you to your interview as long as you use them strictly as a quick visual reminder.

- In applying for jobs, a man increases his chances by trying to enter a field that has previously been primarily a female domain (e.g., nursing). Similarly, a woman increases her chances if she applies for a position that has previously been primarily a male domain (e.g., electronics).

- Don't be afraid to reapply and reinterview at the same company. Your interview skills will probably have improved in the meantime, and different areas of the company may be interested in you for different positions.

- Bring a hard copy of your portfolio to demonstrate your capabilities.

- Before the interview, verify the particulars. Write down the interviewer's name, the location, and the time and date of your appointment. Last-minute nervousness can block such details from your memory. Plan on arriving at least 15 minutes early.

- Apprehension, tension, and anxiety are a normal part of the preinterview jitters. Relaxation techniques, deep breathing, and chatting with the receptionist may help.

- The successful job candidate demonstrates how he or she is the best person for the job via the resume and the memorable answers to interview questions.

3. **Why should I hire you?** Be prepared to use your own words and examples to convey the fact that "Because, with my skills, experience, positive attitude, and enthusiasm, I am the best person for the job. I agree with your philosophy/ mission statement and I believe that I will fit in and be an asset to your enterprise." (Reemphasize your strengths.) Also emphasize how you can contribute to the company.

4. **What are your career plans? Where do you see yourself three years from now?** Even though it is common to change jobs frequently these days, employers generally tend to assume that you will be with them for some time; you can't make any promises, but you can indicate you would like to be with a company that encourages growth, rewards performance and increasing responsibility, and offers challenge.

▲ Although a job interview can be stressful, careful preparation on your part will enable you to relax, respond to questions more naturally, and make a good impression.

5. **What salary do you expect?** If you have done your research (check out monster.com, salary.com, glassdoor.com) you will have an idea of the general range for the position. Try to defer the discussion until you know more about what the job entails. If the interviewer does not mention salary, it is best not to bring up the subject at a first interview.

6. **Why did you leave your last job?** If asked why you left your last position, provide a positive response such as "I felt I had gone as far as possible in that company and I was ready for more responsibility." If your work history reflects numerous job changes, explain how you have developed and transferred existing skills to each opportunity and how these can benefit this employer.

7. **Do you have any questions?** You might ask what kind of person the interviewer is looking for and then show how you fit the bill. It is very important to ask key questions about the company's goals and objectives. Ask, "Given all that we covered, can you offer me this position?" or "When can I expect to hear about the position?" Refer to the "Success Strategies" feature titled *Sample Questions to Ask at the Interview* later in this chapter.

TIPS FROM THE PROS

Never speak or write negatively about former employers or coworkers. You never know who may be your next boss!

🌐 Practice Questions

The following additional questions may be asked during interviews, some are intended to create a *stress* response. Often they are asked out of pattern, intended to throw you. The interviewer sometimes is more interested in *how* you respond than in what you say, to observe how you react and how you think on your feet. Review the following questions that are likely to be asked of you. **Practice**!

1. Why did you choose this company over our competitors?
2. What qualifications do you have that make you feel you will be successful in your field?
3. Do you prefer working with others or by yourself?
4. Describe how you handle stress.
5. How do you react to criticism?
6. What is your major weakness? (What are three of your strong points? Three of your weak points?)
7. Are you willing to go where the company sends you? Travel? Relocate?
8. What kind of job do you expect to hold three years from now? Five years?
9. How would you describe yourself as an employee?
10. If you were me, why would you hire you?

Leave the interviewer convinced that you are ready and able to do the job. Never answer a question "No" without qualifying it positively. Here are a couple of examples: "Are you familiar with Excel?" "No, but I have mastered other software, and I'm certain I won't have any problems learning." "Can you 10-key?" "No, I didn't realize it was part of the job description. If it's necessary, I can learn. Just how much numerical data entry will be involved?"

🌐 Interview Guidelines

The interview, and ultimately a job, is the goal of your job-search strategy. Generally, people who are interviewed are assumed qualified to do the job; the question becomes one of an appropriate meshing of personalities. Both the interviewer and interviewee are relying on their communications skills, judgment, intuition, and insight. It is a two-way process. While you are being evaluated, you should be evaluating the position and the people offering it. Remember that a good interview is a dialogue, an exchange of information.

DRESSING FOR SUCCESS

The moment we see someone, we form powerful first impressions that are hard to change. Much of a first impression comes from the visual impact of an individual, and much of the visual impact comes from what that individual chooses to wear. Your clothes and accessories speak—and sometimes *shout*—volumes about you.

Many workplaces have become increasingly more casual in dress norms. You may be looking forward to this more casual attire, but it is generally a good rule to dress a bit more formally for the interview. This also communicates a sense of respect for the potential interviewers who are evaluating you and comparing you with other candidates. You are communicating that this is not just another casual encounter but a meeting that has importance to you.

 **FACTS & FIGURES** : **Company Knowledge**

A recent survey reveals that a lack of company knowledge is the most frequent interview mistake. The chances are great in any given interview that you will be asked some variation of the question, "What do you know about our company?" The questions could be "What attracted you to our company?" or "Why do you want to work for our company?" or one of a number of other variations. Employers want to see that you've done your homework; in fact, 44 percent of executives recently surveyed by Accountemps said the most common interview pitfall for today's candidates is insufficient company research.

WHAT DO *YOU* THINK?

1. What steps can you take to make sure you know about the company where you are interviewing?
2. What sources, besides the Internet, can you use when you have to find out information about a company or industry?

It's always best to check out the work environment before the day of your interview to get a general sense for the "look" of employees. Take a good look at yourself and ask others you trust for their opinions. If you are serious about getting a job, then you had better look and dress the part. No interviewer will tell you what you are supposed to wear, but the person will measure your maturity and judgment partially by your appearance. Remember, *you never get a second chance to make a good first impression!*

PRACTICAL PREPARATION

Get specific directions to the location, building, and parking, and if possible, drive by the interview site a day or two before so you'll know where it is, where to park, and how long it takes to get there. Be aware that your GPS does not tell you how long it will take to find parking and get to the right building! Plan to arrive for your interview at least 15 minutes early. Make time to stroll around, look, observe, try to have a brief conversation with the administrative assistant and any other individuals you encounter. This time will help you relax, feel comfortable in your surroundings, and may provide some positive feedback about the organization that you want to share during the interview. Develop a firm handshake (practice), and use it when being introduced. Practice good eye contact. Above all, smile and relax. Remember, you will be talking about someone you know very well—you!

> Tomorrow is often the busiest day of the week.
>
> —*Spanish Proverb*

Sometimes interviewers are just as nervous about the process as you. Feel free to make the first attempts to break the ice. Say something about the office decor, the cordial welcome, whatever makes sense. If you are nervous, you will find that focusing on the question "What would it be like to work here?" rather than "How am I being perceived by them?" will relax you. If it is a panel interview where several people are interviewing you, maintain eye contact with all the interviewers by scanning the room from time to time rather than focusing exclusively on the person asking the question.

In answering questions, use your knowledge and past experience to transmit the idea that you are the best person for the job, allowing strengths such as goodwill, flexibility, enthusiasm, and a professional approach to surface. Take your time. It is acceptable to pause, reflect, and ask for clarification if needed.

Bring samples of your work portfolio if they are related. On an index card, note your strengths or key selling points in addition to the questions you may have and some cue words like "smile, speak up, relax"; review them from time to time, especially just before you go into the interview. Forthright statements about what you do well, with examples of accomplishments, are of key importance. Talk with pride, honesty, and confidence about your accomplishments and your potential, your interest and commitment, and your readiness to learn on the job.

Express yourself *positively*. You are selling yourself; allow your personal *energy* and *enthusiasm* to surface.

Segments of an Interview

Although every interview is different, most follow a general pattern. A typical half-hour session can be roughly divided into **four segments**:

1. The first 5 or 10 minutes are usually devoted to establishing rapport and opening the lines of communication. Instead of wondering why the interviewer is taking valuable time chatting about the weather or parking problems, relax and enjoy the conversation. He or she will get to deeper subjects soon enough. The interview begins the moment you and the interviewer introduce yourselves and shake hands. Don't discount the initial period. Your ability to converse, expressing yourself intelligently, is being measured.

2. The adept interviewer will move subtly from a casual exchange to a more specific level of conversation. The second part of the interview gives you a chance to answer some "where, when, and why" questions about your background or to supply information that does not appear on your resume.

Now is the time to describe any relevant extracurricular activities, volunteer, internship, or work experience, or relate changes you brought about as a member of a campus organization or community group. This is your chance to elaborate on your strong points and emphasize whatever you have to offer. Don't monopolize the conversation; let the interviewer lead. But don't confine your statements to yes-or-no answers. Ask some questions to let the interviewer know you have researched the firm thoroughly and have a keen interest in the position.

The interviewer will be interested not only in what you say but also how you say it. Equally as important as the information you communicate will be the evidence of logical organization and presentation of thoughts. The interviewer will be mentally grading your intelligence, motivation, communication skills, leadership potential, and ability to function as part of a team.

3. The third segment begins when the interviewer feels your skills and interests have been identified and can see how they might fit the organization. If a good match seems possible, the interviewer will discuss the company and the opening available.

4. At the end of an interview, try to find out where you stand. "How do you feel I relate to this job?" "Do you need any additional information?" "Given all that we covered, can you offer me this position?" or "When can I expect to hear from you?"

After you leave, take 10 or 15 minutes to analyze how you did. What questions did you find difficult? What did you forget to say? How can you improve on the next interview? You might even keep a diary or log with written notes on each of these concerns as well as a list of the specific interview questions asked and a note about how you responded. Also list any specific things that you can do in following up with an employer to increase your chances of getting the offer you want.

Send a thank-you letter to the interviewer, recalling a significant fact or idea of the interview that will set you apart from the other applicants. Write the letter while the interview is still fresh in your mind. One paragraph is usually sufficient. Even if all your communication has been via e-mail, send a handwritten note that has been mailed right after the interview, besides an e-mail thank you. This will have a positive impact and set you apart from most other candidates who will only use e-mail.

How to Handle Illegal Questions

Certain hiring practices, employment application form questions, and specific interviewing procedures are illegal under the Fair Employment Practices Act, the Americans with Disabilities Act, and other governmental regulations. Review Exhibit 11.1 to familiarize yourself with the subject matter and specifics of the illegal issues.

EXHIBIT 11.1	Preemployment Inquiries: Lawful and Unlawful	
Subject	**Acceptable Preemployment Inquiries**	**Unacceptable Preemployment Inquiries**
Photograph	Statement that a photograph may be required after employment.	Requirement that applicant affix a photograph to application form.
		Request that applicant submit photograph at applicant's option.
		Requirement of photograph after interview but before hiring.

EXHIBIT **11.1** *CONTINUED*

Subject	Acceptable Preemployment Inquiries	Unacceptable Preemployment Inquiries
Race or Color		Complexion, color of skin, or other questions directly or indirectly indicating race or color, such as color of applicant's eyes and hair.
Citizenship	Request that applicant state whether residency status is: (a) U.S. citizen. (b) Legal right to remain permanently in the United States. Statement that, if hired, applicant may be required to submit proof of citizenship.	What is your country of citizenship? Inquiry whether an applicant or applicant's parents or spouse are naturalized or native-born U.S. citizens; date when applicant or parents or spouse acquired citizenship. Requirement that applicant produce naturalization papers or first papers.
National Origin	Inquiry into applicant's proficiency in foreign language must be job related.	Applicant's nationality, lineage, national origin, descent, or parentage. Date of arrival in United States or port of entry; how long a resident of the United States. Nationality of applicant's parents or spouse; maiden name of applicant's wife or mother. Language commonly used by applicant; "What is your mother tongue?" How applicant acquired ability to read, write, or speak a foreign language.
Education	Inquiry into academic, vocational, or professional education of an applicant and schools attended.	Any inquiry asking specifically the nationality, race, or religious affiliation of a school.
Name	Inquiry about having worked for the company under a different name. Maiden name of married female applicant, assumed name, or change of name, if necessary to check education or employment records.	Former name of applicant whose name has been changed by court order or otherwise.
Address or Duration of Residence	Inquiry into place and length of residence at current and previous addresses.	Specific inquiry into foreign addresses that would indicate national origin.
Gender		If not based on a bona fide occupational qualification, it is extremely unlikely that gender would be considered a lawful subject for a preemployment inquiry.
Birthplace	Requirement that applicant submit, after employment, a birth certificate or other proof of legal residence.	Birthplace of applicant, applicant's parents, spouse, or other relatives.
Age	Requirement that applicant submit, after employment, a birth certificate or other document as proof of age.	Requirement that applicant produce proof of age in the form of a birth certificate, baptismal record, employment certificate, or certificate of age issued by school authorities.
Religion		Inquiry into applicant's religious denomination, affiliation, church, parish, or pastor, or which religious holidays observed. Applicant may not be told, "This is a Catholic/Protestant organization."
Workday and Shifts	Request that the applicant state days, hours, or shift(s) available to work.	It is unlawful to request applicants to state days, hours, or shift(s) that they can work if it is used to discriminate on the basis of religion.

Source: United States Equal Employment Opportunity Commission, Discrimination by Type. Retrieved August 19, 2011 from http://www.eeoc.gov/laws/types/index.cfm http://www.bls.gov/opub/mlr/2006/01/art1full.pdf; additional information: http://www.bls.gov/opub/ooq/2004/winter/art03.pdf; http://www.bls.gov/opub/ooq/2004/winter/art03.pdf

If the question is on an application, you always have the option to put "not applicable" (N/A) in the blank. If you are asked illegal questions in an interview, try to anticipate the concerns a potential employer might have about hiring you and bring them up in a manner that is comfortable for you.

Example:

Interviewer: "Do you have any children?"

Interviewee: "I guess you are wondering about the care of my school-age children. I'd like you to know I have an excellent attendance record. You are welcome to check with my past employer, and, besides, I have a live-in sitter. Additionally, I have researched the needs of this position and can assure you that I have no family responsibilities that will interfere with my ability to do this job."

Not only will employers appreciate your sensitivity to their concerns, but your statement provides you with an additional opportunity to sell yourself and to evaluate whether this position is one you want to consider. It is often advisable for you, the interviewee, to bring up any issue that may be on the employer's mind but that, because of legal concerns, will not be addressed unless you mention it. Such issues as age, children, gender, and qualifications can all be addressed by you in such a way as to enhance your chances of getting the job. Basically, you want to show how your age, qualifications, or gender will be an advantage to your employer. This requires some thinking on your part before the interview. The payoff, getting the job you want, is well worth the effort.

The Behavioral/Situational Interview

Most employers use this type of interview to gain information from you about possible job performance and to ascertain your ability to problem-solve in stressful job situations. It includes a series of questions that challenge you about how job stress was managed in the past to determine the probability of success in the future. Some of the behavioral components that interviewers are looking for include:

- **Listening skills.** Giving active and caring responses that show empathy and concern for others.
- **Writing skills.** Communicating clearly and concisely to resolve issues utilizing shared action plans with suitable outcomes.
- **Organizational/teamwork skills.** Assuming responsibility for self and others; developing mutual agreements, monitoring progress, and evaluating results.

For each of these behaviors, the interviewer challenges the candidate to provide examples of real situations where concerns were addressed and resolved. A sample question related to working effectively with others might be: "Can you give me an example that would show you have been able to develop and maintain productive relations with others, even though they may have differing points of view?"

TIPS FROM THE PROS

Regardless of the behavioral interview question, formulate your answer in terms of a brief statement of the specific situation, a review of the actions you took using your skills and personal strengths, and end with a description of the results.

Because these types of questions cannot always be clearly anticipated, you can best prepare by analyzing the requirements of the job before the interview and thinking of situations that occurred in previous job settings. By preparing in advance, you will be better able to provide clear and concise examples that will impress the interviewer.

Body Language

Your body language speaks just as loudly as your words. Eye contact is crucial. Remember that at a distance of 5 or 6 feet from another person, you can be looking at the person's nose or forehead or mouth and still maintain the sense of eye contact. Try it with friends.

Voice tone, volume, and inflection are important. A soft, wispy voice seldom convinces another that you mean business; a loud or harsh voice tends to be blocked out. Before you interview, prepare a practice interview on YouTube. Look, listen, and ask yourself if you would hire this person. Remember that your own recorded voice always sounds odd to you, so ask others for their comments. The instant feedback is very helpful, particularly if you use the form set out in Exhibit 11.2 to critique your performance. If you are in a class, practice with one or more classmates, evaluating your own and your classmates' interview

▲ Look interested by maintaining eye contact and being enthusiastic.

techniques according to the critique form. If you want to improve, courses in drama, voice and diction, speech communications, as well as workshops through the college career center are available in most colleges.

TIPS FROM THE PROS

Try varying your voice pitch and volume while reading something into a tape recorder. Strive for some variation in your pitch and tone, as this tends to convey interest and enthusiasm, whereas a monotone voice tends to convey disinterest. Try accenting your words with appropriate hand gestures to gain emphasis.

EXERCISE
11.1   Practice Interviewing

You can maximize your chance of successful interviewing by doing practice interviews and being prepared to answer an employer's typical questions. Always be prepared to support your general answers with specific examples from your experience. This strategic focus and preparation will give you the competitive edge. Go to **http://practice.interviewstream.com** for a free interactive practice site. (Be aware of the Consent for Video/Audio Recording and Digital Media Production.)

QUESTION REVIEW
Use the form in Exhibit 11.2 to critique your performance.

EXHIBIT 11.2   Interview Critique Form

Name _____
(individual being interviewed)

	Very good	Satisfactory	Fair—could be better	Needs improvement	Comments
1. Initial, or opening, presentation (impression).					
2. Eye contact.					
3. Sitting position.					
4. General appearance: grooming (hair, makeup, shave, beard, mustache, etc.), clothing.					
5. Ability to describe past work experiences, education, and training.					
6. Ability to explain equipment, tools, and other mechanical aids used.					
7. Ability to explain skills, techniques, processes, and procedures. Ability to emphasize how skills are related to job.					
8. Ability to explain personal goals, interests, and desires.					
9. Ability to explain questionable factors in personal life (functional limitations, frequent job changes, many years since last job).					
10. Ability to answer questions or make statements about company or job being applied for.					
11. Ability to listen attentively to interviewer's questions and to notice and respond to interviewer's body language.					
12. Manner of speech or conversation (voice, tone, pitch, volume, speed).					
13. Physical mannerisms (facial expressions, gestures).					
14. Enthusiasm, interest in this job.					
15. Attitude (positive?), confidence.					
16. Overall impression. Would you hire this applicant?					

Alternative Interviewing Formats

Video interviews

Many companies request a candidate to submit a video as a prescreening and screening tool. You receive questions in advance and address them in your video. *Video interviewing* occurs most often in the fields of education, government, and private manufacturing. According to *EEO Bimonthly* (*Equal Employment Opportunity Magazine*) and many career coaches, six factors are important to consider:

1. How do you come across on videotape?
2. Be prepared; practice what you will say before you are taped.
3. If you are a person who usually plays off another's body language in an interview, you will need to practice to make your answers and conversation flow as if you were actually talking to someone.
4. Dress professionally and conservatively; pay attention to the colors and patterns you wear. Solid colors work best on video.
5. Communicate with enthusiasm and confidence through facial expressions and voice tone.
6. Do not exaggerate your movements. Overdone gestures can be distracting.

Some companies conduct interviews via *videoconferencing*. In this instance, the better you understand the equipment, the more comfortable and confident you will be. Practice beforehand using the microphone and talking to one or several people until it feels natural. You can set up a similar situation using **www.Skype.com**, which enables free video phone conferencing. Give some friends sample interview questions and practice your responses via Skype. Interviewers know that many people have not used videoconferencing before. If you can adapt quickly to this new situation, it reflects well on your communication skills and technical flexibility.

> Videoconferencing interviews

Telephone interviews are sometimes used when distance or other circumstances prevent an in-person contact as well as to screen out questionable candidates. They are often conducted without prior warning so being prepared is of critical importance. First, consider your voicemail message. Make sure it is appropriate and professional before you start interviewing. Then review your usual greeting when someone calls. Unless you are sure of who is on the other line, greet your caller as if you were at work. If the call is inconvenient, agree on an alternative time and be ready. Eliminate any other distractions and background noise. This call must have your full attention. Be aware of your body language even though it is a strictly audio communication. Remember to smile as you speak. You will sound more confident when you have confident body language. Have your resume and any other pertinent notes readily accessible so you can think and answer in a concise, businesslike manner. Before ending the call, ask for an in-person meeting to further discuss the position.

> Telephone interviews

Panel or group interviews can occur in two distinct ways. First, you could be the only candidate in a room full of interviewers. This is much like a traditional interview with similar questions. You need to be particularly skilled at using your eye contact to address the questioner and scan the room so that you are talking to all the panelists. It is your goal to establish rapport with everyone. The second kind of group interview consists of you and other potential candidates in the same room at the same time being interviewed together. You are typically given a situation called a simulation and, as a team, you are asked to respond. The most important challenge for you is to stand out in a positive way. You need to find a balance between leading and following, This is your chance to demonstrate these skills in a simulated work context.

> Panel and group interviews

REAL stories — Meet José

"I can't believe how poorly I did on my interview," José said to his friend Debra. "My hands were so sweaty and I know the committee members tried not to notice when I shook their hands, but I could see it in their eyes."

José had just finished his first interview after graduating with his bachelor's degree in applied science. He had asked a friend to help him rehearse his answers to a list of general questions he found in a career planning pamphlet, and he felt confident going into the interview. But everything went downhill from the moment José sat down. He lost his concentration a couple of times and had to ask for the question to be repeated, and he completely forgot the questions he had prepared to ask the committee. He did feel that he connected with the committee on a couple of questions, and they seemed pleased that he did. After the interview, José was given a tour of the facilities but he was still so upset that he missed several opportunities to redeem his previous behavior.

At home that night, José thought about his preparation for the interview and how he could have prepared differently. He was so upset and sure that he would not be called for a second interview that he didn't bother to write thank-you notes.

WHAT DO *YOU* THINK?

1. What suggestion would you offer José regarding his interview preparation?
2. Was José being too critical about his interview performance?
3. What advice would you give José to reduce his stress level for future interviews?
4. What could José do after the interview to address some of the items more effectively?

SUCCESS strategies — Sample Questions to Ask at the Interview

Going one step further than just *answering* the interviewer's questions involves being prepared to take the initiative in *asking* several questions.

- Where does this position fit into the organization?
- What experience is ideally suited for this job?
- To whom would I be reporting? Can you tell me a little about these people?
- What have been some of the best results you have received from people in this position?
- Who are the primary people I would be working with?

- What are your expectations for me?
- What are some of the problems I might expect to encounter on this job (e.g., efficiency, quality control, declining profits, evaluation)?
- What kind of on-the-job training is allocated for this position?
- What is the normal pay range for this job?
- Given all we've discussed, can you offer me this position?
- When will I hear from you about the outcome of this interview?

Learning from the Interview

As much as they are interviewing you, you are in turn interviewing the representatives of a company. Ideally, you will do only about 40 percent of the talking. In the remaining time, you can listen and assess whether or not you want to work for that company. Although an interview tends to be rather formal, you can still gain a feeling about the climate of the organization. Entering its offices, you can observe the interaction between staff, people talking or not talking in the hallways, their style of dress, and the overall feel of the place. This is both a left- and right-brain activity. Pay attention to all of your senses as you develop your first impression of a possible new work site.

Factors Influencing Hiring

Many factors are involved in a hiring decision. You can control some of these factors, but other considerations are beyond your control. Review these factors in the next "Success Strategies" box to distinguish between the two and determine which factors in your control you have addressed.

A review of multiple surveys of employers indicates the 10 top qualities that employers seek in new employees. To make an outstanding and lasting impression, emphasize the traits listed here during any contact with a company (e.g., information or formal interview). As you review the list, check each item you feel comfortable discussing in an interview:

_____ 1. Communication skills (verbal and written)
_____ 2. Honesty/integrity
_____ 3. Teamwork skills
_____ 4. Interpersonal skills
_____ 5. Strong work ethic
_____ 6. Motivation/initiative
_____ 7. Flexibility/adaptability
_____ 8. Analytical skills
_____ 9. Computer skills
_____ 10. Organizational skills

Each of the traits you checked will strengthen your chances for a successful interview. Those you did not check need to be addressed in order for you to sharpen your competitive advantage.

SUCCESS strategies   Factors That Influence Your Success

FACTORS Out of Your Control

- Too many applicants.
- Cannot pay you what you are asking.
- Indecisiveness on part of business owner.
- Only trying to fill a temporary position.
- A current employee changed plans and decided not to leave.
- Introduction of new personnel policies.
- Looking for a certain type of person.
- Lack of experience on part of interviewer.
- Accepting applications only for future need.
- Looking for more experience.
- Looking for less experience.
- Further consideration of all applicants.
- A more important position must be filled first.
- Company went bankrupt.
- The company is downsizing.
- All positions are frozen.

FACTORS You Can Control or Guard Against

- A poor personal appearance.
- An overbearing, overaggressive, conceited attitude; being a know-it-all.
- An inability to express yourself clearly; poor voice, diction, or grammar.
- A lack of career planning; no purpose or goals.
- A lack of interest and enthusiasm; appearing passive, indifferent.
- A lack of confidence and poise; nervousness, being ill at ease.
- An overemphasis on money; interest only in best dollar offer.
- An unwillingness to start at the bottom; expecting too much too soon.
- Making excuses; evasiveness, hedging on unfavorable factors in record.
- Lack of courtesy; being ill-mannered.
- Talking negatively about past employers or coworkers.
- Failure to look interviewer in the eye.
- A limp, fishlike handshake.
- A sloppy application form.
- Wanting job only for short time.
- Lack of interest in company or in industry.
- An unwillingness to be transferred.
- Arriving late for interview without good reason.
- Failure to express appreciation for interviewer's time.
- Failure to ask questions about the job.

A greater range of jobs now require a college degree. Often a degree is required primarily because so many applicants have degrees. Your liberal arts degree can compete with a specialist degree if the following factors apply:

1. You have a good grade-point average.
2. You have a record of extracurricular activities, ideally with leadership roles.
3. You worked your way through college and/or have volunteer and internship experience.
4. You have a minor or a few classes that taught you marketable skills (e.g., accounting, social media marketing).
5. You've made contacts who can serve as positive references.
6. You have defined goals, you exude enthusiasm and confidence, and you can verbalize these characteristics in an interview.
7. You indicate that you are a fast learner (back this statement up with an example) and are willing and able to train for whatever the job requires.

For example, Walt Disney World Company employs thousands of new college graduates each year; more than a third are liberal arts graduates.

College graduates are expected to demonstrate intellectual ability (written and quantitative) and skills in planning, organizing, decision making, interpersonal relations, leadership, and oral communication. The less your major is related to the job desired, the more effectively you must be able to discuss your transferable skills as related to the job.

If You Are Offered the Job

If you are offered the job—Congratulations! Your career fitness program has paid off. Before deciding to accept a job offer, determine how well the position meets your needs. Consider the following questions before making a decision:

- How does this job fit into your long-range career goals?
- If it doesn't fit well, are there factors that may influence your decision to accept the position anyway?
- Have you considered the scope of the job, the reputation of the company, the possibility for growth and advancement, the geographic location, the salary and benefits package?

SUCCESS strategies

Summary: Reviewing the Interview Process

Preparation

- Have multiple copies of resumes and portfolios.
- Make an interview log for contacts; compose an initial contact e-mail.
- Make appointments with contacts.
- Make notes on each interview on 3 × 5 cards or enter into your computer database.
- Maintain "I can do it" attitude. Visualize that you have the job.
- Dress the part.
- Research the company (use the company website, Facebook site, *Dun and Bradstreet, Moody's, Standard & Poor's, Fortune 500,* annual report, online articles).
- Prepare five or six questions. Know when to ask them.
- Keep a computer log or journal.
- Relax and enjoy the process.
- Be on time and turn off your cell phone before the interview begins!

The Introduction

- Maintain good posture, shake hands, breathe.
- Use direct eye contact and smile.
- The first few minutes are key: Establish rapport and demonstrate enthusiasm.
- Emphasize what you can do for the company, your major strengths, your accomplishments.
- Be positive: Convert negatives to pluses.

The Interview

- Smile.
- Supply information, referring to your resume.
- Anticipate and overcome objections.
- Keep answers brief.
- Ask questions about the position, field, and company.
- Be positive.
- Ask "When will you make a decision?"

After the Interview

- Debrief yourself: Make notes (name, address, phone, impressions; if a panel of interviewers, write down names and positions of all panel members). Update online journal.
- Thank the employer or panel chairperson by a handwritten letter.
- Plan a follow-up strategy. If you don't hear from the interviewer, call and ask if a decision has been made. If you were not hired, ask for feedback and express gratitude for her or his honesty (which will enable you to improve).
- Don't be defeated—keep interviewing!

Alternatives

- Continue learning and searching.
- Consider volunteer work to gain more experience.
- Join or create a job support group.
- Keep your career interests current and updated.

NEGOTIATING FOR SALARY AND BENEFITS

Although you may be excited and eager to accept a job offer, you must realize that your prospective employer is trying to hire the most talented individual at the lowest possible salary. If you are offered a position, your aim should be to start at the highest possible salary. To achieve your goal, first determine what the salary range is for comparable positions. Numerous sites on the Internet can assist you in this research. Check out the WWWebwise exercises at the end of each chapter for specific sites.

It is always wisest to wait for the employer to bring up the topic of compensation, which includes salary and benefits. In some instances, the salary is fixed, as with government jobs, but in most cases there is a range. You will usually be offered a salary at the bottom of the range, and it is up to you to move it up. The most effective way to do that is to hold off accepting the first offer by saying, "I'll think about it," or "Is that the very best you can offer me?" Don't worry about offending your employer. This is an expected negotiation and will only confirm in your employer's mind that you know your value in the job market.

Even if the initial salary cannot be raised, you can ask for an earlier performance review date, which normally has a raise attached for good performers. In addition to or instead of a higher salary, you may be able to negotiate a fringe benefit package that is uniquely tailored to your needs and preferences. Such fringe benefits as flexible working hours or reimbursement for continued education may be equal to or far more valuable than a pay increase! Remember that the best time to negotiate is before you accept the job offer. Summon up your courage and assertiveness, and ask for what you want and deserve.

▲ Act positive and offer a strong handshake at the end of each meeting.

YOUR FIRST MONTH ON THE JOB

Your first day on the job is filled with excitement, hope, uncertainty, and anxiety. All of what you have learned in this process will stand you in good stead as you make your first impression on your work team. Remember that every job is part of your career. Take it seriously, no matter what your tasks. The work ethic that you demonstrate from day one is part of your first impression. It is critical and will set you apart from the average worker. Show up on time, well groomed and appropriately dressed. Be prepared to meet people with a firm handshake and a smile. Recognize that generational differences are a part of most work groups, and demonstrate by your enthusiasm and eye contact that you can relate to everyone on the team. Repeat each name as you are introduced, and be prepared to take notes as new information comes flooding in. Listen carefully and do not hesitate to ask questions. You are not expected to know it all. Your openness and desire to get it right will reflect on the positive self-esteem and success attitudes you have been developing.

You will have many opportunities to demonstrate your emotional intelligence as you begin to forge relationships with your colleagues and supervisors. This part of the job is just as significant as performing your job duties well, so keep alert for chances to build relationships by going to lunch with colleagues and joining activities sponsored by the company. These informal discussions will allow you to collect information on the political underworld that exists in every workplace. It will help you sniff out the spoken and unspoken norms that in fact determine success in the company. This information is never written down in a company manual, but it is crucial to your surviving and thriving in your new work setting. Norms exist around every aspect of corporate life from dress, to when you arrive and leave, to how and who you talk to, to how tasks get assigned, to how raises and promotions are determined. Ideally, you will have identified some of the corporate culture before you accepted the job so that your values will be consistent with what you experience on the job.

Now, as an employee, you will have an opportunity to confirm these values as being part of the way this company does business.

Now, as you get acquainted with your work team and the job, you will have opportunities to express who you are and what your preferences are and, in some ways, tailor the job to fit your uniqueness. You can volunteer for tasks, projects, assignments, and committees that reflect your interests, and personality. This will give you visibility and demonstrate your natural talents. In team meetings and in conversations with your supervisors, be sure to express what your preferences and competencies are so they can be used whenever possible. Also, look for opportunities to learn and grow on the job. This will keep you interested in your work and interesting to the company in terms of new assignments that you are qualified to undertake.

> When you have completed 95% of your journey, you are only halfway there.
>
> —*Japanese Proverb*

🌐 If You Do Not Get the Job

Should you find that, despite your best efforts, you did not get the desired job, remember that all your dedicated preparation will pay off in time. If you are turned down for the position, consider calling to get information to improve subsequent interviews: "I realize this is a bit unusual and I am aware you've chosen someone else for the job, but could you spend a few moments giving me some feedback as I continue my job search?" You could end up with some valuable information and possible leads; it's worth a try!

The next interview will be easier; you will benefit from your experience. The key is to keep a positive attitude and not to give up. Keep your goals in mind, and remember that persistent people achieve their objectives by focusing on the target and believing in the future.

Unfortunately, continuing unemployment can undermine a person's confidence. You will be better prepared to handle temporary setbacks and rejection if you remember that your situation is far from unique; everyone with a job was once a job searcher. As you persist in your job search, remind yourself that you *will* find a job and build a career.

How well you cope with stress and rejection will depend on your attitude and actions. Put any anger or frustration you feel to positive use. Concentrate on your strengths; review them each day. A healthy diet, physical exercise, adequate rest, social interaction with supportive friends and family and meaningful volunteer work are time-tested prescriptions for overcoming undue worry and anxiety.

One of the best antidotes for feeling depressed is doing something to help someone else. You have time, talents, and skills that will mean a great deal to others. And remember, each time you volunteer, you gain valuable experience and contacts.

Finally, try to accomplish something every day. Accomplishments are activities that make you feel good about yourself. Even minor tasks such as cleaning out a closet or refining your resume can invigorate you and give you new direction.

When you take care of yourself and strive to maintain a positive attitude, your self-image is enhanced, and you improve your chances of success.

⚙ *EXERCISE* your options

You be the judge! Search for job interviews on YouTube and other video sites. Review several. Using Exhibit 11.2, Interview Critique Form (p. 258) and the contents of this chapter, develop your own awareness of the factors you observe that lead to a positive hiring decision. Who would you hire and why? Apply this insight to practice and improve your own interview savvy. Create your own online video.

Summary

Although a job interview can be stressful, strategic preparation will enable you to relax, respond to questions more naturally, and make a good impression. When you accept a job, be prepared to begin work with a great attitude, determined to do your best and to exceed expectations.

PURPOSE OF EXERCISES

The written exercises that follow serve to prepare you for a job interview. Exercise 11.1 asked you to maximize your chance of successful interviewing by doing practice interviews and being prepared to answer an employer's typical questions. In Exercise 11.2, you are encouraged to create and post an interview on your favorite social networking site. Exercise 11.3 , WWWebwise, is an online research site to try out. And finally, you will rate your Student Learning Outcomes to reinforce what you learned in this chapter.

EXERCISE 11.2 Create an Online Video for Your Career Portfolio

After reviewing and practicing your interview skills in Exercises 11.1, prepare an interview to post on your favorite social networking sites. Ask a classmate, friend, colleague, mentor, parent, or relative to act as the interviewer. Give him or her the sample questions to use and create a sample interview that you are proud of and that you can then post and use as a reference for potential employers. (You may also use a website such as the one mentioned in Exercise 11.1, **http://practice .interviewstream.com**, to create your sample.)

    Add this sample interview to the Career Portfolio that you started with the chapter summaries. Keep Exercise 11.3 with your other entries so that you can retrieve and add to your portfolio as you continue to refine your Career Fitness program.

EXERCISE 11.3 WWWebwise

Go to **http://www.rileyguide.com**. Click on Network, Interview, & Negotiate. What can you practice to improve your chances of making a favorable impression? What did you read that made the biggest impression on you?

(*Note:* Please be aware that websites can change without notice. If a link does not work, find a similar site to complete the activity.)

REINFORCING YOUR LEARNING OUTCOMES

Review and Rate Your Chapter Outcomes. Indicate in the right-hand column how well you do the following items (from 1 = very well, to 5 = not at all). If you rated yourself 4 or 5, review the material on the pages in parentheses to ensure your career success.

How Well Can You Do the Following?

- Describe the art of interviewing. (pp. 249–253)   1   2   3   4   5
- Recognize essential steps preparing for an interview. (pp. 253–260)   1   2   3   4   5
- Use guidelines and techniques for effective interviewing. (pp. 260–265) 1   2   3   4   5

Go to the Career Fitness Portfolio at the end of the book and complete this chapter summary to build and record your personal Career Fitness Portfolio.

Additional Opportunity: Your instructor may choose to assign the Career Fitness Portfolio for in class or online completion. If so, they will provide the handout or link for you to access.

Focusing on the Future

Keep the Momentum Going

12

STUDENT LEARNING OUTCOMES

At the end of the chapter you will be able to . . .

- Understand the concept of lifelong career management and career fitness.

- Recognize the role of the future in your current career-planning efforts.

- Explain the philosophy of personal empowerment and career flexibility.

As you reach this chapter in your career fitness workout, you may find that your career is in shape and you are exercising your options in a career of your choice. If you are still exploring, you now have the skills to identify a field that resonates with your career fitness profile.

This book has provided tools and strategies to help you discover who you are; define what you want to do; research, identify, and develop your skills; and create a context in which you are able to find meaningful work. Following the book's guidelines puts you in full control, for you are creating your own possibilities instead of spending time preparing for the "predicted future" only to find that it does not exist. The only predictable future is the one that you create for yourself. During robust economic times there are plenty of opportunities for you to find your ideal position; during tough economic times, you are guaranteed nothing but your own determination to succeed. With the right attitude, you can stay focused on the need for constant self-renewal, continuous lifelong learning, and deliberate lifelong networking.

Although congratulations are in order for completing this book, you haven't completed your Career Fitness Program—you've just started it! The job of managing your career has just begun.

> I am always doing that which I cannot do, in order that I may learn how to do it.
>
> *—Pablo Picasso*

Managing Your Career

Every job or work activity, whether it's your dream job or not, is a step in your career. You have the choice every day merely to get by or to put all of your values, interests, skills, and unique personality into your work. For various students, the transition from college to career presents real challenges. Although it's possible for some students to get through college with a decent grade-point average while skipping classes, disregarding deadlines, and "doing their own thing," this will typically not be tolerated in the work world. Employers are eager to acknowledge and reward individuals who have a strong work ethic. These individuals routinely arrive on time, display an optimistic, can-do attitude, and are not only willing to do their job but are eager to take on additional assignments. They are savvy enough to know that they are responsible for their own career development. These individuals recognize that in these uncertain times, a promotion may not be around the corner, but there are always opportunities to grow on the job. This willingness to take on new challenges not only results in job enrichment for the employee but it also sets that individual apart from others who may not be as willing to jump in when needed. This attitude is what often determines whom an employer chooses for a promotion, above and beyond the required skill.

It is, in fact, your career fitness profile—your *brand*—that makes the difference when a promotion, another opportunity, or a pay raise is available. Not only are these qualities essential to getting the right job, they are also critical in managing your career successfully. It is in your best interest to cultivate a strategic outlook on your current job. Every opportunity you take to learn, grow, stretch, and further develop your skills is an opportunity that no one can take away from you. The experience becomes part of your portfolio. You are enriched and your marketability is enhanced. Yes, there are cynics who might think you are being taken advantage of if you choose to do tasks that are not technically part of your job. You may be putting in some of your own time to learn and demonstrate your newly acquired skill sets. But the successful career decision maker knows that as you build mental muscle and develop your skill sets, you have a better chance of sustaining a lead in the competitive job market. Even more important, you become more deeply connected to your profession and you demonstrate the courage to be the person in your work who you really want and need to be. We are using the word *courage* because it is derived from the Old French *cuer*, which means "heart." To be courageous means to be heartfelt. It is only when your heart connects with your work that you become the best person that you can be—and others will respond.

Refining Your Relationship Savvy

It's often been said that it's not what you know but who you know and who knows you. In today's world this must be accomplished not only through in-person contact but also online through social networks, blogs, and your own website. As you move up and around the career ladder, you often move away from technical tasks to jobs where people skills and communication skills are essential to success. Take every opportunity to participate in meetings and special projects that will put you in contact with people outside your everyday work team. According to the manager of accountancy at Sony, 80 percent of her job is dealing with people. Her associates also deal with these people, and they are developing managing skills as a result. In fact, the more your job is involved with people, the less likely it is to be replaced by technology. So regardless of your field, take every opportunity to hone your people skills.

Consider taking a leadership position whenever appropriate. Develop and nurture your relationships at work. Remember that the differences among individuals must be acknowledged and appreciated. If an individual is puzzling or perplexing, take the extra effort to try to understand this person and to cultivate a relationship. This exercise will develop your relationship skills and provide you with a rich network of associates and colleagues. You will cultivate mutual

▲ People skills, communication, and teamwork are essential to career success.

respect and appreciation for each other's uniqueness, and you will develop a strong support network in the process. Appreciating and celebrating differences is the foundation of the global economy.

Although many employers encourage you to think and act as if you owned the company so you will feel empowered to make wise decisions on their behalf, you will also be expected to be part of a team. As a team player you will be expected to act as a part of something bigger than yourself. There is a unique energy that a team experiences when its members are working well together. It's called *synergy*, and it means something bigger and better can come from combining the force of people working together.

Can you think of a time when being part of a group or team was a definite advantage in accomplishing a goal? There are endless examples from the sports world and the performing arts. Think about your favorite singer. Could he or she be a success without the many people who make up the team? Being a team player means being willing to listen to and learn from others, even when their ideas or approaches to solving a problem seem very different. It also means contributing your ideas and thoughts genuinely, demonstrating your enthusiasm and willingness to be a part of the process.

Developing Career Stamina

Even if you are following your passion, doing what you love, there will be some times in the course of your work when you may feel stuck, frustrated, unmotivated, burned out, stressed out, or bored. It's similar to what happens when we are on a physical fitness path. There are times when we've peaked and may be in a slump or at a plateau. According to George Leonard (1991) in his book *Mastery*, the cycle of learning, growth, and mastery has ups and downs. Because plateaus are part of the process of regrouping, reflecting, and getting ready for another leap, accept them as part of the cycle, and use them to reflect and recoup your physical and mental resources. Again, think about some of your favorite sports and entertainment figures. They have all experienced painful public moments before going to ever greater heights.

Embracing Career Fitness as a Way of Life

You are responsible for your own development. Learning to learn is the most essential survival skill in anyone's work life. If you are continuously on the lookout for new ways to use your current skills and develop new skills, you will remain in demand in the job market. Even if you feel content and secure in your current position, you must constantly be aware of emerging trends, opportunities, and warning signals that may affect your situation. In essence, make the world your classroom; learn something new from everything you do and from everything that happens to you!

Your future is determined by the choices you make in the present. For that reason, this book has emphasized the development of your decision-making skills. This takes the focus away from *predicting* your future and puts the emphasis on *creating* your future. The world is in flux and you are continually changing, so why shouldn't your career evolve as well?

Unfortunately, however, it is human nature to resist change. Many people do not turn to career counselors or books about career change until they are terminated from what they had assumed was a secure job. If you are wise enough to prepare for change before it is forced on you, you have a head start. The time to seek the career of your choice is while you are still employed or in school!

Life transitions and unemployment can lead to feelings of desperation and a closed or confused mind. The anxiety and confusion generated by a life crisis make career planning difficult if not impossible. If you are unemployed or underemployed, you are likely to feel depressed,

TIPS FROM THE PROS

Much of the emphasis in career planning is on moving forward, looking ahead, striving and stretching. Equally important for balance, optimal performance, and happiness is enjoying the present. Happiness researchers caution that most of us think "I'll be happy when…(I finish this course, I get a new job, I get a promotion, I lose ten pounds)." We put happiness off into the future, contingent on some external event or condition, when in fact, it is only available to us in the present. Happiness is a state of mind that is largely independent of external factors. People often consider even illness or unemployment a blessing because it forced them to realign their values, priorities, and worldview. They chose to be happy despite their circumstances.

lethargic, and hopeless about the future. It is precisely during this time that you need to immerse yourself in the career-planning process. During times of personal transition and uncertainty, this process will give you a structure to cope with anxiety and depression and to reconnect with your dreams and passions. It is during these times of confusion, upset, turbulence, and life transition that you can rely on the many resources that will help put your life in perspective and that will allow you to focus in on what is genuinely meaningful to you. Additional books that address this issue are *The Power of Now* and *A New Earth* by Eckhart Tolle.

EXERCISE your options

Evaluate your current happiness level. From 1 to 10, what is it right now? What three things could you do today to increase your score?

1. _____

2. _____

3. _____

Sustaining Mental Career Fitness to Continue Exercising Your Options

Cultivating the "*now*" in your life is the secret to developing your resiliency throughout your life. Here are some of the keys to unlock this powerful presence. These tips will enable you to develop the stamina you need to sustain a lifetime of career fitness.

Recognize, respect, and rejoice in YOU. Yes, you are a work in progress but you already possess the keys to your happiness. These fundamentals come from the personal assessment you've completed as part of the Career Fitness Program. Knowing and believing in your values and true nature will enable you to express and feel the joy of being alive today.

Value your work and find work you value. Consciously make the connection between what you are doing and how it contributes to the world. A hairdresser is a self-esteem coach, a cook is part of the hunger project, a plumber keeps things flowing. Every job has intrinsic worth and value. Rather than diminish your role by using the word *just* to describe what you do, think of how you improve one or many lives.

Choose your attitude. An optimistic outlook is not inborn but cultivated by positive self-talk and deliberate reflection. When something or someone upsets you, listen to your self-talk. If you tend to overreact, take a few deep breaths, force yourself to smile, and ask yourself if the awful consequences you fear are likely to happen. Chances are you can be your own best coach in moving from an imagined disaster to a manageable situation.

Cultivate all parts of your being. Make time daily to nurture your body, mind, spirit, and social self. Humor, physical exercise, wholesome food, uplifting music and reading, time in nature, prayer, meditation, yoga, time with friends and family all contribute to a sense of well-being and happiness that will increase your resilience and longevity.

Experience the joy of giving. Regardless of how bad things seem in your life, you have the power to give something of yourself. It could be a compliment, an offer of help, a visit, a call, a smile. It's always a win-win situation. Inevitably, you will make someone's day and your day will be brighter too!

 The World Is Your Oyster

This phrase, **The world is your oyster**, has been used to capture the fact that opportunities abound everywhere. Perhaps this has never been more true than today. Because of our interdependence in every facet of our existence from the air we breathe, to the climate we experience, to the food we eat, to the water we drink, to the language we speak, to the clothes we wear, to the technology we consume, to the work we do, to the people we know, we must think and act globally. Although this might sound overwhelming, it actually all starts with you. Where have you always dreamed about visiting or living? Be it Nashville or Nairobi, or anywhere else, you can experience the world in many ways. Consider a summer or semester or year of study abroad. Volunteer and/or find an internship. Community organizations such as the Rotary International and church groups offer many international opportunities to study and or volunteer at little or no cost to you. Establish friendships online and plan to exchange home visits. Reach out to classmates or members of the community who represent a different culture and discuss

▲ The world is full of opportunities.

the similarities and differences in lifestyle and philosophies. Extend your job search to the cities and countries that fascinate you. Regardless of your major, there are always job opportunities to teach English in schools and businesses abroad.

Plan to explore the world now, before you have a family and financial obligations. The experiences derived from travel will enrich your life. You will become a more competitive job candidate and you will lead people one step closer to world peace through the powerful lens of cultural understanding and appreciation. Reach out and become a citizen of your world!

 Summary

Each time you begin a job search, review the accomplishments and skills you recorded in this book. This may help relieve your apprehension about another job search. You will be reminded of the skills you have and the many alternatives that lead to satisfying career goals. Your emotional intelligence will enable you to recognize that the uncertainty of transition provides you with fertile ground on which to learn and grow. In fact, a change of direction now may become the best opportunity of your lifetime.

In the course of reevaluating your personal strengths and skills, your self-confidence will blossom. You will regain a sense of purpose and direction by setting meaningful and achievable goals. Through networking, information interviewing, and volunteering, your interaction with people

▲ Become a citizen of the world.

will enable you to choose, confirm, or change current goals and be energized and inspired by people who are doing the kind of work you find challenging and rewarding.

Exercising your options may take more effort than crystal-ball gazing, but the results are worth it. Building a career is a lifelong endeavor. This book will continue to serve as your coach in the most engaging journey of your life!

PURPOSE OF EXERCISES

Now that you have completed your career fitness program, Exercise 12.1 invites you to take in the power of an inspiring world entrepreneur, Steven Jobs. Finally, we ask you to reinforce the lessons learned from this last chapter.

EXERCISE
12.1   WWWebwise

Steve Jobs, founder of Apple, died recently at the age of 56. In his commencement speech to the Stanford University graduating class of 2005, entitled "You've got to find what you love," he said he asked himself every day, "**If today were the last day of my life, would I want to do what I am about to do today?**" If his answer was no, and that was his answer several days in a row, he knew change was needed.

Here are his words of wisdom for each of us today: "Your time is limited, so don't waste it living someone else's life…Don't let the noise of other's opinions drown out your own inner voice….And most important, have the courage to follow your heart and intuition. They somehow already know what you truly want to become. Everything else is secondary." *Read his entire speech for a jolt of inspiration!* ***http://tinyurl.com/dfbkvo***.

REINFORCING YOUR LEARNING OUTCOMES

Review and Rate Your Chapter Outcomes. Indicate in the right-hand column how well you do the following items (from 1 = very well, to 5 = not at all). If you rated yourself 4 or 5, review the material on the pages in parentheses to ensure your career success.

How Well Can You Do the Following?

- Understand the concept of lifelong career management and career fitness. (pp. 267–269)   1 2 3 4 5
- Recognize the role of the future in your current career-planning efforts. (pp. 269–270)   1 2 3 4 5
- Explain the philosophy of personal empowerment and career flexibility. (pp. 271–272)   1 2 3 4 5

REAL stories   Meet Brian

Meet Brian, who wrote this essay as part of his work experience class at a community college. As you read, think about the career fitness journey you have just completed with this book and how Brian is using the lessons he has learned in his workplace.

For most adults over the age of 21, the majority of our time is spent at the workplace or with work-related things. So I felt I needed to make the best of my time at work. A lot of people dread going to work, and until recently, I was no different. I have been working with a worldwide copy and print company for about two years and felt I needed to step up my responsibilities. I wanted to show people that I have potential to change the way others work in my store, and how they spend their time in what I call "Our home away from home." With a recent promotion, I took this work experience class to allow me to work full time and gain college credit simultaneously. Little did I know this course would turn out to be more of a benefit than just another class.

Over the past few months, I have been on a path to develop my operating skills, to be a little more self-motivated, and most importantly to develop leadership skills, so I may motivate others to want to work and look forward to coming into work every day.

Besides copying, the company accepts packages to pack and ship at the same time as maintaining a store with lots of machinery, and serves customers who need assistance. When I first started working at the store, I felt overwhelmed with what was expected of me, and I felt the weight every day I had to step foot into my store. Work was very repetitive and difficult, but I knew I couldn't continue to view my workplace in such a way.

For my objective on self-motivation, I started coming into work with a positive attitude, ready to take on any obstacle the day may bring my way. I had set my goal to make every customer happy, no matter what it takes, and to build a trust with them. I have found that if we build a relationship with the customers, they are more likely to be lenient and patient with any situation that may come up. This also makes the workload a lot easier for my coworkers because we are able to handle our work without stress and/or worry. In turn, the customer's patience allows us to focus more on getting our jobs done right.

My position is titled lead project coordinator. My job is to manage all store operations as far as production goes. It is my responsibility to make sure jobs are getting done correctly, on time, all the while completing multiple jobs in a timely manner. I must make sure all our sources of operation are available to us for whatever we may need them for, and keep track of all workers and what they need to focus on. Along with the position, I also do the production, and attend to the mailing portion of the store, as well as the graphics stations and technical work. My skills have developed tremendously since my first year working here. In my store, I am the go-to guy of my shift. Even the assistant managers ask me for advice from time to time. That alone is a good feeling. Although I am knowledgeable about most everything in my store, I know there is still much to learn. My skills are an aspect of myself that will never reach an end. That being the case, I can only hope to become stronger, not only for myself, but for everyone around me, so that they may enjoy working and feel they have someone to depend on.

Taking this work experience course allowed me to experience some operations of the store that only a manager would be involved in. I presented the idea of developing my leadership skills to my assistant manager and with that she granted me minor assistant manager responsibilities. It may sound like even more weight on my shoulders, but I understand that with every step up you make in this company, you take on new responsibilities as well as needing to maintain your old ones. When managers take time off I was left responsible for all workers on my shift, as well as the store. It felt great. My coworkers looked up to me to get things done right, and we had fun while doing our daily routines. I got comments from my coworkers saying it was the most fun they have had while working. We even finished all the work with time to spare in the end, which allowed us to better attend to every customer who walked through our doors.

During this work experience class, I have learned that everything truly works in a cycle. We take care of ourselves, and it helps us take care of our coworkers and customers. When we are positive, customers are positive in return, ultimately resulting in a positive end. Everyone is satisfied and has a lot less stress when coming to work. Also, with this course, it helped me prove to my managers that I am capable of doing more. In the near future, I plan on applying for an assistant manager position at one of the many new stores opening around the area. For the time being, I will stay with this company and further develop my skills. When it comes time to move on, I will have a lot to show for myself through my improved skills.

REAL stories   *CONTINUED*

WHAT DO *YOU* THINK?

1. Describe how Brian has used the information in this book to improve his attitude and performance on the job. Think about his positive success profile, his brand, his values, skills, interests, personality type, and decision-making and goal-setting abilities.

2. How did Brian demonstrate his relationship savvy? And his understanding of generations and personality types?

3. If you were an employer, would you hire Brian? Explain your answer.

4. What might be the benefit to you in taking a work experience course at your college?

Go to the Career Fitness Portfolio at the end of the book and complete this chapter summary to build and record your personal Career Fitness Portfolio.

Additional Opportunity: Your instructor may choose to assign the Career Fitness Portfolio for in class or online completion. If so, they will provide the handout or link for you to access.

Career Fitness Portfolio

Putting it all together to create a Career Fitness Portfolio and reach a tentative career goal.

A career portfolio is an essential tool in your career fitness program. It will help you track your thinking, collect your work products and prepare you to present your most professional self to the work world. It will be useful to you as you begin your career planning and search. Create a file on your computer and/ or a hard copy in a binder in which you can collect information about yourself—your skills, interests, and abilities. Get into the practice of collecting and documenting information about yourself. Include any reports, projects, job appraisals, notes or awards of recognition or other information that will support your self-assessment.

Many of the following exercises are excerpted from their respective chapters in the text. This is done deliberately.

This is your opportunity to review your responses and reflect on how true they are for you today. If your responses today are different from those you recorded when you initially completed these exercises, note your current responses below. These summaries will help you integrate the information from each chapter and put together your unique Career Fitness Portfolio. The last question in each chapter gives you space to record the website that you found the most useful and what type of information you learned from it. ***Note:*** Use extra paper as necessary to complete exercises.

CHAPTER 1   Testing Your Career Savvy

Refer back to original Chapter 1 answers.

1. I am _____

2. I need _____

3. I want _____

4. My generational preferences that may influence the career I select can be summarized as _____

5. The Holland Type most like me is:

   ____ Realistic   ____ Enterprising   ____ Social

   ____ Artistic   ____ Investigative   ____ Conventional

6. Five adjectives that best describe me are _____

7. My favorite school subjects include _____

8. In the WWWebwise exercise, I found _____ useful for
                                               (list website)

   _____.
              (learning outcomes/gaining what type of information)

2 Building Your Career Success Profile

Refer back to original Chapter 2 answers.

1. I am proud that _____
   _____
   _____

2. Five positive attitudes I bring to the job are _____
   _____
   _____

3. I admire the following characteristics in people: _____
   _____
   _____

4. I am developing the following success qualities: _____
   _____
   _____

5. My affirmations are _____
   _____
   _____

6. In the WWWebwise exercise, I found _____ useful for
   (list website)
   _____.
   (learning outcomes/gaining what type of information)

3 Confirming Core Values

Refer back to original Chapter 3 answers.

1. My top values are _____
   _____
   _____

2. A societal issue that concerns me is _____
   _____
   _____

3. My most important considerations in a job are _____
   _____
   _____

4. I am energized by the following types of activities (from my past jobs, volunteer experiences, or hobbies): _____
   _____
   _____

5. My ideal job would be (if you don't have a title, list the job tasks, activities, or lifestyle) _____
   _____
   _____

6. In the WWWebwise exercise, I found _____ useful for
   (list website)
   _____.
   (learning outcomes/gaining what type of information)

CHAPTER

4   Assessing Your Personality and Interests

Refer back to original Chapter 4 exercises.

1. Circle the term in each of the following pairs that best describes your personality type:

   extravert / introvert   sensing / intuitive   thinking / feeling   judging / perceiving

2. Circle your top three Holland Interest Environments from Chapter 4:

   realistic   enterprising   investigative   conventional   artistic   social

3. List the results of any assessments or inventories you have taken during the past year. For example:

   a. Strong Interest Inventory: Holland Type letters _____ _____ _____

      General Occupational Themes:

      _____

      Three highest Basic Interest Scales:

      _____
      _____
      _____

      Very similar/somewhat similar occupational scales (job titles). List five:

      _____
      _____
      _____
      _____
      _____

   b. Career Occupational Preference Survey (COPS) or other interest inventory:

      _____

      List your three highest occupational groups from this survey or from any other interest inventory used:

      _____
      _____
      _____

      List five related job titles that sound interesting:

      _____
      _____
      _____
      _____
      _____

4. After reviewing your interests, list your three tentative career choices:

   _____
   _____
   _____

5. In the WWWebwise exercise, I found _____ useful for
   (list website)
   _____.
   (learning outcomes/gaining what type of information)

CHAPTER

5   Evaluating Your Skills

Refer back to original Chapter 5 exercises.

1. Three of my accomplishments are _____
   _____
   _____

2. A summary of the skills I most enjoy using: _____
   _____
   _____

3. The skills I want to use in my future career are _____
   _____
   _____

4. The skills I plan to develop in the next few years are _____
   _____
   _____

5. In the WWWebwise exercise, I found _____ useful for
                             (list website)
   _____
        (learning outcomes/gaining what type of information)

CHAPTER

6   Examining the World of Work

Refer back to original Chapter 6 exercises

1. The advantages of my age, sex, race, or physical limitations in looking for a job or working toward my career goal are
   _____
   _____
   _____
   _____

2. The disadvantages of my age, sex, race, or physical limitations in looking for a job or working toward my career goal are
   _____
   _____

3. Occupations that interest me (based on the trends described in Chapter 6):
   _____
   _____

4. In the WWWebwise exercise, I found _____ useful for
                             (list website)
   _____
        (learning outcomes/gaining what type of information)

CHAPTER
7 Exploring Career Information

Refer back to original Chapter 7 exercises.

1. List the one best job from Exercise 7.7: _____
_____

2. Choose a job you researched and list the titles or names of sources used in each category:

   a. Newspapers, bulletin boards, magazines _____
   _____

   b. Trade journals (name one) _____

   c. Directories (name one) _____

   d. Internet addresses _____
   _____

   e. Career and placement centers _____
   _____

3. In the WWWebwise exercise, I found _____ useful for

   (list website)

   _____.

   (learning outcomes/gaining what type of information)

CHAPTER
8 Refining Your Decision Making

Refer back to original Chapter 8 exercises.

1. I use the following decision-making strategies: _____
_____

2. My limiting beliefs include _____
_____

3. My belief about the future is _____
_____

4. The best use of my time right now (according to time management strategies) is _____
_____

5. A long-range goal related to my career is _____
_____

6. A short-term goal related to my career is _____

   I will complete it by (indicate a date): _____

7. External factors that can affect these career decisions include _____
_____

8. Internal factors that can influence these career decisions include _____
_____

9. In the WWWebwise exercise, I found _____ useful for

   (list website)

   _____.

   (learning outcomes/gaining what type of information)

CHAPTER

9   Targeting Your Job Search

Refer back to original Chapter 9 exercises.

1. Identify your ideal job situation and then list an entry-level job related to your ideal:

    _____

    _____

2. Identify volunteer, freelance opportunities or part-time opportunities:

    _____

    _____

3. Identify people who are doing what you would like to do:

    _____

    _____

4. List your information interview questions:

    _____

    _____

    _____

5. What did you learn from interviewing someone:

    _____

    _____

6. List your contacts and professional associations for this ideal job:

    _____

    _____

    _____

7. In the WWWebwise exercise, I found _____ useful for
    (list website)

    _____.
    (learning outcomes/gaining what type of information)

CHAPTER

10   Crafting a Winning Resume and Portfolio

Refer back to original ch. 10 exercises
Create your own professional website and/or blog and include your resume and a list of your references.

CHAPTER

11   Interviewing Strategically

Refer back to original ch. 11 exercises
Add a sample video interview to your website

12   Focusing on the Future

Refer back to original ch. 12 exercises

Add your mission statement and your philosophy of life to your website and practice it daily as part of your Career Fitness Program

Now complete the following exercises to integrate this information and set a tentative career goal.

EXERCISE

Quick Impressions

Read each category and respond quickly by recording the first three thoughts that come to mind in each one. Then list short- and long-term career goals.

Career Values _____

_____

_____

Career Interests _____

_____

_____

Career Skills / Abilities _____

_____

_____

Possible Careers _____

_____

_____

Career-Related Leisure-Time Pursuits _____

_____

_____

SHORT-TERM CAREER GOALS AND OBJECTIVES	LONG-TERM CAREER GOALS AND OBJECTIVES	SUPPORTIVE PEOPLE TO HELP ME IMPLEMENT MY CAREER GOALS
1. _____	1. _____	1. _____
2. _____	2. _____	2. _____
3. _____	3. _____	3. _____
4. _____	4. _____	4. _____
5. _____	5. _____	5. _____

Review your Quick Impressions with three supportive people in your life. Ask for their input and help in working toward your goals. As a final step in confirming your career goal, complete the next exercise, "Information Integration and Goal Setting."

Information Integration and Goal Setting

Complete the form provided using the sample following the exercise as a guideline.

Long-range career goal: _____

Present short-range career goal (one-to five-year goal): _____

I look forward to *majoring* or *getting training* in _____

so that I can become _____

because I *value* _____

and my *interests* include _____

_____

and this career would allow me to _____

_____

Summary of strengths and weaknesses related to goal:

PERSONAL STRENGTHS ("YOUR TYPE")

_____
_____
_____
_____
_____

PERSONAL WEAKNESSES (NEED TO IMPROVE)

_____
_____
_____
_____
_____

FAVORABLE EXTERNAL CONDITIONS RELATED TO CAREER CHOICE

_____
_____
_____
_____
_____

UNFAVORABLE EXTERNAL CONDITIONS RELATED TO CAREER CHOICE

_____
_____
_____
_____
_____

STRATEGIES TO REACH GOAL

_____
_____
_____
_____
_____

RESOURCES AVAILABLE TO HELP REACH GOAL

_____
_____
_____
_____
_____

Alternative short-range career goals that would be equally satisfying: _____

_____

_____

Training needed to enter this career alternative: _____

_____

_____

SAMPLE

Information Integration and Goal Setting

Long-range career goal: To enable people to use their resources.

Present short-range career goal (one- to five-year goal):

I look forward to *majoring* or *getting training* in psychology

so that I can become a social worker or counselor

because I *value* helping others, serving people, being resourceful, variety, creativity, and continually learning.

and my *interests* include communication, holistic health, adult development, higher education, and career counseling.

and this career would allow me to share, keep informed, serve people, be an expert.

Summary of strengths and weaknesses related to goal:

PERSONAL STRENGTHS ("YOUR TYPE")

Have a B.A., willing to study, quick learner, self-confident, able to present before groups, eligible for credential programs, have already volunteered and resourceful

PERSONAL WEAKNESSES (NEED TO IMPROVE)

Impatient, lack money for further education, fear taking the Graduate Record Examination, need time Management instruction

FAVORABLE EXTERNAL CONDITIONS RELATED TO CAREER CHOICE

Many education programs available, many counselors retiring in next three years, already working, volunteer experiences are available, graduate programs exist

UNFAVORABLE EXTERNAL CONDITIONS RELATED TO CAREER CHOICE

Not many openings now, not many paid positions available now, many people with this degree out of work

STRATEGIES TO REACH GOAL

Talk to graduate adviser, obtain application to graduate school, discuss alternatives with adviser, identify volunteer opportunities, volunteer, seek part-time job related to counseling (e.g., teacher's aide)

RESOURCES AVAILABLE TO HELP REACH GOAL

Faculty, counselors, college career and placement centers

Alternative short-range career goals that would be equally satisfying: Work in the Student Activities Office as a club organizer or be a student affairs assistant in the Career Center helping students find resources, leading orientations, and organizing outings to industry

Training needed to enter this career alternative: Working in Student Affairs or the Career Center while in college

Now that you have selected a career goal and identified your strengths and weaknesses, answer the following questions:

1. What can you do now (or in the next six months) to address one or two of your weaknesses? List one weak area here (e.g., test anxiety), and list one method to help you improve (e.g., see a counselor to learn how to reduce anxiety).

    Weakness: _____
    _____
    _____
    _____

    How to improve: _____
    _____

    By when will I complete this goal: _____
    _____

2. What can you do now to start working toward your career goal? List three activities you can do to move you closer to your goal (e.g., see a counselor to find out requirements for the major; sign up for major-related classes).

    To do: By what date:

    a. _____   a. _____

    b. _____   b. _____

    c. _____   c. _____

3. When you complete these activities, what can you do to reward yourself for your efforts?
    _____
    _____
    _____

If you are still confused about which career to focus on, start with the one that is most easily attainable. Work through your job search strategy in Part III of this book using that career as your focal point. Once you understand the job search process, you can use it to explore additional career goals.

References and Suggested Readings

Betrus, Martin. 2009. *The Complete Book of Perfect Phrases for Successful Job Seekers*. New York: McGraw-Hill.

Bolles, Richard N. 2009. *The Job Hunter's Survival Guide*. Berkeley, CA: Ten Speed Press.

Bolles, Richard N. 2009. *Job Hunting on the Internet*. Berkeley, CA: Ten Speed Press.

Bolles, Richard N. 2006. *Quick Job Hunting Map*. Berkeley, CA: Ten Speed Press.

Bolles, Richard N. 2012. *What Color Is Your Parachute? A Practical Manual for Job Hunters and Career Changers*. Revised edition. Berkeley, CA: Ten Speed Press.

Bridges, William. 2003. *Managing Transitions*. Cambridge, MA: Perseus Publishing.

Brooks, Katharine. 2009. *You Majored in What?* New York. Penguin Group.

Brown, Lola. 2007. *Resume Writing Made Easy*, 8th edition. Upper Saddle River, NJ: Prentice Hall.

Bureau of Labor Statistics. 2007. "20 Facts on Women Workers." *Statistical Abstracts of the United States*. Washington, DC: Bureau of Labor Statistics, U.S. Department of Labor, Women's Bureau.

Bureau of Labor Statistics. 2008. *Tomorrow's Jobs*. Accessed at www.bls.gov.

Business Week Online. 2007, August 20, 27. *The Future of Work*. www.businessweek.com.

_____2009, March, Bloomberg-Business Week issue "Work-Life Balance" article found at http://www.businessweek.com/managing/content/mar2009/ca20090327_734197.htm?chan=careers_special+report+--+work-life+balance_special+report+--+work-life+balance

Career Opportunities News. 2004. Garrett Park, MD: Garrett Park Press. (Six issues annually.)

Career Planning and Adult Development Newsletter. San Jose, CA: CPAD Network. (Six newsletters and four journals annually.)

Career Planning Program Handbook. 2003. American College Testing Program.

Covey, Stephen. 2006. *The 8th Habit: From Effectiveness to Greatness*. Philadelphia, PA: Running Press Miniature Editions.

Crispin, Gerry, and Mark Mehler. 2002. *Career X Roads*. New York: MMC Group.

DeBack, Allan. 2010. *Get Hired in a Tough Market*. New York: McGraw-Hill.

Dictionary of Occupational Titles. 2009. Washington, DC: U.S. Department of Labor, Employment and Training.

Dyer, Wayne. 1992. *Real Magic*. New York: HarperCollins.

Edwards, Paul, and Sara Edwards. 2007. *Middle-Class Lifeboat: Careers and Life Choices for Navigating a Changing Economy* Nashville TN: Thomas Nelson.

Eikleberry, Carol. 2006. *The Career Guide for Creative and Unconventional People*, 3rd edition. Berkeley, CA: Ten Speed Press.

Elliott, Myrna. 1982. *Transferable Skills for Teachers*. Moorpark, CA: Statewide Career Counselor Training Project.

Enelow, Wendy, and Louise Kursmark. 2009. *Expert Resumes for Career Changers*. Indianapolis, IN: JIST Works.

Farr, Michael. 2006. *Best Jobs for the 21st Century*. Indianapolis, IN: JIST Works.

Farr, Michael, 2010. *100 Fastest-Growing Careers*. Indianapolis, IN: JIST Works.

Farrell, Warren. 2005. *Why Men Earn More: The Startling Truth Behind the Pay Gap and What Women Can Do About It*. New York: AMACOM.

Fields, Jonathan. 2009. *Career Renegades*. New York: Broadway Books.

Fein, Richard. 2005. *Cover Letters! Cover Letters! Cover Letters!* Franklin Lakes, NJ: Career Press.

Fortune Magazine. 2011. "100 Best Companies to Work For." (Updated annually.)

Friedman, Thomas. 2005. *The World Is Flat: A Brief History of the Twenty-First Century*. New York: Farrar, Straus and Giroux.

Friedman, Thomas. 2007. *The World Is Flat 3.0. A Brief History of the Twenty-First Century*. New York: Farrar, Straus and Giroux.

Galinsky, E. A., K. Kuman, and J. Bond. 2008. *The National Study of the Changing Workforce: Times are Changing: Gender and Generation at Work and at Home*. New York: Families and Work Institute.

Gardner, Howard. 1993. *Frames of Mind: The Theory of Multiple Intelligences*. New York: Basic Books.

Gardner, Howard. 2000. *Intelligence Reframed: Multiple Intelligences for the Twenty-First Century*. New York: Basic Books.

Gawain, Shakti. 2000. *Creative Visualization*. Novato, CA: New World Library.

Gelatt, H. B. 1991. *Creative Decision Making: Using Positive Uncertainty*. Menlo Park, CA: Crisp.

Gehlhaus, Diana. "What Can I Do with My Liberal Arts Degree?" *Occupational Outlook Quarterly* 2007-8 Washington, DC: U.S. Department of Labor, BLS.

Goleman, Daniel. 1995. *Emotional Intelligence.* New York: Bantam Press.

Goleman, Daniel. 2002. *Working with Emotional Intelligence.* New York: Audio Renaissance.

Graber, Steven (Ed.). 2005. *Adams Job Almanac 2005.* Holbrook, MA: Adams Media Corporation.

Half, Robert, and Max Messmer. 2005. *Job Hunting for Dummies.* Chicago: IDG Books Worldwide.

Hammer, Allen L. (Ed.). 1996. *MBTI Applications: A Decade of Research on the Myers-Briggs Type Indicator.* Palo Alto, CA: Consulting Psychologists Press.

Handy, Charles. 2002. *The Future of Work.* Malden, MA: Blackwell Publishing.

Harrington, B., Van Deusen, F., & Ladge, J. (2010). *The new dad: Exploring fatherhood within a career context.* Chestnut Hill, MA: Boston College Center for Work & Family. Retrieved from http://www.bc.edu/centers/cwf/metaelements/pdf/BCCWF_Fatherhood_Study_The_New_Dad.pdf; also see http://wfnetwork.bc.edu/business.php

Hayes, Cassandra. 2002. *Black Enterprise: Guide to Building Your Career.* New York: John Wiley & Sons.

Herzberg, Frederick. 1966. *Work and the Nature of Man.* New York: World.

Hewlett, Sylvia A., and Carolyn B. Luce. 2005. "Off-Ramps and On-Ramps: Keeping Talented Women on the Road to Success," *Harvard Business Review,* vol. 83, no. 3, p. 14.

Hill, Napoleon. 2007. *The Law of Success in Sixteen Lessons by Napoleon Hill* (Complete, Unabridged). Accessed at www.bnpublishing.net.

Hirsch, Arlene. 2005. *Interviewing.* New York: John Wiley & Sons.

Holland, John. 1985. *Making Vocational Choices: A Theory of Vocational Personalities and Work Environments,* 2nd edition. Englewood Cliffs, NJ: Prentice Hall.

Howe, Neil, and William Strauss. 2000. *Millennials Rising: The Next Great Generation.* New York: Random House.

Jensen, Eric. 2007. *Enriching the Brain: How to Maximize Every Learner's Potential.* Indianapolis, IN: Jossey-Bass.

Job Choices. Bethlehem, PA: National Association of Colleges and Employers 2006. (Annual publication.)

Journal of Career Development. 2007, November. New York: Human Sciences Press.

Judge, Timothy A. and Charlice Hurst, "How the Rich (and Happy) Get Richer (and Happier): Relationship of Core Self-Evaluations to Trajectories in Attaining Work," *Journal of Applied Psychology,* 93 (4): 2008. Information accessed 8/18/11 from Strategy+Business, http://www.strategy-business.com/article/re00046?gko=ed2a4

Jung, Carl. 1923. *Psychological Types.* New York: Harcourt Brace.

Kaye, Beverly L., and Sharon Jordan-Evans. 2008. *Love 'Em or Lose 'Em: Getting Good People to Stay.* San Francisco: Berrett Koehler.

Keirsey, David, and Marilyn Bates. 1984. *Please Understand Me: Character and Temperament Types.* Del Mar, CA: Prometheus Nemesis.

Kleiman, Carol. 2006. *Winning the Job Game.* New York: John Wiley & Sons.

Kreigel, Robert, and Marilyn Kreigel. 1985. *The C Zone.* Garden City, NY: Fawcett.

Krumholtz, J. D. and A. S. Levin. 2004. *Luck Is No Accident: Making the Most of Happenstance in your Life and Work.* Atascadero, CA Impact Publishers.

Lancaster, Lynne and David Stillman. 2010. *The M Factor.* New York: Harper Collins.

Leonard, George. 1991. *Mastery.* New York: Dutton.

Levinson, D. J. 1978. *The Seasons of a Man's Life.* New York: Knopf.

MacKay, Carleen, and Brad Taft. 2006. *Boom or Bust.* Scottsdale, AZ: Cambridge Media LLC.

Matherly, C, ad D. Robinson, 2000, "Get Ready for the Global Workplace" Accessed on August 19, 2011 from http://www.black-collegian.com/career/wsj/getready902.shtml

Maslow, Abraham. 1987. *Motivation and Personality,* 3rd edition. Upper Saddle River, NJ: Pearson Education.

Miller, Dan. 2010. *48 Days to the Work You Love.* Nashville, TN: B&H Publishing.

Mitchell, Susan. 2005. *American Generation: Who They Are, How They Live.* Ithaca, NY: New Strategies.

Monthly Labor Review. 2007, November. Washington, DC: U.S. Department of Labor, Bureau of Labor Statistics.

Myers, Isabel. 1962. *Manual: The Myers–Briggs Type Indicator.* Palo Alto, CA: Consulting Psychologists.

National Business Employment Weekly. P.O. Box 300. Princeton, NJ 08543. (Published quarterly.)

Occupational Outlook Quarterly. 2010–11. Washington, DC: U.S. Department of Labor, Bureau of Labor Statistics.

Parker, Yana. 2006. *The Damn Good Resume Guide.* Berkeley, CA: Ten Speed Press.

Peters, Tom. 1999. *The Brand You.* New York: Random House.

Peterson's Internships 2006. Princeton, NJ: Peterson's Guide Publisher.

Phelps, Stanlee, and Nancy Austin. 1997. *The Assertive Woman, A New Look.* San Luis Obispo, CA: Impact.

Pink, Daniel. 2002. *Free Agent Nation: The Future of Working for Yourself.* New York: Warner Books.

Pink, Daniel. 2006. *A Whole New Mind: Why Right Brainers Will Rule the Future.* New York: Penguin.

Radcliffe Public Policy Center. 2000, July. "Life's Work." Harris Interactive Poll.

Reich, Robert B. 2002. *The Future of Success: Working and Living in the New Economy.* New York: Vintage Books.

Renner, Michael, and Scott Mackin. 1998. "The College Undergraduate Stress Scale (CUSS)," *Teaching of Psychology*, vol. 25, no. 1, pp. 46–48.

Rocks, Celia. 2001. *Organizing the Good Life: A Path to Joyful Simplicity—Home to Work and Back.* New York: Demand Press.

Rolie, Linda K. 2009. *Getting Back to Work.* New York: McGraw-Hill

Rosen, Lucy. 2010. *Fast Track Networking.* Franklin Lakes, NJ: Career Press

Salvador, Evelyn. 2011. *Step-by-Step Resumes.* Indianapolis, IN: JIST Works

SCANS (*Secretary's Commission on Achieving Necessary Skills*): *What Work Requires of Schools: A SCANS Report for America 2000.* 1991, June. Washington, DC: U.S. Department of Labor.

Schepp, Brad and Debra. 2010. *How to Find a Job on LinkedIN, Facebook, Twitter, Myspace and Other Social Networks.* New York: McGraw-Hill.

Seligman, Martin E. P. 2011. *Flourish: A Visionary New Understanding of Happiness and Well-Being.* New York: Free Press

Sheehy, Gail. 1996. *New Passages: Your Life Across Time.* New York: Ballantine.

Simon, Sidney B., Leland W. Howe, and Howard Kirschenbaum. 1995. *Values Clarification.* New York: Warner Books.

Snodgrass, Jon. 1996. *Follow Your Career Star: A Career Quest Based on Inner Values.* New York: Kensington.

Stangler, Dane. 2009, The Economic Future Just Happened. Kansas City: Ewing Marion Kauffman Foundation.

Super, Donald E. 1957. *The Psychology of Careers.* New York: Harper.

Super, Donald E., M. L. Savickas, and C. Super. 1996. "A Life Span, Life-Space Approach to Career Development." In D. Brown, L. Brook, & Associates (Eds.), *Career Choice and Development* (3rd edition, pp. 121–128). San Francisco: Jossey-Bass.

Tieger, Paul, and Barbara Barron-Tieger. 2007. *Do What You Are: Discover the Perfect Career for You Through the Secrets of Personality Type.* New York: Little, Brown.

Tischler, Linda. 2004, March. "Where Are the Women?" *Fast Company*, vol. 79, p. 52.

Tischler, Linda. 2005, January. "Bridging the (Gender Wage) Gap," *Fast Company*, vol. 90, p. 85.

Tolle, Eckhart. 2004. *The Power of Now.* Vancouver: Namaste.

Tolle, Eckhart. 2006. *A New Earth.* New York: Penguin Group.

Tracy, Diane. 2006. *Take This Job and Love It.* Naperville, IL: Sourcebooks.

Tulgan, Bruce, and Carolyn Martin. 2001. *Managing Generation Y.* Amherst, MA: Human Resource Development Press.

Tullier, L. Michelle. 2005. *The Unofficial Guide to Landing a Job.* New York: John Wiley & Sons.

University of Wisconsin Center on Education and the Workforce. 2010. "Help Wanted 2018," www.cew.georgetown.edu/jobs2018.

Whitcomb, Susan, Bryan, Chandlee and Dib, Deb. 2010. *The Twitter Job Search Guide.* Indianapolis, IN: JIST Publishing

Working Mother. 2011. "Annual Survey of Best Companies." Accessed at www.workingmother.com/list/shtml. (Updated annually.)

Yaeger, Neil M., and J. Hough. 2006. *Power Interviews.* New York: John Wiley & Sons.

Index

Notes

Notes

Notes

Notes

Notes

Notes

Notes

Notes

Notes

Notes

Notes

Notes

Notes